The Social Context of Ageing

Why do some people live to an advanced old age while others do not? And what does old age really mean in modern society?

Gerontology is a multi-disciplinary science concerned with the study of ageing, which integrates biological, psychological and social study. This book focuses on the social contexts of ageing, looking at the diversity of ageing and older people, and at different factors that are important to experiences of old age and ageing.

This comprehensive text includes chapters on:

- theoretical and methodological bases for the study of ageing
- demographic context of the 'ageing' population
- health and illness
- family and social networks
- formal and informal care and other services for older people

The book provides an invaluable introduction to the major issues involved in the study of ageing and is essential reading for students of sociology, gerontology, social policy, health and social care, and professionals working with older people.

Christina R Victor BA MPhil PhD Hon MFPH has worked in social gerontology for over twenty years. She is professor of Gerontology & Health Services Research, and Acting Head, School of Health & Social Care, University of Reading, Reading, UK.

In loving memory of my father
Idris Windsor Ronald Victor
12 February 1914 to 24 August 2003

The Social Context of Ageing

Christina R. Victor

Routledge
Taylor & Francis Group

LONDON AND NEW YORK

First published 2005 by Routledge
2 Park Square, Milton Park, Abingdon, Oxon OX14 4RN

Simultaneously published in the USA and Canada by Routledge
270 Madison Ave, New York, NY 10016

Routledge is an imprint of the Taylor & Francis Group

© Christina Victor, 2005

British Library Cataloguing in Publication Data
A catalogue record for this book is available from the British Library

Library of Congress Cataloging in Publication Data
A catalog record for this book has been requested

ISBN (hardback) 0-415-22139-0
ISBN (paperback) 0-415-22140-4

Composition by Wearset Ltd, Boldon, Tyne and Wear

Printed and bound in Great Britain by TJ International Ltd,
Padstow, Cornwall

Contents

Illustrations

Figures

Boxes

Tables

Acknowledgements

This book was started while I was Professor of Social Gerontology in the Department of Community Health Sciences at St George's Hospital Medical School in London and I am grateful to the department for their support for this literary enterprise.

Particular thanks are due to Loretta Hall for her help in the preparation of early drafts of the manuscript and to the various groups of students who provided feedback on the material to be included in the book. I also wish to take this opportunity to thank my colleagues in the School of Health and Social Care at the University of Reading for providing the encouragement to complete the writing of this book. Amanda Harvey provided valuable help in preparing the final manuscript, including deciphering the almost illegible alterations written in my unique handwriting style! As always David and Christopher provided moral support, encouragement to finish the task and invaluable technical help.

1 The social perspective on ageing

Gerontology is the science concerned with the study of ageing. Also encompassed within the term is a more expansive definition of the study of ageing to include the study of later life, old age and older people. As such it is a comparatively 'young' science: the term 'gerontology' was first used by a Russian biologist Metchnikoff in his book *The Prolongation of Life* published in 1908. However, the recency of the identification of the science of gerontology masks an interest in old age and older people that has existed for thousands of years. Distinguished scientists such as Francis Bacon, Benjamin Franklin and Francis Galton all wrote about ageing. There have always been 'older' people present within societies. The oldest reported lifespan is that of Methuselah, who is supposed to have lived for 969 years. The longest verifiable lifespan was that of Jeanne Calment, who died in 1997, aged 126. Individuals living to advanced age is not a feature unique to contemporary society: Thomas Parr was presented to Charles I as being 152 years old, but such claims were largely unverifiable because individuals were not always certain as to their exact date of birth. As a society we have always been interested in what it is about certain individuals that means that they can survive to very advanced old age while others do not. Writers from the times of Aristotle onwards have been interested in the attributes required for living to old age and the first question many are asked upon achieving their centenary is what do they ascribe their long life to.

Perspectives upon ageing

Given the breadth of the topic under study it is, perhaps, not surprising that there are a number of different perspectives upon the study of ageing. These are usually defined as the biological, the psychological and the social. Thus gerontology is a multidisciplinary field of investigation in which each of these perspectives has a valuable contribution to make. One of the many challenges confronting the gerontologist is to be able to integrate these differing approaches to enhance and develop our understanding of ageing and later life. The bio-social-psycho model initially advanced by Engel (1977) is one way of developing a more integrationalist framework towards the study of old age. He argues that in order to understand ageing and the experience of old age, and to develop interventions to compensate for the vicissitudes of old age, we need to be able to integrate these differing perspectives. This model for understanding ageing was developed in response to the dominance of the biomedical model of ageing. This later model is imbued with notions of decline and deterioration, is focused upon disease and is highly reductionist in its thinking about later life. In contrast the bio-psycho-social model focuses upon health, integrates notions of both mental and physical health, and emphasises the influence of contextual factors upon the experience of old age.

The biological perspective

The biological approach to ageing is concerned with how the passage of time affects physiological systems (see Kirkwood, 1999). We are all aware of how older people illustrate specific physical changes such as wrinkles or grey hair. The key question is whether such changes are a result of 'ageing' or growing older or whether they represent potentially modifiable changes resultant from social and environmental factors. For example the presence of wrinkles is seen by many as arising from growing older. However, we know that, in part, wrinkles reflect lifestyle and environmental factors such as sun exposure and smoking. Physiological changes attributed to ageing may, in part, be attributable to social and environmental influences or mediated by them. In theory, at least, this offers the potential to develop interventions to ameliorate such factors, if not eradicate them entirely.

Biologists are interested in longevity and the varying life spans of different species. Longevity refers to the maximum lifespan that a species could attain under 'optimal' conditions. Lifespan refers to the period between birth and death and the maximum verified to date for a human is 126 years. Life expectancy refers to the 'average' number of years remaining to a person of a specific age. This is an actuarial calculation often calculated at birth but can also be calculated from any given age. Biologists refer to ageing as 'senescence'. This describes decreases in the efficient functioning of an organism with age as a result of natural processes rather than abnormal processes which bring about pathology and disease (Ebrahim and Kalache, 1996). There have been various attempts to define the biological changes and characteristics which accompany growing older in all forms of life. Strehler (1962) defines ageing as the changes which occur in the post-reproductive phase of life that result from a decrease in the ability of the body to maintain homeostasis, that is to regulate the functions of the body within the very precise limits required for efficient functioning and survival. Consequently the body becomes less able to adapt to physiological stress and less resistant to disease and pathology. Ageing is viewed as an involuntary phase in the development of the organism which brings about a decrease in adaptive capacities and, ultimately, death. Although there is still considerable debate about the precise biological definition of ageing, Strehler (1962) again suggests that four criteria distinguish ageing from other biological processes and which can also be used to distinguish 'ageing' from 'disease'. For a physiological change to be considered part of 'ageing' and not some other process, Strehler (1962) suggests that it should demonstrate the following attributes: universality (it must happen to every member of a population), internality (it must result from internal processes and not reflect lifestyle or environmental factors), progressiveness (it is progressive, rather than acute, with cumulative effects) and harmfulness (it should demonstrate a deleterious, rather than benign, effect upon the organism and its ability to cope with its environment). Using these criteria, Box 1.1 illustrates that dementia is clearly a disease rather than an ageing effect as it fails to fulfil most of the Strehler (1962) criteria.

There are at least twelve different theories advanced to account for why we age and it is neither appropriate nor practical to examine all of these here. We shall illustrate the range of theories in this area by using examples from the two major approaches to theories of ageing: 'error theories' and 'programming theories'. Error-based theories of ageing develop the proposition that ageing results from the development and replication of errors within the physiological system. Perhaps the oldest manifestation of this approach to theorising biological and physiological ageing is the 'wear and tear' theory which can be traced back to the ideas of Aristotle. This perspective likens the human body to a machine, which eventually wears out, with this process being expedited by 'overuse'. A popularist development of this theory is that all individuals have a fixed amount of time 'allocated' to them and that vigorous exercise or lifestyle will use up this energy, leading to premature death. The second set of theories relate to the notions of 'programmed' ageing which hypothesises that

---

Box 1.1   Ageing and disease

Ageing is	Disease is
• universal	• random
• internal	• intrinsic and extrinsic
• progressive	• acute and chronic
• harmful (death)	• may be halted

Dementia (impaired cognitive function) is not part of the ageing process because it is

• selective not universal (prevalence of about 5 per cent – but depends upon threshold)
• intrinsic (variety of causes – vascular)
• progressive (slow onset, drugs may reverse)
• harmful (causes disability or dependence not necessarily death)

---

ageing and the maximal life span are programmed into the genes of the particular organism and derives from the work of Hayflick (1996). Ageing and death are 'pre-programmed' events with an inherent biological clock, which keeps track of time and initiates the ageing process when certain limits are met.

Ageing is a 'normal' process; distinguishing this normal process from pathology and disease remains a key challenge. Much work in gerontology has tended to conflate these two distinct notions so that we have not always clearly distinguished between them. Disease and age-related change have been linked together and have contributed to many of our negative views of ageing by a concentration upon decline and dysfunction. Increasingly we are aware that the physical changes we have attributed to 'ageing' are age related but not causally. Such changes may be linked to the social and environmental context and that they may be modified.

The psychological perspective

The psychological approach concentrates upon examining person-ality, mental function and notions of self and identity. The psychologist is interested in both differences in behaviour between individuals and changes within individuals with the passage of time. Hence this perspective is distinguished from the cellular/organ systems approach of the biologist and the structural/social factors approach of the sociologist. This is a diverse area of research which embraces topics such as cognitive function, health psychology (health beliefs and behaviour), mental illness and personality and adjustment. The biomedical model has influenced this area of work in that there has often been a very negative, decline and loss orientated approach to the subject. The focus has been upon adjustment to loss rather than more positive notions of self-development in later life. This topic is dealt with in more depth in Chapter 6.

The social gerontological perspective

The sociology of ageing is concerned with using sociological perspectives to understand ageing. Social gerontology is a wider discipline in that it is concerned with approaching ageing from a variety of social science perspectives in order to achieve a better understanding of ageing and old age rather than for developing sociological theory and insights. As such social gerontology incorporates three distinct perspectives – individual, social and societal – at two levels of analysis, the microscale and macroscale which illustrates the complexity of the subject area. The microscale approach is concerned with understanding and explaining ageing as an individual experience by investigating such topics as changes in perceived age identity as the individual progresses through the lifecourse. Here we are trying to elucidate what it is like to be an older person within contemporary society.

However, few individuals grow older in isolation from the rest of society. Rather, ageing occurs within a social context ranging from the microscale of the family to the macroscale of the whole society or culture or increasingly of a globalised world (Estes *et al.*, 2004). Hence the second approach to the study of ageing examines the social context which defines ageing and seeks to understand the position of and experience of older people within society and how this is shaped by major structural factors such as class, gender and ethnicity. The meaning and impact of the constraints operating upon the older adult are highly dependent upon the social environment in which the individual encounters them. It is now evident that ageing is not a homogeneous experience which affects every individual within the same society in a monolithic fashion. All 'old people' are not alike and pre-old-age characteristics such as class and gender continue to exert a strong influence across the lifecourse. To conceptualise old age as an undifferentiated experience is both naive and unhelpful. We all bring to the experience of old age access to various resources – material, health and social – and these are strongly influenced by our experiences prior to 'old age'. Indeed, with the development of the ideas of the 'successful ageing' (Rowe and Kahn, 1999) the importance of the social context for the shaping of the experience of old age has assumed greater prominence. These authors argue that successful ageing is defined by both longevity and quality of life and that these are promoted by the interaction of three sets of factors: social engagement and participation, reduction of disease, and promotion of high levels of physical and mental functioning.

The third facet of social gerontology is concerned with 'societal ageing'. This is concerned with the demographic, structural, cultural and economic transformation resultant from the increase in the number and proportion of 'older' people within society. How do social institutions respond to the changes in the nature and composition of our population? How will society respond to the increased number and visibility of older people? In this chapter we consider the different approaches which have been adopted towards the definition of old age and we examine the characteristics of these competing perspectives. The chapter then provides a summary of some of the dominant values that characterise society, which are of importance for understanding the experience of ageing and the position of the older people in contemporary society.

What is old age?

Both professionals and the lay public, when describing people in the later phases of life, often use terms such as 'the elderly' or 'older people'. These are terms which are common currency in both popular usage and more academic environments. Despite the frequency with which they are used, the definition of exactly what constitutes 'old age' and when it starts remains problematic. These terms are a shorthand way of identifying the group of interest and little more. We cannot presume that the identified group is homogeneous as it may encompass an age range of 40 years or more from, for example, 65 to 105 years. It is totally unrealistic to expect such a group to be homogeneous in either character or attitudes.

There are a number of different ways, in theory at least, to determine when old age starts and to identify our group of interest. There is no readily agreed biological definition of ageing or of the onset of old age. The physiological manifestations of biological ageing occur at different rates in different people with the result that the older age groups are very varied in terms of senescence. Hence the potential for using biological markers or some notion of functional age remains problematic for theoretical, conceptual and technical reasons.

Perhaps the easiest measure of old age is 'chronological' or calendar age. Of itself chronological age simply conveys the number of birthdays that an individual has accumulated. Clearly for this measure to be used it requires a society to be sufficiently well organised that its members know their chronological age. Although this is frequently used to define the onset of old age it is, at best, only a very rough guide to the ageing of the individual in biological terms because of the variability across individuals in terms of senescence. In addition chronological age of itself has no innate 'meaning' but is derived from the social and historical context within which it operates. Hence the interpretation and meaning of specific chronological ages vary both historically and culturally. Because of the ease with which information is presented, chronological age is by far the most accessible definition of old age, but we need to remain alert as to the limitations which this approach poses.

Another approach to the definition of old age is via the concept of the lifecycle or life stage. This is usually conceived as an orderly progression from infancy to old age with biological and socio-cultural factors interacting to govern the sequence of progression. Old or middle age are broad social categories that encompass changes of role (from child to adult), physical changes and other forms of social transition (becoming a grandparent). Although these life stages are often perceived as a simple universal progression from one well-defined set of social roles to another, it is in reality a highly complex concept. Within the broad term lifecycle it is possible to distinguish between a variety of sub-lifecycles related to different aspects of life such the family or work. The family dimension of the lifecycle involves numerous transitions including courtship, newly married, new parents, parents of teenagers, 'empty nesters' and widowhood. Not everyone will experience all these phases of the family cycle; there may also be enormous variations in the age at which individuals experience these transitions. For example, some people marry at 18 and have three children by the age of 25; others may not marry until well into their thirties, while others have their children in their forties at an age when others are becoming grandparents. Furthermore this trajectory is based upon notions of monogamy across the life course. Neugarten (1974) describes how the lifecycle has become increasingly differentiated into smaller segments with the emergence of the subgroups of 'adolescence', 'pre-school' and 'middle age' as distinct phases. It was not until industrialisation in the seventeenth and eighteenth centuries that childhood emerged as a specific phase of life with its own special needs and characteristics, while adolescence did not become widely recognised until the early part of the twentieth century. More recently middle age has become recognised as a distinctive phase and, increasingly, there is a trend to differentiate between the 'young' elderly (those aged between 65 and 74 years) and the 'old' elderly (those aged over 75 years). There is also the distinction between the 'third age' (those aged 50–74) and the 'fourth age' (Laslett, 1989). From the lifecycle perspective, in describing someone as old (or juvenile) we are locating them within a specific social environment, which expects particular roles and provides opportunities and barriers. While these are interesting ways to conceptualise the lifecourse, such life-stage definitions of old age are of limited practical and policy relevance as they are almost impossible to operationalise. Hence, for all its limitations, we are usually left with using chronological age to define the group of interest.

Conclusion

Gerontology is concerned with the study of ageing, later life and old age and is an area of both academic and policy interest that has experienced a considerable expansion in the post-war period, largely in response to the perceived 'problem' of an ageing population. Within this broad area of study, there are three main perspectives towards the study of ageing: the biological, the psychological and the social. In this book we focus upon the social context within which old age is experienced. However, it is important to recognise that this is just one of the perspectives that may be brought to bear upon the ageing experience. Old age, while it is a term that is very widely used, remains an entity that is difficult to define, operationalise and measure. Biological definitions of the onset of old age are not yet well developed, although many of the theories such as vitalism have been rejected because of their simplistic approach. The biomedical model which conceptualises old age as a time of inevitable decline have had a very important influence upon the development of the subject. Chronological definitions of old age are essentially shorthand terms used as a surrogate measure for biological and functional ageing, reflect social ascriptions and norms or relate to statutory provision such as retirement pensions. These definitions of old age are all culturally and historically specific. There are many assumptions about old age and the use of terms such as 'the elderly' can imply a false sense of homogeneity within this population. In this book we examine the diversity of the ageing experience, and consider how the social context, especially issues of gender and class, influences this.

2 Theoretical perspectives on the study of ageing

Social gerontology is a multidisciplinary enterprise that involves the social sciences and arts and humanities in the study of the social context of ageing. It also includes insights gained from research, policy and practice. Given the variety of disciplinary perspectives involved in social gerontology, and its comparative recency as an academic discipline, it is hardly surprising that the development of theory within gerontology remains limited. Indeed social gerontology does not possess an extensive theoretical framework in its own right. The systematic development of theory, and subsequent application and testing, are activities that have been largely absent from many social scientific studies of ageing, especially in the United Kingdom where there is a very strong tradition of 'applied' gerontological work. Frequently, researchers have been content simply to describe aspects of behaviour in later life, or the characteristics of various subgroups of the older population, without trying to organise the findings into a coherent theory of social ageing. The focus in much social gerontological investigation has been upon identifying, classifying and describing the experience of later life rather than understanding and theorising. Much of the explanation of this largely atheoretical nature of much gerontological work derives from the essentially applied and/or policy related nature of much gerontological research. This dominance is encapsulated by the still relevant comments of Fisher (1978), who wrote:

> Social gerontology has not succeeded in creating a body of theory. . . . Probably, gerontology will never be a theoretical discipline in its own right, but rather a consumer of theory from other sciences. Its major function seems to be that of an applied social science. . . . Its major role, perhaps, has been to destroy the

myths which so thickly encrust the study of ageing, to oppose the
age prejudice which has grown so strong. . . .

(Fisher 1978: 194–195)

More recently Estes *et al.* (1992: 50) commented that we still have
'no common thread or tie to a common core of knowledge to unify
the field' (of gerontology). Bengston *et al.* (1999) suggest that this
reflects the fact that gerontology has been a bottom-up discipline that
groups observations into models rather than theories and because of
the different levels of gerontological research – individuals, populations and processes. However, there is a clear need to enhance the
theoretical bedrock of our subject of study. Perhaps some of the reti-
cence about the development and utilisation of theory in gerontology
derives from the practical focus of much of the work and our
concern with describing the characteristics of older people (Estes,
1979). This is contrasted with the 'irrelevance' of the development of
theory. Yet theory is important because it is concerned with explaining rather than simply describing, in this instance, the social world of
older people. Implicitly or explicitly we all use theory to 'explain' the
facts of ageing. For example the 'fact' that older people report higher
levels of physical disability may be explained in terms of either physiological and biological changes in musculoskeletal integrity (biological theories) or as a response to the expectation of increased
problems of mobility (sociological theory). Theory is also important
because as well as attempting to explain observations it may suggest
intervention to ameliorate particular problems. Biological explanations of chronic disease may suggest either no intervention (as physiological change is both inevitable and irreversible) or medical
interventions such as drug therapy or surgery. Sociological explanations of the same observations may suggest social interventions such
as more positive attitudes towards ageing and older people.

This failure to formulate a systematic theory within social gerontology is perhaps not surprising given the complexity of the field, its
relatively recent development as a substantive area of academic
endeavour and the importance of the policy agenda in the development of research questions. There is a further complication that has
made the development of theory in gerontology challenging. Gerontology, like sociology, operates at both macro- and microlevels of
investigation, which adds to the complexity of our subject. Gerontology is interested in questions of microlevel individual adaptation to
the experience of ageing such as 'how do individuals adjust to widowhood?' or decide when to consult their doctor. At the macro-level

social gerontologists are concerned with questions such as the implications for the health care system of population ageing or the economic purpose of retirement (Phillipson, 1982), or with how factors such as class and gender influence the experience of ageing (Arber *et al.*, 2003). In attempting to evaluate and understand theoretical perspectives and frameworks upon social ageing we need to establish at which level the theoretical proposition is operating at – micro or macro. In reality, of course, the distinction between these two perspectives is much less clear cut than the dichotomy described here – it reflects a continuum rather than a clear division. It is not that one perspective is superior to the other. They both contribute different, but complementary, approaches to our understanding of the experience of old age and serve to enrich our subject.

In establishing the utility of any gerontological theories we need to consider three major factors. How well does the theory explain current events? How well does the theory predict future events? How well does it generate new theoretical insights? Bond *et al.* (1993) give examples of these three different attributes of theory in gerontology. They indicate how theories of loss and adjustment can be used to explain and understand three apparently unrelated events: bereavement, retirement and amputation. This indicates how theory can be used to generalise far beyond the initial area of study. Theoretical propositions should then be able to predict future outcomes or trajectories after these three very different events. Finally, good social theory should lead to future areas for research and scholarship. In considering theoretical propositions in gerontology we need to consider how well our theories match these three criteria. We also need to establish the assumptions and ideologies that underpin the various theoretical positions. In the rest of this chapter we examine the major theories and frameworks which have been used to study ageing and consider the levels at which such theories operate and the assumptions which underpin them.

Old age as a social problem

While not a specific theory as such, the consideration of old age and later life as a social problem is a framework which has consistently informed social gerontological research, especially that carried out in Britain. This perspective with its focus upon the problematic nature of ageing, both for individuals and societies, has had a profound effect upon the types of questions which have been researched and hence in the generation of knowledge about ageing and old age in

Britain. This framework is an approach that operates at both micro-
and macrolevels of analysis as it can investigate both the problems of
ageing individuals and ageing societies. This type of approach has
been applied frequently in social gerontology and relies heavily upon
the biological model of ageing with its emphasis upon decline and
deterioration in function.

Clearly in using this perspective the definition of which aspects of
ageing are defined as 'problematic' is crucial. At the most obvious
level social problems are what people think they are. If conditions are
not defined as social problems by the people involved in them, then
they are not problems to those people although they may be problems to policy makers or to scientists. Hence there is an issue of
power and ownership at the heart of the 'social' problem approach
to the study of ageing. Problems may be defined as being perceived
either by the individual or by society at large. In this tradition, who
defines which 'problematic' aspects of ageing are worthwhile
researching is of key importance. Additionally we must consider why
the identified problems, for example loneliness or isolation, are seen
to be problematic for older people but not to other segments of the
population. The essence of this approach is that it is concerned with
the problematic and difficult aspects of ageing and the knowledge so
generated is concerned with these areas, thus this approach will yield
very little evidence as to the 'non-problematic' or 'normal' aspects of
ageing. Indeed the focus is upon the 'deviant' or difficulty aspects of
ageing rather than to 'non-problematic'. We can draw few inferences
from work in this tradition about 'normal' ageing, except, perhaps,
by counter-example. A concentration upon this problem-focused
research agenda, while undoubtedly for the best of possible motives,
has perhaps served to perpetuate the very negative stereotypes of old
age and later life which is so pervasive in Britain.

At the macrolevel older people in Britain emerged as a specific
'problem group' for which specific social policies were required in the
late nineteenth century (Thane, 2000; see also MacIntyre, 1977).
Prior to this older people were not differentiated from the rest of the
pauper classes: old age per se was not seen as a social problem;
rather destitution, irrespective of age, was the issue. What prompted
the emergence of older people as a specific problem group in the late
nineteenth century? Demographic changes are an insufficient explanation because the major period of growth in the absolute and relative number of older people in the population did not occur until the
early part of the twentieth century. Thane (2000) demonstrates how
the awareness of older people as a particular problem group arose

from three interrelated factors: a growing awareness of the complexity of the causes of poverty (of which old age was one), the difficulties of older workers remaining in the labour force, and the concentrations of older people, especially in rural areas, brought about by the outward migration of the young. A variety of interlinking social trends combined to increase the social and physical visibility of older people within society and drew attention to the problems of old age for both the individual and society as a whole. There was not, however, the same impetus to examine the 'non-problematic' aspects of the newly visible population of elders.

Within the British research tradition there are two distinct forms of the 'old age as a social problem' perspective – the humanitarian and the organisational – and these two approaches reflect the macro- and microlevel approaches towards the study of ageing (MacIntyre, 1977). The humanitarian perspective emphasises an interest in the problems of old age and ageing for the individual while the organisation approach is concerned with the problems for society of an ageing population. Again while for the purpose of discussion and description these two approaches are presented as distinct dichotomies, in reality such sharp divisions are less clear cut and a specific piece of research may be addressing both aspects of this perspective.

There is an extensive British academic tradition of work in the humanitarian or microlevel framework and it is an approach with a long and honourable pedigree. At the most general level this type of research tradition has concentrated upon describing the circumstances of the poorest and most disadvantaged sections of the community as a means of changing attitudes towards these groups and to argue for the provision of welfare resources and interventions. The surveys of Mayhew in London, Booth in London and Rowntree in York provide some of the earliest examples of this tradition of academic research. There are many examples of work in this traditional 'social arithmetic' tradition in the study of ageing and later life. The classic surveys of Tunstall (1966) into loneliness and isolation and Townsend's work on residential homes and the social world of older people (Townsend, 1957, 1964) are of particular note. These publications are exemplars of this tradition and there is much for the modern gerontologist to learn from reading such 'classic' studies.

Within this tradition, the process of ageing is not defined as the problem. Rather, the focus of attention is upon the individual older person and the problems which old age by implication 'inevitably' brings. Old age is implicitly conceptualised as a time of declines in physical, mental and social functioning and not as a time of life characterised by new opportunities or challenges. These functional declines are seen as being universal and inevitable and there are obvious parallels with the 'biological' model of ageing with its emphasis upon loss, deficit, decline and decay. Research in this framework has focused upon five main areas: morbidity, quality of life, social relationships, use of services and employment.

Where issues other than these have been addressed, the focus has been on describing the differences between older people and other age groups, rather than looking at either continuities between age groups or differences within the older age groups. Old age is segregated or separated from earlier phases in the life course and is not often seen as representing a continuation and development of previous phases of life. Few of the investigations carried out considered the contributions made by older people. Research undertaken from this 'social problem' perspective often, by the very nature of the questions they are seeking to answer, portray a very one-sided picture which often focuses upon the negative aspects of ageing and which is of only limited generalisability. While undertaken for the best of reasons, social problem-focused research has contributed, in part at least, to perpetuation of negative attitudes towards old and older people and has not looked at the positive aspects of how older people organise and manage their daily lives.

The second manifestation of the 'old age as a social problem' perspective is as an organisational problem for society and is a macrolevel approach to the 'problems' of ageing. This tradition emphasises the ideology that old age is a 'burden' for society, especially for those people who are in employment and who will have to shoulder the 'burden' of paying to support the legions of pensioners. Despite the recent interest in the notion of 'intergenerational conflict' resultant from the burden which younger people are going to face in supporting future cohorts of elders, this is not a particularly new approach. Good examples of the orientation of this approach are demonstrated by titles such as *The Rising Tide*, a report concerned with projected numbers of older people with dementia in Britain (Health Advisory Service, 1982). This report was concerned that we would be 'swamped' by the health care demands of older people with dementia. Another example, *Averting the old age crisis*, a report from the World Bank (1994) concerned with the economic problems resultant from having to pay pensions to an increasing number of old people. This concern about the burden of population ageing has been termed 'moral panic' by Jefferys (1983) or the 'elderly avalanche' by

Russell (1990). This is an approach which has been highly distinctive of many British government reports, especially those produced in the 1940s and the 1980s, and is rooted in concerns about the consequences of the changing nature of the British population, especially the very low birth rates of recent years. Forward projection of these rates suggested that there would insufficient young people entering the workforce to provide for the increasing number of older people (often referred to as the demographic time bomb). Indeed, concern about the ageing nature of the wider European population has prompted a debate as to whether immigration should be encouraged in order to ease the burden of caring or supporting all these 'unproductive' elders.

The approach of Beveridge is an exemplar of the negative way that older people are often conceptualised. His 1942 report upon social security provision saw old age as a one-way drain on resources from other more important areas of social need. He wrote that 'It is dangerous to be in any way lavish to old age, until adequate provision has been assured for all other needs such as the prevention of disease and the adequate nutrition of the very young' (Beveridge, 1942: 96). These comments indicate that the primary focus of social policy as manifested by the creation of the post-war welfare state was towards the young. The post-war Royal Commission on Population (1948) stressed this point further by observing that the old consumed without producing, thereby reducing the overall standard of living. This report recommended ways of reducing the social costs of old age by getting older people to do more to maintain themselves but there was no recognition of the past contributions that they had made to society, or indeed any awareness of their current contributions, especially in terms of informal care. As such this report is typical of the arguments advanced more recently about the 'parasitic' nature of older people which fail to acknowledge the contribution of older people to the social and work-based economy and to society more widely.

This emphasis upon older people as a burden which society cannot afford re-emerged in the 1980s and is illustrated by the debate about the ability of the nation to 'afford' the various health and welfare benefits provided for them. This has been manifested in the development of the notion of 'intergenerational' conflict over the distribution of welfare and other social resources. Demographic and ideological factors largely explain the re-emergence of this perspective. As with the immediate post-war period, there has been considerable worry about the perceived ageing of the population. In particular there have been fears expressed about the growth in numbers of the very old (i.e. those over 85 years of age). Decreasing fertility rates and family size have raised fears about the possible lack of workers in the future to maintain the elderly population (and other dependent groups) and that there will develop 'intergenerational conflict' between the young and the old for welfare and other transfers of resources (Johnson *et al.*, 1990; Arber and Attias-Donfut, 2000). Ideas of intergenerational conflict arose first, perhaps, in the 1960s when the youthful 'baby boomers' challenged many of the then current social norms and the established social order. In its more recent manifestation, there are concerns over the emergence of 'grey power' with older people monopolising political activity and securing resources for themselves to the detriment of other groups. At its most basic the notion of intergenerational conflict is reduced to the simple question, 'are the aims of young and old sufficiently different to make them political and social adversaries?' This presumes that political groups would develop around the basis of age and that these age-based parties would have different agendas: the young lobby wanting support for education and the older age groups pensions or health care. In a time of limited resources conflict may erupt between age groups for control of scarce resources. However, this requires people to act and vote along simple age lines. Older people present diversity in terms of class, ethnicity and gender. Indeed the diversity of the older age groups is increasing and this probably militates against the development of a simple voting lobby organised upon the basis of age, but older people are more likely to vote than younger people and all parties woo the 'grey vote' (Vincent, 1995, 1999).

Ideological factors have also influenced this debate. In Britain older people account for about half of the current health and social welfare budget. With the election of a Conservative government in 1979 deeply committed to the reduction of public expenditure, combined with economic recession and high unemployment, the ability of the nation to 'afford' the 'burden of the elderly' has been questioned. In addition the philosophy of the 'new right' is centred upon the responsibility of individuals to provide for their old age. Both the ability of, and the appropriateness of, the state providing for old age have been questioned and the post war consensus between political parties concerning welfare provision has been questioned. Administrations following on from 1979 have all, to a lesser or greater degree, sought to reduce the responsibility of the state in supporting older people and have moved more towards promoting a policy of 'self-sufficiency' in old age with the state stepping in only as matter of 'last resort' (see Victor, 1997; Means and Smith, 1998).

In the United Kingdom in particular this framework has had a profound influence upon the study of ageing and in generating knowledge about the social context of ageing. The emphasis upon the 'problems' of ageing means that our knowledge and understanding of other non-problematic dimensions of ageing remains sparse. This type of framework can also be seen in the priority areas identified for research by bodies such as the Economic and Social Research Council (ESRC) and the Medical Research Council (MRC) who are concerned with the potential 'future burden' of health and illness among older people and advances a research agenda that is concerned with such matters. The ESRC Growing Older programme also demonstrated a concern with many of the perceived 'problematic' dimensions of growing older and has a heavily social policy focus. There remains little interest from funding bodies or research organisations in the 'everyday life' of older people nor in the study of problems identified by older people rather than policy makers (Gubrium and Holstein, 2000; Bytheway, 2003).

Developing theory in social gerontology

There are a number of different explicit theoretical frameworks concerned with the study of ageing. Psychological and physiological perspectives upon ageing focus upon the changes which happen to individuals. However, when focusing upon the social context within which ageing occurs, both for groups and individuals, then theories derived from sociological perspectives are most pertinent. As noted earlier, a concern with examining and understanding the social context of ageing involves studies which look at questions concerned with the adaptation of individuals (a microscale approach) and of questions posed at the macroscale (i.e. concerns with the impact of ageing upon social structures and vice versa). Social theories of ageing are characterised both by the level of explanation at which they operate and by the assumptions and ideologies that underpin them. Aroni and Minichiello (1992) developed a typology of theories including both the level of analysis (micro versus macro theories) and nature (interpretist contrasted with normative theories such as role theory). When evaluating the theories summarised below, and when encountering others not covered here, the student of gerontology needs to consider four basic questions: What is the level of explanation at which theory x operates? What does the theory try to explain? What type of questions is this theory trying to answer? What are the assumptions and ideology underpinning the theory? Using this basic framework helps us to clarify the robustness of the results and explanations proposed and expose the degree to which we can have confidence in their generalisability and reveal the assumptions upon which the research is based.

Functionalist theories and ageing

Functionalist perspectives have been highly influential in the development of theoretical frameworks in social gerontology. Theories such as disengagement, activity theory, continuity theory, the thesis of modernisation and age stratification theories of ageing all developed from the structural-functionalist premises. As such this has been a powerful influence upon gerontological thinking and the key assumptions of this approach are, therefore, summarised before examining the major ageing theories which derive from this perspective. Structural functionalism is a macrolevel theoretical stance that is concerned with analysing elements of society (social institutions and structures) in order to elucidate how society is maintained and developed. The appropriate analogy here is with the body. In order to understand how the body works you need to understand how each organ works, how the organs are interrelated and how they relate to the body as a whole. Functionalists adopt a similar approach to understanding and theorising about society and are concerned with identifying the functions that particular social arrangements fulfil for any given society. This approach views the elements of society as being functionally interdependent, with the individual and society always seeking to maintain a state of equilibrium between them. In this perspective society is seen as being analogous to a biological system in that it is conceptualised as a number of identifiable and interrelated constituent parts. Each of the individual parts responds to changes in the other elements of the system. Hence within society different groups are conceptualised as interrelated and respond to changes in other parts of society. Society is seen as an 'open' system where different component parts adapt and function to ensure that the overall system remains both unified and (relatively) stable and unchanged. In very broad terms functionalism may be seen as analogous to biological and natural sciences where there is an emphasis upon the creation and maintenance of (social) order. Specific behaviour patterns within a social system can be viewed as either functional or dysfunctional. Functional patterns help to maintain and integrate the social network while dysfunctional patterns lead to breakdown and disintegration. The functional operation of each organ or unit within society (such as older people) has implications for the well-being of society as a whole. It is assumed that there is an agreed and universal set of values within society that determine the goals and norms through which social order is maintained. Hence this is a theory which posits that social order is maintained via consensus rather than conflict. Social order is maintained by the existence of powerful social norms (the expectations given to specific social roles) which are internalised via a system of 'socialisation' and social control that suppresses deviance from expected norms via agencies of social control such as the police, schools and other state bodies.

Before considering the major gerontological theories that have developed out of functionalism it is necessary to outline the meta-critiques which have been made of this approach. The implicit emphasis within functionalism is upon social order, equilibrium and the maintenance of the status quo rather than upon possible change and conflict. Hence the functionalist perspectives, and resulting theories of ageing, are seen as being essentially conservative. In reading functionalist theories, with their stress upon determined nature of many social actions, the power of individuals to influence their social environment is highly limited. Individuals are seen as little more than passive social actors or 'cultural dopes' (Aroni and Minchello, 1992). Furthermore society is conceptualised almost as a separate entity, with its own set of needs and desires, and an existence separate from the individual members. However, despite these critiques, functionalism has been important in gerontology given that much of the emphasis in our area has been towards investigating and understanding personal and social adjustment to old age, changes in social roles which often accompany later life and life satisfaction. Given these concerns it is, perhaps, hardly surprising that functionalism has been so important to the development of theory in gerontology. Hence we consider the major functionalist theories which have influenced gerontological thinking and have had a very profound influence upon the types of research questions posed and the development of our knowledge base.

Disengagement theory

This is a theory which links both micro and macro approaches to the study of ageing. Disengagement was the first explicit social theory that was concerned with ageing and was originally formulated in *Growing Old* by Cumming and Henry (1961). This theory posits that, independent of other factors such as poor health or poverty, ageing involves a gradual but inevitable withdrawal or disengagement from interaction between the individual and her/his social context and that this process is mutually beneficial. Thus disengagement would be seen as functional or useful, because it facilitates a smooth transfer of power from the old to the young. From this perspective, retirement is seen as a mechanism by which companies can predetermine levels of employee turnover, gives the individual a 'graceful' exit from the pressures of employment and creates employment opportunities for younger workers. Hence disengagement, as illustrated by retirement, is a mechanism for ensuring equilibrium within society and the transition of social power across generations.

By disengaging from activity, either employment or social, individuals prepare themselves for death. At the same time, society also prepares the individual for the later phases of life, by withdrawing the pressure to interact and facilitating the entry of younger cohorts into the social world and the disruption caused by the death of the individual is minimised. Disengagement therefore implies a triple loss for the individual: a loss of roles, a restriction of social contacts and relationships and a reduced commitment to social mores and values. Successful ageing, from the viewpoint of disengagement theory, implies a reduction in activity levels and a decrease in involvement, until the individual withdraws from all previous activities and becomes preoccupied with the ultimate withdrawal of death. Central to this theory is the assumption that both the individual and the wider society benefit from the process. Withdrawal for the individual may mean a release from social pressures that stress productivity, competition and continued achievement. For society, the withdrawal of older members permits younger, more energetic individuals to take over the roles that need to be filled. Disengagement therefore is seen as a way of permitting an orderly transfer of power between generations. The mutual withdrawal of the individual and society from each other is presented as a necessary condition for both successful ageing and the orderly continuation of society. This involves a triple loss – of social roles validated by society, restricted social contact and a reduced commitment to social mores.

Disengagement theory had a profound influence upon the development of gerontological research partly because it was the first major theory and thereby generated considerable debate and discussion within the gerontological world. It has also been influential because it appeared to indicate the pathway to 'successful' ageing. In this latter manifestation it is the first of many apparently prescriptive pathways offering the key to successful ageing. In this case the way to age 'successfully' was to reduce social involvement and social interaction. Although a negative pathway to the nirvana of successful ageing, it is not conceptually different from other ways to a successful old age such as dietary adaptations (such as eating yoghurt) or religious or physical activity. It was also highly influential at a time when the first stirrings of apocolyptic demography were being heard and it clearly resonated with the negative concerns which were linked with population ageing.

Disengagement influenced the direction of research as investigators sought to establish the veracity of this particular theory. The empirical evaluation of disengagement as a theory of ageing must address three core aspects of the theory. First, disengagement is a lifelong process; for most individuals, it takes place over a period of time rather than suddenly. Throughout the life course the individual is continually acquiring and dropping particular social roles. Hence it is problematic to design a research study which could easily incorporate this 'lifelong' perspective. Second, there is an implicit statement that disengagement is inevitable because death and biological decline are inevitable, although the nature and timing of disengagement will vary between individuals, historically and culturally. Again to establish the inevitability of reduced social engagement poses methodological challenges. How can 'inevitable' disengagement be differentiated from reduced levels of social participation resultant from ill health or poverty? Third, disengagement is seen as adaptive for both society and the individual. Reduced social engagement is seen as being beneficial. Further measurement challenges are posed by the requirement to measure disengagement. How does one develop a measure to record disengagement? Against what preexisting standard does one determine if disengagement is present (is it the individual's previous levels of activity or some population norm?).

Given these very problematic methodological issues this may be a theory it is impossible to test empirically, clearly a major flaw with any theory. There is some empirical evidence to support disengagement theory in that older people do experience a loss of roles with ageing, whether through retirement, the death of a spouse or the departure of older children from home. However, older people, like other groups within the population, use strategies of substitution and compensation to offset for losses of role. The widowed may remarry, or older people may replace a widespread and loose-knit pattern of interaction with more intense, locally based networks. While empirical data may demonstrate reduced social activity with increasing age, the inevitability, universality and essentially adaptive nature of these changes remains unproven. Indeed the veracity of disengagement theory is further compromised because of the involuntary nature of many disengagements, such as mandatory retirement and the failure for disengagement to be demonstrated universally (for example there are some societies where social roles increase in later life). However, Daatland (2002) has suggested that disengagement theory was an important stage in the development of gerontology because it identified old age as distinct and important phase of life and because it was an essentially multidisciplinary perspective.

Several commentators argue that disengagement theory has had profound negative impact upon older people because of its influence within social and health policy formulation. Blau (1973) argues that disengagement theory has been used to avoid confronting and dealing with the issue of older people's marginality in American society and to condone indifference towards the problems of older people. Estes *et al.* (1982) and Estes (2001) consider that the popularity of disengagement theory has had a marked influence upon the formulation of policy for older people in the United States. They argue that this concept of old age prescribes either no policy response to ageing or interventions that achieve the separation of the older person from society. Similar arguments could be constructed for the United Kingdom where many services for older people are often discrete or separate from the mainstream (the argument being that specialist services offer better services by concentrating expertise). Such separations may be spatial as well as conceptual with, for example, health services for older people located off main hospital sites, in former workhouse premises or symbolically in the oldest hospital buildings. Disengagement theory has implicitly formed the justification and intellectual basis for age-segregated policies and the separation of older people from other forms of welfare development. The notion of disengagement has been used to legitimise policies that have sought to exclude older people from social arenas and services and enabled professionals dealing with older people to rationalise their often-negative stereotypes. This theory has further enabled the erection of 'barriers' between older people and other social groups and the professionals dealing with them, with the inevitable consequence of poor quality services and inadequate education and training for the staff working within them (Biggs, 1993, 1999). It has also provided the theoretical justification for a culture of indifference for both the problems experienced by older people and the policy formulations developed in response to these. Poor quality services, low pensions and inadequate standards of care can be justified by theorising that old age is a time of disengagement and that older people are no longer to be evaluated against current social mores. Hence it is perfectly acceptable to provide them with marginal or substandard care and concern.

The response to disengagement: activity theory

The presumed inevitability of the process of disengagement, with its basis in the biomedical and sickness model of ageing, has also been subject to extensive academic criticism. While disengagement theory has been highly influential in the development of social gerontology, empirical testing and debate have exposed its essential frailty. It has, however, had an important impact in stimulating the development of counter-theories of which activity and continuity theories are the most significant. These two theories are concerned with the ageing of individuals although, again, approached from a macrolevel theoretical perspective. However, it still remains within the structural functionalist paradigm in that it is concerned with the maintenance of equilibrium within society. The focus is upon adaptation and integration into the social system and, again, it is prescribing a route to successful ageing.

Diametrically opposed to the notion of disengagement is activity theory. Developed by Havighurst (1963) this perspective maintains that normal and successful ageing involves preserving, for as long as possible, the attitudes and activities of middle age. Here mid-life is conceptualised as the nirvana of 'success' to which we are always looking back and always trying to regain. To compensate for the activities and roles that the individual surrenders with ageing, substitutes must be found. Upon retirement from paid employment the retiree must find other roles, such as voluntary work, to compensate for this loss. It is assumed that any type of activity can be substituted for the lost role. The assumption is made that the meaning and value attached to different activities are the same and that all members of society share these meanings. Both these assumptions may be unfounded. Activity theory is a prescriptive view of ageing which argues that activity and engagement offer the path to successful ageing. This is a socially based manifestation of the 'use it or lose it' conceptualisation of successful ageing and is the mirror image of disengagement but is equally judgemental and prescriptive.

There are two central assumptions of activity theory. First, that morale and life satisfaction are positively related to social integration and high involvement with social networks: those with high levels of activity and integration are more satisfied. Second, role losses such as widowhood or retirement are inversely correlated with life satisfaction and such losses need to be compensated for by the substitution of compensatory activities. Again the empirical evidence in support of these assumptions has been ambiguous. Activity theory suffers from the problems of measurement and research design noted for disengagement theory. It also is a good example of the difficulty resultant from using cross-sectional research designs to make assertions about causal relationships. Studies may well demonstrate that those who are most active are also the most satisfied with life and we can demonstrate a statistical association between these two variables, but we cannot determine if activity 'causes' satisfaction. It may well be the case that activity promotes satisfaction. However, it could equally well be argued that satisfaction with life causes activity or that some other confounding (or intervening variable) such as health or income influences both activity and satisfaction. Furthermore, research has demonstrated that individuals can maintain high levels of satisfaction and quality of life with both declining levels of activity and with low levels of activity. Again, one may question the value judgements inherent in the theory that interaction and activity in old age is a 'good thing'. The social policy implications of this perspective are rather more positive than disengagement theory, for at least it argues for the integration of older people as full members of society.

The response to disengagement: continuity theory

Continuity theory holds that, in the course of growing older, the individual will attempt to maintain stability in the lifestyle he/she has developed over the years. Continuity theory suggests that in the process of ageing, the person will strive to preserve the habits, preferences and lifestyle acquired over a lifetime; that there will be a process of evolution of activities as the individual grows older (Atchley, 1999). Both disengagement and activity theory suggest that successful ageing is achieved by movement in a single direction. Continuity theory, in contrast, starts from the premise that the individual will try to preserve the favoured lifestyle for as long as possible. It then suggests that adaptation may occur in several directions according to how the individual perceives her/his changing status. The theory is rather less dogmatic in that it does not assert that one must disengage, or become active, in order to cope with the ageing. Rather the decision regarding which roles are to be disregarded and which maintained will be determined by the individual's past and preferred lifestyle and potentially by structural factors such as income and health. Unlike activity theory, this approach does not assume that lost roles need to be replaced. Continuity theory, therefore, has the advantage of offering a variety of patterns of successful ageing from which the individual can choose. The disadvantage is the problem of trying to test this theory empirically. Each individual's pattern of adjustment in old age or retirement becomes a case study in which the researcher attempts to determine how successfully the individual was able to continue in her/his previous lifestyle. Building a generally applicable theory from this basis is, therefore, difficult. From a research and policy perspective, it stresses the need to understand the biography and lifecourse of the individual in attempting to understand her/his experience of later life. As such it is a more person-centred approach and stresses the links between 'old age' and earlier phases of life.

The importance of social roles in functionalist theory

Both disengagement and activity theory embrace the structural-functionalist concept of social roles. Social role theory originated within the interpretist perspective derived from anthropology and the theories noted earlier are concerned, as is much gerontological work, with the meaning, content and organisation of social roles in later life. Disengagement, activity and continuity theory are all, to a lesser or greater degree, concerned with how older people adjust to changes and losses in social roles. However, such concerns are also evident in other phases of the lifecycle – role loss is not exclusive to old age. All three theories offer a profoundly negative view of old age in which all role changes are the result of loss. There is little reference to new positive roles such as becoming (great) grandparents.

Social role theory assumes the existence of a set of rules, regulations and roles and that as an individual ages there will be a change (adaptation) in the number of social roles an individual has and how these are executed. Here roles are conceptualised in the Parsonian sense and are defined in terms of both expectations of the role and orientation of the role. Roles are part of the normative order of society and are powerful determinants of behaviour as there are sanctions for deviation from 'social expectations'. Put at its most straightforward a social role can be conceptualised as a pattern of behaviour expected from an individual who holds a particular social status (defined in terms of social position) – in our examples that of an older person.

However, the social world is a complex entity and any individual has a multitude of roles to play simultaneously. An individual could be involved in the roles of spouse, parent, sibling or employee at the same time. All of these roles stress different aspects of the individual's persona. In the broadest sense, competing social roles differ in three main ways. First, roles will emphasise varying qualities. Some roles are defined in terms of the task undertaken, such as the worker role, while others are defined more in terms of emotional content, such as wife or husband. Second, social roles vary in the type of reward offered, such as money, prestige, status, emotional support or satisfaction. Third, roles are evaluated according to the values of the society. For example, in capitalist societies strongly imbued with the Protestant work ethic, the role of the retired person or the mother staying at home looking after small children may be ascribed little value. Similarly, the retired person may be ascribed little status in a society, which places its major emphasis upon economic activity and financial independence. The notion of social roles is complex and a dynamic area of social world which not all theories acknowledge. In attempting to understand later life we clearly need to be able to integrate our understanding of the different roles that older people play and how they make sense of them.

Age stratification theory

This is another good example of a theory which is concerned with the adaption of groups, rather than of individual older people. Again the concern is with examining social integration but from the basis of age-based groups and it flows out of the consensus approach. Society is often conceptualised as being stratified, or divided, along a number of dimensions such as social class or ethnic status and these factors are used to allocate social roles. Age stratification theory uses chronological age as the defining and role allocation variable (Riley, 1971; Riley *et al.*, 1973; Riley, 1987). Three basic issues dominate age stratification theory: first, the meaning of age and the position of age groups within any particular social context, second, the transitions which individuals experience over the lifecycle because of these social definitions of age, and third, the mechanisms for the allocation of roles between individuals.

Riley (1971) argues that each age group (young, mid-life and old) can be analysed in terms of the roles that members of that group play within society and how these are valued. For example within the employment field, workers may be classified as 'older' and 'younger' and the latter valued more highly because of their perceived greater productivity, innovation and vitality. The use of chronological age in guiding the allocation of social roles is probably universal to all cultures, but the precise nature of these age norms reflects the culture, history, values and structure of specific societies. For example, over the twentieth century there have been substantial variations in some aspects of the lifecycle. Childbearing and child-rearing are now confined to a much shorter period than previously when women were 'reproductively active' for twenty-five to thirty years. This has been matched by the creation and increase in the duration of the 'empty nest' phase of the lifecycle. Similarly, within specific societies the size, composition and history of particular cohorts influence both the timing and order of the major life events. The existence of compulsory national service will 'delay' the major life transitions such as marriage, going to university or starting a career.

These age norms in behaviour may originate in tradition, factual regularity or negotiation. Whatever the origin, they are based upon assumptions, either explicit or implicit, about age-related abilities and limitations. These norms may, however, vary with social class, ethnicity or sex, historically or culturally. For example, members of the working class traditionally marry at an earlier age than members of the professional classes. Similarly, age at first marriage is usually older for males than for females. Because of these variations, age norms have different realities and meanings for varying social groups. Despite this, age is a universal criterion for role allocation.

The age grading of roles within an age stratification system creates age differences and inequalities. Each age group is evaluated, both by itself and others in the society, in terms of the dominant social values. This differential evaluation of roles will produce an unequal distribution of power and prestige across the age groups. Thus when societies value the accumulated experience and wisdom of the old, and allow them to undertake roles that capitalise upon this experience, then the aged will be accorded a position of respect. Riley and Riley (1994a) have developed the notion of structural lag as a way of responding to the observation that individual lives, in relation to age-graded roles, change more rapidly than social norms or institutions. They argue that social institutions lag behind major social changes such as the institutionalisation of formal retirement. Now people can anticipate fifteen or twenty years of retirement without the development of social opportunities and clear roles. Similarly a policy of 'lifelong learning' does not fit easily with the completion of formal education for most people between 18 and 25 years. This approach can be used to argue for a review of our formalised age norms, such as retirement, which can lead to the loss of the potential contribution of older people across the life course.

The value of this approach is that it allows the gerontologist to look at any age group in terms of its demographic characteristics and its relationships with other groups. The system of age stratification in any society is complex and dynamic and linked in with other systems of stratification such as class or ethnicity. The task of understanding the effects of age stratification is complicated by these interactions. Furthermore the usefulness of this approach is weakened by the use of chronological age rather than 'actual' ageing to define cohort membership; the 'meaning' attached to particular ages is both historically and culturally specific. This is very much a macroscale approach to the study of ageing for, while it tells us about the attributes of different cohorts, it is of limited value in explaining individual behaviour. This approach can often be seen as being deterministic and allowing little freedom of action for the individual social actor because of the themes' macrolevel orientation and of being an essentially static theory which neglected political processes (Quadagno and Reid, 1999). Riley *et al.* (1999) developed the ageing and society paradigm to address the static nature of age stratification. This new paradigm distinguished the notions of changing lives and changing structures as two interrelated sets of processes. However, this remains an essentially functionalist stance which emphasises balance, integration and norms and one in which factors such as class and gender are conspicuously absent.

Modernisation theory

The position of older people in pre-industrial society is usually described as one of respect and authority. Typically, pre-industrial society is depicted as the 'golden age' of ageing and older people, although every stage in history seems to look back to its own 'golden age'. This stereotypical view of the past is usually contrasted with their position in modern society where older people are thought to be worse off because they are consigned to meaningless retirement, neglected by their family and ignored by the prevailing youth culture. The basic thesis of modernisation theory is that as society moves from rural to industrial, the position of older people deteriorates as urbanisation and industrialisation combine to undermine the extended family and replace it with the nuclear family as the primary unit of society and isolate older people from both society and the family.

Cowgill and Holmes (1972) developed these ideas further. The process of modernisation was defined by four parameters: improvements in medical technology, the application to the economy of science and technology, urbanisation and mass education. Cowgill and Holmes (1972) argued that improvements in health care led to an ageing of the population. The decrease in the potency of death results in an ageing of the working population and a decrease in job opportunities for the young. Thus intergenerational tensions are created by the competition for jobs. Retirement then becomes a social substitute for death and creates job opportunities for the young. However, the dominance of the prevailing work ethic results in a 'devaluing' of retirement. Additionally economic and technological developments devalue the employment skills of the old. Urbanisation attracts young people from the rural areas, resulting in a break-up of the extended family. Finally, the development of mass education reduces the hold that older people have over younger people. Changes in these four factors contributed, it was argued, to a decrease in the status of the older people in modern society. In such developing social settings, youth and progress are extolled while the traditions and experience of the old are developed and seen as irrelevant and their reduced power and prestige places them at a disadvantage. The old become socially and physically abandoned and live a marginal existence on the fringes of society. First, implicit within this theory is the notion that pre-industrial societies are uniform and are characterised by a positive attitude towards older people. Second, it assumes there has been a before-and-after situation within societies with regard to the position of older people and that there has been a smooth, uniform, linear translation from one type of society to another. Third, and perhaps most important, there is now a significant body of empirical research which indicates that the presence of an extended family does not guarantee the status and care of older people (Thane, 2000). Again pre-industrial societies illustrate a degree of diversity in the attributes displayed towards older people and it is unwise to presume a homogeneity that is more fable than fact.

Conflict theory and ageing

As its name suggests, conflict theorists take a rather different view of the organisation of society than functionalists who stress the values that different social groups have in common. In contrast conflict theory, which derives from neo-Marxist and neo-Weberian views of society, stresses discord and conflict. Social groups are conceptualised as having opposing views and are seen as being in conflict over control and access to social resources. However, this is still a macrolevel group of theories in that the concern is with society overall rather than individuals. Society is conceptualised as being stratified into specific groups and classes and society is seen as the result of the conflict between these different groups. The neo-Marxists explain this conflict as a result of economic inequalities resulting from the concentration of economic power within specific groups (which then seek to retain control of them). Neo-Weberians take a more expansive view of the roots of social conflict, which include not only economic power but also social status and ideology. Gerontological applications of this theoretical perspective are much less common than theories from the functionalist perspective but include the highly influential structured dependency theory and political economy approach to ageing. This perspective upon ageing became very important in the development of the 'radical' dimension of British gerontological developments and has key protagonists in the United States (Estes, 2001) and Europe. Such themes were not, however, unique to the field of ageing but demonstrated a wider resonance across the social sciences (see Estes *et al.*, 2001).

Structured dependency and the political economy approach

The approach to old age from a conflict theory perspective emphasises the continuity into later life of the inequalities that characterise the earlier phases of the lifecycle. To oversimplify the case, those who were poor in mid-life will be poor in old age (perhaps even poorer) while those who were rich and powerful remain so. A good example of this was Queen Elizabeth, the Queen Mother. Although she lived to be a centenarian her wealth, power and prestige were not compromised by her experience of ageing. The structured dependency theory was initially proposed by Townsend (1981) and then enthusiastically taken up by others such as Estes (1979), Walker (1980, 1981), Myles (1984) and Pampel (1998). Structured dependency theory has been especially influential in British gerontology during the latter part of the twentieth century while in the United States similar views were described as political economy.

Political economy is concerned with the interaction between the state, the economy and various socially defined groups, in this case older people, and in particular with the way 'social goods' are distributed between groups and the mechanisms by which they are allocated. Those working in the broad field of political economy were informed by four main areas: conflict theory, critical theory, feminism and cultural theory. What both political economy and structured dependency are concerned with is the proposition that the dependent social position of older people and the problems they experience are socially constructed and derive from conceptions of ageing and health. This approach to the study of old age is essentially structural and macrolevel in nature although Estes (2001) now claims that it can be used to study micro- and meso-level (organisational) aspects of ageing. This perspective offers a sharp contrast to the potentially 'victim blaming' and 'biomedical' philosophy of old age as a time of loss and decline which was at the heart of some manifestations of structuralist theories. Political economy theorists argued strongly against these assumptions and developed a theoretical framework in which age is conceptualised as a social rather than biological construct and one which is located within the explicit study of capitalism. Social policies, which shape old age, are seen as the product of economic, social political and cultural forces.

The political economy approach, as exemplified by Estes (1979), Walker (1981) and Olson (1982), argues that old age is defined neither by chronology nor by biology but by the relationship between older people and the means of production in general and social policy in particular. The organisation of production, social and political institutions, social processes and the social policies pursued explicitly (or implicitly) by society is seen to be, in this approach, the key relationships. It assumes a structural relationship between older people and the rest of society, with society constructing the institutions and rules within which old age is defined and the experienced of ageing contextualised. Estes (2001) argues for the importance of the state in defining and experience of old age because (a) the state is important in the distribution of power and resources, (b) it intervenes to mediate relationships between different social groups, and (c) it intervenes to ameliorate conditions which threaten the overall stability of society. From this perspective, older people are seen not as a group separate from the wider social context, but as an integral, if marginalised, part of society. Capitalism and the state combine to marginalise and dominate older people (Walker, 1999). However, in this perspective older people cannot be analysed in isolation from the society within which they are located.

Central to this perspective is the notion of structured dependency (Townsend, 1981). This approach argues that in order to understand the dependent situation of groups such as older people we need to understand the essentially 'socially constructed' nature of this status. Dependency is viewed as a socially constructed entity best understood in terms of relationships between the dependent group, in this case older people, capitalism and the state. Policies for social security, retirement and pensions assume particular importance in this perspective because they determine the duration of the working life and assign dependent status to specific phases such as retirement (or child-rearing) or to groups such as the long-term sick or to handicapped people. This dependency is enhanced and reinforced by the exclusion of older people (or young mothers) from employment, the major means of economic status in advanced capitalist societies. As a result of this socially constructed exclusion from the labour market, and their reliance upon welfare and pensions for their source of income, older people experience wider social exclusion such as poverty, reduced community involvement, institutionalisation and marginalisation. This exclusion of older people from the social mainstream could, therefore, be overcome by changes in social policy, most notably a major increase in the level of the state pension.

The political economy and structured dependency approaches have several positive aspects. First, it has offered a powerful set of counter-arguments against the demographic 'doom and gloom' analysts who portray the increasing numbers of older people as an inevitable social and economic catastrophe. This perspective has important new questions for research and has done much to overturn the assumption that the experience of old age is homogeneous and that those factors such as class, gender and ethnicity do not matter. This perspective has also been instrumental in raising questions about the nature and quality of services offered to older people. Second, structured dependency has, at its heart, a focus upon the full integration of older people into society and, as such, offers a sharp contrast to the notions of disengagement so characteristic of earlier gerontological studies. It has certainly been one of the most influential gerontological theories and excited a whole generation of scholars.

There are drawbacks to this approach which are well summarised by Gilleard and Higgs (2000). Conceptually it is a macrolevel theoretical framework concerned, as it is, with the analysis and explanations of the workings of the social system and its problems. The key concept of structured dependency is rather deterministic and fails to address the issue of the power of individuals to challenge such classification and control mechanisms. By focusing upon relationships with the labour market and issues of retirement, which for current generations of elders largely concerns men only, this perspective has failed adequately to deal with issues of gender. Perhaps most importantly this approach has largely ignored questions concerning the meaning and purpose of the experience of ageing. Its focus upon structure has led to the relative neglect of the experiences of older people and the ways that they make sense of old age, although this is now changing. By focusing upon a 'mass' solution to the key problem of poverty in old age, structured dependency theorists end up homogenising older people by proposing a simple 'one size fits all' policy solution. This has been somewhat undermined by the discovery of significant variations among the current cohort of elders in terms of class and gender. Phillipson (1998) responds to this challenge by developing a dichotomy in the history of old age (Gilleard and Higgs, 2000); up to the 1970s the welfare state and retirement were central to the development of a 'secure' old age, while after this period the institutions of the welfare state were radically transformed by recession and the rupture of the consensus on the role of the welfare. This, combined with increasing diversity of the older population, has led Phillipson (1998) to argue for the creation of 'critical gerontology', which marries the political economy perspective with its recognition of the importance of class, gender and biography to provide a more rounded perspective upon old age and later life. Estes (2001) has significantly developed this approach by developing a complex multilevel analytical framework that incorporates (a) financial/post-industrial capitalism and globalisation, (b) the state, (c) sex/gender system, (d) citizen/public and (e) the ageing enterprise/ medical industrial complex. These are located within the interlocking systems of oppression – class, race, gender and ideology. Despite the refinements, it remains a theory which is problematic at the microlevel of analysis.

Interpretist theory and ageing

In contrast to the macrolevel theories of ageing are those developed from the interpretative tradition in social science and which have a microlevel focus where the individual is the key focus of theoretical attention. As noted in the development of Phillipson's (1998) notion of critical gerontology, there are now explicit attempts to link these different theoretical approaches in a more integrated fashion. At the heart of the differing manifestations of the interactionist perspective is the notion that we should understand those we study and that we can do this best by trying to view and understand the world as they do. These approaches, with their emphasis upon individuals, offer a very different way of theorising about social phenomena from the structuralist perspectives. In a structuralist theory individual actions are framed within a broad social system which governs social interactions and is understood within a specified top-down framework. In contrast interactionism has a very different individual-based focus. From this perspective social life, social action and social processes derive from the bottom-up and out of the cumulative actions of lots of individuals rather than being 'prescribed' by external factors. Society and social life does not take on the autonomous, independent characteristics attributed to it by structuralists. Society is not seen as a rigid external structure but as a series of loosely overlapping groups and is seen as coming from within: society is not conceptualised as an external force. There are various manifestations of interpretist approaches to the study of ageing and later life and these are summarised in the following sections. The types of research questions that this type of approach would pose focus very much upon the social world of older people and often cast their gaze upon the commonplace and taken for granted.

Symbolic interactionism

Symbolic interactionism was developed by Mead (1956) and is a key sociological theory. Proponents of this view argue that communication with others is a means of both transmitting and receiving cultural norms and values. It is via the communication of symbols that we learn vast numbers of social meanings and ways of acting and this perspective implies that most adult behaviour is learnt from symbolic communication with others. In the process of social interaction, the individual is both an actor and a reactor. Through the communication of symbols, individuals learn the values and meanings of their culture and therefore ways of acting from others. Essential to the interactionist perspective is the view that individuals construct realities or social worlds in a process of interaction with others. Meanings are socially defined but the social actor defines the social world as well as being defined by it.

The symbolic interactionist perspective on ageing is concerned with the reciprocal relationship between the individual and her/his social environment. Old people, like other social actors, construct their own social reality. Consequently this approach sees ageing as a dynamic process that is responsive to both structural and normative contexts and individual capacities and perceptions. This perspective is essentially a microscale approach to the study of ageing for it stresses the need to understand the nature and impact of ageing at the individual level. Thus an understanding of the impact of ageing requires an understanding of the meaning and interpretation of the events which accompany old age and which are articulated and defined by older people.

Labelling theory

It has been suggested that old age may usefully be conceptualised within the framework of the labelling theory of deviance. Labelling theory (Berger *et al.*, 1976) suggests that other groups attribute social status to individuals and/or groups by the successful application to them of negative 'labels' to confer stigma or deviant status. In a youth- and health-conscious society, old age may be defined, or labelled, as a deviant and stigmatising condition. Indeed, those who work with older people may also attain this damaged or spoilt identity by contamination with the stigmatised group. Coming into contact with the 'deviant' group is sufficient to compromise the status and professional identity of individuals as well as the older people themselves. The basic assumption of labelling theory is that the concept of self is derived from interaction with others in our social environment: we get our sense of worth and identity from how others react and interact with us. Thus the behaviour of older people is seen to depend largely on the reactions of significant others in their immediate social world, which depend upon how they define, classify and value older people. Such interactions may communicate a stereotypical image of older people as useless, dependent and marginal. The individual who accepts this negative labelling is inducted into the dependent negative position, learning to act as older people are supposed to and losing previous skills, confidence and independence; finally the external label is accepted and the person defines her/himself as inadequate, thereby creating a vicious circle. Thus once people are 'labelled' as old because they are retired, they have to play the role of a 'retiree' and accept their pension and not seek gainful employment. Similarly the failure of older people to consult their doctor for specific symptoms because they think they are 'due to old age' rather than interpreting them as signs of disease is another negative way that social labelling may affect older people. Although the example here is of a negative image of old age, it is clear that from this theoretical perspective the adoption of positive labelling could have the opposite effect; attempts to rebadge old age as a positive and rewarding phase of life have met with little success to date.

Social exchange theory

Symbolic interactionism concentrates upon the nature of the individual–society relationship; exchange theory provides a more detailed explanation of why individuals behave as they do in particular situations. The notion of social behaviour as exchange can be traced back to the anthropological work of Mauss (1954) who considered that interaction constituted an exchange of material and non-material goods and services. There are four key assumptions which underpin this theoretical stance: (a) individuals 'choose' interactions which maximise benefit and minimise 'cost', (b) individuals use past experiences of exchanges to predict the future, (c) interactions will be sustained only if they are beneficial, and (d) power is derived from 'imbalances' in social exchange – if an individual is 'dependent' upon another then he/she loses 'power' and the other party accrues it. The centrality of exchange in the relationships of older people is now well recognised (Gubrium and Holstein, 2000).

All three of these related theories concentrate upon the detail of human behaviour and interaction without locating this within some notion of the structural impact of society as a whole. There is no link with the macrolevel of analysis which may be defining the overall social context. As such this contrasts markedly with the structural theories considered earlier. Some critics argue that interactionist perspectives find it problematic to deal with large-scale structures and social processes. Like the structural theories, however, this approach is also ahistorical in that it neglects the influence of life experiences and lacks a biographical or lifecourse perspective and does not address issues of class or gender in any detail.

Lifecourse perspectives on ageing

Age is an important organising factor within society and is used to allocate social roles and to determine entry into specific social activities. Most countries have laws regarding age of entry into formal education, driving, voting, purchase and consumption of alcohol or tobacco, and marriage. The precise ages that are used to determine entry into these different social activities vary both between different societies and historically. The age at which subjects in Britain can vote has changed from 21 to 18 (and there is now a lobby to reduce this still further to 16) as has the age of consent for gay sex (from 18 to 16) (see Bytheway, 1997, for a discussion of age-related roles). These 'formal' age-related roles are supplemented by a series (and obviously fluid) set of informal social norms and expectations. These combine to form what Neugarten (1974) termed a 'social clock' that is now more commonly referred to as the 'lifecourse'.

What is the lifecourse?

The notion of the lifecourse is one of the oldest and most enduring of all our conceptual frameworks concerning ageing and has been important in the development of gerontological theorising and frameworks for analysis. At its most straightforward the lifecourse consists of a series of stages (or social roles) which all individuals pass through as they age; this idea is not new or confined to the erudite discourse of gerontologists. The notion that the pattern of life is divided into distinct phases is prevalent across cultures and throughout different historical time points. Most of us are familiar with Shakespeare's seven ages of man. There are various different models as to the number of 'stages' which constitute the life course. The lifecourse has become increasingly differentiated into smaller segments with the emergence of subgroups of 'adolescence', 'pre-school' and 'middle age' as distinct phases, and more recently 'empty nesters'. The distinction between the 'young' old (those aged between 65 and 74 years) and the 'old' old (those aged over 75 years) is now often described as the third and fourth ages.

An idea that has held considerable currency is the notion that the later phase of life may be divided between the 'third age' and the 'fourth age' (Laslett, 1989). Laslett advanced the thesis that it is possible to differentiate a 'third age' characterised by a time of opportunity and leisure for the increasingly affluent older person freed from the necessities of paid employment and dependence upon the state. In contrast the fourth age is a time of decrepitude, dependence and ill health before death. The seductive image of the 'third age' lifestyle is clearly evident. It celebrates the agency of older people as it recognises the less rigid post-work world that requires active planning by older people in the construction of a 'third age' post-work identity. However, it neglects to take into account the broader social context of ageing and the way that factors such as class and gender impact upon our ability to enjoy a post-work lifestyle.

The lifecourse is not a single entity but consists of several different spheres such as education, occupation and family dimensions. In understanding the lifecourse we need to distinguish and interrelate three different types of time: historical, biological and social. Historical time refers to the precise historical context, biological time links the physiological and biological timetable to life stages such as infancy, adolescence and maturity, while social time relates to the definition, expectation and meaning that is attributed to the different stages of life. These different dimensions interrelate to produce a pattern of lifestages that is historically and culturally distinct. The (fairly) recent emergence of stages such as childhood, adolescence and retirement demonstrates the essentially dynamic and fluid nature of the lifecourse concept and its location within specific cultural and historical contexts. There is nothing inevitable or universal about this way of thinking about the process of ageing: it is a dynamic and constantly evolving framework.

Although the lifecycle is often perceived as a simple universal progression from one well-defined set of social roles to another, it is in reality a highly complex concept consisting of several interrelated trajectories. We need to distinguish between the different arenas within which we can identify different stages of development and how these different stages overlap and sometimes are in conflict. For example, the family lifecycle element may involve numerous transitions including courtship, newly married, new parents, parents of teenagers, 'empty nesters', retirement and widowhood. Importantly not everyone will experience all these phases of the family cycle; there may also be enormous variations, between cultures and different historical time points, in the ages at which individuals experience these transitions. The primary focus of lifecourse research remains, however, at the individual level of analysis.

Social roles and social norms

In using a lifecourse perspective, to describe someone as old (or juvenile) we are locating them within a specific social environment, which expects particular roles and provides differing opportunities, rights, privileges and barriers. Chronological age serves as the basis for proscribing or permitting admission to various social roles and behaviours. The entry into, and exit from, specific social roles such as adolescent or retiree is influenced by the existence of 'age norms'. All cultures have rules (either explicit or implicit) which define what are appropriate (and inappropriate) forms of behaviour for people of particular ages. These rules are generally referred to as norms and allow us to predict the behaviour of others in specific situations, as well as allowing others to predict our behaviour. For example, in British culture the norm, or expected behaviour, upon being introduced to someone for the first time is to extend our hand and shake hands. This seems perfectly natural to British people but in some cultures it would be interpreted as a gesture of hostility, not friendship, or an indication of extreme rudeness.

Age norms are concerned with the linking of specific chronological ages to expected (and inappropriate) behaviours. Three features characterise age norms: they identify appropriate and inappropriate behaviours, they are shared by particular social groups (ranging from entire societies to specific subgroups) and they imply some element of social control and social sanction for transgression. At the formal level there are established age norms concerning voting, driving, alcohol consumption or school attendance. There are also informal norms concerning the appropriateness of behaviours for different age groups (and not just older people). For example we are not surprised, but might be embarrassed, to see a young child having a tantrum if her mother refuses to buy her some sweets. However, we would consider it most surprising if a teenager behaved in the same way. Similarly we expect certain behaviours and attitudes from older people such as lack of interest in sex or romantic involvement and to thinking and dressing in a conservative fashion. Neither are they expected to engage in heavy manual labour. Informal behaviour rules also provide suggestions about appropriate behaviour towards older people. We are expected to help old ladies across the street, give them our seat on crowded buses and trains, and carry their shopping or luggage. Similarly, older adults have social obligations such as showing an interest in their (great) grandchildren. The erring or uninterested grandparent would be subject to considerable social sanction and gossip, both from within the family and from the wider social environment.

In looking empirically at the concept of age norms there are at least four potential research questions. What do people do (can we identify regularity in specific events such as marriage, birth of children or widowhood), what do people say they do and what do people think they (or other people) should do and what are the consequences of not observing norms? We can look both at what people do and what people say they do. Demographic data show fairly consistent patterns of behaviour in terms of timetables for marriage and birth of children. The classic studies of Neugarten (1974) identified empirically that non-institutionalised age norms are well recognised by the population, and appropriate behaviours are ascribed to them. In a study of residents in a US Midwestern city she demonstrated that adulthood was seen as consisting of four periods – young adulthood, maturity, middle age and old age (Neugarten, 1974). Five dimensions defined progression from one stage to the next: health, career, family responsibilities, and psychological and social factors. Respondents could easily answer questions such as 'What is the best age for a woman to marry?' Greatest agreement among respondents was observed on the timing of major role transitions such as marriage or retirement. Most middle-class men and women felt that men should be prepared to retire between the ages of 60 and 65 and that the right age for a man to marry was 20–25. More recent research from New Zealand and North America seems to confirm the existence of these types of age norms (Byrd and Bruess, 1992; Settersten and Hagestad, 1996a, 1996b), but the research illustrates the complexity of this concept. Certainly research participants can identify idealised 'timetables' across the lifecourse, but it seems likely that these may form a generalised framework, a type of cultural template, but not necessarily one that individuals would feel the need to conform to.

Individuals are aware of such norms in their own timing of life events, and make role transitions when they think they have reached the most appropriate age or when they think they ought to. Individuals are aware of how their pattern of timing varies from the norm with such comments as 'I married late' or 'I had my children late'. There is less evidence that people feel constrained to conform to the norms or that they feel any social sanction for not adhering to the 'ideal' path. It has been suggested that this is because individuals accept the general notion of 'cultural' lifecourse timetables but do not necessarily use these to construct a personal timetable. Such dissonance between views about appropriate behaviour for oneself and for the wider population is evident in, for example, attitudes for HIV testing (i.e. it should be available for everyone but I would not choose to be tested). Clearly the notion of the lifecourse is a very powerful organising concept within gerontological theory and research. It is, however, problematic for many of the reasons already outlined. Operationalising this concept is problematic because of lack of consensus as to the number of stages involved and in defining entry or exit points to the different stages. There are also problems in determining the universality of the concept because of cultural and historical variations in the 'meaning' ascribed to different ages. However, it remains a powerful idea because of the way that it seeks to locate the understanding and explanation of the behaviour of individuals and societies within a temporal perspective. Individuals and societies are not simply 'old'; rather they are ageing with a past (and with a future) and it is this dynamic perspective which a lifecourse approach to ageing emphasises.

Conclusion

Theoretical formulations in the social sciences display a marked variation in terms of complexity and sophistication. The theories used by social gerontologists reflect these varying levels of sophistication and complexity. We have also indicated that most of the theory used by gerontologists to inform their work has been derived from other disciplines such as sociology or psychology. Thus there are sometimes difficulties in applying the concepts involved across disciplinary boundaries. Additionally it is important for the European reader to remember that the majority of these theoretical approaches have been developed in North America, which may limit their utility and explanatory power when applied elsewhere.

The earliest formulations in social gerontology such as activity and disengagement theory, although not derived from other academic disciplines, were simplistic in approach. Considerable empirical evaluation of these two theories indicates that neither is sufficient to explain the experience of ageing. Indeed these perspectives seem to be as much if not more philosophical than theoretical. Both activity and disengagement theory appear to be prescriptive recommendations about how to live in the later years of life, rather than theories attempting to explain human behaviour. Nevertheless, these two theories have had considerable impact upon the development of gerontology and the formulation of social and medical policies for later life. In particular, disengagement theory has been used to justify the age-segregated policies for older people that characterise many modern industrial societies. They have also been highly influential in determining the types of research questions which are informed by a focus upon loss and adjustment.

The early theories of ageing were very proscribed and prescriptive as to how individuals should age. Successful ageing was to be achieved variously by remaining active, prescribing a middle-aged lifestyle and reducing engagements. Theoretical formulations which offer the path of successful ageing re-emerged in the 1990s with the proposal of Rowe and Kahn (1997). They suggest that successful ageing, which is never really defined, is to be achieved by the promotion of three factors: low probability of disease, high functional and cognitive ability, and active engagement with life. These formulations take little account of the influence of wider structural factors upon the experience of ageing nor do they fully take into account the influence of race, gender and class in predicting the experience of age. As with so many theoretical formulations the notion of 'successful ageing' assumes a homogeneous population and does not acknowledge the existence and importance of the existing inequalities with which cohorts enter old age. Encompassing the diversity that the older age groups demonstrate remains a challenge to all those who theorise about this aspect of life.

Social gerontology has not been isolated from the wider developments of theory within the social sciences. Gerontologists have adopted theories of human behaviour developed by other scientists. Symbolic interactionism, labelling theory, exchange theory and age stratification approaches all offer considerable scope for future evaluation and testing. Of such developments the symbolic interactionist approach may prove to be one of the most useful theoretical perspectives for the gerontologist to employ. This approach has the advantage of viewing ageing as a dynamic process. It is also value free: it does not offer a philosophical mandate about how to live the later years of life. A particular advantage of this theory is that it suggests that the influence of negative labelling, low expectations and negative stereotypes of old age can be overcome by more positive attitudes from the rest of society. However, we need to be realistic in what can be achieved. As with the debate about the third age, here is a fine balance to be drawn about the experience of old age.

Given the complexity of social gerontology, it seems unlikely that a single perspective will adequately explain the experience of ageing. It seems probable that a composite theory of ageing will develop using aspects of a number of these different viewpoints. Before we are able to formulate a composite theory of social ageing, these competing approaches require much more empirical investigation to test their explanatory power. In particular we need to develop cross-cultural and cross-national perspectives in order to test the veracity of our theoretical formulations. In addition, as Bytheway (1997) argues, we need, as gerontologists, to recognise the ageist assumptions which underpin many of our theoretical perspectives upon ageing. He argues that we need to develop a theoretical base, which breaks free from the ageism implicit within popular culture, if we are ever to be able to understand how people manage and experience age and to be able to evaluate the social context within which this takes place. Furthermore we need to develop research and theoretical perspectives that view the issue of ageing and the topics to be researched from the perspective of the older person. So much gerontological research has, for the best possible motives, been concerned with the 'problems' of later life and how older people care with loss and adversity. Clearly there is room for the development of a research agenda which examines the issues and topics of concern to older people themselves rather than being a top-down approach imposed by the concerns and preoccupations of policy makers. By focusing upon the concerns of older people themselves we may gain greater insight and understanding of the challenges and rewards of ageing and later life.

3 Methodological aspects of the study of ageing

In a survey of attitudes towards the prospect of Britain adopting the euro, 61 per cent of those aged 65+ were against this, compared with 32 per cent of those aged 25–34. Such data are routinely presented as evidence of the inherently conservative nature of older people. From this an inference is drawn to suggest that it is the process of ageing which has brought about the politically, economically and socially conservative views implied here. This leads to the conclusion that, upon entry to old age, we will all become socially and politically conservative regardless of our previous social or political beliefs. Using this line of argument social and political conservatism is seen as being constructed as a universal and inevitable aspect of the 'social' component of the ageing process. Similarly social commentators and the media often produce reports of the relationship between diet, such as eating yoghurt, and the longevity of populations. It is the prime function of the gerontologist to look critically at such suggestions and to draw conclusions as to the veracity of such claims. Hence the major focus of the study of gerontology, or ageing, is to identify and understand how and why individuals (or societies) age and to look critically at any such factors that are hypothesised as demonstrating the effect of ageing or factors which are proposed as 'causing' ageing. These deceptively simple goals are fraught with methodological challenges and this chapter concentrates upon the problems posed by the study of ageing, in which age is taken as the independent variable, and upon the techniques used to respond to these challenges. However, all of the issues such as the importance of clearly defining study populations or maximising response rates, which characterise other social science research, also apply to the study of ageing and later life and readers are referred to the standard research methods literature for these (Bowling *et al.*, 2002). The focus of this chapter is upon the special challenges of gerontological research and working with older people. There are now several texts concerned specifically with research in social gerontology (Lawton and Herzog, 1989; Peace, 1990; Wallace and Woolson, 1992; Jamieson and Victor, 2002) where further details about the major methodological issues pertinent to the study of ageing may be found and which serve to complement and enhance the points raised in this chapter.

Types of research

Gerontologists are primarily interested in identifying, investigating and understanding the effects of ageing. As indicated in the introduction, the definition of gerontology and the gerontological field of interest are often extended to include the study of the experience of 'old age' as well as ageing. In very broad terms in gerontological research, age is the independent variable and, for example, measures of social, psychological or physical function operate as the dependent variable. Within this broad research paradigm, there are a variety of different methodological approaches and different types of research questions which require consideration. It is important for the student or scholar of gerontology to understand these different approaches for these influence greatly the type of information gathered. The types of research design used influence our overall knowledge about ageing and also the areas where our knowledge and understanding are more patchy. The extent and nature of our knowledge about old age and ageing is greatly influenced by the types of questions that we ask and how we choose to answer them.

The first distinction between different types of research questions considered by gerontologists that needs to be drawn concerns the distinction between the study of ageing and the study of old age. There is an extensive body of research that has concentrated upon enumerating the many and varied characteristics of older people. For example Bury and Holmes (1991) studied 200 people aged 90 and over, providing an informative and stimulating description of the health, social circumstances and quality of life of the 'very old'. However, such studies tell us little about the process of ageing: rather they provide an often-detailed description of the key characteristics of older people at particular time points in particular settings and in particular cultures. There is also now a body of work emerging investigating ageing: there is a different emphasis here from classifying and describing the group of interest to trying to describe and understand the processes of ageing. This is a more dynamic approach that raises a variety of different questions. Again when evaluating the quality of research in gerontology we need to distinguish between these two types of approaches and interpret the findings from these types of studies appropriately and in context.

Within the broad-shared objectives of gerontological research there are, at the most simplistic level and in common with other social science disciplines, three broad types of research: theoretical research, empirical research and applied research. The distinction between these categories is somewhat artificial: a single research project, such as a study of loneliness and isolation in old age, may contain elements of each type of research. For example, the sampling framework for such a study might be derived from theoretical principles, empirical data collected to demonstrate the extent of loneliness and applied research undertaken to evaluate the most effective ways of combating loneliness. Although each type of approach is considered separately the interrelationships between these different strands of research must be borne in mind. Again each of these research traditions and approaches can consider both the process of ageing or consider the characteristics and attributes of populations of older people.

Empirical research is broadly concerned with the generation of knowledge about the world of older people. Such research may, for example, look at the prevalence of loneliness in later life and seek to determine the 'risk factors' for loneliness. This type of research is often seeking to enumerate the extent of specific aspects of the experience of ageing or to describe the characteristics of particular populations. Much British gerontological research has been of an empirical variety that has sought to challenge and confront the many myths and stereotypes that abound about the experiencing of ageing. Examples of this type of empirical research include the work of Claire Wenger (1984) who has carefully documented and theorised about the social networks of older people in North Wales (Wenger and Burholt, 2004). Empirical research in this sense does not have to be totally quantitative or highly statistical in nature (although most of it is!). Qualitative research such as that by Thompson *et al.* (1990) provides useful and revealing insights into the social world of older people and meets the criteria for empirical research in that they are generating knowledge and data about older people, their world and their experiences. In the case of qualitative research the data or knowledge generated may take the form of words or actions, while quantitative research is concerned with numerical data of various types and with statistical analysis. They are both providing us with description and analysis of the social context and social world of older people.

Theoretical research in British gerontology is much less well established than either empirical or applied research. As Chapter 2 indicated, gerontology is not a strongly theoretical discipline, although this partly reflects the academic 'immaturity' of gerontology as a discipline for scholarship, teaching and research. In gerontology much of the theoretical work has been derived from related social science disciplines; developments such as feminism are having an increasing influence upon the nature of the questions posed by gerontologists, the types of methodology employed and the explanations for the observations noted (Arber and Ginn, 1995). Social theory is concerned with developing theories that can explain and predict either (or both) individual or macrolevel social behaviour. As Chapter 2 indicated, gerontologists have developed theories and have undertaken empirical research to attempt to refute them. It is the role of the research scientist, regardless of discipline, to attempt to disprove (rather than prove) a particular theory. The scientific method requires that the emphasis is upon disproving rather than proving the various theories and hypothesises advanced. However, theoretical propositions are also important because they influence the questions posed and methods used at given points in time. For example, the predominance of the activity and disengagement theories in the 1950s and 1960s influenced the development of a research agenda concerned with measuring quality of life in old age and the adjustment to the losses which were inevitably seen as part of ageing. This reflected the acceptance by researchers of the biomedical view of ageing as a time of inevitable loss and decline. Proponents of the 'successful ageing' paradigm might ask a different set of questions.

Applied gerontological research is a particular strength of British researchers, perhaps because of the emphasis of research-funding bodies upon evaluating service-based interventions. This type of research focuses upon questions of policy and practice and seeks to determine the 'best' way to provide care or improve practice. Applied research could be characterised as 'research for action' and is usually undertaken to provide the answer to a specific question of policy or practice. Such questions may be examined at local, regional or national levels or some combination of these. For example researchers have evaluated the effectiveness of different types of preventive services such as the evaluation of health visiting service by Vetter *et al.* (1984) or screening older people (Smeeth *et al.*, 2001). The aim of this essentially applied body of research is to provide policy makers with information on the most appropriate and effect-ive models of care for older people. This is research for action, although the recommendations of researchers are not always imple-mented for political or financial reasons. Again this type of research is highly influenced by the key policy questions at the time the research was undertaken. A general concern with optimising the use of hospital beds may prompt a series of research studies looking at 'inappropriate' bed use, the utility of early discharge schemes and the relationship between secondary care services and the primary care and social care interface. The implementation of pre-hospital dis-charge assessment may prompt research to examine which profes-sional group is most appropriate to lead the assessments process (Healy *et al.*, 1999) or how best to organise assessments. The emphasis in much of this type of research is not upon understanding the experience of ageing or old age but is driven by the needs to eval-uate the interventions under study and inform service development and implementation. Consequently the types of data collected are informed by the applied nature of the research question rather than with wider concerns of 'understanding' ageing or old age. A study concerned with evaluating a specific intervention may ask extensive questions about how the service affected carers but is not at all con-cerned with any role the older person may play as a 'carer' of either another older person or younger family members. Such studies often employ extensive structured questionnaires based upon the use of standardised health outcomes measures which may be of limited use for older people and do not allow for the expressions of the concerns of older people. Applied research studies are usually restricted to particular populations such as older people in hospital or those receiving specific services. Hence the generalisability of much of this research about, for example, the prevalence of dementia to the wider population of older people is of questionable value and the insight such studies can offer on the experience of old age is clearly limited.

In each of these approaches, different drivers are at work in gener-ating the research question posed and the methodology and types of empirical material collected to answer it. For example the broad acceptance of the stereotype that old age is a time of isolation and loneliness could result in the development of a research programme by gerontologists to establish the empirical evidence to support or refute this assumption. Such an approach could provide data upon the extent of loneliness among older people. Whatever the findings, the availability of evidence would be preferable to the reliance upon commonly held but possibly incorrect stereotypes. However, the danger in such types of research is that we focus upon the issues of later life, which form the basis of myths and stereotypes and forget the larger agenda. For example, a focus upon loneliness in later life may result in the neglect of examination of loneliness among other groups within the population such as young mothers, students or 'empty nesters'. A focus upon the issues we think are problematic in later life may result in a neglect of the issues which really matter to older people such as transport or environmental matters. Similarly, theoretically driven research is informed by the theories which are current at the time of the research. The widespread popularity, especially in North America, of activity and disengagement theories informed an extensive body of research about roles and functions in later life. Key to many of these investigations was the notion of life satisfaction, a concept that is much less prominent now where the current emphasis is upon quality of life and successful ageing, but which spawned the development of a variety of different measures and studies. Finally, concentration upon applied or policy research often means focusing upon issues which are important for policy makers but which tell us little about the social world and experiences of older people. Hence the types of insights about ageing that these different types of research can provide vary and the reader of such research needs to be able to identify these. Identification of the orientation of the original research helps us to interpret the results presented and evaluate the veracity and authenticity of the insights about ageing and old age generated.

Researching old age and ageing: identifying age, period and cohort effects

It is blatantly obvious that there are clear differences between people of different ages in numerous dimensions such as dress, social norms, diet and lifestyle, political attitudes and physical appearance. Such differences are clearly evident from our everyday experiences. The simple observation that many older people have grey hair may well be represented in the media (or elsewhere) as demonstrating the effects of ageing and determining the onset of 'old age'. The observation of differences between people of different ages in terms of how many have grey hair may well reflect the process of ageing (this may also be termed an age effect). However, the simple observation that something is more common among older people does not automatically mean that we may attribute the cause of this difference to ageing or that it represents an age effect. What makes gerontology especially challenging is that such observations may be alternatively explained as being the result of either period or cohort effects. These different explanatory frameworks each reflect the influence of different sorts of time: individual time (the maturation and growing older of the individual as illustrated by a focus upon developmental time) and historical time (which influences both cohort and period effects). This duality of potential explanations complicates the study of social aspects, and indeed other dimensions, of ageing and creates the potential for the misleading interpretation of research findings. However, this complexity greatly enhances the intellectual challenge involved in the study of ageing and adds to its academic appeal! For example, variations in health status between age groups may be attributed to the 'effect' of ageing when they may be the result of birth cohort differences or period effects such as wartime restriction of diet. Each of these explanations is considered further. Although these three sets of explanatory variables are discussed separately there is obviously the potential for interaction and overlap: this complicates the study of gerontology still further and makes the search for simple solutions and explanations highly problematic.

Age effects

Human physiological development may be divided into three broad phases – maturation, maturity and later life. As individuals move from maturity into 'later life' they may change physically, socially and psychologically and it is these changes which may be conceptualised as the process of ageing and be classified as 'true' age effects. For such changes to be seen as a part of natural ageing they must fulfil several criteria including not being pathological or related to disease states nor resultant from hazardous lifestyles such as smoking or excessive use of alcohol and be both universal (i.e. happen to everyone) and harmful (not amenable to 'reversal') (Strehler, 1962). Hence, for example, ageing is conceptually differentiated from disease or pathology as Box 1.1 illustrated. Dementia does not fulfil the criteria for an 'age effect' because, for example, it is not universal. Ward (1984) distinguishes between two, in theory at least, types of age effects: intrinsic and reactive. Intrinsic age effects are changes that naturally, and inevitably, accompany the ageing process, irrespective of the social context. In contrast reactive age effects are fashioned by the social environment within which ageing takes place. Reactive age effects are, therefore, both culturally and historically specific. Although conceptually distinct, in practice it is often extremely difficult to differentiate between the two different types of age effect. Within the subdiscipline of social gerontology there is less focus upon the identification of age effects as these are much less obvious than in the biological field where the focus of research is concerned very much with developmental time. Age effects are 'independent' of historical time and Wadsworth (2002) suggests that menarche and menopause are two rare examples which merit this classification although they do not entirely meet Strehler's requirement of 'harmfulness'.

Cohort effects

Despite its long folk history and appeal as a way of understanding society, Mannheim (1997) was the first scholar to point to the importance of what he termed generations (a group of people born within a specific time) in understanding differences between age groups. He hypothesised that a generation would develop a common identity and social consciousness (Mannheim, 1997). He suggested that it was exposure to formative events while young (not specifically defined) which was the key factor. Hence the observation of differences between age groups may be due not to the ageing process itself but to the influence of generational or birth cohort effects. This explanation emphasises the influence of historical time and events, rather than developmental time, upon the attitudes of groups of individuals and links the individual experience to the broader social context of the peer group. The nature of the group, in terms of gender balance or size or ethnicity, can also influence the experiences of specific cohorts as they grow up and grow old together. The cohort explanation of age-based differences links both individual and historical time.

A cohort consists of a group of individuals born at similar times, perhaps a ten-year age band, whose members experience the same historical events at roughly the same point in the lifecycle. Good examples of the types of events which might have created the development of distinct birth cohorts, with a particular shared consciousness, are the interwar depression, the Second World War, Vietnam and the 'swinging sixties'. Perhaps the classic example is the post-war 'baby boomers', whose progress can be tracked across time. Mannheim's hypothesis would be that exposure to the 'liberal' attitudes of the 1960s when young would lead to develop of a generational specific ideology and consciousness which would be manifest in their future social attitudes and behaviours and which would mark them out from other generations. Hence as the 'baby boomers' age their supposedly distinctive social and political attitudes may be distinguished from younger and older age groups.

There are four main criticisms which have been advanced to counter the suggestions of Mannheim (1997). First, there is little evidence to support Mannheim's thesis that it is exposure to formative events while young that develops generational differences. Experience of formative effects at other phases of the lifecycle may be equally as important, such as becoming a student in the 1960s or being conscripted into the army as young men in the 1950s. Second, events experienced by one cohort may not be experienced by subsequent groups. The generation born in 1900 lived through the great interwar depression while the 1950 cohort did not. The sequence of historical events experienced by each successive cohort is unique. Third, there is variation within, and between, cohorts in their experience of the same historical event. Several cohorts will experience a seminal event such as the Second World War at different stages of development. Those born in 1920 experienced the Second World War as young adults while those born in 1935 were young children during the war. However, it would probably be foolish to conclude that the Second World War had a formative influence only upon children born between 1939 and 1945. A key event, such as the interwar depression in Britain, was not a monolithic experience for all those who lived through it. Any one historical event is likely to be experienced in many different ways because cohorts consist of subgroups differentiated in terms of class, gender or ethnic origin. A historical event will provoke a variety of responses, of varying degrees of intensity, within a single generation and between different generations. Consequently they relate to them differently and the influence the events will have is variable. Fourth, for the Mannheim thesis to work, generations need to retain their collective consciousness and ideals across the lifecourse and there is, as yet, little empirical evidence to support this hypothesis (Pilcher, 1995).

Period effects

The point that specific and self-limited historical events, such as war or depression or radical social change, can affect the entire population is the source of the third explanatory framework for the observation of age differences: period effects. Period effects also relate to historical time and its influence upon entire populations and offer another framework for explaining differences between age groups. This explanatory framework suggests that certain processes and events may stimulate changed attitudes throughout the whole of society and not just in a single age group. Period effects are events and trends affecting the attitudes of all ages and cohorts at a particular point in historical time. As the groups affected by this age die out, the period effect may appear to be an age or birth cohort effect. Examples of important period effects could be economic depression, widespread religious revival or war or the development of a policy of home ownership as the preferred type of housing tenure. Food rationing during the Second World War in Britain is a good example of a period effect as is the London smog of the 1950s, although this was geographically limited in extent.

Developing on from the notion of birth cohorts to develop the notion of cohort analysis further and drawing a link with period (or historical) based explanations for age-based differences, society can therefore be conceptualised or modelled as a series of cohorts moving through historical time. Each cohort will have been influenced by a unique configuration of events (Ryder, 1997) and will have experienced different historical events at different ages. The cohort born in 1900 experienced two world wars, lived through the depression in early adulthood and experienced the culture shock of the 1960s 'permissive society' in old age. The cohort born in 1930 experienced the Second World War as young children, grew up with the welfare state, experienced the permissive society as young adults and experienced mass economic recession in late middle age. We can only speculate as to what the formative events for future generations might be, but the principle remains the same: experiencing major historical events can have a formative influence upon future attitudes and behaviours, although not necessarily in a monolithic or inevitable fashion. The task of the gerontologist is to try to distinguish between these different explanatory frameworks or at least to recognise the complexity of trying to disentangle the relative influence of developmental time from historical time in seeking to understand the experience of old age and ageing.

Distinguishing age, cohort and period effects

These three explanatory frameworks for the existence of variations between different age groups have been presented as distinct and separate entities. However, there is clearly the potential for interaction between them. This makes the task of the social gerontologist in explaining, identifying and interpreting age differences extremely complex. Indeed it is not just within social gerontology that such complexity exists. Similar conundrums confront the biological gerontologist or geriatrician. How much of the differences we see between people of different ages is the result of ageing and how much is due to period or cohort effects. Thus when presented with an observed difference in, for example, political attitudes or the performance of activities of daily living, the gerontologist has to consider whether this observation is due to age, cohort or period effects (or indeed some combination of all three) and how these explanatory frameworks may vary across the older age groups.

Glenn (1974), taking the example of the apparently more conservative attitudes of the old compared with the young, observes that this finding may be subject to a variety of interpretations. This serves to demonstrate yet again the intellectual and methodological problems in identifying the effects of ageing and may, in part, explain why researchers have looked at the characteristics of older people rather than at the process of ageing per se. Biological ageing, which results in a decrease in energy and loss of brain tissue, may result in increased cautiousness and resistance to change; this could be interpreted as an intrinsic age effect. Accumulated family responsibilities and possessions as one passes through the lifecycle may lead to an increase in conservative values. This could be seen as a reactive age effect. Older people may have been born into a more conservative society. Consequently their more conservative attitudes could be interpreted as a birth cohort effect. Alternatively they may have experienced a society-wide conservative/religious revival resulting in their adoption of more conservative values. This example illustrates well the problems that the gerontologist faces in attempting to enumerate and explain age differences and draws attention to the intellectual challenge of the study of ageing. While gerontologists may not always be able to separate out these different causal factors for observed age differences, the articulation of cohort or period explanatory frameworks is important in dispelling the negative myths and stereotypes that characterise attitudes towards ageing. Such explanations also highlight that future cohorts of older people may not demonstrate the same types of characteristics as current elders. How much of what we now see in the older people is the 'true' result of ageing and how much is the result of birth cohort and period effects remains the subject of speculation.

Study design and the study of ageing

Given the potential complexity of differentiating age, period and cohort effects, particular care needs to be given to the methodological aspects of the study of ageing. In this section we consider aspects of study design and how this influences the inferences about ageing which may be drawn from particular studies. These methodological issues are raised, not to turn all readers into practising researchers, but to develop the critical and reflective faculties when assessing any claim that observation *x* is a result of ageing. Research design is influenced by the nature of the question the researcher wishes to pose. However, in general terms in designing studies of ageing, the researcher ideally needs to be able to distinguish age from period and cohort effects. There are two main designs employed in the study of ageing and old age: cross-sectional and longitudinal (see Box 3.1). The merits of these perspectives are considered below and examples of different types of these major approaches to the study of ageing are illustrated.

Cross-sectional research

Cross-sectional studies make inferences about the effects of ageing by comparing the characteristics of groups of people of different ages at a single point in time (see Box 3.1). They represent a summary of information about a cross-section of the population at a specific

---

Box 3.1 Idealised schema of different types of study design in ageing research

Year of birth	Dates of data collection			
	1970	*1980*	*1990*	*2000*
1910	A	B	C	D
1920	E	F	G	
1930	H		I	

Cross-sectional study (study of people of different ages at single point in time) = comparison of cells A, E, H (ages 60, 50, 40).

Longitudinal study (study of cohort over several time points) = comparison of cells A, B, C, D (ages 60, 70, 80 and 90).

Time-lag study (comparison of people of same age but measured at different time points) = comparison of cells A, F, I (ages 60) or B and G (ages 70).

moment in time. Table 3.1 presents typical data from a cross-sectional study with different age groups within the adult population of Great Britain compared on the percentage reporting that they have a longstanding illness or disability, a longstanding limiting illness or an acute illness. The percentage reporting that they have a longstanding (and limiting) illness or disability clearly increases with age and such data are used as evidence for the 'fact' that ageing causes disability. The fundamental assumption underpinning the cross-sectional approach to the study of ageing is that observing people of different ages at a single point in time is the same as observing a single age group (say all people born in a specific week like the National Child Development Surveys (NCDS) in the United Kingdom which are based upon all births in specific weeks in 1946, 1958 and 1970) over time. This assumption is questionable because people of different ages at the same point in time vary along dimensions other than age, such as social class, gender or ethnic minority status. For example the percentage of women in each of the age divisions increases so that for age 75+ most are women. It is well known that women report more chronic illness than men do, so an alternative explanation for the trend demonstrated in Table 3.1 is that it reflects gender differences in the composition of the age groups rather than the influence of ageing. We cannot be certain, from the evidence presented in Table 3.1, that the observed differences between age groups do not reflect other differences in the composition of these groups such as gender, social class or ethnicity. This single point in time snapshot approach does not offer any insights into, for example, how many of the older people with a longstanding limiting illness also had this when they were younger. This type of study, while pro-

Table 3.1 Longstanding limiting illness by age, Great Britain, 2001

Age	% reporting		
	Longstanding illness or disability	*Longstanding limiting illness*	*Acute illness*
0–4	15	4	10
5–15	20	8	9
16–44	24	13	12
45–64	45	20	18
65–74	63	41	20
75+	72	53	26

Source: Rickards *et al.*, 2004: Table 7.2

viding copious information about the characteristics of older people, may be of less utility in illuminating the process of ageing or for locating responses within a life course or biographical context. Consequently this research approach is of more utility in exploring the characteristics and distinguishing features of the older population than in illuminating the process of ageing.

This research design, while it can show differences between age groups, cannot determine whether such differences are due to age, cohort or period effects. As Box 3.1 shows, cross-sectional studies cannot distinguish between age, period or cohort effects. For example the observation of differences between young and older people in the prevalence of longstanding illness may reflect (a) an age effect such as decreased physiological function, or (b) a birth cohort effect resultant from the poor nutrition experienced in childhood by this group, or (c) a period effect whereby current generations of elders, like other groups, experienced limited nutrition because of war or social conflict. Using a cross-sectional research design we can never disentangle these differing explanatory frameworks and so cannot determine if developmental or historical time is responsible for the observed pattern (or indeed some combination of the two). However, if the research question posed is simply concerned with description rather than explanation, such conceptual limitations are less problematic.

Cross-sectional studies, for all their limitations, can offer some insights into the experience of ageing in a more dynamic context. Developments in social science methodology and analytical techniques offer the potential to develop more sophisticated ways of analysing cross-sectional data more rigorously. Two methodologies are considered here: time trend analysis and the construction of pseudo-cohorts. The existence of surveys repeated over a period of years, using similar questions, can facilitate the examination of trends over time. The General Household Survey (GHS), a generic survey of a random sample of approximately 10,000 members of the adult population of Great Britain resident in the community, has been running continuously since 1971. Throughout the life of this survey several topic areas such as health status and use of health services have been asked consistently using very similar, if not identical, questions. This offers the potential to examine trends over time in, for example, the percentage of people aged 65 and over reporting that they have a longstanding (limiting) illness or an acute illness in the previous two weeks (see Table 3.2). Such data may, therefore, offer us the possibility of examining the compression or expansion of morbidity hypotheses. The percentage of people reporting the presence of longstanding illness or disability fluctuates annually, but there is a clear trend over time for reported rates of acute illness or longstanding illness to increase while longstanding limiting illness demonstrates little change over time. Interpretation of such trends are not straightforward for all the reasons of confounding noted earlier and we can make few inferences about the potentially changing morbidity patterns of older people from such routine information.

As well as including a consistent bank of questions the GHS has included specific topic modules, such as older people living at home, and then repeated them at various time points. This also provides data from which trends over time can be examined. In 1980, 1985, 1991, 1994, 1998 and 2001 the GHS has included a special set of questions for people aged 65 and over. These questions cover living arrangements, ability to undertake activities of daily living, housing and consumer durables, health, use of health services, sources of support, use of transport and social networks. Comparison of data from these surveys, but without constructing pseudo-cohorts, can provide some evidence as to changes in, for example, the housing circumstances of older people. For example, the percentage of people aged 65 and over living in private rented accommodation decreased from 12 per cent in 1980 to 3 per cent in 2001. Data like these can

Table 3.2 Trends in health status over time, Great Britain, 1972–2001 (%)

	Longstanding illness		Longstanding limiting illness		Acute illness	
	65–74	75+	65–74	75+	65–74	75+
1972	48	62	—	—	10	13
1975	52	62	38	48	11	13
1979	51	61	37	51	14	20
1981	55	67	38	52	14	19
1983	61	69	43	54	16	19
1985	56	63	38	48	16	21
1988	58	66	37	50	17	23
1991	58	65	37	49	15	20
1993	60	67	40	50	18	21
1995	55	63	37	48	19	24
1996	59	66	41	52	20	24
1998	59	66	38	50	21	26
2001	57	63	36	46	19	25

Source: Rickards *et al.* 2004: Table 7.2

illustrate changes which are taking place within society generally and, more specifically, among older people and in the social context within which they experience ageing. As such these types of continuous social surveys are useful social barometers and provide insights into the changing nature of society and how this is reflected among older people. One example of this is the increasing percentage of older people who have experienced divorce. However, from such analyses we can never be fully certain that the changes observed do not reflect variations in the composition of the samples interviewed. Furthermore this survey, because it excludes those residents in institutions such as residential and nursing homes, is not necessarily a representative sample of all older people. This is an important limitation when considering either the nature of very old age or the health status of older people. In both cases exclusion of the most frail from the sampling frame will result in the understatement of health problems in advanced old age. This also serves to remind us that the utility of much research is contingent upon the population from which they are derived. We shall return to this point in our discussion of longitudinal studies.

The popularity of cross-sectional research arises because, compared with longitudinal studies, it is comparatively cheap and easy to undertake. Although it has limitations, cross-sectional research is not entirely inappropriate for the study of ageing, for as well as looking at trends over time such data may be subject to cohort-style analysis by the creation of pseudo-cohorts (Evandrou and Falkingham, 2000). Using data from the General Household Survey, Evandrou and Falkingham (2000) created four birth cohorts (people born in 1916–1920, 1931–1935, 1946–1950 and 1961–1965). Clearly these cohort boundaries are somewhat arbitrary but the rationale was to identify broad groupings who experienced differing social and political climates. Taking the example of the 1916–1920 cohort these individuals were aged 55–59 in the 1975 GHS survey and approaching retirement; they would be at least 80 by the year 2000. Each cohort group is tracked across the various waves of the survey. Hence the 1916–1920 cohort was aged 60–64 in the 1980 survey, 70–74 in the 1990 survey, 76–80 in the 1996 survey and 81–85 in 2001. This method tracks groups rather than individuals: the unit of analysis is the group or cohort and the data presented represent or summarise the average experience of the group. The prevalence of, for example, longstanding limiting illness will be calculated for each age cohort. Evandrou and Falkingham (2000) traced the experiences of their four pseudo-cohorts with regard to three main areas: health, living arrangements and access to resources over the period 1974–1996. As an example of this approach they examined trends in the percentage of women classed as 'never married' among the four cohort groups. At age 30 a much higher percentage of women, approximately 25 per cent of the 1961 cohort, are classed as unmarried compared with 20 per cent for the 1916 cohort, 8 per cent for the 1931 cohort and 4 per cent for the 1946 cohort. This approach does not indicate whether the 1961 cohort will 'catch up' by marrying later but does show that the characteristics of older people in the future will not, necessarily, follow the same pattern as for our parents and grandparents. This serves to emphasise, using fairly simple data and methods of analysis, the dynamic nature of the population defined as 'old'. The advantage of the pseudo-cohort approach, over a straightforward cross-sectional analysis, is that it focuses attention upon the whole life course and not just a single point in time and investigates the changing nature of the experience of old age. While this is a useful approach it still remains limited by the cross-sectional nature of the original data and by its dependence upon the calculation of 'group means' and the averaging out of group experiences, which say nothing about variation within different cohorts in terms of class, gender or ethnicity.

Secondary analysis

Time trends analysis and the construction of pseudo-cohorts are both excellent examples of what is termed 'secondary data analysis' and it is appropriate to deal with this methodological approach, having examined the potential of the GHS previously. Secondary analysis may be simply defined as the analysis and interpretation of data initially collected for another purpose (Victor 2002). This type of analysis is most commonly associated with 'quantitative' studies but can be employed for the reuse of qualitative material). The General Household Survey was designed as a general 'social barometer' survey of the living conditions of the British population. It was not designed for the specific study of ageing or later life, but it has provided British gerontologists with a rich source of data for examining gender variations in the experience of old age (Arber and Ginn, 1991), social class inequalities in later life (Victor, 1991) or financial resources in later life (Falkingham and Victor, 1991). Secondary data analysis can take two forms. First, it can involve reanalysis of studies set up to examine specific issues. For example the Health Survey for England has been reanalysed by Shah and Cook (2001) to examine class variations in the detection and management of hypertension in later life. However, the original objective of this group of surveys was to monitor progress towards the original *Health of the Nation* targets. The second type of secondary data analysis involves the analysis and interrogation of entire surveys to investigate research questions they were never intended to answer. The use of GHS for the development and analysis of pseudo-cohorts is an excellent example of the novel and challenging reinterpretation of large-scale general social surveys.

The popularity of secondary data analysis among gerontologists, and other social scientists, reflects the easy availability on CD-ROM (or other electronic formats) of such studies from archives such as the Data Archive at Essex University. The easy availability of these data sets does not mitigate their major conceptual limitation, which is that their content, in terms of variables measured and populations studied, reflects the original purpose of the study. Thus the concepts and variables measured by any specific survey do not always correspond to the question which the gerontologist wishes to answer. For example to study 'women in the middle', the group of women with childcare and parent-care responsibilities and work, age of youngest child is taken as a proxy for 'childcare' and marital status as a proxy for domestic role (Agree *et al.*, 2002; Evandrou and Glaser, 2002). Many of the government-sponsored surveys such as the GHS, FES and Health Survey for England are characterised by large sample sizes, good response rates and high data quality, So they have considerable potential for secondary analysis. However, limitations in topic areas covered and questions asked means that they have only limited potential. For example inequalities in health remains a key public health topic in Britain with several reports into the area. In theory the Health Survey for England, which includes a wealth of physiological, condition and other data could offer the potential to look at inequalities in later life in the prevalence of disease, its detection, management and treatment by doctors. However, the survey is limited because it focuses upon three specific disease areas: cardiovascular disease, accidents and stroke. Consequently the research has to compromise by trying to develop surrogate measures of the desired variable(s) if it is not present in the original data set. The major limitation of secondary analysis for the gerontologist is that most surveys rarely contain sufficient numbers of older people and non-response rates tend to be highest among the older age groups. This criticism is less relevant to the major government-sponsored surveys, which often include substantial numbers of older people. However, even the

GHS has a sample of only 285 people aged 85+ in 2001 and it excludes those in this age group who are resident in care homes. The researcher must remember who collected the data set and why this has an important influence upon the conceptualisation of old age presented by the data and the questions asked. Illustrative of this limitation have been the GHS carers' supplement surveys undertaken in 1985, 1990, 1998 and 2000 which are concerned with quantifying the help given to, but not help given by, older people.

Longitudinal research

The central concern of gerontology is the enumeration and explanation of ageing and age-related changes. Longitudinal research design is the theoretically most appropriate approach for the study of ageing. Put at its most basic, longitudinal research involves following a group of people over a period of time that may range from a few months to an entire lifetime, depending on the topic under investigation. Hence this is a prospective type of study in that we are following participants forward in time. During the period of follow-up the participants in the study may be interviewed or assessed several times over the lifetime of the investigation. The schematic plan of a longitudinal study is shown in Box 3.1. While longitudinal studies are especially appropriate for the study of ageing they can be used to study other change type variables such as child development. Indeed the major British studies were concerned initially with child development (Wadsworth, 2002). Furthermore the length of follow-up in longitudinal studies is not prescribed and could, if it was appropriate, take place over periods of months, years or decades. There are also examples of 'historical' longitudinal studies in which the discovery of a set of historical records can prompt the follow-up many years later of participants. A good example of this was the discovery of birth records that were subsequently linked to mortality and health status in adulthood. It was studies of this nature that led to the recognition of the importance of the fetal environment for health status in mid- and later life (Barker, 1998). While longitudinal studies are often associated with large-scale, longterm, statistically sophisticated data, such approaches are used in qualitative settings. The longitudinal or prospective design can be used in a variety of settings and is, perhaps, a more versatile research approach than it is often given credit for.

To illustrate the philosophical and practical differences in approach between cross-sectional and longitudinal studies we can consider the example of a researcher interested in investigating the effect of retirement. A cross-sectional study design would involve the comparison of a group of workers and retired people at a single point in time. Such a study might observe differences between the two groups in, for example, self-reported loneliness or social isolation, but using this methodology we could not state, with precision, whether the differences were due to the effect of retirement or variations in the composition of the two groups. Given that retired people are older and more likely to be widowed than younger age groups, any differences in loneliness and isolation between the two populations might reflect differences in the size of their social networks because of bereavement rather than because they were 'retired'. In contrast a longitudinal research design would select a sample of workers and collect data from them while they were employed and as they moved into retirement, and then look to see if patterns of loneliness and isolation changed over time.

Longitudinal designs are not without their conceptual limitations. The observation of differences in outcome variables over time may, indeed, be the result of ageing, but when using this type of research design we cannot be certain that the observed differences do not reflect measurement effects such as variations in the environment in which the measures were taken or the increased familiarity of the study participants with the measurement regimen. For example, longitudinal study participants may perform better on a psychological test when it is conducted in a familiar environment such as their home in comparison to when it is undertaken in a research laboratory or medical school. Similarly, as longitudinal studies involve the repeated administration of tests and questionnaires (otherwise there is nothing to compare longitudinally) it is possible that participants may become familiar with the tests or remember their previous responses. It is also possible, in theory at least, that participation in a longitudinal study will alter the behaviour of participants and thereby compromise the main outcome variables. Longitudinal studies cannot disentangle the effects of historical time and 'ageing', and, like other types of research, are influenced by period effects influencing the research process from design to analysis and interpretation (Wadsworth, 2002). Such factors are important in cross-sectional studies, but the prospective and enduring study period of many longitudinal studies means that such influences are manifest over a long time period. The questions posed, measures collected and methods used are all influenced by secular change and the current state of scientific knowledge and the socio-political environment.

In order to be able to accurately distinguish age, cohort and period effects, Schaie (1967) proposed using a combination of approaches which involved three types of analysis: cross-sectional, longitudinal and time-lag. Time-lag study involves comparing people of the same age (for example 75) at different times so that they belong to different cohorts. In the example in Box 3.1 this would involve taking measurements from people aged 60 in 1970, 1980 and 1990 and comparing the results, but this method confounds cohort and measurement effects. Schaie (1977) proposed a further modification with his 'most efficient' design, which is an amalgamation of all three approaches. This involves starting with a 'simple' cross-sectional study of two (or more) age groups measured at the same time point. These initial subjects are then retested at a latter time point to provide longitudinal information on two cohort groups. At the second time point, two (or more) new cohorts are recruited and followed up (see Box 3.2). This cycle continues for as long as the study lasts. Using this sophisticated type of design, the researcher can

---

Box 3.2   'Most efficient' research design for studying ageing

Baseline (1960)	1970	1980	1990	2000
Cohort 1 (born 1900)	age 70	age 80	age 90	age 100
Cohort 2 (born 1910)	age 60	age 70	age 80	age 90
Cohort 3 (born 1920)	—	age 60	age 70	age 80
Cohort 4 (born 1930)	—	age 50	age 60	age 70

A – cohort sequential analysis – compare dementia prevalence at ages 70 and 80 for two cohorts (born in 1900 and 1910), which confounds period effects

B – cross-sequential analysis – this examines cohort and period effects but confounds age (comparison of three different ages 70, 80 or 90 but for two cohorts and two time points)

C – time sequence – two different age groups at two different time points those aged 70 and 80 in 1990 are compared with same age groups in 2000

interrogate the data to evaluate the differing contributions to age, cohort and measurement effects.

Using the example of cognitive function we could investigate the influence of age and cohort upon our outcome dependent variable (see Box 3.2). A cohort sequential analysis involves enumerating changes in ability among those aged 60–70, from a group born in 1910, with that of the same age group but from a cohort born a decade later. A simple cross-sectional analysis can identify the interaction between cohort and measurement effects. In this case we could examine changes in cognitive function in all four groups between, for example, 1980 and 1990. This is clearly a much more sophisticated way to look at the process of ageing, but the sophistication and rigour are the result of a far more complex research design which is expensive to design, maintain and analyse.

Major longitudinal studies of ageing

The scientific merit of this method of studying ageing is generally recognised and there have been longitudinal studies of ageing undertaken in most parts of the developed world including the Netherlands (Rotterdam), Sweden (Göteborg), Germany (Berlin), United States (Duke, NC, and Baltimore, MD), Australia (the Australian Longitudinal Study of Ageing and Australian Women's Health Study), Italy, Israel and Latin America (see Schaie and Hoferson, 2001, for a summary). Few large-scale longitudinal studies of ageing have been funded in Britain, although the English Longitudinal Study of Ageing is in its initial phases. There have been several locally based longitudinal studies in Nottingham (Morgan, 1998) and East London/Essex (Boothby *et al.*, 1994; Bowling and Grundy, 1997) which provide useful insights into the experience of ageing. Older people also form a significant element in general health surveys such as the Health and Lifestyle Survey and which have been followed up longitudinally (Pendry *et al.*, 1999). The major national longitudinal studies undertaken have been concerned with child development and the initial NCDS cohort was established in 1946 so the study participants are now in mid-life (Wadsworth, 2002). The Office for National Statistics (ONS) longitudinal study which is concerned with following up a 1 per cent sample of the population from the 1971 census is limited by the reliance upon census data for its baseline and by the restricted nature of the outcome variables (death or emigration or cancer registration or changes in key census variables such as household). However, this study has been used to monitor movements into institutional care and changes in household formation (Grundy and Glaser, 1998).

Other studies initially intended to be cross-sectional studies have been developed to look at aspects of ageing. Examples of this include the Whitehall 2 study of cardiovascular disease among civil servants (Breeze *et al.*, 2001). Such developments are useful but the utility of such studies to reveal much about the nature of ageing is compromised by the limitations of the original design. For example, the Regional Heart Survey excluded women and the Whitehall study, because it is based upon an occupational group, excludes those who did not participate in the labour force and might understate ill health in the population because of the 'healthy' worker effect. The context within which the initial study was framed and the types of policy questions it was initially intended to answer also limit studies such as the 1946 NCDS. For example, because smoking was not seen as problematic in 1946, the initial survey did not include parental smoking, something that would now be considered essential in any large-scale study of child development.

Gerontology in general and longitudinal research is usually striving to identify evidence concerning ageing, which can be transferred to the general population of older people. However, the generalisability of any research may be compromised by bias. This may be summarised as systematic, as opposed to random errors, errors within the research and the way it has been carried out. Within longitudinal research, bias may be introduced from a variety of different sources such as the source of the study population and sample attrition rates because of non-response. In addition there is a more subtle type of bias which may impinge upon gerontology (and other aspects of science). This relates to prejudice in the posing of the question, methodology or interpretation of the findings, because of the ideological orientation of either the researcher or the funding body. When reading any research report the gerontologist should be aware of the possibilities of prejudice in the way that the findings are presented and interpreted. The gerontologist should also be aware of the nature of the body funding or undertaking, the research and any interest they may have in the findings proving a particular case. For example, if the sponsoring body for a research survey was a lobby group which wished to argue the need for more money for older people, they might include only questions which asked abut financial problems (and did not survey or ask about levels of affluence).

Researchers can minimise the potential for bias, or systematic errors, in longitudinal and other forms of research by careful research design. Bias, because it is a systematic error, affects some parts of the data more than others. This may lead to erroneous results and the subsequent misinterpretation of findings. Thus it is distinguished from random errors, which occur with equal frequency throughout the sample and its subgroups and which, therefore, may not bias the reported results. The systematic exclusion from studies of people from minority communities, because participation in the study is contingent upon the ability to read or write English, is an example of bias. Similarly, the use of samples of very old people which exclude those resident in institutional settings will bias the results by the exclusion of the most frail.

The first main area where bias may be introduced is in the identification and selection of the study population. The Berlin study was designed to provide information about ageing among the general population. In addition to these general surveys there are also longitudinal studies of 'special' populations, designed to answer specific questions or investigating specific groups. Examples of these include the McArthur studies of successful ageing (Seeman *et al.*, 1995), the 'Nun' ageing study (Snowdon, 2001) and the Hispanic-ageing cohort (Abbott, 1997) or to look at the development of particular diseases such as the MRC cognitive function and ageing study (Meltzer *et al.*, 1999) or changes in the health status of particular disease groups such as older people receiving dialysis (Lamping *et al.*, 2000). Clearly the focus of these special interest studies limits the generalisability of the results. In addition some applied or evaluation studies often involve a longitudinal element. For example, the evaluation of the effectiveness of health visitors involved a two-year follow-up of study participants to identify the long-term effects of the intervention. Such studies may provide some insights into the processes of ageing, although this is always secondary to requirement to evaluate the intervention under review (Vetter *et al.*, 1984).

All the studies summarised are based upon samples of the target population, as rarely is it necessary to include an entire population to answer a specific research question. This issue encapsulates two distinct elements. The first is the source of the study population and the second relates to identification and sampling. The source and definition of the study population is a crucial factor in determining the generalisability of research. The definition of this population will depend upon the specific research question under investigation. For example, a survey of older people living at home will require a sample of older people normally resident in the community. In contrast a study of satisfaction with the hospital service will require a sample of those in contact with the service. Thus it is crucial that the population the researcher studies is accurately specified so that we can immediately determine the generalisability of the results and could, if required, reproduce the study within our own area. The clear description of research methodology such that the study could be replicated elsewhere is one of the key aspects of the scientific method.

Obtaining samples of older people living in the community (in Britain) is problematic because there is no complete and accurate list of the population readily available to researchers. One list often used by researchers in Britain as a sampling frame is the electoral register. This lists, for each electoral area, the name and address of those individuals eligible to vote in elections and is updated annually. However, it does not list the age of voters. The electoral roll is used as the basis for selecting citizens for jury service. Currently, individuals over 70 may exclude themselves from jury service and are thus identified on the electoral roll. However, not all those over 70 choose to identify themselves. It is unclear as to exactly what percentage do exclude themselves from jury service, but it is highly probable that those who do exclude themselves are in some way different from the general population of those aged over 70. For example, they may be less healthy than those who indicate that they are available for jury service. Thus any sample selected from the electoral roll may be subject to bias and may not be representative of the total population in which the researcher is interested.

In Britain primary medical treatment is provided free under the National Health Service (NHS). Most of the population is registered with a general medical practitioner (GP). Older people (or other age groups) are identifiable from the age-sex registers maintained by practices, but access to such data is fraught with ethical and practical difficulties, especially for the non-clinically qualified researcher. In addition the researcher must also take into account the inaccuracies inherent in this sampling frame, especially the presence in the records of patients who are either dead or have left the area, although this is less problematic now (Cook and Shah, 2001). If we are interested in the overall experience of ageing it is important to note that the population resident in nursing and residential homes are usually excluded from such studies. This exclusion is probably not very important for the under-75 age group, where few are resident in such forms of care, but this could be a crucial omission if we are studying survival into very old age, say those aged 90 (or 100) and over. Accessing sampling frames for this population can be problematic.

As a cautionary note, when reading the literature, it is important to remember that samples of older people drawn from membership lists of clubs and organisations will usually over-represent the healthy and the middle class. Studies based upon lists derived from those in institutions or receiving social services will overemphasise the chronically ill and dependent. Observations based upon such samples must not be inferred as being attributable to all elderly people but may only safely be extrapolated to the population under investigation. An example of a longitudinal study based upon an unrepresentative sample is the Harvard Alumni Health Study, which has followed up 14,998 male alumni who entered Harvard during the period 1916–50 (Lee and Paffenbarger, 1995). This study provides some interesting insights into the experience of ageing among an affluent and elite group of males but it is difficult to generalise findings from this study to uneducated minority groups or to women.

The second major area of longitudinal studies that can compromise their scientific robustness is that of sample size, response rates and sample attrition (or loss to follow-up). Longitudinal studies are often large, involving thousands of subjects. However, large sample sizes are an absolute necessity because the effects of non-response and sample attrition which can reduce the numbers included within the study drastically (Wadsworth, 2002). Like any study the first stage of a longitudinal study is the identification of potential participants. The research team then need to maximise participation in the baselines assessments. It is not always clear from studies as to what the initial sample was and what percentage the number at baseline represents. The studies from Nottingham (Morgan, 1998) and East London (Bowling and Grundy, 1997) report initial participation rates of 70 per cent or more, which contrasts with the Australian Women's Health Survey where the initial participation rates were only about 40 per cent (Brown *et al.*, 1998). This means that the vast majority of those invited to participate in the study declined to do so. If there is a low uptake of the invitation to participate at baseline this can also compromise the robustness of any results. Taking the example of the Australian survey how confident can we be of the generalisability of their results when only one-third of those selected to participate actually did so?

The initial take-up rate is of importance because it indicates what percentage of the study group failed to complete a baseline assessment. It is not correct to assume that those who do not respond to a survey possess characteristics identical to those who do respond. Non-responders may well be an unrepresentative fraction of the sample. Consequently the measured results may be subject to bias.

For example non-responders may be less (or more) healthy than responders. Hence researchers need to try to establish if a low response rate has introduced bias, the direction of the bias and develop analytical strategies to take this into account. Researchers can estimate the degree of bias in the results brought about by non-response if they know something of the characteristics of the non-responders. There are few data available about the characteristics of non-responders in surveys of older people. Work by Shah *et al.* (2001) demonstrates how the content of questionnaires may increase or decrease response rates. For most studies we know that bias is present but are unclear as to the extent and direction such bias may take and therefore are unable to take this into account in either analysis or interpretation of data and results.

Longitudinal research involves repeated contact with, and the tracing of, sample members often over lengthy time periods; the NCDS 1946 birth cohort has been followed for almost fifty years to date. This is expensive, labour-intensive and time-consuming. Taking part in such a study requires a high level of commitment from the researchers involved in the project and from the study participants. For example, in the Berlin Ageing study each assessment involved seven days at a university institute while each assessment for the Baltimore study took 2.5 days and participants may not be paid for their time or travel and accommodation expenses. Hence it is legitimate to question how representative of the general population are such participants. Furthermore we do not know how participation in a long-term follow-up survey influences sample members either generally or with regard to the variable under study. A sample involved in a long-term health study may become more health conscious and modify their behaviour thereby compromising the major study outcome variable.

Enthusiasm for the study, by either researchers or researched, may well decrease over time resulting in low levels of follow-up and participation in second (and subsequent) waves of the survey. Loss to follow-up (or sample attrition) occurs for four main reasons: deaths of study participants, withdrawal of participants for health or other reason, moving house, area or type of residence, and non-response. With any longitudinal study it is inevitable that not all those recruited at baseline will be included in the subsequent assessment points. From the researcher's perspective, sample attrition needs to be minimised. Using the example of the Berlin Ageing study we see that the study started with 222 participants and had only thirty-four left at the seventh follow-up. Similarly in the Seattle study only 10 per cent of the initial participants remained in the study twenty-one years after baseline (Schaie, 1993).

If we take the example of Bowling and Grundy's (1997) study of people aged 85 and over, we can see how sample attrition works to greatly reduce the size of the population studied. Of the 900 people aged 85 initially selected, 70 per cent (630) participated. At follow-up 70 per cent of these (441) participated. This means that the final results are based upon data from 441 of the original sample of 900 – 41 per cent of those originally approached. Again loss to follow-up may render participants no longer representative of the original sample if there is a systematic pattern to those who no longer participate such as the poorest, frailest or fittest, but this is usually less problematic as previous data can be used to determine the nature and extent of sample attrition and allow for this in the analysis. However, good follow-up rates as demonstrated by the Australian Women's Health Study cannot compensate for the paucity of the initial response of less than 40 per cent. When considering the veracity of evidence from longitudinal studies we need to consider both the response to the initial invitation to participate and subsequent follow-up rates.

Given all these methodological and practical challenges large-scale longitudinal studies are usually undertaken by government or research institute funded research teams. There are many technical and statistical challenges, which such studies pose. Here we need to conclude by outlining the types of questions which such studies can answer. Data can be analysed cross-sectionally and the nature and characteristics of the population studied. Then we can investigate the developments of specific diseases in relation to risk factors/protective factors (Lee and Paffenbarger, 1995), look at the non-pathological changes, consider changes in social roles and relationships and investigate the timing of specific events such as bereavement or entry into residential or nursing home care. Also we should caution against the idea that only quantitative numerical studies can be conducted longitudinally. There is nothing, in principle, which says that qualitative studies cannot incorporate the prospective dimension.

Qualitative research designs

The emphasis in this chapter has been upon quantitative numerical approaches towards the study of ageing. While such methods are useful for describing the nature and characteristics of older populations or enumerating the process of ageing and analysing material statistically, such approaches are of limited utility for understanding the experience and the meaning of old age (or indeed any other age group). In addition quantitative studies assume a cultural and social homogeneity which few populations meet. There is an important role for qualitative research approaches in gerontology where the emphasis is upon the analysis of words, concepts and meanings of individuals. Qualitative research still collects data but it is usually in the form of words or actions rather than numbers. The broad objective is to represent reality as seen by the study participant rather than impose that of the researcher or the project goals. It is far too easy to see these two different approaches as opposing and in conflict. Rather they represent two different ways of investigating the social world of older people and are more appropriately viewed as complementary. Here we do not dwell upon the details of qualitative research but we concentrate upon providing a brief summary of the major qualitative approaches that have been used with older people and consider the special issues concerned with their use in a gerontological setting.

Life history research

Life history research is one method by which gerontologists have examined the interrelationship between ageing, time and social change at the level of the individual. This technique can obviously be used to examine the processes of social change as perceived by the individual with any subgroup of the population and not just with older people. In life history research we are inviting respondents to look back over their lives and evaluate key transitions and changes. By considering a number of life histories collected from different respondents the researcher can then look for patterns of similarities and differences in the experience of ageing. A life history approach focuses upon the individual who is providing the history rather than upon the historical or social context, which distinguishes life history from related activities such as oral history, reminiscence (which often has a therapeutic function) and biographical interviewing (Bornat, 2002).

Life history research is still relatively rare in the British gerontological literature, although the studies by Thompson *et al.* (1990) and Hockey and James (1993) are notable exceptions. The development of interest in life history approaches to understanding old age and ageing stems from a variety of different sources. These include a desire to 'reveal' what is hidden or obscured in large-scale surveys or official records and with a democratic and emancipatory concern to examine the experiences of hidden populations such as working-class women or people with disabilities. Life history approaches also developed in response to broader developments within sociology as manifest by the development of more reflexive forms of data collection which were more responsive to the needs of individual respondents as well as part of a broader concern to develop more egalitarian and collaborative approaches to research.

Life history research has been used in a variety of research contexts and to answer many different research questions. Examples of life history approaches can be found in investigations of individual or group autobiographies, studies of particular topics or experiences such as women's lives, sample-based studies, evaluative research, experimental and longitudinal or studying particular aspects of social change (Bornat, 2002). This is versatile research technique but it is not without limitations. It is clearly very time consuming, study respondents may need to prepare for interviews, it may be difficult to find respondents for 'difficult' topics, and the data generated are complex. There are also issues of the 'representativeness' of samples and the generalisability of results. Those people interviewed may be the most articulate and represent the 'survivors' of their generation (an observation that holds true for all gerontological studies), but there is scope for the further development of life history research within gerontology. In particular, as well as being an important approach in its own right, used in conjunction with official data or large-scale surveys it can provide the context within which such statistical data can be interpreted. Such approaches offer the potential for the development of a more 'egalitarian' approach to research with an emphasis upon emancipatory and empowerment research traditions.

Biographical interviewing

The tradition of the biographical approach to research in British gerontology can be traced back to an article written by Johnson in 1976 in which he lamented that gerontologists had failed to incorporate the voices of older people themselves. Gerontologists had largely ignored the meaning attributed to ageing by older people, although there is now evidence emerging of a greater interest in the 'everyday' lives of older people (Gubrium and Holstein, 2000; Askham, 2003). The biographical approach centres upon the notion of the 'careers' of individuals and how these are shaped by biographical events such as marriage, divorce, work, parenthood, grandparenthood, etc. As such the biographical approaches integrate key concepts from interactionist theory (a concern with how individual study participants interpret and construct the world) and aspects of the life history tradition.

The biographical interview is a rather discursive enterprise with the emphasis firmly placed upon the participants constructing (and reconstructing) their own lives. This type of approach contains elements of a structured or programmed interview; a clinical interview and a conversation between friends can be used in reminiscence work, although not everyone wishes to talk about the past. It has also been used in service assessment setting, although some individuals do not feel that they need to recount their life history before they are considered for services such as home care or mobile meals. This approach has also been used in 'pure' research settings. Many of the advantages and disadvantages of life history research apply to the broad area of biographical interviewing. It is a type of interviewing which requires the disclosure of highly personal information to 'strangers' and, as such, is not an approach which all potential participants will relish.

The case study

Another interesting methodological approach to the study of ageing is the case study. As its name implies this is an in-depth study of a single case and is strongly rooted in the psychological tradition. Typically, such studies are pursued over a long period of time and are highly intensive. The case study may be a single person, or a detailed account of a social process or event, such as case conferences for the allocation of services to older people or the review and interpretation of an individual life. Detailed case studies can be used, as by Coleman (2002), to test the veracity and authenticity of differing theoretical models, in understanding the lives of individuals. Such studies often provide considerable insight into the social aspects of ageing and it is, again, an approach that can be integrated within a wider research project. The disadvantage is that it is difficult to generalise from the findings of case studies unless the individual cases can be co-ordinated into a substantial integrated sample and, again, there may be only a limited numbers of potential participants for this type of research.

Observational techniques

Another methodological technique, which has been used to only a limited extent by British gerontologists, is that of ethnographic and observation-based studies, a research tradition which has its origins in the academic disciplines of sociology and anthropology. Observational studies can use either participants or non-participants and, again, the central focus is upon understanding the social world of study participants (Latimer, 2000). In participant-based observation researchers become part of the group or event that they are studying. These types of studies require the researcher to have a very close and lengthy involvement in the activities of those under study. This approach could be used, for example, to study the interaction among residents of an institution by a researcher who was employed as a staff member in the home under study. Staff–patient interaction or the 'culture' of different types of institutional setting or professional group dealing with older people are aspects of gerontology that could be approached by participant observation. Observational studies have been most frequently used in settings where older people are grouped together in clubs, homes or hospitals; it is clearly more difficult to undertake within the individual homes of older people. Participant observation studies have been used particularly within care settings where the researcher occupies a dual role as 'impartial' observer and professional such as nurse.

Conclusion

Within the broadly shared objectives of gerontologically focused research there are a number of different ways that research can be categorised. We can distinguish quantitative from qualitative research or differentiate theoretical, empirical and applied research. Differentiating these categories is somewhat artificial as a single research project, such as a study of loneliness and isolation in old age, may contain elements of each type of research. What is important for the critical (in the sense of being reflective) student of gerontology is that each different approach to research generates different types of information about old age or ageing and that these limit our state of knowledge about our chosen field of interest. The production of knowledge about old age or ageing takes place within a specific social, political and cultural context. Hence the humanitarian political economy tradition in British social research results in a huge body of research about the 'problems' of old age and rather less attention being paid to the 'non-problematic' aspects of ageing. In this example, policy makers and researchers and *not* the older people define the problems. When considering the state of knowledge about a specific aspect of ageing or older people, such as the provision of 'informal' care or the need for chiropody services, we need to consider the implicit assumptions, ideological positions and potential biases resultant from the social context within which the research has taken place. What we don't know or have never researched may tell us as much as documenting what we do know.

In this chapter we have seen that observed age differences may be attributed to three mechanisms – age effects, cohort effects and period effects. For an age difference to be classified as an intrinsic age effect the causative mechanism must be an inevitable consequence of growing older which is neither culturally nor historically specific. Age effects must be universal, that is displayed by all populations, and inevitable (i.e. not the result of a hazardous lifestyle or environment). Reactive age effects are fashioned by the social context in which ageing is experienced and therefore demonstrate variation between, and within, cultures. However, within the field of social gerontology age effects are extremely difficult to identify with any certainty. An alternative explanation for age differences in behaviour is to be found in period effects. There are those who doubt the existence of period effects and they do seem to be the most difficult to evaluate. Cohort effects are probably responsible for some of the observed variations between groups in social behaviour and attitudes. We have shown that it is unwise to group whole birth cohorts together upon the basis of an assumed common experience. Cohorts are subdivided in terms of a number of parameters including class, ethnicity and gender. These variables will influence the experience of a particular historical event such as the interwar depression or the progressive society of the 1960s. In attempting to offer cohort explanations for age-related variations in attitudes or other phenomena, we must remember that the group commonly referred to as 'the older population' includes at least three separate cohorts; the views and attitudes of a centenarian may (or may not) be very different from a 70 year old. Taken in combination these three different explanatory factors serve to underpin the difficulties which face the gerontologist and also serve to remind us to look critically at evidence which claims to prove that *x* or *y* is the result of, or is caused by, ageing. It is common to see these three explanations for age differences as competing perspectives that are mutually exclusive. This is rather extreme and it seems likely that many age differences reflect the influence of both cohort and reactive age effects and, as gerontologists, we need to develop methods of study design and analysis which facilitate the identification and understanding of this complexity. As yet there has been insufficient cross-national, cross-cultural and historical research for us to determine whether any of the observed age-related changes are intrinsic age effects.

In designing specific research studies, social gerontologists must use appropriate research designs, measurement techniques and samples in order that they may unambiguously investigate their specific research question. Without being unnecessarily prescriptive gerontologists need to consider a series of questions before embarking upon their research. These questions include the following.

How much is already known about the subject? Areas where there is already an extensive body of knowledge enable the researcher to build on previous research by replicating methodologies. Such studies may be very highly specific. More exploratory, groundbreaking research is more broadly focused and may use in-depth exploratory methods. Additionally we need to consider if there are already data in existence that we could use to answer the question by undertaking secondary data analysis.

What type of research is being planned? Is this applied research which is linked to a particular policy initiative or is it knowledge or theory generating? Applied research is often 'quick and dirty' and is usually much more constraining in terms of time than other types of research.

What is the nature of the research question? This includes a number of issues. First, is the study concerned with enumeration and empirical matters (for example looking at the relationship between numbers of doctors and mortality) or is it concerned with understanding the social meanings and behaviours (such as why do people call for an emergency ambulance during GP surgery hours)? It is usual to undertake qualitative studies when the research is focused upon the meanings attributed to social factors or why understanding behaviours, while quantitative studies are usually concerned with counting the distribution of specific events and outcomes. These two approaches should not be seen as mutually exclusive but as complementary and both may be used in the same project. Second, is the focus of our research upon older people as a distinct social category or group or are we concerned with the processes of ageing? For the former, cross-sectional research is adequate but for the latter a longitudinal design may be required. Again both types of study design can be used in quantitative and qualitative contexts.

How should we collect the data? This links to the above aspect concerning the nature of the research question. Depending upon the specific question there is a number of different ways of collecting data: observation, experiments, interviews, review of health or social care records. Again a variety of different data collection techniques may used in a single project, thus a study of rehabilitation after stroke may involve review of patients' case notes, observation of patients during therapy sessions, setting specific 'tasks' for them to undertake as well as interviewing them. Triangulation of data from a variety of sources can help reveal the complexity of many issues. In addition social gerontological research can be undertaken using a variety of designs and approaches. Here we have confined our attention to the more conventionally used 'social research' techniques that are widely used in social gerontology, but the potential for other sources of 'data' to shed useful insights onto the experience of old age and the process of ageing is readily acknowledged. Cultural products such as painting (Blaikie and Hepworth, 1997), photographs (Johnson and Bytheway, 1997), literature (Zeilig, 1997) and historical material (Troyansky, 1997) can all be used to facilitate our understanding of gerontology. In addition historical material can provide a rich source of data and enables us to locate the current experience with that from historical times.

The precise research design to be employed depends upon the question that the researcher wishes to answer. As with other forms of social research, it is important that the gerontologist minimises the bias within the data by selecting appropriate samples and achieving adequate response rates and follow-up rates. Simply because the subjects of investigation are older people does not excuse the poor research design, inadequate questionnaires and low response rates that some investigators have reported. The gerontologist must be aware of the limitations imposed by the type of sample population and measurement techniques employed. Populations should not be researched simply because they are readily available. In particular, studies based upon samples of volunteers should be avoided as data based upon such study groups tell us nothing about the wider population of older people. Erroneous generalisations and extrapolations should not be made from inappropriate study populations. Perhaps one reason why old age is viewed in such a negative way by society is that many early research studies were based upon samples drawn from institutions, thereby giving a highly biased picture of the nature of old age. As gerontologists we have a responsibility to see that research is properly designed, conducted and interpreted so that we do not contribute to the validation of the myths and stereotypes of later life. Yet, at the same time, this laudable aim must be balanced by the obligation to report the results of research truthfully and completely however much they represent a challenge to cherished ideologies.

4 The demographic context

Much of the stimulus for the development of social gerontology as an academic discipline, and as an area of social and political concern, has come from the increase in the number and proportion of the population categorised as 'old' or 'elderly'. Indeed issues concerned with the demography of ageing are central in understanding many of the social, political and policy-related issues characteristic of twenty-first-century Britain. The backdrop for much political and policy-related debate is the concern about 'the demographic time bomb'. This is a rather pejorative term for the changing age composition of our population and of the balance between different age groups. As this chapter demonstrates, over the past 150 years there has been a profound change in the age composition of the British population with the 'ageing' of the population and a decrease in the number of children. This is represented in some quarters as an impending social disaster for two reasons. First, 'ageing' populations are attributed many of the negative stereotypes given to ageing at an individual level. All the negative attributes ascribed to an individual older person have been transferred to ageing populations. These are characterised as lack of energy, enthusiasm, innovation and artistic and intellectual achievement. Ageing populations are seen as being unresponsive to change and traditional in approach. Second, the increase in the number of older people is seen as having negative, perhaps even dire, consequences for the social and health services. These arguments taken together have been used to describe what Jefferys (1983) termed the 'moral panic' of population ageing which focus upon the perceived 'burden' which the increased numbers of older people will impose upon the state and younger people. Another way of describing this negative perspective is apocalyptic demography (Vincent, 1999) – the perception that we will be overwhelmed in social, political and welfare terms by the increasing numbers of old people.

In this chapter we examine the demographic trends which have brought about the growth in the number of older people in society by considering how populations 'age' and examining ways of measuring 'population ageing'. We then describe the demographic characteristics of the older section of the population and consider how the characteristics of this segment of society may change in future decades. The majority of the data presented relate to the United Kingdom, but many of the points raised have a wider resonance and parallels may be drawn with many countries in Europe, the Americas and Australasia. Hence the changing of the age profile of the population towards an increase in the number and proportion of older people is not unique to the United Kingdom but has a much wider resonance.

The ageing of populations

Demography is concerned with describing, analysing and understanding trends in the structure of populations. In this context populations are usually defined in terms of nation-states as these are the units for which data are collected, but demographic analysis may be undertaken with various subsets of national populations such as regions, counties or specially constituted populations such as inner cities (or rural areas). The structure of a given population is rarely static as the relationship between the key drivers of demographic change; birth rates, death rates and migration are highly fluid and subject to considerable variation over time. It is the interaction between these three sets of factors that brings about demographic change. In the case of the United Kingdom, population ageing has largely come about because of changes in birth and death rates.

The ageing of the British population

Perhaps the most striking demographic trend during the twentieth century in Britain, and many other parts of western Europe, has been the 'ageing' of the population. This refers to the processes of demographic change which results in an age structure which is characterised by increasing numbers (and percentages) of older people and decreasing numbers (and percentages) of younger people. Leaving aside the question of how precisely 'older' and 'younger' components of the population are defined, what are the processes which result in this demographic shift and what are the measures we use to describe the age profile of populations? Considering the processes that bring about population ageing, at the most basic level the distribution of age groups within any given population are function of mortality (death) rates and fertility rates. Population ageing occurs when large numbers of people survive into old age and comparatively few children are born.

There are a number of different measures that are used to summarise the age distribution of populations. These are percentage population classed as 'old', mean and median ages, population pyramids, dependency ratio. We examine the factors involved in demographic ageing and the measures used to describe this in more detail by considering the changing nature of the population of Britain.

Percentage aged

The most straightforward way of summarising the ageing of any given population is to record the percentage of the total population that is categorised as 'old' or 'elderly'. The key issue with this measure is the age taken as defining the index group. Ultimately the selection of a specific chronological age taken as the indicator of entry into 'old age' is arbitrary given the variable nature of the link between chronological age and ageing. In addition the specific age selected is subject to both cultural and historical variation. The 'meaning' of any specific chronological age is subject to variation both between different cultures and historically. Hence the experience of being age 60 in 1841 was almost certainly very different from the experience of the current group of 60 year olds. However, this measure does have the advantage of simplicity and facilitating comparisons both over time and between and within countries. It provides an easily understood and accessible way of summarising the relative contribution of older people, or indeed any other age group, to any given population at any particular point in time. The limitations of this measure need to be borne in mind when examining demographic data and in drawing inferences about the implications of any given distribution.

When considering the relative importance of older people, or indeed any other age group, within the total population we can present data in terms of total or absolute numbers in the age group of interest or the percentage of the total population aged, for example, 60+. Typically we present data in terms of the percentage of the total population represented by a particular group. This enables us to examine how the relative importance of those aged 60+ has changed independent of changes in the total population. If we present data only in terms of absolute numbers, any increase in the age group of interest may simply reflect an increase in the size of the total population. It is sometimes also helpful to consider the absolute numbers within particular subgroups, especially when large percentage changes in the relative size of particular elements of the population are being presented. This may be especially helpful when looking critically at the large recent increases predicted for the number of people aged 85+.

Estimating historical patterns of population structures in Britain is subject to considerable error because of the paucity of national data sets and the reliance upon parish records and other local rather than national data sets. There are always assumptions made in extrapolating from local data and generalising this to the entire population. Greater confidence can be placed in data from 1831 onwards as this marks the start of statutory registration of births, deaths and marriages in the United Kingdom. This is supplemented by the implementation of the decennial census from 1841 onwards which provides accurate and complete information on the age structure of the population, alongside other important information about the housing and economic circumstances of the population.

Given these caveats, the percentage of the English population aged 60 and over appears to have been remarkable stable at about 5–7 per cent, although the absolute number fluctuated for almost 400 years from about 1540 to about 1920. Indeed the percentage population aged 65+ increased from 4.8 per cent in 1851 to 5.1 per cent in 1931 while the total population approximately doubled over the same period (20.8 million to 40.8 million). Since 1931, however, the percentage had doubled to 18 per cent in 2001 (Shaw, 2004). Before considering the explanations for this increase in the percentage of older people we need to dissect the population aged 60 and over into its constituent parts and examine what has been happening to the size of these different subgroups. For example how have the numbers of the 'very old' (those aged 85 and over) changed in absolute terms and relative to both the total population and the population aged 60 and over?

The significant increase in the numbers and percentage of the older population of Britain took place in the early decades of the twentieth century. This is illustrated empirically in Table 4.1. Between 1901 and 2001, the number of people aged 60 rose four fold from 2.8 million to 12.1 million. It could be that the entire population was also rapidly increasing. We can put these data about the older age groups into context by looking at the change in the

Table 4.1 Growth of the population aged 60+, United Kingdom, 1901–2001 (thousands)

Age	1901	1931	1951	1971	1991	2001
60–64	1064	1897	2422	2935	2876	2800
65–74	1278	2460	3668	5193	5027	4937
75–84	470	844	1555	2674	3111	3280
85+	61	113	224	601	890	1124
Total	2873	5314	7869	11,403	11,904	12,141

Source: Askham *et al.*, 1992: Table A; ONS, 2003

total population over the same period. This reveals that over the same period the population of the United Kingdom grew by 55 per cent from 38.2 million (1901) to 58.7 million (2001). Hence the increase in the number and percentage of older people is not simply a reflection of general population growth but reflects other changes within the population.

The pattern of growth in the numbers of older people fluctuated over the course of the twentieth century and reflects the varying size of the different birth cohorts and the timing of changes in mortality. The first three decades of the twentieth century saw the numbers of older people in each subgroup virtually double while the largest percentage increase in the numbers of those aged 85 and over was between 1951 and 1971. When examining these apparently large percentage increases it is important to look at the absolute change as well. For example, between 1951 and 1971 there was a 268 per cent increase in the numbers aged 85 and over. However, the increase is much less spectacular when presented in absolute terms: an increase from just under a quarter of a million individuals (224,000) to a little over half a million (601,000). This reinforces the need to examine both relative and absolute numbers when reviewing past (and future) changes in population structure.

In addition to the slightly over fourfold increase in the twentieth century in the number of United Kingdom subjects aged 60 and over a second trend is observable and was hinted at in the earlier paragraph. This relates to the 'ageing' of the older population and is characterised by the increase in the numbers of very old, usually taken as aged 85 years and over, and centenarians. We can see that the number of people aged 85 and over has increased from just 61,000 in 1901 (0.16 per cent of the total population and 2 per cent of the population aged 60 and over) by 1839 per cent to 1,124,000 (1 per cent of the total population and 9 per cent of those aged 60 and over) (Table 4.1). The profound change in the nature of the age structure of the British population is, perhaps, best encapsulated by the growth in the number of centenarians. According to Thatcher (1999) centenarians were a rarity in the early years of the twentieth century and this probably reflects the situation for preceding populations. Persons of extreme longevity were very rare although not entirely unknown, but before compulsory national registration of births it is not clear what the precise chronological age of the 'very old' in historical times actually was. Thatcher (1999) estimates that, in 1911, there were 102 people in England and Wales aged 100 years (or more) and these numbers remained fairly constant until after the Second World War when they started to expand rapidly. In 1951 there were an estimated 295 aged 100+ compared with 8500 in 2001. Future projections rest upon assumptions about changes in mortality rates. Official projections from the Government Actuary Department suggest there will be 39,000 in 2036 and 95,000 by 2066. Thatcher (1999) suggests that this increase is due to the interrelationship between increased survival to age 80 and then, most importantly the increase in survival after age 80 as illustrated by rapidly decreasing death rates in this age group. Calculation of the probability of survival to age 100 illustrates the significance of this change. Aldwin and Gilmer (2004) report that an American born in 1879 had a 1 in 100 chance of becoming a centenarian compared with 1 in 8 for the 1980 birth cohort.

The increase in the number of older people in the population of Britain since the early 1950s is not something that has taken the government (or demographers) by surprise. In 1954 the Phillips Committee estimated that the numbers of pensioners, men aged 65+ and women aged 60+, would increase from 6.9 million in 1954 to 9.5 million by 1979. This estimate was remarkably accurate: the actual number of pensioners in 1979 was 9.46 million. Thus the current numbers of the very old are completely in line with population predictions. Protestations by governments of all political persuasions that they have been taken by surprise by the increase in the numbers of older people are not, therefore, very convincing.

The increase in the proportion of the population defined as elderly during the twentieth century is not unique to Great Britain. Rather, it is characteristic of most advanced industrial societies, and is now approaching the status of a global phenomenon (Table 4.2). Indeed it is estimated that one in three people in the world in 2050 will be aged 65+. Within Europe, Greece and Italy have almost a quarter of the population aged 60 and over while Ireland has the lowest percentage

Table 4.2 Population aged 60+, and life expectancy at birth for selected countries, 2000

Country		Life expectancy at birth	
	% aged 60+	Male	Female
European Union			
Belgium	22.2	74.8	81.2
Denmark	20.2	74.8	79.5
Germany	23.7	75.1	81.1
Greece	23.7	75.5	81.8
Spain	22.0	75.3	82.6
France	20.5	75.6	83.9
Ireland	15.3	75.8	79.2
Italy	24.1	76.2	83.2
Luxembourg	19.4	74.5	81.8
Netherlands	18.4	75.8	81.7
Austria	21.1	75.9	81.8
Portugal	21.0	72.7	80.1
Finland	20.2	74.5	81.2
Sweden	22.7	77.7	83.1
UK	20.7	75.1	79.9
Other developed			
USA	16.2	74.3	79.5
Canada	16.9	76.6	81.9
Australia	16.5	77.4	82.6
Japan	23.8	77.6	84.2
Lowest life expectancy			
Botswana	4.6	39.3	38.6
Sierra Leone	4.7	32.7	35.9
Zimbabwe	4.7	37.1	36.5
Zambia	4.5	36.7	37.0

Source: WHO Annual Report, 2002: Annex Table 1
Accessed from website www.who.int/whr/2002/en/whr2002_annex1.pdf

at approximately 15 per cent. In only two African countries, Botswana and Zimbabwe, did male life expectancy exceed that for females.

Mean and median ages

Mean and median ages are summary statistics that are used to succinctly summarise the structure of a population and, again, facilitate examination of both changes over time and between different countries. The mean age is simply an arithmetic average of the age distribution and, as such, is subject to influence by the extremes of the age distribution. Hence a high absolute number of children (or older people) will influence the resultant mean figure. The median is the midpoint of the age distribution, the age at which half the population is younger and half older. In 2002 the median age of the population of the United Kingdom was 38 and the mean age was 39 (Shaw, 2004). The median age of the United States was very similar at 36 in 2000 while in Italy it was 40; in contrast the median age in Malawi was 17 (Aldwin and Gilmer, 2004).

Population pyramids

Simply presenting the percentage of older people (or indeed any other age group) within a population gives only a limited perspective upon the composition of the whole population. The above measures of summarising population structure are limited in that they do not give a clear 'overall' summary of the structure of the population and the relative contribution of the different age groups. None of these measures gives a good summary of the overall structure of a population or of the relationship of the constituent elements. The population pyramid is a graphical representation of the age and sex composition of a given population (see Figures 4.1a to 4.1c) usually (but not always) divided into five-year age bands. Population pyramids can

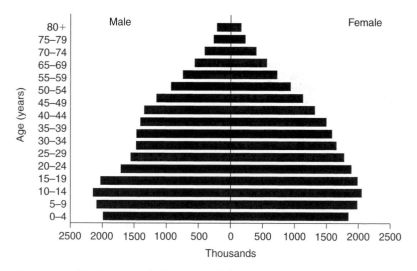

Figure 4.1a Idealised population pyramid for Great Britain in 1990.

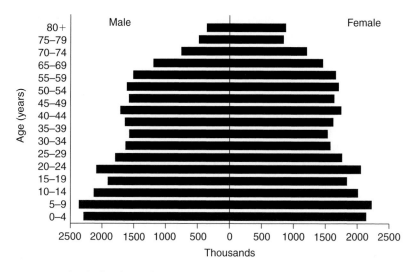

Figure 4.1b Idealised population pyramid for Great Britain in 2000.

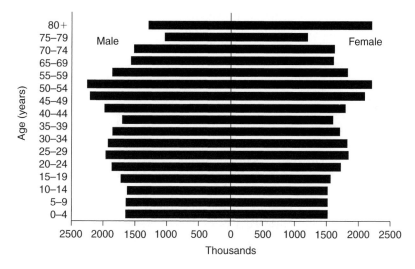

Figure 4.1c Idealised populaton pyramid for Great Britain in 2050.

show the influence of previous variations in fertility as well as the influence of mortality 'birth bulges' and years when there were fewer births are clearly evident. This method also demonstrates the gender balance within different age groups.

The population pyramid for 1901 demonstrates a 'classic' pyramid shape, with lots of children and young people at the base and comparatively few older people at the apex (Figure 4.1a). Such a population distribution is characteristic of populations with high rates of mortality and high birth rates. How can we explain the change in the shape of the population distribution to that illustrated by 2000, which is a 'beehive' type shape reflecting a situation of low fertility and mortality (Figure 4.1b)? This change from a situation of high mortality and fertility to low mortality and fertility is known as the demographic transition and is proposed as a part of a 'package' of interrelated social and economic changes that accompany the development of modernisation and industrialisation. The demographic transition theory explains the development of population ageing and is exemplified by the changes that took place in western Europe during the nineteenth and twentieth centuries. In the first stage the economies of, for example, Great Britain moved from being agriculturally to industrially focused. As a result of economic development, improved (general) prosperity and environmental improvement 'such as clean water and sanitation' mortality rates declined. Lagging behind declines in mortality are decreases in fertility. Once fertility declines, the transition is complete and population ageing occurs because of the combination of low mortality and fertility. It is profound decreases in fertility that, in this model, are the engine driving population ageing.

The notion of demographic transition forms a plausible model for how societies (or populations) move from high mortality/fertility to low patterns. However, theories attempt to go beyond description to explanation and prediction. There are many debates as to the veracity of the demographic transition theory (as opposed to the model of different stages). Certainly in the developing world we can see a pattern of declining mortality rates, but these have not always been accompanied by the decreases in fertility, as this is often contingent upon cultural, ideological, religious and social factors that are not very well understood. In many developing countries because of the medical and technological inflows from the developed world, such as contraceptives and childhood immunisation, population ageing can be driven by changes in mortality (rather than fertility) and can occur in advance of, rather than after, economic development.

Is there a 'correct' population shape?

Although there is often intense political debate about what the 'correct' age distribution for any given population should be, there is no easy answer. Interpretations of the implications of the different types of population distribution are rarely evidence based or value free. Each of these types of population distribution illustrated by Figures 4.1a and 4.1c, a projected distribution for twenty years hence, poses social and public policy challenges. The 1901 type of distribution implies lots of children, large families and high death rates. The major focus for public policy would be around child-related services (schools and child–maternal health) and reducing mortality and improving public health. The 'beehive' distribution suggests that caring for older people would be the major challenge for public policy. Based upon current age distributions we can make limited predictions about the likely nature and characteristics of the population in the future. For example, we can see that one of the most significant influences upon the structure of the British population will be the 'ageing' of the baby boomer generation (Evandrou, 1997). This mirrors the profound influence this group has had at earlier phases of the lifecycle and is not something unique to later life, although it is sometimes presented as such.

Dependency ratio

Another numerical, rather than visual, way of summarising the structure of a given population is via the use of the dependency ratio. This refers to the measures which express the 'dependent' population, defined as those not considered to be potentially active in the labour market, as a percentage of the population classed as not being dependent on or in relation to the overall total population. It is customary to calculate two distinct measures. One is concerned with children and is termed the 'youth dependency ratio' and the second is concerned with older people. In each the number in the population aged 0–15 (the age range which approximates to childhood) or 60/65 (the current ages for British women and men to become eligible for retirement pension) is expressed as a ratio (usually per 1000) percentage of those classified as economically active (i.e. 16–59/64) or as a ratio of the total population. Clearly there are many assumptions which underpin these measures and such assumptions should be explicitly stated and subject to critical analysis. The major assumptions are (a) all children are economically dependent (which ignores the participation of many in these age groups in part-time employment), (b) all those aged 16–59/64 are economically active (which ignores the early retirement of men from the labour market, the non-participation of women resultant from caring responsibilities or participation of young adults in higher education), (c) it is a single point in time, cross-sectional snapshot-type measure which ignores the previous contributions of older people. While these can be useful ways of summarising population structures we must be wary of the ideological assumptions which underpin such measures. These are simply numerical summaries without any intrinsic meaning or value. The meaning we attribute to these numbers reflects the value of specific societies or groups.

Given these caveats in the United Kingdom, the youth ratio has decreased from 438 (1971) to 3227 (2001) while the old age ratio has increased only marginally from 288 to 298 over the same period (Dunnel, 2000; Shaw, 2004). If we were to calculate an overall dependency ratio there has probably been little change in the number of 'assumed dependants' in comparison to the size of the assumed working population, although the nature of the 'dependent' group has switched from predominantly children to predominantly older adults. However, this pattern of no overall change in the dependency ratio does not fit easily with the alarmist scares which, by calculating dependency ratios for future decades, predict crisis of modern western society because of the ageing of the baby boomer generation and the expanding duration of later life (and the number of individuals achieving this).

What has brought about these changes in the structure of the population?

The key question is what has brought about this increase in the percentage of older people within the population? We have, in previous sections, alluded to the two major mechanisms that have brought about changes in population structure: fertility and mortality. We now consider each of these in turn. In addition we also need to acknowledge the third, but less important factor in the United Kingdom, which is migration.

As noted earlier, the age structure of any population is the result of the complex and dynamic interrelationship between three factors: fertility, mortality and migration. The increase in the proportion of the population classified as older in Britain is largely attributable to changes in fertility and mortality rates, especially infant mortality; migration has had much less of an impact upon the age structure of our population (although this is not true for all countries and may not be true in the future). The important changes in fertility and mortality that have characterised Britain over the past 150 years are summarised in turn as they each represent a major change in the British demographic context.

Fertility

Fertility simply refers to the numbers of children born in any given population. There are various ways of describing and analysing patterns of fertility within and between populations. At the most basic level we can calculate the total numbers of children born in a given year. In 2002 there were 669,000 live births in the United Kingdom (Summerfield and Babb, 2004). This was 202,500 less than the number recorded in 1971 (ONS, 2004b). This example demonstrates how the annual numbers of birth, in the United Kingdom and elsewhere, fluctuates and there are both peaks and troughs. In the United Kingdom the largest annual number of births recorded was in 1920 when 1.127 million babies were born: 300,000 more than the previous year (ONS, 2004b). The lowest was in 1997 when 657,000 were born. This annual difference in total births has been as large as 300,000, which has obvious and profound social policy implications. These peaks and troughs in the number of births also exert an influence upon the age distribution of the population by the creation of 'baby booms' or 'birth bulges' as the population pyramids described earlier illustrate. The largest 'birth bulge' experienced in Britain occurred between 1918 and 1920. This post-First World War baby boom was larger than that which occurred after the Second World War, although it was not maintained for as many years. The British population shows two further 'birth bulges' in the years immediately following the end of the Second World War and in the 1960s. The post-war bulge is characterised by 1946 and 1947 when almost 1 million babies were born each year (Falkingham, 1997). This increase in the numbers of births created the population bulge that is often collectively known, in Australia, Britain and North America, as the 'baby boom' and its members as the 'baby boomers'. Even examination of variations in the total number of births can offer insights into potential changes in the shape of our population. While it is comparatively easy to enumerate the numbers of births it is much less easy to explain variations in births or, very importantly, predict future patterns of births. People remain highly capricious in deciding whether to have children and how many children to have.

One important factor influencing both the current (and future) patterns of births is the number of women within the population, as the number of births is clearly limited by the number of women of childbearing age. Comparing crude numbers of births over time is not a reliable way of assessing trends in fertility as any variations observed may simply reflect variations in the numbers of women of the relevant age. Hence demographers calculate a number of different measures of fertility to examine trends over time, to make inter-country comparisons and consider future trends. These measures include the number of births per 1000 population (the crude birth rate), the number of births per 1000 females aged 15–44 years (the years usually considered to be the ones associated with childbearing) and the total period fertility rate (i.e. the number of children a woman would have if current patterns of fertility were maintained across her lifetime). Regardless of how it is described, the fertility rate is a crucial element in determining the age structure of a population. A decrease in fertility or numbers of children born, by definition, reduces the numbers in the younger age groups and consequently increases the percentage in the older age groups, even if the absolute number of older people remains the same.

Fertility rates in England and Wales, as measured by the number of live births per 1000 population, were fairly stable at about 31–35 per 1000 from about 1841 until the end of the nineteenth century (ONS, 2004b). The rates then started to decline such that, in 2002, there were 11.4 births per 1000 (ONS, 2004b). Effectively this measure of fertility has decreased to one-third of the 1900 rate over the course of the twentieth century. This decrease is reflected in other measures of fertility. The rate of live births per 1000 women aged 15–44 decreased from 115 at the start of the twentieth century to 57 at the start of the next (Summerfield and Babb, 2004). For the United Kingdom as a whole the total period fertility rate has decreased from 2.4 in 1971 to 1.6 in 2001 compared with 4.8 in 1871 and 3.1 for the period 1901–1905 (Grundy, 1997). These levels of fertility are well below the level of 2.1 children per woman required for 'natural' replacement of the population and well below the post-war peak of 2.93 recorded in 1964 (ONS, 2004b). Irrespective of the measure used there is a consistent trend of decreasing rates of fertility. This trend may be observed internationally. In 1990 the average number of children per woman worldwide was 3.3 – by 2002 this had decreased to 2.6. Hence decreasing fertility is a global rather than a national or international phenomenon.

Changes in fertility rates are reflected in the size of real families.

People born in 1871 would have had, when they became parents, an average of 4.8 children and of these children 2.7 would have survived until age 45. When the generation born in 1921 became parents the average number of children was 2.0, and 1.6 survived to age 45; for the generation of women born in 1960 average family size is estimated at 1.94 and virtually all will survive into old age (Pearce, 1999). In Britain there have been two further trends which have influenced fertility: the increase in the percentage of women remaining childless from about 10 per cent for the cohort born in 1940 to 20 per cent for those born in the late 1950s (Pearce *et al.*, 1999) and the 'delay' in childbearing.

Within the overall general trend of declining fertility there is some variation within age-specific rates. Fertility for women in the 20–24 age group has declined markedly from about 154 live births per 1000 in 1971 to 68 in 2002 (ONS, 2004b), but rates for older women have increased. For example the rate for women aged 35–39 decreased consistently from 1961 (48 per 1000) until 1981 (22) but has since steadily increased to 43 in 2002. Similar trends are observable for those aged 40 and over. This trend has increased the mean age of first-time mothers from 27.6 in 1961 to 29.2 in 2001. This means that, of the 590,453 live births in England and Wales in 2002, 15 per cent were to women aged 35–39 and 3 per cent were to mothers aged over 40, a situation very close to that recorded in 1961. So, although age-specific fertility rates for the over-35s have increased since the early 1980s, the majority of births are still to women aged 20–29. Again these two apparently contradictory trends reflect the influence of using absolute and relative rates in the analysis. The decline in fertility demonstrated by the British population reflects both the increases in the number of women who are remaining childless and, for those who do opt for children, a predominance of one- and two-child families.

In combination the pattern of fertility in Britain in the past 100 years has been for fewer women to have children, for those women who do have children to have smaller families and for fertility to be delayed. It is not clear as to why these changes in childbearing have taken place but they are also not specific to Britain. Pearce (1999) reports the very dramatic declines in fertility which have characterised post-Second World War Europe. Although the timing of the decline varies between countries, fertility and family sizes have decreased markedly across Europe regardless of the religious tradition of the countries (Table 4.3). Hence we see low fertility rates in Italy and Spain as well as Germany and Scandinavia. Clearly this a

Table 4.3 Fertility data for selected European countries

	Total fertility rate		Average family size for women born		% childless	
	1960	1999	1940	1960	1940	1960
Belgium	2.6	1.6				
Denmark	2.5	1.7	2.24	1.88	10	12
Germany	2.4	1.3				
Greece	2.3	1.3				
Spain	2.9	1.1	2.59	1.73	8	10
France	2.7	1.7	2.41	2.09	8	8
Ireland	3.8	1.9	3.27	2.39	5	16
Italy	2.4	1.2				
Luxembourg	2.3	1.7				
Netherlands	3.1	1.5	2.21	1.84	12	18
Austria	2.7	1.4				
Portugal	3.1	1.4	2.61	1.87	6	7
Finland	2.7	1.7	2.03	1.94	14	18
Sweden	2.2	1.6				
UK	2.7	1.7	2.36	1.95	11	21

Source: Walker and Maltby, 1997: Table 2.1, Pearce, 1999: Table 3

pan-European trend which extends across the developed world and a variety of explanatory factors are involved including decreases in infant mortality and increased education about methods of birth control and profound changes in the role of, and opportunities for, women in society. The variation in the timing of fertility changes across the different countries of Europe illustrates how these wider societal changes have been experienced differentially across the continent. Taken in combination these trends show that for women born in 1955 in England and Wales, approximately 20 per cent have no children, 10 per cent have one child and 40 per cent have two children, with the remainder having three or more children compared to women born in 1940, where only 10 per cent were childless and 37 per cent had three or more children.

Mortality

The second major influence upon the age distribution of a given population is the pattern of mortality or deaths. Again detailed examination of these trends are contingent upon an accurate and complete system of death registration. In the United Kingdom in 2001 there were 602,300 (ONS, 2004a) deaths, giving an excess of births over deaths of 70,800. In examining patterns of mortality, and how they have influenced the age composition of society, we need to examine three distinct elements: changes in overall mortality, changes in infant mortality and changes in adult mortality. Here we are concerned with mortality as a driver of population change rather than as an indirect measure of health status, this will be considered in Chapter 5.

When examining trends in mortality we need to look at changes in rates rather than crude numbers to determine changes over time and to make comparisons within (and between) populations. To make sense of patterns of mortality we need accurate details of deaths (the numerator) and accurate details of the population (the denominator). The most straightforward measure is the crude mortality rate that describes the number of deaths per 1000 total population. This indicator has approximately halved since the 1840s. For the quinquennia 1841 and 1845 the overall death rate in England and Wales was 21.4 per 1000 Office of Population Censuses and Surveys (OPCS), 1992) compared with 10.2 per 1000 in 2002 ((ONS, 2004a). Crude death rates were relatively stable until about the turn of the century with rates decreasing most rapidly in the period 1901–1931. Since this time, rates have continued to decline but at a slower rate, although the trend remains inexorably downwards.

Crude death rates present only a limited analysis as it is related to the age structure of the population. The changes outlined above may simply reflect changes in population structure or a decrease in size rather than in mortality. However, given that the population over this period was characterised by a doubling in the number of older people, this halving of the crude death rate is all the more remarkable. We might consider that large absolute increases in the older age groups might have resulted in increases in mortality. A better way of looking at overall changes in mortality is to examine age-specific rates that describe death rates in particular age and sex subgroups of the population. Here we look at two specific areas – deaths in childhood and deaths in later life – although it is, of course, possible to look at other age and sex groups as well.

Over the period 1841–2002 there has also been a massive decrease in the numbers of children dying within the first year of life. This is known as the infant mortality rate and is usually expressed as a rate per 1000 live births. In the period 1841–1845 the infant mortality rate was 148 per 1000 (OPCS, 1992). Put into perspective this means that about 15 per cent of all babies died in the first year of life. Applying this to the 590,543 births in England and Wales for 2002 means that 88,581 babies would have died. The actual recorded infant mortality rate of 5.2 per 1000 in 2002 meant that only a little over 3000 babies died (ONS, 2004a). The scale of the decline of deaths of children in the first year of life is remarkable; the rate is now only 3 per cent of the 1841 level even given the birth of very premature and low birth weight babies. This decrease in infant and early childhood mortality has resulted from the decreased potency of childhood diseases such as measles and diphtheria, and other communicable diseases such as smallpox, cholera and typhoid, resultant from improvements in public health measures and the changed natural history of these diseases. McKeown (1979) argues that the majority of the decrease in mortality over the past 150 years can be attributed to the control of infectious diseases. Looked at in this light the ageing of the population resultant from the decline in infant mortality may be viewed as a triumph for public health, rather than a demographic disaster.

Similar decreases in mortality have been observed throughout childhood but especially in the pre-school years. In 1861–1865 the annual mortality for children in the 1–4 age range was a little under 4 per cent compared with 0.02 per cent in 2001. Again it is the scale of change which is remarkable and which has had a profound impact upon family formation. In the middle years of the nineteenth century the high rate of mortality in childhood meant that over one-third (37 per cent) of children died before the age of 15. This contrasts to the current situation where less than 1 per cent of children die before this age. Taken together the decreases in early childhood mortality have been highly influential in changing patterns of fertility as we now presume that children born will survive into old age; this is a total contrast to the previous generations when high childhood mortality was a fact of life and most families experienced deaths of children in infancy or childhood. This is a profound social change which we have not always fully recognised or celebrated for the advances in public health that it demonstrates.

When analysing changes in mortality less attention has usually been given to examining changes in late-age mortality. Mortality in all three age subgroups of the older population has declined by between 60 per cent (for those aged 65–74) and 45 per cent (for those aged 85+) between 1841 and 2001. In comparison to both general mortality and infant mortality, the declines in late age mortality have been much more recent. For all three age groups, but especially that aged over 75, the decrease gathered pace from the 1960s onwards. We will return to this point in Chapter 5. It is sufficient here to note the enhanced survival for those people now reaching later life.

Taken overall the changes in mortality rates at different ages have combined to bring about a profound change in the epidemiology of death in Britain (Table 4.4). In 1841 children under 14 accounted for 37 per cent of deaths. This contrasts with the situation in 2002 where 80 per cent of deaths were accounted for by people aged 65, and over 1 per cent by deaths in childhood. One result of this skewing of death into the later years of life has been to develop the stereotype that old age is linked with death and decline. At previous points in our history death was not so closely linked with old age. We can illustrate this very profound change in the distribution of mortality by considering the probability of individuals surviving to specific ages. Of a cohort of 10,000 males born in 1841, 40 per cent would survive to age 55 and 14 per cent to age 75 compared with 92 per cent and 56 per cent for a cohort born in 1994–1996. Clearly most of us will now live to old age, a situation unheard of in previous generations. Furthermore, our children now take for granted the presence of grandparents (and great-grandparents) within their family groups. Yet this was not the case even in the 1940s and serves to highlight the novelty of the type of population structure characteristic of contemporary Britain. This demonstrates how changes in a fairly abstract and academic concept such as mortality rates are translated into 'real effects' in the lives and families of contemporary society.

Life expectancy

Life expectancy refers to the average number of years members of any specific population can expect to live. This measure is not to be confused with life span which refers to the maximum length of time humans (or other species) can expect to live under optimal conditions. Life expectancy is based upon the application of current mortality rates to different age groups within the population to

Table 4.4 Deaths by age, England and Wales, 1841 and 2002 (%)

	Deaths *1841*	*2002*
Infancy and childhood (0–14)	37	1
Young adults (15–34)	25	2
Mid-life (35–64)	33	17
Later life (65+)	15	80

Source: derived from OPCS, 1992: Table 3; ONS, 2004a: Table 6.1

establish likely rates of survivorship. Hence we are applying current rates of mortality to predict survival. These estimates may be upset by changes in the patterns of mortality resulting from the emergence of new diseases such as AIDS or the better identification and treatment of existing diseases. In response to changing social and economic conditions, life expectancy can go down as well as up, as the case of Russia exemplifies. (Aldwin and Gilmer, 2004).

Expectation of life, the average number of years individuals can expect to live, is commonly calculated for birth cohorts but can also be calculated from other ages as well. For example, we can calculate for a 60 year old how many more years the 'average' individual can expect to live. The limitation of this measure is that, while we can estimate the number of years remaining for the average individual, we cannot accurately apply these estimates to specific individuals. This is an illustration of the 'ecological fallacy' the difficulties of applying information about groups or areas to specific individuals. Hence we cannot identify which individuals will live beyond the average (nor those who will not), which is a characteristic of population level research.

Clearly the changes in mortality rates described earlier have had a profound influence upon average life expectancy in Britain. Life expectancy at birth in England between 1530 and 1800 was estimated at between 40 and 45 years, although there were variations between different social groups and the estimates would vary because of the influence of epidemics of infectious diseases upon rates of mortality. In particular, females had a shorter life expectancy than males because of high maternal mortality. As late as 1901–1910 life expectancy for a newborn male was still only about 48 years and 52 years for a newborn female (Table 4.5). By 2001 this had increased by almost 26 years, or a little over 50 per cent, for both sexes, compared with about 24 per cent change in the previous 60 years. Life expectancy in the United Kingdom at birth in 2001 is 75.7 years for men and 80.4 years for women (ONS, 2004a). Hence the changes in life expectancy at birth in the twentieth century seem to be continuation and acceleration of a pre-existing trend. These increases reflect the sharp decline in childhood mortality noted earlier and the fact that the number of people who manage to live to old age has increased. This increase in expectation of life at birth does not, necessarily, tell us anything about possible changes in the extent of the potential human life span.

We can also calculate life expectancy for any other age other than simply at birth. Life expectancy at age 65 has increased during the twentieth century. In 1841 a 65-year-old male could expect to live

Table 4.5 Expectation of life, England and Wales, 1841, 1901 and 2001

Expectation of life	1841		1901		2001	
	M	F	M	F	M	F
At birth	40.2	42.2	48.5	52.4	75.9	80.6
Age 65	10.9	11.5	10.8	12.0	15.3	19.1

Sources: Victor, 1994; Summerfield and Babb, 2004

another eleven years compared with fifteen years in 2001. For females the increase over the same period was from twelve to nineteen years, again increases in the order of 50–60 per cent in a little under a century (Grundy, 1997). This trend seems to be one that is exclusive to post-nineteenth century as there was little change in expectation of life at age 65 between 1841 and 1901. We can calculate expectation of life for the various subgroups of the older population. For those aged 80 and over in the United Kingdom at the turn of the millennium women could expect to live for another 8.7 years and men for another 7.1 years (ONS, 2004a).

One of the most interesting demographic changes over the past 150 years has been the development of a profound imbalance in the percentage of males and females surviving to old age. Ancient populations were characterised by an approximate balance between the sexes in later life or possibly a slight excess of males. As late as the 1930s the population of Britain was characterised by approximately equal proportions of elderly men and women. In 1901 women lived, on average, only two years longer than men did. Now women live, on average, seven years longer than men. This male–female difference in life expectancy is now accepted by many as being one of the 'objective facts' of ageing when it is, in fact, a recent phenomenon of almost certain multifactorial causation. Indeed there are still four countries where males have a slightly longer expectation of life than females. These are Zimbabwe (40.9 years versus 40 years), Namibia (43.3 years versus 43 years), Eritrea (46.6 years versus 46 and Botswana (39.5 years versus 39.3 years) (World Health Organisation (WHO), 2002). As the examples of Russia and Africa demonstrate, life expectancy can go down as well as up and there is nothing 'inevitable' about the observed increases in expectation of life nor in the gender difference in life expectancy.

Three sets of reasons have been advanced to account for this gender imbalance: 'biological superiority' of women, environmental factors and social factors. For the biological superiority thesis to be the answer, we would expect to see universal and significant differences in mortality between men and women and that this would have been present throughout history. However, many countries show only very small life expectancy advantages towards women and, in other countries, the mortality advantage of women has been of fairly recent origin. So while there might be some truth in this thesis it is not the entire answer. It seems likely that environmental and social factors are also important. Until recently men's participation in the labour market exposed them to more environmental hazards than women. In social terms men, again until recently, have been more likely than women to indulge in habits such as smoking, excess drinking and risk-seeking behaviour. Data from North America suggest that the increased differential in life expectancy between the sexes is due to the high prevalence of smoking and its related diseases among males. The generation of women now experiencing old age has very low rates of smoking. This, therefore, seems to be a plausible explanation for this differential. Women took up smoking in large numbers during and after the Second World War. Indeed women are still continuing to smoke while men are giving up the habit. It is interesting to speculate about how these changed patterns of smoking behaviour will influence the life expectancy and health in later life of future generations.

Although in Britain over the past century crude mortality rates have declined markedly and life expectancy has increased dramatically, there is nothing 'inevitable' about this process. It is important to remember that (like stock market investments) mortality and life expectancy can go up as well as down! We can see evidence for the reversal in mortality and life expectancy from the case of the former Soviet Union. Shkolnikov *et al.* (1997) report that male life expectancy at birth in Russia decreased by 6.2 years between 1990 and 1994 (to 57.6 years) with rapidly increased rates of alcohol-related and accidental or violent deaths and the re-emergence of infectious diseases implicated in the decline. This reversal of a substantial period of mortality decline in Russia serves to remind us of the fragility of our apparent control over death and the need for public health interventions to control infectious diseases via immunisation and environmental protection remain a priority for all populations.

Migration

Migration is the third main influence upon the demographic profile of any given population. Large outflows of young people can bring about the ageing of a population while the immigration of the young will have the opposite effect. In Britain, migration, either into or out of the country, has had only a very marginal impact upon the national demographic profile, but given the projected changes in the age composition of the UK population this may become a much more important 'driver' of demographic change. Migration, especially the emigration of the young in search of employment, has been an important influence upon the demographic profile of many areas within Britain and can result in some areas having a higher percentage of older population because of the exodus of the young. In future decades it is likely that inward migration might exert a more profound influence upon our population structure, although this depends upon political decisions about the nature and extent of migration within a European context.

How will the population change in future decades?

It is fairly straightforward to undertake the analysis of changes in population structure, fertility and mortality as the data are readily available and we are describing changes that have taken place in the past. Predicting what will happen to the structure of the United Kingdom population (or indeed any other population) is more problematic as we have to make assumptions about the maintenance of current trends into the future (Shaw, 2004). Predicting the number of older people in future populations is contingent upon the application of current rates of mortality. Hence changes in mortality (either upwards or downwards) will affect the accuracy of the projections. Predicting the percentage of total population that older people will represent is even more problematic as this requires estimates (or predictions) of future patterns of births. Predicting the numbers of children that future generations will have is notoriously difficult. Will future generations of women show the same trends for deferral of fertility and small family sizes? Will governments intervene and develop 'pronatalist' policies to encourage increases in fertility and will such policies be 'successful'? Can social engineering and social policy incentives reverse what has been a century-long decline in fertility?

The 2002 projections for the United Kingdom, based upon forward projection of current patterns of mortality, life expectancy and fertility, suggest only a slight increase in the total population from 59.2 million in 2002 to 61.8 by 2031 (Shaw, 2004). If the low levels of fertility are maintained, and this is not offset by significant in-migration, the population will start to decline after this peak and this trend is expected to be demonstrated by most countries in Europe and the developed world (Shaw, 2004).

Assuming that current rates of mortality apply, the absolute numbers of those aged over 60 are projected to increase from 12.2 million in 2002 to 19.4 million in 2031 (Shaw, 2004), an increase of approximately 7.2 million (59%). It is the projected rise in the proportion of the over-85s that has aroused perhaps the most interest from politicians and government policy makers. This growth in the numbers of the very elderly is seen as having dire consequences for the British economy, living standards and welfare state provision. The numbers of those aged 85 years and over are projected to increase from 1.1 million in 2001 to 3.1 million by 2051, an increase of just over 2 million people in 50 years. This indicates that a significant proportion (about one-third) of the overall increase in the population over 60 will be accounted for by increases in those aged 85 years and over. These changes will be reflected in the gradual increase in the median ages of the population to 43 in 2031.

More problematic than estimating the absolute number of older people in the future, as we at least are already born, is predicting the number of children. Fertility rates are notoriously volatile and difficult to estimate. The data in the 2002 estimates are based upon an assumed fertility rate of 1.7 children per woman, but these are based upon forward projection of current trends, which may (or may not) be accurate. The presentation of details of the older age groups as a percentage of the total population is based upon assumptions about the size of elements of the denominator which may (or may not) prove to be correct, especially if there are changes in the migration element of the population size equation.

Broken down by age and sex: the diversity of the population

In this section we examine some of the more detailed demographic characteristics of this group and consider the extent to which this profile varies from historical characteristics of the older population. Factors such as gender, class, age and ethnicity are important because they provide the social context within which people experience old age and, indeed, shape the experience of the earlier phases of the life-cycle. One key issue to consider throughout this volume is to what extent old represents a continuation of previous life experiences. For example, are class, gender or ethnic differences in health (or access to financial resources) continued into old age and do such differentials increase or reduce? It is not always possible to answer such questions because of the paucity of data, but such issues require detailed examination if we are to develop a fuller understanding of the context within which people experience old age. In addition such factors are important when considering the appropriate type of service and policy response to the problems and issues experienced by older people. In this section we deal with sex structure, ethnicity, civil status and household composition as these provide the 'demographic' context that frames old age and later life.

Sex structure

Given the differences in mortality and life expectancy noted previously, it is not surprising that 57 per cent of those aged 60 and over are female, reflecting their earlier retirement age and greater longevity (Table 4.6). At all ages from 60 years and over there is a marked imbalance between the sexes and the number of females per 100 males increases with age. For those aged 60–64 there are 104 females per 100 males while for the 85 and over age group there are 278 females per 100 males. Of the 8560 centenarians in England and Wales in 2001, 80 per cent were female, but the imbalance between males and females has been decreasing and this trend is projected to continue. In 1971 for the 65–74 age group there were 112 females per 100 males and this is predicted to decrease to 106 by 2008; for those aged 75 and over the sex ratio was 213 in 1971 and is predicted to be 157 in 2008. This trend indicates that mortality differentials are decreasing and the gap between the sexes is narrowing. The

Table 4.6 Sex distribution of population aged 60+, United Kingdom, 2001 (thousands)

Age	Male	Female	Ratio*
60–64	1409	1470	96
65–74	2301	2636	87
75–84	1300	1980	66
85+	310	814	38

Source: ONS 2003 available from http://www.statistics.gov.uk/census 2001/ default.asp?

Note: * Ratio – males per 1000 females

experience of old age is for current (and future) cohorts of elders predominantly a female one. Scholars of gerontology have not always
noted this predominance; feminist scholars (Arber *et al.*, 2003) and
those interested in the lives of older men (Davidson *et al.*, 2003) have
only recently addressed the issue of gender in later life. In the future,
it seems that the sex imbalance will be greatly reduced, which draws
our attention to the diversity of the ageing experience and how it is
not always constant and can vary across generations. Furthermore it
illustrates how the social context within which future generations of
elders will experience 'old age' will show considerable variation from
the current pattern.

Ethnicity

Perhaps the most profound and readily apparent aspect of the changing socio-demographic profile of the older population will be related
to ethnicity. Currently the older population of the United Kingdom
consists of only a small minority of 'non-white' subjects. The 2001
Census estimates suggest that overall 4 per cent of the population
aged 65+ define themselves as belonging to minority groups (ONS,
2003). This, perhaps, is the most homogenised dimension of the
older age groups. This situation is likely to change in future decades
as the population of individuals who moved to Britain after 1945
starts to age. In comparison to the 'white' population where 17 per
cent of the population are aged 65+, no minority groups have over
10 per cent of their population in this age group. Several communities have substantial percentages of their population in the 45–59 age
group such as the Indian, Chinese and Black Caribbean groups; it is
likely that there will be more ethnic diversity in the composition of
future generations of elders as the generation of post-war migrants
'ages'. This is especially likely to be the case in specific locations such
as London and other large cities where there are well-established
concentrations of minority groups (Evandrou, 2000). The term
'double jeopardy' has been coined to describe the double discrimination that older migrants are thought to face, being negatively evaluated twice on account of their age and minority status (Blakemore
and Boneham, 1994). While it is clear that older ethnic minority
people are disadvantaged in Britain it is not yet clear if they are more
(or less) disadvantaged than their white counterparts. The research
base is rather limited and, as yet, it is difficult to be definitive on this
subject. We can be certain that the ageing of the minority populations will exert a considerable influence upon the diversity of the

ageing experience and the response from policy makers and services. This is another manifestation of the diversity of the population that is classified as old or elderly: we must be cautious in assuming that the population is homogeneous and that the experience of 'old age' in the future will be the same as it is currently. Although each of these important aspects of the composition of the older population is discussed separately, they all intersect. We need to be developing a more sophisticated research agenda that can examine the relationship of age, gender, class and ethnicity: these dimensions do not exist in isolation and research, policy and practice need to recognise this diversity.

Civil status

Civil status refers to the legal classification of the population as married, widowed, divorced/separated and single (or never married). The civil status of the older age groups varies, as with other sub-groups within the population, with both age and sex. There are also historical and temporal variations, which need to be taken into account in researching ageing and old age and the area of civil status and its measurement in social research offers some elegant examples. Period effects are illustrated in the way data about civil status have been collected in a variety of censuses and surveys. In his 1945 survey, Sheldon (1948) did not have a category for divorced/ separated while the 2001 Census distinguishes between first and sub-sequent marriage as well as cohabitation. In this section we consider age and gender variations as well as trends over time. In addition we consider how variations in the nature of the population can produce different answers to the same questions. This illustrates how the nature of the population surveyed can greatly influence the results produced, an important principle of all social research.

Table 4.7 demonstrates the well-observed gender and age-based variations in the civil status of the older population. For the older age groups, men are more likely to be married than women, while women are more likely to be widowed. By the age of 75 years the majority of women are widowed. For men, widowers do not become the statistical majority until the age of 85 years and over. This vari-ation reflects both the tendencies for women to marry men older than themselves, the average age difference at marriage being several years, and the gender difference in mortality. For both sexes the pro-portion classified as widowed increases markedly with age as does the fraction of females classified as single. This latter characteristic of

Table 4.7 Civil status of population aged 65+ living in the community, Great Britain, 2001 (%)

	65–69		70–74		75–79		80–84		85+	
	M	F	M	F	M	F	M	F	M	F
Single	7	5	7	6	5	7	6	7	3	9
Married	83	62	73	49	69	41	68	23	40	10
Widowed	4	25	14	35	22	45	25	67	55	79
Divorced	6	8	6	10	4	7	2	3	2	2

Source: Walker *et al.*, 2002

the population is a cohort effect reflecting the lack of marriage opportunities for many now elderly women because of the high mortality of men in the First World War. The 'dying' out of this generation is clearly seen in Table 4.8, which shows that this group has decreased from 14 per cent to 7 per cent in approximately thirty years. We can also see how the percentage of elders classed as divorced or separated has increased from 1 per cent to about 7 per cent over two decades and it is to be expected that, in future generations of elders, this percentage will increase.

We may, in the future, see the re-emergence of the single (i.e. never married) older person and the single post-divorce older person. Evandrou and Falkingham (2000) offer some interesting insights into the possible profile of older people in the future. They indicate that for those aged 65+ in 1971 (i.e. born in 1906 or earlier) marriage was almost universal. However, for those who were born in 1960 the suggestion is that far fewer will marry or establish a permanent long-term relationship. They argue that up to 20 per cent may remain 'unpartnered' and we may well see the renaissance of the 'spinster'. This has implications for the sources of support and friendship that older people can access in later life and in times of crisis, as is discussed in Chapter 7.

One important factor to remember when considering tables such as these is that they represent the situation at a particular point in time, giving a rather static perspective upon the experience of ageing and the circumstances of older people. One way of taking a more dynamic perspective upon, for example, patterns of civil status among older people is to look at trends over time. If we consider civil status in 1980 in comparison to 2001 we can see several trends emerging: the decline of the 'spinster', the slight increase in the percentage of women still married and the emergence of the divorced

Table 4.8 Civil status of population aged 65+, Great Britain, 1980 and 2001

| | All aged 65+ community residents | | | | All aged 65+ | |
| | 1980 | | 2001 | | 2001 | |
	M	F	M	F	M	F
Single	7	14	6	6	7	7
Married	73	35	72	42	70	40
Widowed	19	50	17	44	17	48
Divorced	1	1	5	7	6	5

Source: ONS 2003; Walker *et al.*, 2002

older person. This offers three different dimensions in which the civil status of older people is changing and which may have a profound influence upon how current and future cohorts experience old age.

We can also use the example of civil status to reflect upon how the nature of the population surveyed can influence the results. Table 4.8 compares the civil status of the population aged 65+ from the General Household Survey, which is based upon community residents only, and the total population in this age group derived from the 2001 Census. Exclusion of the non-community residents from the GHS results in an underestimate of the percentage of single and widowed people and an over-estimate of the percentage who are married. When making inferences about the population we must consider the nature of the population surveyed and whether this is likely to influence the results and their generalisability. Systematic exclusion from research studies can significantly bias the results and lead to erroneous conclusions.

Widowhood is now a feature that is associated mainly with later life, for both men and women. This represents a change from earlier times in history when higher mortality rates in the earlier phases of the lifecycle meant that widowhood was a feature of almost every phase of the lifecycle. Probably as many as one-third of all women would have been widowed before the age of 55 in the nineteenth century. While it is now uncommon for a man to be widowed before old age, it would have been an accepted feature of everyday life in previous centuries. The experience of widowhood in later life varies between males and females. By the age of 70 almost 50 per cent of women have been widowed compared with less than 10 per cent of men. Even in the oldest age group, the over-80s, 56 per cent of males are married compared with only 18 per cent of females. Thus women in later life have to experience a longer period of widowhood than men. Among ever-married women, widows constitute a majority of the population by the age of 72 in England and Wales, compared with 86 for men.

Household composition

The type of household that older people live in is influenced by several factors including their age, gender, civil status and health status. The first distinction that needs to be drawn is between those living in the community and those older people resident in institutions such as long-stay hospitals, nursing and residential homes. These are termed 'non-private households', 'communal establishments' or the 'institutional' population and represent approximately 5% of the older population. Contrary to popular belief, there has been little change in the percentage of the elderly population living in institutions over the course of the twentieth century, although clearly the absolute number has increased substantially. In 1911 about 5 per cent of the population aged over 60 was resident in some form of institution, usually the workhouse. The percentage of the older population classified as resident in an institution increases with age from 1 per cent of those aged under 75 to 25 per cent of those aged 100+. There is a variation with gender in the proportion of elderly people classified as living in non-private households. At all ages after 75 years, a higher percentage of females than males live in residential homes. As Table 4.9 indicates these percentages have been remarkably stable in the post-war period, until 2001 when there is a decline in those aged less than 80 living in institutional settings. It is only

Table 4.9 Percentage enumerated in 'non-private' households, England and Wales, 1921–2001

	60–64		65–69		70–74		75–79		80+	
	M	F	M	F	M	F	M	F	M	F
1921	2.5	1.7	3.7	2.2	4.5	2.8	5.1	3.7	6.1	5.4
1931	2.6	1.7	3.4	2.1	3.9	2.7	4.9	3.7	6.4	6.1
1951	2.1	2.0	2.6	2.5	3.4	3.4	4.9	5.0	7.5	9.4
1971	2.5	2.2	2.8	2.6	3.7	3.8	5.2	6.1	10.9	13.3
1981	1.9	1.6	2.1	1.9	2.8	2.9	4.2	5.4	9.8	15.6
1991	1.8	1.5	2.2	2.0	3.1	3.1	4.5	5.5	12.0	19.9
2001	0.67	0.49	0.8	0.71	1.2	1.4	2.3	3.3	7.4	14.9

Sources: Grundy 1997; ONS 2003

with very advanced age that older people in any significant proportion are not living in the community with the rest of the population. This is illustrated by the case of the 8560 people in England and Wales aged 100 where 53 per cent still live in the community. Given the increases in the number of older people within the population, there has been an absolute increase in the numbers of people living in care environments since the early 1920s, but in relative terms there has been little change in the overall balance between those living in care situations and those living at home.

The vast majority of the older population is, therefore, resident within private households in the community. For those living in private households approximately 35 per cent live alone, 55 per cent with their spouse and the remainder, 10 per cent, lived in a variety of other different forms of households including living with children or siblings. The vast majority of older people, approximately 90 per cent, live in 'simple' types of household structure. Although this 'other' category represents only a minority of older people, it does consist of a myriad of different types of household. The reality of everyday life for older people in terms of the types of households in which they live may be more complex than the social commentators simple summaries might suggest.

The type of household in which older people live shows substantial variation with both age and gender. With increasing age the percentage living alone increases while that living with a spouse decreases (Table 4.10); indeed by the age of 85+ almost three-quarters of women live alone. At all ages women are most likely to be living alone while men are most likely to be living with a spouse. This reflects the tendency for women to marry men who are several years older, combined with their superior longevity, as was noted earlier in regard to marital status.

The type of household in which older people live has attracted considerable attention from politicians, policy makers and social

Table 4.10 Household composition of population aged 65+, Great Britain, 2001 (%)

	65–69		70–74		75–79		80–84		85+	
	M	*F*	*M*	*F*	*M*	*F*	*M*	*F*	*M*	*F*
Alone	15	30	24	39	27	51	27	63	54	69
With spouse	66	52	59	42	61	37	63	21	37	10
Other	19	18	17	19	12	12	10	16	9	21

Source: Walker *et al.*, 2002: Table 3

commentators. As we have already noted, the romantic view of the past presents pre-industrial society as a society in which the extended family was the basic building block of the social fabric. Protagonists of this viewpoint argue that the nuclear family has replaced the extended family with a resultant increase in the neglect of the old. It is quite clear that there have been changes in the types of households in which older people live. This has been the most marked change in the nature of the older population over the twentieth century. In pre-industrial England probably less than 10 per cent of the older population lived alone. Thane (2000) suggests that approximately 11 per cent lived alone in Britain in the period 1684–1796 while Sheldon (1948) reports it was very similar at 10 per cent. In 1998 the percentage was 36 per cent. Even in the space of two decades the type of households in which older people live has changed markedly, with the virtual halving of the percentage of older people living in other types of households and the trends towards either living alone or with a spouse consolidated (Table 4.11).

These changes in the household composition of older people reflect wider social changes in household and family formation patterns, especially in the post-war period. This trend towards solo living is not unique to older people nor is it unique to the United Kingdom (Tomassini *et al.*, 2004). Indeed one of the most pervasive trends of the post-war period has been the increase in solo living. In 1901 it is estimated that only 5 per cent of households consisted of single persons. This had increased to 11 per cent in 1961 and to 29 per cent by 2002 (Summerfield and Babb, 2004). As well as increases in the number of this type of household, their composition is changing. In 1961 64 per cent of single-person households were 'pensioners'; by 2002 this had decreased to 48 per cent (Summerfield and Babb, 2004). Hence there has been an increase in the number of younger people living in single-person households. This type of household is no longer the prerogative of the older person.

Table 4.11 Household composition of population aged 65+, Great Britain, 1980 and 2001 (%)

	1980		2001	
	M	F	M	F
Alone	17	45	24	47
With spouse	62	33	70	43
Other	21	22	6	10

Source: Walker *et al.*, 2002: Table 3

Social class

Perhaps the most important axis of social differentiation at earlier phases of the lifecycle is social class. Within British society social class profoundly influences life expectancy, health status, employment and access to material and economic resources (Marmot, 2004). Until fairly recently, social class has been an unacknowledged factor in the experience of ageing. Part of the reluctance, in the United Kingdom at least, has arisen from the difficulties of applying occupational base class measures to a non-economically active population. This is especially problematic for older women who may never have worked except, perhaps, either during the war or before marriage. In addition to this technical difficulty of applying an occupationally based classification system there has been a more profound reluctance to incorporate class into later life. We may speculate that the widespread assumption of old age being a homogenising experience has resulted in the late arrival of the analysis of the experience of old age which acknowledged the diversity of the experience and which addressed issues of class and gender. It is clear that class position, as defined mainly in terms of occupation, profoundly effects the chances of surviving to experience old age and the quality of the experience in both Britain, North America (Pampel, 1998) and Europe. Hence it is a variable which needs to be integrated into the understanding of the experience of old and later life and which, again, needs to be linked with gender and ethnicity in order to fully capture the complexities of the experience of ageing. However, there is still only a limited research base, largely concentrated in the health field, which has taken seriously issues of class in later life.

Conclusion

In this chapter we have seen that the proportion of the population categorised as being in the 'older' subgroup of the population has increased since the 1930s, prior to which it had been fairly constant at about 5 per cent. This increase has taken place within the context of a stable or very slowly increasing total population. The 'ageing' of the population has done much to prompt the perception of older people as a 'social problem' and stimulated research into the perceived problems of an ageing population. All the negative stereotypes associated with the ageing of individuals are attributed to populations and we are presented with a highly negative scenario, which is summarised concisely in the concept of apocalyptic demography.

The increase in the percentage of the population defined as old has arisen in response to the very profound decreases in mortality, especially infant mortality, and fertility rates that have characterised the twentieth century. A combination of low mortality and low fertility have combined to ensure that fewer children are being born but that those who are have an over 60 per cent chance of reaching the age of 75 years. We must not be complacent about the seemingly inevitable decrease in mortality and the inexorable rise in life expectancy. These gains have been brought about by a combination of improvements in 'public health', living standards and developments in health services. As the example of Russia and other countries illustrate, our 'control' over death is fragile and the failure to maintain public health and social protection can reverse these hard-won gains.

Future projections as to the likely composition of the population of Britain in the future assume the continuation of low mortality and fertility. If current low rates are maintained then Britain, along with many other developed countries, will experience population decline. Within this overall trend of a decrease in total population we will experience a further 'ageing' of the population. Average age will rise and the number and percentage of older people is expected to increase. Certainly the likely increase in the number of older people is a demographic fact because we are already born, but the social and political implications of this are less certain.

The composition of the older population demonstrates several interesting features. Most striking is the marked imbalance in the numbers of men and women surviving to old age. Thus any discussion of old age and ageing within the developed world context is very largely concerned with women rather than men. Far from this being a demonstration of the biological superiority of females, it seems to be a reflection of the differences between the sexes in terms of smoking patterns and the resultant health effects in combination of greater exposure to social and environmental risks and occupational exposures. This example illustrates rather neatly the need to link the biological, social and psychological perspectives when investigating old age. It also demonstrates the huge significance of the social environment in influencing both whom survives into old age and the nature of the experience of old age. It remains to be seen whether the widespread adoption of smoking by women during and after the Second World War will reduce the difference in life expectancy. We can also see that, again, this greater life expectancy of women is neither inevitable nor universal. Several African countries still demonstrate a greater life expectancy for men because of the high mortality associated with childbirth.

Again it is only within the last three generations that childbirth has become 'safe' in the sense of maternal mortality. We must not become complacent about such important public health advances: they are neither inevitable nor universal and, in the event of the collapse of current social protection arrangements, may be reversed.

Demographic data can illustrate the importance of cohort effects in the study of ageing and later life. The age-related increase in the fraction of women classed as never married is a cohort effect reflecting the lack of marriage opportunities in the years after the First World War. This population is now 'dying out' to be replaced by the increase in the percentage of older people who are divorced, a feature virtually unknown in earlier times. We may speculate that future cohorts will see the re-emergence of the 'new spinsters' – a group of women who have opted to remain unpartnered. It is a popular belief that the old are condemned to spend their final years living in an institution of some type. However, we have seen that, even in the very oldest age groups, only a minority of the older population are resident in non-private households. In Britain this fraction has shown comparatively little change over the past century. There has been a substantial change in the types of households in which those resident in the community live. Older people, like younger age groups, express a marked preference for living in their own household rather than living either with other older people or with members of younger generations. This reflects a general societal trend for individuals to establish single households rather than living in larger groups. This trend reflects a desire for autonomy and independence among those of all age groups rather than being a demonstration of lack of interest between members of different generations. While most elderly people either live by themselves or with their spouse, the elderly are also resident in a great variety of different types of households. These diverse groups tend to be various forms of 'extended' household and involve a variety of generations living together. Thus it is important to remember that, even in something as mundane as household composition, the older population is characterised by a considerable diversity of experience. Indeed demographic data provide hints as to how this diversity will be manifest in future decades with the ageing of minority communities, the baby boomers and the growth in older people who are either divorced or not in a long-term relationship. While demography can provide a picture of the current population of older people it can also provide an indication of how the experience of ageing may be different, or at least experienced within a different set of social parameters.

5 Health and illness

In considering the 'resources' that older people bring to the experience of ageing, one of the most fundamental is health. Central to most studies and models of successful ageing is the concept of health status, which reflects the interaction of numerous factors including genetic make-up, individual behaviours (such as diet, exercise or smoking), exposure to environmental and occupational hazards and the availability of health care. Social factors such as gender, ethnicity and social class are also important for both health status and access to health care. Health in old age, or other phases of the lifecycle, can be viewed as a result of a complex interaction between both individual level and macrolevel social and environmental factors as well as factors concerning the organisation of health (and social) care. In this chapter we examine the health status of older people and consider how the experience of health in later life is shaped by macro-social factors such as gender, class and ethnicity.

What is health?

Health, although it is a factor of importance for both individuals and society as a whole, is a difficult entity to define. Culyer (1981) distinguishes between four main approaches to the definition of health: health as the absence of disease (a medical model approach); health as the absence of illness (a sociological perspective); health as an ideal state (the World Health Organisation model); and health as a pragmatically defined entity. While conceptually it is important to distinguish between the different concepts of 'disease', 'illness' and 'health', there are no universally valid, comprehensive and agreed definitions of these terms. We need to distinguish between these different concepts because they result from different theoretical conceptualisations of this topic area and hence give rise to different types of research knowledge and different types of 'knowledge' about ageing. Each of these three major concepts is considered and their implication for the study of health in later life examined.

Disease and the medical model of ageing

The medical model of health focuses upon the identification, diagnosis and treatment of disease. The term disease is usually used to describe the medical concept of a defect or abnormality in function or structure of any part, process or system of the body. This is the province of physicians and specialists in the treatment of older people. In this conceptualisation individuals (or groups or entire societies) are healthy if they are characterised by the absence of disease. Hence health is defined by what it is not, i.e. health is not having a disease. If you are not 'sick' then you are 'healthy'. This is a rather limited conceptual framework for the study of ageing; the medical model offers only limited insights into the complex phenomena of health for three major reasons. First, this approach is highly reductionist. Explanations for the presence or absence of disease in individuals is sought in terms of physiological and biological functions without reference to the social or psychological context within which individuals live. Hence we have a theoretical position whereby it is possible to imagine the doctor, using only signs based upon 'objective' physiological indices, deciding whether disease is present or absent, irrespective of the state of perceived well-being of the individual concerned. Diseases are conceptualised as having a specific, and usually, single cause or aetiology which ignores the multifactorial nature of much disease causation. A consequence of the medical model approach is that we search for the specific cause (or causes) of disease *x* or *y* and ignore or downplay the influence of wider social and environmental factors. For example the 'causes' of fractures in older people may be identified as osteoporosis. Such a focus ignores the wider social context by ignoring levels of nutrition in older people, adequate dietary calcium being of importance in protecting against osteoporosis or the financial resources which may influence the opportunities older people have to access an adequate diet or to participate in exercise. Furthermore the medical model seeks specific explanations for the cause (or aetiology) of diseases rather than looking at the importance of contextual factors. Second, and related to this focus upon physiology and biology, the notion of health as simply the mere 'absence' of disease is highly limiting. There is no role within this model for positive aspects of health. Third, this model presumes a dichotomy between 'mind' and 'body'. A clear and unambiguous distinction is drawn between 'physical' health and the psychological status of individuals. No link is drawn between psychological well-being and physical well-being. Hence there is an emphasis upon disease as a physical entity with disorders of the mind given much less attention.

There are a number of further empirically based problems with this theoretically 'objective' definition of disease. First, there are few universally valid norms of physical functioning because of the enormous range of variability among individuals and because of changes over time which may reflect 'normal' ageing. Determining what is, and is not, disease can be highly problematic. Second, the 'objective' physiological measures may not correlate with subjective perceptions of health status, or with features such as pain or debility. The correlation between physiological measurements and physiological changes and causes of death may also be poor. Third, using this type of objective approach, disease may be so prevalent that almost the entire group under study would have to be classified as 'diseased'. Fourth, the medical model conceptualises the individual disease sufferer as a rather passive 'recipient' of disease: the person is powerless and passive while the disease agent 'attacks' the specific cell, organ or structure. Whether individuals subsequently succumb or repel the 'attack' is largely seen as out of their control. This model of disease offers little opportunity for individuals to promote or maintain their own health and is highly negative about population level interventions aimed at promoting health. Another dimension to the critique of the medical model is via the presumed relationship between health care interventions and provision and the health of populations. Acceptance of the medical model would suggest that the provision of health care services would improve and promote the health of the population if the interventions focus upon the 'causes' of disease. There are several very powerful challenges to the medical model of disease, which contest the basis premise that the provision of medical care is related to the health of the population. For example McKeown (1979) has observed that the declines in mortality noted earlier (see Chapter 4), largely attributable to the declines in infectious diseases, started before the introduction of major immunisation and vaccination programmes. Rather, most of the decline in infectious diseases results from improvements in the social and environmental context such as improved sanitation, housing, environmental factors and wealth. While the value and contribution that medical interventions can make to the health of individual patients is acknowledged we cannot uncritically extrapolate such benefits to entire populations and must give due weight to wider 'public health' type measures which promote interventions aimed at the macrolevel.

The medical model of ageing is extremely widespread and has had a highly pervasive influence upon all aspects of the health care systems of most western societies and this affects all of us in various ways. The medical model influences the design of health care systems, the systems for collecting health-related information, the organisation of treatments and the education of health professionals and, perhaps, influences what we as patients and consumers expect from our health care service. Hence health care systems are dominated by hospital-based 'curative' medicine, with preventive medicine and public health given much less emphasis. As we shall see later in this chapter routine health data are concerned with monitoring the health care system or concerned with patterns of mortality. Research in health care is dominated by the search for 'cures' for major diseases such as cancer and heart disease with much less emphasis upon chronic diseases. For example, as consumers and voters we are more reluctant to support health care funding for preventive activities than for high technology acute 'heroic' interventions. We also favour expending health care resources on groups such as children as opposed to smokers. Older people themselves are less likely to prioritise research into the diseases of old age than other causes of disease or health problems of other age groups.

The medical model, via its reductionist focus upon 'defects' (or 'natural' changes or variations) in physiological parameters, may result in 'normal' physiological processes or changes being labelled as 'pathological' and therefore as medical problems. Examples of the 'medicalisation' of normal life include the developments in childbirth and menopause. Childbirth has become increasingly seen as a medical problem rather than as a 'natural' process; with the developments of hormone replacement therapy, the menopause has been seen as a medical problem and the 'male menopause' is being similarly characterised. Indeed Estes and Binney (1989) suggest that 'ageing' has also been medicalised with the result that older people and old age are pathologised and ageing is constructed as a medical problem with a consequent emphasis upon medical research and medically based 'solutions' to the problem of ageing. Emphasis is placed upon identifying the 'abnormal' rather than the 'normal' in the experience of ageing. By defining aspects of old age as 'disease states' rather than normal ageing extends and legitimises medical control over this aspect of life and older people. If something is defined as disease then there is an impetus to search for a cure and an imperative to provide treatment and interventions. For example if having grey hair was defined as a disease, we would be funding research to look for a test to identify grey hair, be developing a screening programme to identify the early disease state and establishing a research programme to find a cure, usually a pharmacological one, which could then be prescribed to the sufferers. Hence the colour of an individual's hair is 'medicalised' and becomes an aspect of life over which doctors and health care professionals are seen as having a legitimate interest. Many aspects of the experience of ageing, therefore, are 'problematised' and become the domain of experts and problem solvers rather than being seen as part of a normal transition or changes that characterise the post-mature individual (Tulle-Winton, 2000).

Illness

In contrast to the 'theoretically objective' physiologically based concept of disease, illness is a more subjectively defined state in that it usually refers to the feelings of individuals as to whether they are, or are not, in good physical or mental health. The focus in research looking at illness is to identify perceived health status and the prevalence of features such as pain or disability. We may distinguish between disease, where the focus is upon 'objectively' defined physiological parameters with no relationship to the feelings of the individuals and illness where the focus of attention is upon more diffuse and subjective manifestations of ill health and how they impact upon the individual. For example, for an individual with a clinically diagnosed condition such as diabetes or epilepsy the problem may not be the 'disease' per se but how the condition is manifest in terms of symptoms or restrictions on their daily lives and how society responds to such individuals that is the problem. Hence the illness perspective is concerned with both the individuals and societies response to the identified clinical condition. The correlation between disease and illness is not perfect. Individuals may be diseased without feeling ill and vice versa. There is a parallel with disease definitions of health in that health is defined as the absence of illness. Hence it is still a theoretical position in which health is being defined as the absence or lack of something else.

Illness affects both society and the individual in a variety of ways. For society, ill health exacts a high cost in economic terms through both lost economic production and the provision of health care services. Illness also has consequences for the individual, regardless of age. Talcott Parsons (1951) argued that those who are ill are not required to perform their normal social roles but adopt the 'sick role' that is characterised by the adoption of a dependent rather than an independent status. This transition may be very distressing for the individual concerned given the heavy emphasis placed in our society upon remaining independent and autonomous. The sick role is not expected to be of long duration. The long-term sick, or those with particular illnesses such as epilepsy or various mental disorders, can come to acquire a highly stigmatised status because of the extensive duration of their illness. A similar stigmatising status may be ascribed to older people because of the perceived widespread prevalence of chronic illness and its extensive and debilitating nature that can compromise independence and autonomy.

Illness behaviour is a complex aspect of social interaction that involves the individual in monitoring their body, interpreting symptoms, taking curative action and seeking help from the health care system or other appropriate agencies. Even in Britain, which has a national health care service which provides care free of charge, the vast majority of illness is not presented for consideration by the health care services. Only an estimated quarter to one-third of all illness episodes result in a medical consultation (Ford, 1985). The decision to seek medical aid is only one illness behaviour strategy out of a whole range of possible options, which includes self-care, folk remedies, consultation with friends or relatives or use of 'alternative' or complementary over-the-counter therapies.

Sociologists interested in illness behaviour have largely focused upon the younger members of the population. Ford (1985) has attempted to review illness behaviour in later life and its variation from that characteristic of younger age groups. One of the enduring stereotypes about old age is that treatable illnesses are mis-ascribed by older people to the process of ageing rather than being the manifestation of 'disease'. Consequently, it is argued, older people do not seek appropriate treatment. In support of this view a variety of studies have demonstrated that there are a large number of previously unidentified medical conditions to be found among older people living at home (Williamson *et al.*, 1964). Researchers have not undertaken such 'case finding' exercises comprehensively with younger populations and so it is not clear that these levels of 'unreported' health care problems are higher or lower than other groups within the population. These types of exercise are conceptually rather simplistic in that the focus of attention is upon enumerating the number of previously undiagnosed medical conditions. Such studies rarely consider if the previously undiagnosed condition was identified as important by the older person or causing them inconvenience or disability. They may well not have drawn it to the attention of their GP because it was not a problem for them and not because they ascribed it to the inevitability of ageing. Hence it is too simplistic to explain health behaviour of older people only in terms of their age. Rather there is clearly a complex interplay between a whole variety of factors including, but not exclusively, age in understanding health behaviour. Rory Williams (1990) in his study of ageing in Aberdeen also sheds some light upon this stereotype. He argues that older people do not ignore symptoms but are equally as likely to seek treatment for these health problems as any other age group and that illness behaviour in later life does not differ significantly from that in earlier life. Older people are every bit as diverse in their illness behaviour as other age groups, and illness behaviour in later life represents a continuation of previously established patterns. Just as for other age groups, health behaviour in later life is mediated by social factors such as gender, class and ethnicity as well as the broader social context. Independent of physical or mental morbidity, social networks appear to be implicated in the consultation and health seeking behaviour of older people. Our understanding of the health and illness behaviour of older people needs to take into account the wider social and environmental context, factors such as class and gender are located within a life course perspective.

Health

Health is a more conceptually complex entity to define than either disease or illness. From this perspective it is regarded as being insufficient to think of health as simply being the absence of disease or illness. Rather health represents an ideal state as exemplified by the World Health Organisation model of health as a state of physical, social and psychological well-being. This framework sets out an 'ideal state' to which all can aspire. The advantages of this type of conceptualisation of health are that it acknowledges the link between mind and body and the importance of social and environmental factors for health. The downside of such aspirational conceptualisations is that they are very difficult to define and measure and it is not clear how well such definitions link with the experiences and expectations of people.

The whole area of the definition and measurement of health in given populations, of which older people form but one subgroup, is methodologically complex. However given the frequency with which such measures are used some familiarity with these measures is required by the student of gerontology. Many of the most commonly available generic health status measures such as the SF-36 or the Nottingham Health Profile follow the WHO definition in distinguishing between physical and mental health but less rarely do they incorporate social well-being. However, what is included within these broad domains shows substantial variation. While there may be some agreement between measures in terms of the broad domains to be included there is huge variation in how these domains are operationalised. There are several critiques which can be made of these generic health status measures, a considerable number of which relate to technical properties of such measures. Here we are concerned with more fundamental questions regarding the appropriateness of such measures for use with older people. Many of the most widespread measures such as the SF-36 were developed in the United States. Hence we might wish to consider the appropriateness for use with a UK or European context because we know that notions of health are culturally specific. We also need to consider the age groups with which such measures were developed. Scales such as the SF-36 were developed from 'middle-aged' populations. Are they relevant to older populations? We should probably be cautious in using such measures with UK populations of older people. It is important to remember that definitions of health are historically and culturally specific. Epilepsy is now regarded as an illness and sufferers are largely stigmatised and marginalised from certain spheres of life, but in ancient Arabic societies epileptics were glorified and attributed extensive status; they were not considered as ill and would not have been included in any enumeration of sickness nor symptoms of epilepsy included within any measure of health status.

Disability, impairment and handicap

Another perspective upon the complex area of understanding the health status of older people, or indeed any other age group, is provided by the concept of disability. WHO (1980) defines disability as the lack of ability or restriction in ability of individuals to undertake activities considered 'normal' for a person. Central to the whole notion of this measure is that of the reference criterion of 'normal'. Given this caveat WHO have constructed a simple model of disability which involves three stages. Disease (or some other stressor) can lead to impairment such as osteoarthritis resulting in loss of the range of movement in the knee joint. This impairment may result in disability, as the individual may be unable to undertake a range of normal activities such as shopping, housecare or walking. Handicap is the disadvantage that then flows from the inability of individuals to fulfil a 'normal' role. The distinction between these three stages is conceptually very useful in that it emphasises that disability and handicap are strongly influenced by the environmental and social context. Disability is concerned with examining stresses upon the ability of individuals to lead independent lives within the community: the primary goal of older people themselves and successive governments. Although the WHO model is presented as a linear developmental model we must remember that this presents an 'idealised' schema. Disability does not inevitably follow impairment: individuals may have impairments but never develop either disability or handicap. This, in part at least, reflects the 'socially constructed' nature of disability that relies upon judgements about what are 'normal' activities for individuals within any specific age group. Disability and any resultant handicap are seen as being very strongly mediated by the social and environmental context. Disability may also result from the interaction of several different impairments, hence disability may have a multifactorial set of 'causes'. Disability is seen as a dichotomous variable: individuals are conceptualised as either disabled or not disabled. However, as discussed below this represents an oversimplified version of reality as disability is rarely easily categorised into 'present' or 'absent' and may well demonstrate temporal or seasonal variation, especially with some conditions which are characterised by periods of remission.

Measuring the extent of disability, impairment and handicap within populations is both methodologically and conceptually problematic. There is no universally accepted method for assessing disability within the population irrespective of the age of the population under review. Rather a variety of different approaches may be identified. One approach is that exemplified by the national studies of the prevalence of disability within the population undertaken by OPCS (Martin *et al.*, 1988). This examined the prevalence of different types of disability such as sight, hearing, communication and locomotor functions and derives from the nine major areas of disabilities identified by WHO. Hence it was a mixture of problems with specific parts of the body (such as eyes and ears) and activities such as walking and self-care. Martin *et al.* (1988) also attempted to classify the severity of disability within the population on a scale ranging from one (least) to ten (most severe). From this work national estimates of the type and number of disabled people within the population were derived.

Estimating the number of disabled people within the population remains a contentious area of work because of conceptual debates about the definitions of disability used and suspicions as to the use that will be made of the resultant data. Disability does not fit easily within the biomedical model of health and illness, which is based upon the notion of a simple distinction between the two states. Disability and, indeed, many other health issues are best understood as a continuum rather than a simple dichotomy. At one extreme we have individuals who are 'not disabled' and at the other there are individuals who are clearly disabled. Where the line is drawn (in epidemiology this is known as the case definition threshold) is ultimately a matter of judgement. At what threshold the line is drawn will greatly affect the number of people subsequently defined as disabled with consequences for both the individual and the wider population.

Perhaps the most frequently used measures to determine the extent of disability within populations are the measures of functional ability; that is how well can people undertake a range of activities considered essential for the maintenance of an independent life in the community. There are many scales and measures, which record the functional status of individuals. Some have been designed to summarise the ability of older people to function independently in the community while others such as the Bartel index were designed to determine the need for nursing staff in hospital wards. Usually these measures include three major aspects of daily life: self-care, mobility and instrumental activities such as shopping, cooking and cleaning. Inevitably such measures have been developed from the top down. Many of the items measured reflect the concerns of policy makers with estimating the need for different types of services and enumerating the factors which place older people 'at risk' of entering institutional care rather than reflecting the concerns of older people. Consequently these types of measures may not, necessarily, reflect the concerns of older adults and have only a tangential relationship with more clinical measures of physiological function or 'disease'.

How do older people define health?

Older people, like any other group within the population, value their health. Health is a key element of well-being and quality of life (Sidell, 1995; Bernard, 2000). Given the problems academics have in defining what constitutes health, how do 'ordinary' people understand and define concepts such as health and illness. At the most superficial level of analysis lay notions of health include elements of both the negative definition of health (health as the absence of disease) and the more positive and holistic concept implied within the WHO definition. Classic studies by both Herzlich (1973) and Williams (1990) provide evidence that older people subscribe, in part at least, to the idea that health may be conceptualised as the 'absence' of disease. Regardless of the age of individuals, attitudes towards health beliefs are complex and often, apparently, contradictory. Views of, and definitions of, health are culturally and historically rooted and related to the values and expectations of particular groups. Furthermore health related beliefs and attitudes almost certainly vary with regard to class, gender, age, and ethnicity (Bernard, 2000) and, taking this complexity one stage further, a single individual may hold apparently conflicting, and mutually exclusive, beliefs at the same time (Sidell, 1995).

Given this complexity there does seem to be some consistency in the trend for older people to define health in functional terms rather than in terms of fitness. Williams (1990) in his study of elderly Aberdonians provides examples of the notion of health as involving ideas of functional fitness such as being able to undertake 'normal' or conventional activities such as gardening or keeping house and an emphasis upon coping and the ability to undertake 'normal' activities. Here health is being defined more positively by what an individual 'can do' rather than by what they cannot, or in terms of signs or symptoms. The importance in lay definitions of psychological elements of health, in stark contradiction to the premise of the medical model, is also evident (Cornwall, 1984; Sidell, 1995). However much the biomedical model seeks to distinguish between mind and body, the general population appears to conceptualise physical and mental well-being as being essential for good health and not to operate a rigid mind–body distinction. We need to reflect upon the social and cultural context within which such definitions and conceptualisations are articulated and how much these are informed by assumptions and expectations concerning the likely (negative) health status to be enjoyed in old age. Do older people define health in functional rather than fitness terms, because they expect to be unfit in later life? Does a functionalist definition reflect the concerns of older people with maintaining themselves in the community and the onus they feel to demonstrate their 'competence' to remain independent autonomous adults. Do notions of stigma and spoilt identities require that they articulate functional rather than fitness-based definitions of health?

Will future cohorts of older people hold similar views concerning health in later life? We cannot answer these questions but they need to form the critical backdrop against which we interpret and evaluate current methods for measuring the health status of older people and how we interpret the resultant empirical evidence. We also need to consider if there are important variations with gender, class or ethnicity in how older people think about their health.

Describing and analysing the health of older people

As we have seen health is a wide-ranging notion encompassing more than the mere absence of disease and, at its most basic, includes some notion of physical, mental and social well-being. When we attempt to describe and analyse the health status of populations, or of particular groups within defined populations, we are usually forced to use more limited disease-orientated measures. This largely reflects the dominance of the medical model within the areas of routine health information collection and epidemiological investigation. From this perspective health is perceived as the absence of disease rather than anything more positive. Within this limitation we can distinguish between physical and mental health status and consider other important aspects of health such as disability and how older people themselves evaluate their own health. We also draw a distinction between acute and chronic health problems as it is presumed it is chronic problems which are especially associated with old age.

Key debates concerning health in old age

Health status is clearly of great concern to older people both as individuals and more collectively (and indeed people of any age group). The health of older people is also an area of concern for governments throughout the developed world because older people are the main users of health services. The increases in the number of older people within the population is seen as posing a considerable challenge for governments in terms of both pension provision and provision of health and social care services. Hence there has been considerable interest in looking at trends in the health status of older people and considering how patterns of health status may change, either for better or worse, in future decades. There are several theories concerning trends in the health status of older people and what is likely to happen in the future. In this section we outline these differing theoretical positions and consider the empirical data.

Rectangularisation of mortality and compression of morbidity

There has been a massive decrease in overall mortality rates over the past 150 years. While there may be debates as to why these changes have happened there is no doubt as to the reality of the very profound changes in the pattern of deaths within the population. One result of this mortality transformation has been the 'redistribution' of death from the young to the old and massive increases in expectation of life at birth. Furthermore mortality rates in mid-life have also declined markedly (see Chapter 4). Olshansky and Rudberg (1997) report that for the United States 52 per cent of those born in 1900 would live to age 65 and 18 per cent to age 85 compared with 85 per cent and 45 per cent respectively for those born in 1990. So profound has this social and cultural change been that we now all expect to live to experience 'old age' and take this to be normal, natural and inevitable. It is very easy to forget the recency of this expectation.

Since the 1850s, the shape of the distribution of mortality has (as we saw in Chapter 4) changed significantly so that with low rates of mortality in childhood and youth, mortality is concentrated into later life. This very profound change in the distribution has been described as the rectangularisation of mortality and can be seen in most developed countries. That mortality has become increasingly concentrated into the later phases of life, in most developed countries, is not disputed. Rather it is the consequences of this 'compression' of mortality into the later phases of life, which are contested and the two major perspectives are discussed below.

Compression of morbidity

The optimistic perspective argues that, as a result of the constriction of mortality into later life, morbidity will also demonstrate a similar trend. Fries (1980, 2003) started from the assumption there is a 'fixed' biological limit to expectation of life, and proposed that this would be 85 years on average, although he did not produce any empirical evidence to support the thesis that the human life span is finite or for the selection of the chosen age. Fries further assumes a 'skewed' distribution of 'natural' mortality and argues that under 'ideal' conditions 95 per cent of deaths would occur between the ages of 77 and 95 years. We are, therefore, advancing rapidly towards this state whereby premature death has been largely eradicated and mortality in later life is as a result of the body 'wearing out' at the end of its 'natural' lifespan rather than because of disease per se. In Britain those aged 75+ account for currently almost two-thirds of deaths (64 per cent). So in Britain there is still some way to go before the situation posited by Fries is reached. His thesis is that morbidity, as well as mortality, would also be 'compressed' into the later phases of life as a result of advances in medicine and living standards because the causes of morbidity and mortality are the same (or at least are influenced by the same risk factors). This hypothesis would see the mean age of onset for chronic disability pushed back from, for example, 55 years to 65 years (Fries, 2003). Fries (1980) argues that there are more people surviving into 'old age' and that those who survive will be fitter because the factors that have delayed mortality will also have delayed morbidity. Hence those people surviving to old age will be fitter for longer with significant levels of morbidity being limited to a short period at the very end of life. This theory has very obvious policy implications. If the compression of morbidity thesis is correct then expenditure on heath care could, in theory at least, be reduced (or perhaps contained) and the 'ageing' of the population does not imply any great challenge to the provision of health and social welfare.

Expansion of morbidity

It is no surprise to note that this notion of the compression of morbidity in later life has not gone unchallenged and the counter-argument to this is much less optimistic and suggests that the result of the compression of mortality will be an increase in morbidity. This approach was termed by some the 'failure of success': lives would be longer but the 'extra' years would be characterised by frailty, disability and ill health. According to Gruenberg (1977) the observed decline in mortality is the result of a decrease in fatality rates for many diseases rather than improvements in population health status. It is further proposed that neither the incidence of chronic diseases nor the rate of progression for these conditions has changed as a result of changes in mortality. Hence as a result of decreased death rates there will be an increase in the morbidity of the population because, although more people will survive into old age, they will do so with much poorer health. Rather than morbidity being compressed into a short period at the end of life it will be extended across a longer period. This scenario has been termed the 'survival of the unfittest'. Kramer (1980) termed this a pandemic of mental disorder, chronic disease and disability while Olshansky *et al.* (1990) and

Olshansky and Carnes (2001) called it the 'expansion of morbidity hypothesis'. Olshansky *et al.* (1990) share the assumption of a fixed maximum average life expectancy of 85 years with Fries (1980), but they do not maintain the concept of skewed mortality distribution. Rather they presume that the distribution of age at death will continually shift towards the highest age groups resulting in an increase in numbers of the oldest old with a consequent increase in the number of people with (multiple) chronic diseases within the population. This is obviously a pessimistic view as to the implications of more people surviving to older age groups: the implication is that there will be a massive increase in the numbers of disabled people experiencing poor quality of life in their later years. The implications for families and societies, especially in terms of health care provision, are dire.

Certainly there are many who are sceptical of the proposition of the delay of morbidity (Verbrugge, 1984; Manton, 1991). To date the debate concerning the validity of these two opposing propositions has been conducted at the population level (Fries, 2003). There has been remarkably little research examining the veracity of the compression/expansion of morbidity theses within subgroups of the total populations. Sidell (1995) argues that the compression of morbidity hypothesis may hold for men but not women. This is a neglected area and there is clearly a large research agenda to examine morbidity trends both within populations and in terms of entire populations. Given our knowledge that the experience of morbidity is not distributed equally within societies, with rates of morbidity elevated among certain groups such as women, those from less privileged backgrounds and from minority communities, it seems unlikely that any changes in morbidity would be equitably distributed throughout the population. If patterns of morbidity are changing among the older populations then some groups will be benefiting from such changes more than others do. Hence we need to examine these hypotheses both in terms of entire populations and in terms of the subgroups within these populations.

Measuring health status: mortality

In attempting to describe the health status of populations and their constituent elements we ideally need measures that allow comparisons between individuals, groups or different points in time (or indeed some combination of these). This latter requirement is especially important if we are to empirically test the two propositions outlined above or develop robust predictions of the likely health experience of future cohorts of elders. The measure that comes closest to fulfilling the technical requirements of being accurate, complete and routinely available for populations over a fairly long historical time span is mortality data or information concerning the distribution of patterns of death. Conceptually this measure is flawed because it is a disease-based measure. Furthermore we are taking patterns of deaths within populations and assume that these are characteristic of survivors of the same ages and that the major causes of death are the principal causes of ill health among survivors. Hence we have to assume that the distribution and causes of mortality mirror that for morbidity.

Despite these conceptual limitations, mortality is probably the oldest and most widely used index of health status, especially as the end state or outcome is unambiguous. As early as the sixteenth century, mortality statistics relating to epidemics of the plague were published in London. Mortality is now widely employed as a health indicator by social researchers for a variety of reasons. The data are easily available in countries such as Britain, which have compulsory and comprehensive national systems of death registration, birth registration and accurate and complete decennial population censuses to provide both accurate numerators (numbers of deaths) and denominators (the numbers of people within specific age and sex groups). Individual death certificates give details of the deceased person such as age, sex, social class and area of residence as well as immediate and underlying cause of death. From the aggregation of the certificates completed for each death it is possible to examine patterns of mortality within the different subgroups of the population. When analysing mortality data for older people, we must be aware of the limitations imposed upon this type of analysis by inaccuracy in the certification of the cause of death among the older age groups.

There were 533,527 deaths in England and Wales in 2002 of which the majority (80 per cent) are accounted for by people aged 65+ (ONS, 2004a). The distribution of mortality across the age groups describes a J-shaped distribution. Mortality is (relatively) high in the first year of life and then remains at under 1 per cent (10 per 1000) until the mid- to late fifties (Table 5.1). Thereafter mortality rates approximately double for each decade increase in age. This age-related increase in mortality is used as evidence to support the notion that ill health and disease are not simple factors associated with old age but that they are 'caused' by old age. Manton (1991) suggests that the pattern of mortality in later life is influenced by two interacting

Table 5.1 Death rates by age and sex, England and Wales, 2002

	Death rate per 1000		
	Male	*Female*	*Ratio M/F*
Under 1	5.9	4.5	1.3
1–4	0.25	0.20	1.3
5–9	0.12	0.10	1.2
10–14	0.16	0.11	1.3
15–19	0.49	0.24	2.2
20–24	0.78	0.27	2.8
25–34	0.94	0.44	2.4
35–44	1.58	0.94	1.7
45–54	3.85	2.54	1.5
55–64	9.7	6.0	1.6
65–74	27.2	17.0	1.6
75–84	73.6	50.5	1.5
85+	188.0	159.8	1.2
All ages	9.9	10.5	0.95

Source: ONS 2004a: Table 6.1

sets of factors: senescence (or the rate of 'natural ageing') and the distribution of risk factors for specific diseases within populations such as the prevalence of smoking, obesity or environmental hazards. Manipulations or interventions which change either (or both) of these factors would, eventually, result in changes in the pattern of mortality within populations. Hence this suggests that there is scope for the further reduction in mortality across the life span and that mortality in later life is not simply a matter of mortality.

Changes in mortality rates over time

As was introduced in Chapter 4, overall mortality rates in Britain have declined significantly over time. The crude mortality rate for England in 1541 was approximately thirty per 1000 (although it was subject to violent fluctuations as a result of epidemics of infectious diseases) compared with approximately ten per 1000 in 2001. Furthermore we have shown that death before age 65 is now highly unusual. Given the concentration of death into the latter phases of life it is easy to see how Hayflick, a pioneering gerontologist, arrived at the conclusion that in later life 'old age' was the major cause of death and one which we can do nothing about (Vaupel, 1997). Acceptance of this proposition leads to the conclusion that death, and by implication poor health, in old age is 'inevitable'; this suggests that health care resources expended on older people are wasted and that there is little we can do to improve the health of older people and so there is no point in trying to promote the health of older people.

As we saw in Chapter 4 mortality rates in later life are by no means static and do not yet seem to have reached a biological limit or final end. For the population aged 65 and over mortality rates have declined since 1950 and especially since 1970 (see Table 5.2). Since the 1850s, mortality rates among older people have approximately halved with the greatest reduction being demonstrated by women (Table 5.2). From the baseline of 1841–1845 mortality rates for men and women aged 65–74 have decreased by 58 per cent and 71 per cent respectively. Taking 1911 as the index point, Vaupel (1997) demonstrates that mortality rates for females aged 85 have halved over the course of the twentieth century in England and Wales. For those aged 90 and 95 the decreases, while less marked, are equally significant. This is not a feature unique to the United Kingdom. Vaupel (1997) presents data which indicate that this general trend is displayed by many western industrial societies including France, Sweden, Japan and the Nordic countries. Taking female octogenarians and nonagenarians from four countries (England and Wales, France, Sweden and Japan), Vaupel (1997) demonstrates that death rates for these populations decreased from about 165–185 per 1000 in 1950 to 90–95 per 1000 in the mid-1990s, an approximate halving of death rates in four decades. As well as changes in overall mortality rates there have been significant changes in mortality from specific diseases. For both males and females aged 65 years and over, mortality from heart disease in the United States decreased by about 15 per cent in the five years 1980–1986. Similarly another way of illustrating changes in mortality rates and survival over time is to examine the age at which average life expectancy is fifteen years. Grundy (1997) reports that in 1901 for men and women this was 55 and 58 years respectively. By 2001 this had increased to 65 for men and 72 for women. This demonstrates that these changes in late age mortality are observed across the entire age range of the older population and many different diseases. This observation stands in sharp contrast to the idea that mortality in later life is intractable and suggests that there is scope for further reduction of mortality and for further rectangularisation of mortality and, perhaps, challenges the notion of a 'fixed' life expectancy.

It is, of course, extremely difficult to test many of the propositions in the mortality/morbidity debates in human populations. One way is to look at patterns of mortality in populations with very low rates. If

Table 5.2 Death rates for population aged 65+, England and Wales, 1841–2002

| | Death rate per 1000 | | | | | |
| | 65–74 | | 75–84 | | 85+ | |
	Male	Female	Male	Female	Male	Female
1841–45	65.5	59.1	143.7	131.8	305.1	288.6
1851–55	66.7	59.7	150.9	137.2	310.9	292.1
1861–65	66.4	59.1	145.9	133.8	316.6	287.9
1871–75	70.1	61.3	149.6	135.3	323.3	293.9
1881–85	68.8	59.1	145.4	129.0	297.9	265.5
1891–95	72.5	63.0	149.2	134.3s	290.8	264.0
1901–05	68.3	54.8	143.1	119.9	282.8	249.4
1921–25	58.2	45.5	135.5	112.9	272.7	241.2
1931–35	56.8	42.8	139.5	108.9	286.3	245.0
1951–55	54.6	33.1	126.7	92.4	265.9	222.0
1961–65	54.0	29.8	121.3	83.6	253.2	206.7
1971–75	51.1	26.4	115.1	74.5	237.1	188.9
1981–85	45.2	24.1	103.5	64.4	220.8	175.9
1991	38.5	21.4	93.6	57.1	197.1	153.1
2002	27.6	17.1	75.4	51.0	190.0	158.8

Source: OPCS, 1992: Table 2; ONS, 2004a: Table 6.1

death rates among the 'oldest old' and other members of the older population were approaching a biological limit, then we would expect that mortality improvements in countries with low rates would be slower than in countries with higher rates. Vaupel (1997) suggests that there is little evidence to support this proposition and countries with low late age mortality rates continue to show improvements. Similarly we can look at gender differences. Women have lower mortality rates than men in late old age. Again examination of improvements in male and female mortality rates provides an indication that this proposition is unproven. Men have higher mortality rates than women, but it is women who have shown the greatest improvements in late age mortality. That there is scope for further reductions in late age mortality is suggested by comparing rates between countries. For example, at age 90, death rates in western Europe and Japan are about 50 per cent higher (0.19 versus 0.13 per cent) than in the Midwestern region of the United States (Vaupel, 1997). Hence it is unlikely that we have, as yet, reached the biological limit upon decreasing mortality rates in later life. Fries (2003) using US data suggests that rates of increase in life expectancy after age 65 will start to slow down but not necessarily cease altogether.

A fixed expectation of life?

The hypothesis of Fries (1980) rests upon a central assumption of a 'maximum' average life expectancy of 85 years, which he posits is the result of the genetic characteristics of humans. This compares with the 'limit' mortality estimate of 91 years suggested by a UN team and estimates of (potentially) 120+ from Kirkwood (1999). Currently in the United Kingdom expectation of life at birth is 80 for women and 75 for men and in fifteen countries expectation of life at birth is 80+ years. Examining data for the United States, Olshansky *et al.* (1991) indicate that mortality rates need to decline by approximately 50 per cent (40 per cent for women and 60 per cent for men) for this goal to be achieved. In the United Kingdom, late age mortality has declined by this amount over the course of the twentieth century and Robine *et al.* (1996) suggest that some countries will achieve an average life expectancy at birth of 85 years by the year 2024 (assuming current trends continue). Manton (1990) has proposed that, for women, if the population demonstrated 'ideal' risk factor profile, mortality would be reduced such that life expectancy increased to 106 years. It is not clear whether populations could be persuaded to adopt the 'optimal' lifestyle pattern or if mortality rates will continue to decrease significantly from the now low base. The prospects for extended survival remain unclear for both the British and other populations; however, maintenance of current trends suggests improvements in mortality and life expectancy at later life for future populations of elders. If these improvements result in decreased morbidity, or if these benefits are shared by all the subgroups of the older population, remains a matter for speculation. Long-term trends in late life mortality in Britain suggests that women have benefited more than men and it seems likely that those from more affluent backgrounds will also have benefited disproportionately from decreases in mortality. This trend may not necessarily continue across future decades.

Causes of death

A central assumption of the use of mortality data to describe the health status of populations is that they accurately reflect the distribution of disease and disability within that population. There are two distinct aspects to this assumption: demographic (i.e. the age and sex distribution of health problems) and the type of health problems identified. By comparing mortality and morbidity data we can test the veracity of these assumptions. In terms of mortality the most important causes of death are circulatory disease (accounting for 40 per cent of deaths), respiratory disease (accounting for 19 per cent of deaths) and cancers (23 per cent of deaths). Overall these three disease categories account for 82 per cent of all deaths among those aged 65+.

Patterns of mortality

To date most debates about the 'compression of mortality/morbidity' hypothesis have been undertaken at the general population level. However, it is also pertinent to investigate whether some subgroups of the older population are experiencing decreases in morbidity/mortality that are not shared by the whole population of older people. For older people in Britain this debate takes place within the context of well-established general variations in mortality (and health more broadly defined) in terms of class, gender, ethnicity, geography or time of year. The empirical data available make it difficult to test these different hypotheses, but we can examine variations in health status within the older age groups and consider the degree to which these well-characterised health variations persist into later life. We can tentatively consider which groups appear to have benefited most from recent changes in mortality.

Overall there are important variations within the older age groups in the probability of death and which largely reflect patterns observed at earlier phases of the lifecycle. We have already noted the increase in mortality rates by age. In addition to this there are variations in terms of gender, social class and ethnicity. How well do these replicate those described at earlier phases of the lifecycle? As Table 5.1 shows, the male–female mortality differential after the age of 65, but over the age of 65 years the differential ranges from 60 to 25 per cent. Hence the differential is less large than for some age groups (note the doubling of male mortality in the 15–34 age groups) but is observed for every age group. Furthermore the gender difference in mortality seems to have increased from about 10 per cent male excess in 1850 to 25–60 per cent in 2001.

Comparative mortality differentials between the different ethnic minority groups and the white population in later life are much less clear cut. This partly reflects the currently relatively small number of ethnic minority elders combined with a lack of systematic data collection. This remains a very under-researched area (Evandrou, 2000) but there is evidence to suggest that some diseases and conditions are higher among minority communities. Bone *et al.* (1995) have produced estimates of mortality among differing ethnic populations. For men aged 65–74 mortality rates range from 439 per 10,000 for black elders, 340 for those from the Indian subcontinent and 374 for the white population. This pattern for elders from the black population to illustrate the highest mortality in later life is also shown for the 75+ age group and for women. The Indian subcontinent population occupies an intermediate position. It is almost certainly the case that the distribution of mortality in later life is not equally distributed throughout the different ethnic minority populations, but as yet we have only limited data with which to examine these trends. Current levels of analysis fail to disaggregate the 'black' and 'Indian subcontinent' into their various constituent groups. It seems probable that variation between ethnic minority communities is as a great as between them in aggregate and the 'white' population.

Within Britain mortality among those of working age is strongly associated with social class. Consistently individuals from the unskilled and semi-skilled manual occupation groups have a mortality rate which is about 75 per cent higher than their professional occupation group contemporaries (Victor, 1991). This difference is reflected in the almost six-year difference in expectation of life at birth observed for boys (expectation of life at birth for social classes 1 and 2 is 74.9 and 69.2 for classes 4 and 5) and differential of 3.4 years for girls (Khaw, 1999b). It is only comparatively recently that this analysis has been extended to the retired population. Two main factors underpin this reluctance to examine the importance of social class in describing the experience of later life. First, there are the very real methodological and conceptual problems of applying occupationally based measures of class to those outside the labour market. Second, there is the tendency to homogenise the experience of later life by presuming that class differences were rendered irrelevant once individuals had entered old age because of the perceived 'universal' experience of chronic illness and disability.

There is now a growing body of evidence pointing to the continuation into later life of these class-based mortality differentials and also expectation of life at ages 65 and over. Victor (1991) has reported that, overall, there is a 60 per cent mortality differential for males aged 65+ according to their social class position. Hence for males over the age of 65, there is a strong class-based gradient in mortality, which mirrors that characteristic of younger age groups. Consistently elders who were employed in professional occupations demonstrate a lower mortality than their counterparts who were engaged in manual occupations. Victor (1984) suggests that these differentials are preserved into the very oldest age groups. Even in retirement it seems that there are strong class-based inequalities in mortality for males that are every bit as strong as that characteristic of earlier phases in the lifecycle. The position is less clear-cut for females, largely because of the inadequacy of the social class classification of older women and the non-participation of many now older women in the labour market. It seems likely that there is a class-based mortality gradient among older women, although it may not be as strong as that for males (Victor, 1991). Supporting evidence for the persistence of class-based differences in mortality in later life is summarised by Khaw (1999b). Using alternative measures of social status, housing tenure and car ownership, Khaw (1999b) illustrates the importance of 'social position' for the experience of health in later life. Smith and Harding (1997) demonstrate mortality rate differentials across the various types of housing tenure (highest among local authority tenants and lowest among home owners). Similarly Marmot and Shipley (1996) demonstrate occupational variations in mortality based upon grade of employment within the civil service. They report excess mortality rates of 75 per cent among those from the lowest civil service grade compared with the highest. Such differentials are, therefore, not inconsiderable. The evidence certainly does not suggest that class-based differences in mortality decrease in potency with the onset of retirement and later life. This is further supported by the observation that, at age 65 years a man from social classes 1 and 2 (the professional occupations) could expect to live for another 15 years while his contemporary from classes 4 and 5 (the semi-skilled and unskilled groups) would live for another 12.4 years (for women the average expectation of life was 18.7 years and 16.7 years respectively) (Hattersley, 1997). Reductions in the class-based mortality differentials would clearly have an impact upon overall mortality and, again, hints that mortality rates have not yet bottomed out.

Data on changes in life expectancy can be used to test the equity of the 'compression of mortality' hypothesis. Have changes in life expectancy at age 65 been shared equally across the social classes and men and women? Hattersley (1997) reports that between 1971 and 1991 expectation of life at age 65 increased by 0.9 years for men and 1.0 year for women. Hence there seems to be a marginal additional mortality decrease 'advantage' to women, perhaps increasing the well-observed gender differential in mortality in later life. Older people from professional backgrounds demonstrate larger 'gains' in life expectancy than their less occupationally privileged contemporaries. For males from classes 1 and 2 the increase in life expectancy was 0.6 years compared with 0.4 years for classes 4 and 5 (0.8 years and 0.1 years respectively for women) (Hattersley, 1997). Hence recent improvements in mortality have not been equally distributed among all older people but rather seem to accentuate existing differentials.

Similarly have the chances of 'surviving' to old age and advanced old age (i.e. ages 85 years and over) changed over past decades and are there gender and class variations? For class 1 men aged 25–29 in 1972–1976, 72 per cent could expect to survive to age 65 compared with 61 per cent class 5. Two decades later 84 per cent of those from class 1 could expect to survive to 65 compared with 64 per cent from class 5. Among women there is a very similar pattern of greatly improved probabilities of those from class 1 surviving to age 65 and virtually no improvement for those from class 5. Similarly for survival into very old age a clear class-based differential in the probability of survival has now emerged for both men and women. Men and women from class 1 now have a significantly higher probability of survival into old age than their less privileged contemporaries. Overall this evidence suggests that increases in life expectancy, resulting from decreases in mortality, have not been equally shared throughput the population of older people. Women appear to have benefited more than men have, and those from professional occupations have benefited at the expense of those from manual occupations. While there are no comparable data on ethnicity it seems highly unlikely that increases in life expectancy, improved mortality and probability of surviving to reach 'old age' will have been shared equally across the major ethnic groups.

Measuring health: physical health status

Mortality is a useful index for comparing health status between groups, areas or trends over time. However, its applicability as a measure of health is obviously limited in that it tells us nothing about the status of those who have not died. The use of mortality as an indicator of health status is predicated upon the assumption that it is a surrogate measure of morbidity. This means that it is assumed that causes of morbidity and mortality in the population are synonymous. This, as we shall see later, is a highly questionable assumption for studies of older age groups, who experience much morbidity in terms of disabling illnesses such as musculoskeletal disease or dementia or resulting from accidents such as falls, which do not inevitably result in large numbers of deaths.

In attempting to investigate and understand patterns of morbidity within the older age groups there are several key epidemiological terms that require definition before considering the empirical material. In enumerating the amount of morbidity among older people we need to distinguish between the total pool of older people with, for example, dementia and the number of new cases appearing over a given period. The former measure is known as prevalence and the latter is known as incidence.

There are a number of different approaches to the development of morbidity indicators and it is only possible to summarise the major approaches here. Three main types of approaches towards the measures of morbidity may be identified. First, there are measures which attempt to determine the incidence and prevalence of various conditions via direct epidemiological studies of general or specific subgroups of the population. Such studies could use measures designed for use with general populations such as the general health status measures used in the General Household Survey (Rickards *et al.*, 2004) although some indices are specific to the older age groups such as the Geriatric Depression Scale (GDS). Examples of this approach include the use of measures designed to establish the incidence and prevalence of dementia in the community or the extent of depressive illness among older people. Studies have also looked at the prevalence of different symptoms and diseases within the older age groups or used more generic measures of health status such as the SF-36 in order to estimate overall quality of life. Second, there has been the widescale development of measures designed to establish the incidence and prevalence of disability and chronic disease within populations as illustrated by the Health Survey for England. Third, there are indirect indices that are based upon the secondary analysis of routine clinical or health service activity data. An example of this is the use of data for hip fractures to establish the extent of osteoporosis within the population. In this section we concentrate upon data derived from general studies of morbidity and disability within the population rather than looking at the epidemiology and burden resultant from individual diseases.

When investigating the health status of populations, especially for studies concerned with older people, it is conceptually important to differentiate between acute health problems and those of a more longstanding or chronic nature. This distinction is drawn because of the differential impact which such conditions are likely to have upon individuals. Chronic conditions are much more likely than acute illnesses to impose restrictions upon the daily activities of individuals and to challenge their ability to maintain an independent and autonomous life in the community. In this section we largely concentrate upon the chronic conditions because these are most likely to compromise the independence of individuals, although we give consideration to acute health problems prior to focusing upon disability and chronic illness.

Acute health problems

Acute health problems are usually defined as self-limiting conditions of short duration, usually three months or less. Included under this heading are such conditions as colds, influenza or accidental injuries and other short-lived episodes of illness. Usually, acute illnesses are characterised by symptoms or causes for which medical techniques or other forms of intervention may effect a cure or which are 'self-curing' within a fairly short period of time. Each year the General Household Survey asks its respondents about acute health problems that have restricted their normal level of activity in the fourteen days before interview. These data demonstrate that, although there is some age-related increase in the reported prevalence of acute illness, this is not especially marked (see Table 5.3). For example, 17 per cent of males aged 45–64 reported acute illness episode compared with 24 per cent of those aged 75+. The number of days annually estimated to be affected by restricted activity is higher among the older age groups, especially the 75+ age group with those aged 65+ reporting 10 days of 'restricted activity' per year. Hence, while the prevalence of episodes does not show a great age-related differential, the duration of each episode seems to be greater among the oldest age groups. Compared with females, reported rates of acute illness by males are approximately 10–15 per cent lower. Evandrou (2000) reports that rates of acute illness are elevated among elders from Bangladeshi/ Pakistani backgrounds but that there are also gender variations within this overall pattern. There is no consistent link between acute illness and social class: the Health Survey for England suggests a slight excess of acute illness among manual workers which is not evident in the General Household Survey. The Health Survey for England collected data from older people resident in both community and long-term care environments. The reported rates of acute illness showed little variation between the two settings (18 per cent for those in the community and 20 per cent for those in care). This affords support for the observation that acute illness varies little with age and that the only major difference seems to be in terms of gender, perhaps reflecting gender differences in how the question is interpreted.

Table 5.3 Prevalence of acute illness (restricted activity in the 14 days before interview), Great Britain, 2002

	%		Number of restricted activity days per person per year	
	M	F	M	F
16–44	11	13	2.3	2.6
45–64	17	19	4.3	4.3
65–74	19	20	5.5	5.2
75+	24	28	7.2	8.2

Source: Rickards *et al.*, 2004: Tables 7.2 and 7.3

Chronic health problems

Chronic health problems are, by definition, long term and not usually characterised by a cure. Implicit within the term is also the notion of inevitable decline or deterioration. Medical intervention may (or may not) alleviate some, or all, of the associated symptoms and may halt (or slow down) the rate of decline. Examples of such long-term health problems are multiple sclerosis, dementia and arthritis. It is this type of health problem that is specifically identified by both the general public and many professional health workers alike as an integral, inevitable, natural and universal feature of old age. How valid is this stereotype?

We can establish the prevalence of chronic illness within the population using several different data sources. Using data from the General Household Survey, we can examine variations in reported levels of chronic ill health within the population and over time. The GHS, and now many other surveys, and the 2001 Census ask two distinct questions about chronic illness. The first establishes the number of people with a longstanding illness (of one or more years' duration). The second part of the question asks if this condition impairs the activity levels or lifestyle of the individual. This is known as longstanding limiting illness and is seen as important for older people in that it may compromise their ability to live independently within the community.

Data from both the Health Survey for England and the General Household Survey suggest that about one-third of men and women aged 65 and over living in the community report that they do not have a longstanding illness (Table 5.4) and this shows little variation with age. A further 40 per cent of people report a longstanding

Table 5.4 Longstanding limiting illness by age and sex, Great Britain, 2001 (%)

	65–69	70–74	75–79	80–84	85	All
	With longstanding limiting illness					
Male	34	39	46	48	51	41
Female	33	41	40	45	57	41
	With longstanding non-limiting illness					
Male	23	20	17	14	19	19
Female	22	17	19	18	14	19
	With no longstanding illness					
Male	43	42	37	38	30	40
Female	45	42	41	37	28	40

Source: Walker *et al.*, 2002: Table 10

limiting illness; this is most commonly reported by women and increases with age. This pattern suggests that the popular stereotype of old age, as a time of universal and inevitable chronic health and impaired activity, is somewhat inaccurate. While the reported prevalence of a longstanding limiting illness increases with age it is not a universal characteristic of later life. A little over half of men and women aged 85 and over living in the community report that they do not have a long-standing disability or illness that impairs their activity levels. However, this is a self-report measure and does depend upon the perception of the individual as to whether their activity level is limited by the condition. It is also a single point in time measure which relates only to the previous year; we do not know for how many respondents the illness was a continuation of a pre-existing condition, a new illness or if it subsequently resolved.

In addition to the common perception of all older people as suffering from chronic illness, there is also the issue of multiple pathology. One of the supposed 'novel' aspects of the medicine of old age is that it can deal with the multiple pathology demonstrated by older people. Unlike the rest of the population older people are supposedly characterised by the presence of multiple conditions. The Health Survey for England indicates that on average those living at home have two chronic illnesses and this was similar in care homes. While older people may present with a pattern of multiple illnesses it may not be as complex a pattern of problems as the stereotypes might suggest.

The data presented earlier are derived from a population of older people living in the community. This will inevitably under-estimate the 'true' extent of morbidity because many of the sickest members of the population will be living in residential or nursing homes. Glaser *et al.* (1997) demonstrates how, using 1991 Census data, rates of morbidity for the institutional dwelling elderly population are in the order of 80–90 per cent. Data from the Health Survey for England in 2002 support this estimate as they show that 82 per cent of care home residents report the presence of a longstanding illness. If we assume that all of those aged 65 and over in residential or nursing home care have some form of longstanding illness which impairs their daily activities and compromises their independence (or else why are they in such care) we can revise the estimates of long-standing illness within the older population. This involves adding in the number of people in nursing and residential care across each age and sex band. The end result of this exercise is to markedly increase the prevalence of chronic health problems among the oldest age groups although the difference is less evident for the younger age groups. This is illustrated by Table 5.5, which suggests that GHS data significantly underestimate the prevalence of chronic health problems when compared with data from the 2001 Census, which included all older people irrespective of place of residence. This is especially notable for the 85+ age group where disability prevalence rates increase by 20 per cent by the inclusion of the 'institutionalised' population. Hence when we are thinking about the very old the exclusion of the 'institutional' population can seriously under-estimate the true needs for care by older people.

The distribution of longstanding limiting illness is not equally distributed across the older population. Women report more chronic illness than men and this differential is at its most extreme among the

Table 5.5 England and Wales: comparison of chronic illness rates between GHS and 2001 Census

	With chronic illness (longstanding, limiting illness)					
	65–74		75–84		85+	
	GHS	Census	GHS	Census	GHS	Census
Male	36	43	47	56	57	70
Female	37	41	42	59	57	78

Source: ONS, 2003

85+ age group where it is 25 per cent. Evandrou (2000) reports that rates of long-term illness are higher among elders from the Indian subcontinent. This is confirmed by preliminary analysis of the 2001 Census data for England and Wales. Of the population aged 65+, 52 per cent of those defined as 'white' report a longstanding limiting illness compared with 54 per cent of the Black/Black British and 60 per cent of the Asian/British Asian populations. The percentage of older people reporting that they experience a longstanding limiting disability varies with social class from 37 per cent of those from a professional occupation background to 47 per cent from the semi-skilled and unskilled occupation groups (Victor, 1991). GHS data indicate that males aged 65+ from non-manual backgrounds have crude rates of chronic illness higher than their manual contemporaries (41 per cent versus 51 per cent and 40 per cent versus 49 per cent for women) (Rickards *et al.*, 2004). Calculation of age- and class-specific disability prevalence rates indicates that an older person aged 80+ from a professional occupational group has a lower rate of disability than those aged 65–69 from unskilled occupations. Similarly work by Khaw (1999b) supports the conclusion that social class variations in health status are preserved into very old age. Reduction of these gender, class and ethnic variations would clearly both improve the health of the population and reduce the demands upon services. The existence of such socially defined differences again serves to highlight that the experience of (ill) health in old age is as much to do with social and environmental factors as it is to do with biology and genetics. Indeed Rowe and Kahn (1997) suggest that in advanced old age, differentials in health status are largely attributable to social, environmental and behavioural factors rather than to biology or genetics: a viewpoint supported by Aldwin and Gilmer (2004).

What are the major causes of chronic illness?

Data from routine surveys also enable us to establish the major health conditions that are bringing about these chronic health problems in both community and institutional populations. Both the General Household Survey and Health Survey for England demonstrate the importance of musculoskeletal conditions, mostly arthritis, and circulatory diseases in compromising the mobility and independence and later life, especially in the community. For those living in the community with chronic illness approximately a third have heart/circulatory disease, a further third have musculoskeletal disorders and 10 per cent respiratory problems and less than 1 per cent have cancers. In the institutional population about one-third have cognitive impairment cited as the major cause of chronic illness, followed by heart disease and musculoskeletal disorders. This pattern of causes of morbidity is somewhat different from that for mortality and we can distinguish three distinct categories:

- high mortality and high morbidity (e.g. heart and circulatory diseases)
- high morbidity but low mortality (musculoskeletal disease and dementia)
- high mortality and low morbidity (cancer).

Measuring health: disability, impairment and handicap

As noted earlier in this chapter there are innumerable measures for recording the prevalence and incidence of disability within the population. It is existence of a plethora of different methods and measures, each with their own systems and thresholds, that results in rather fruitless debates about the 'real' or 'true' number of disabled people within the community. Here, how we look at chronic health problems has been via the collection of data about the ability of older people to undertake a variety of activities and tasks considered essential to an independent life in the community. Hence, in theory at least, these measures relate directly to key government policy objective of enabling older people to lead independent lives within the community. These research instruments are loosely grouped together as measures of functional capacity and a large number of these measures have been devised. Much epidemiological study of later life has been almost solely concerned with the construction and validation of these measures. This interest in the functional capacity levels of older people stems, in part, from a desire to allocate services to those most 'in need' and to estimate current (and future) service requirements. The indices are not usually constructed to demonstrate the level of independence of older people. Rather they concentrate upon measuring dependence and the 'need' for services and consist of items that researchers and policy makers consider relevant to independent life in the community. Rarely do they reflect the views of older people as to the activities they need to undertake to successfully remain in the community nor do they necessarily reflect the things that are important to older people (Askham, 2003).

The Health Survey for England looked at five major types of disability: locomotor, personal care, hearing, sight and communication.

This study suggests that approximately 60 per cent of those in the community report no disability compared with approximately 14 per cent of those in institutional settings (Marmot *et al.*, 2003). As Table 5.6 shows, levels of all forms of disability are significantly higher among the care dwelling population. Typical of these measures of functional capacity is that described by Townsend (1979), a measure that has been widely used in the United Kingdom (Meltzer *et al.*, 1999). The nine items included in his list of activities cover mobility, self-care and instrumental activities of daily living (Table 5.7). This is essentially a dictionary approach in which the ability of the older person to undertake a series of tasks is recorded upon a checklist and older people rate how easily they can accomplish the tasks specified. Collecting data about such activities of daily living (often referred to in the literature as 'ADL') does pose some practical difficulties for the researcher. Performance of tasks such as making a cup of tea in a test setting in a hospital may produce artificially high or low results while collecting the data in an interview situation presents problems of gender bias, especially for current cohorts of elders. In addition there is potential bias introduced because the older person may not wish to admit to an interviewer that they cannot manage a task and compromise their self-image as a competent adult (a potential clash of public and private faces).

Data from the General Household Survey indicate that the majority of older people can undertake these activities without difficulty; only a minority is unable to undertake them without the assistance of another person (see Table 5.7). Thus we find that for the task which presented the most difficulty to this sample of older people, cutting toenails, 30 per cent were unable to undertake this alone and 70 per cent were totally independent. Yet that 30 per cent of approximately 8.8 million people experience problems with this activity indicates

Table 5.6 People reporting varying disabilities, England, 2000 (%)

Disability type	Care homes		Community	
	Male	*Female*	*Male*	*Female*
Locomotor	86	81	30	33
Personal care	58	64	16	14
Hearing	28	34	14	12
Sight	25	28	6	8
Communication	31	35	3	2

Source: Hirani and Malbot, 2002: Table 2

Table 5.7 People unable to manage items in the Townsend Disability Index by age and sex, Great Britain, 2001 (%)

Task*	65–74		75–84		85+	
	M	F	M	F	M	F
Cut own toenails	17	24	29	45	49	72
Wash all over or bathe	3	5	6	10	18	23
Go up and down stairs	1	0	1	2	1	2
Do heavy housework	5	7	11	16	21	40
Shop and carry heavy bags	6	9	11	20	35	44
Prepare and cook a hot meal	4	2	8	6	11	17

Source: Walker *et al.*, 2002

Note: * Three tasks of the Townsend Disability Index not included in GHS – getting on a bus, reaching an overhead shelf and tying a knot in a piece of string

that, in absolute terms, there are substantial numbers of people within the population who may have compromised independence. It is also clear that the ability to undertake these tasks decreases with age. Examination of Table 5.8 reinforces again the very dependent nature of the care home population, with levels of dependence in terms of activities of daily living far in excess of the community population. This important distinction is often not fully recognised when considering the potential for caring for very frail older people in community settings. As these data indicate those resident in care homes represent the 'extreme' end of the disability and frailty continuum.

When classifying the functional capacity levels of the older population describing each of the nine tasks separately is rather time-consuming. Thus responses to the nine items are summed following a standard scoring procedure to produce an overall index of disability which suggests that 15.7 per cent of people aged 65+ in England and Wales are severely disabled; a total of 1.3 million people (Meltzer *et al.*, 1999). This is not too dissimilar to the 13 per cent reported by the Health Survey for England. Women have higher prevalence rates than men (19.2 per cent compared to 10.6 per cent) and represent 72 per cent of the total severely disabled population. Only 18 per cent of this population are resident in institutional care. The percentage with no or slight disability decreases with age from 80 per cent of those aged 65–69 to 15 per cent of the 85+ groups. It is the severe disability category, which demonstrates both the largest age-related increase and the biggest gender differential, especially for those aged 80+. The

Table 5.8 People aged 65+ unable to manage specific tasks: a comparison of community and care home populations, England, 2000 (%)

Task	With severe difficulty	
	Care home	Community
Walking	45	6
Going up 12 stairs	64	8
Picking up shoes	56	13
Getting in and out of bed	40	1
Getting in and out of chair	36	1
Dressing	48	2
Washing	30	0
Feeding	23	0
Getting to and using toilet	42	1

Source: Hirani and Malbot, 2002: Tables 3 and 4

prevalence of severe disability increases from 45 per 1000 at aged 65–69 to 457 per 1000 at age 80+ (341 per 1000 for males and 573 per 1000 for females). How much of this difference reflects a 'true' difference in morbidity and how much is a reflection of the social definition of gender roles and the tasks considered appropriate to those roles remains unclear. Using these data Meltzer *et al.* (2000) demonstrate the existence of socio-economic differentials in both the overall distribution of disability and severe disability which are evident for all age and sex groups and these are confirmed by HSE data where there is an approximate 20 per cent difference in disability prevalence between manual and non-manual occupation groups. Meltzer *et al.* (2000) claim that achievement of the disability prevalence of the most privileged groups by all older people would result in an absolute fall in the numbers of disabled elders despite projected increases in both population and longevity.

Health status: compression of morbidity?

Old age is strongly associated with ill health by both professionals and members of the public alike. The data presented above indicate that while old age is not universally a time of poor health the reported prevalence of chronic health problems does increase with age. However, this is not the same as saying that 'chronic health' problems are the result of ageing. While there is undoubtedly an association with age it is not clear that ageing causes chronic health problems; it could be the other way around. The observation of an association between age and chronic disease may reflect the influence of a third confounding variable such as class or gender. We should also remember the influence that social, environmental and occupation factors have in the genesis of chronic disease. Furthermore the increase in prevalence rates for chronic illness which we observe with age may, in fact, reflect a cohort rather than ageing effect. Given the harsh circumstances that today's elderly people experienced during their formative years, the levels of ill health we have observed may be a reflection of this. Indeed the 'Barker' hypothesis argues for the 'fetal' origin of disease by suggesting that it is the environment in utero and early infancy which establishes risk factors for disease in middle and later life (Barker, 1998). We might suggest that future generations, which have experienced less privation and better health care in infancy and prior to birth, might demonstrate improved health status in later life. The time frame required testing this hypothesis is clearly long term. The widespread acceptance of this type of argument can, of course, be used to argue against health promotion and other interventions in later life, on the grounds that the health status of individuals is preordained and not amenable to change. However, the existence of class, gender and ethnic differences in health status also indicates the importance of social and environmental factors. Rowe and Kahn (1997) suggest that, in advanced old age, social and environmental factors are more important than biology and genetics in determining health status.

As outlined in the beginning of this chapter there are two opposing hypotheses as to the effect that decreasing late life mortality will have upon the health status of the older population. The pessimistic hypothesis argues that as more individuals survive into later life, as a result of decreasing mortality, this will increasing be made up of the 'survival of the sickest'. The development of medical interventions that 'save lives' and increase the period of pre-death morbidity will promote the development of an increasing sick and morbidity older population. This view presumes that there is no biological or genetic programme for death and that the fatal and disabling (chronic) diseases are independent of each other. The optimistic hypothesis argues that success in decreasing mortality reflects the improved initial health status of older populations, that success in decreasing mortality reflects success in postponing morbidity. Hence, as with mortality, morbidity will be concentrated into a short phase at the end of life. Clearly from our highly limited suite of morbidity indices in terms of both veracity of measures and study design imperfections it is extremely difficult to establish the veracity of either of these hypotheses.

Changes in disability over time

There has been an extensive debate in the literature regarding the veracity of these two contrasting hypotheses (Fries, 2003). In order to test these theses we need detailed data on secular trends in morbidity, which are rarely available. It is not possible to test this particular hypothesis using cross-sectional data, instead we require extensive longitudinal data, which are not yet available. One method of considering this is to examine trends over time in routinely collected survey data (as described in Chapter 3). Clearly there are methodological problems in making such comparisons including changes in question wording. Furthermore changes in the reported prevalence of longstanding limiting illness among older people in the community may result from factors linked to the supply and admission to residential or nursing home care and the ability of services to care for more or less disabled and dependent people within the population and not from any changes in overall morbidity. Although the prevalence rates fluctuate there is no evidence for an increase over time for those aged 65–74 and only a 2 per cent increase in prevalence over 25 years for those aged 75+. Similarly, General Household Survey data look at overall and age-specific trends in the ability of older people to undertake selected activities of daily living (Table 5.9). Overall there is considerable stability in the responses obtained over time and no evidence from these data of marked changes in functional ability over the previous two decades. We can use GHS data to construct pseudo-cohorts and this offers another way to examine trends over time. Confining our attention to those aged 85+, there is considerable stability across cohorts. For those aged 85+ in 1980 (born 1895 or earlier), the prevalence of longstanding limiting illness was 53 per cent for men and 59 per cent for women – remarkably similar to the

Table 5.9 People aged 65+ having difficulty undertaking items in the Townsend Disability Index, Great Britain, 1980–2001 (%)

	1980	1985	1994	1998	2001
Cut own toenails	28	29	31	30	31
Wash all over or bathe	9	9	8	7	7
Go up and down stairs	8	9	9	9	10
Do heavy housework	10	12	10	10	11
Shop and carry heavy bags	14	16	16	14	13
Prepare and cook a hot meal	7	8	5	5	5

Sources: Victor, 1997; Walker *et al.*, 2002

51 per cent and 57 per cent respectively for the 1916 cohort (85+ in 2001). This certainly does not suggest any radical changes in disability prevalence since the early 1970s when examined at the level of the entire group. However, it may well be the case that this masks considerable changes within the population.

Manton *et al.* (2000) and Manton and Gu (2001), having examined trends in chronic disability in the United States between 1982 and 1994, conclude that disability prevalence declined by 0.34 per cent per year or by 4.3 per cent for the period 1982–1996. Such decreases are not trivial. These authors observe that there were 1.4 million fewer disabled people aged 65+ in 1994 than if the 1982 rates had been maintained. This provides some tentative evidence that there might be some reduction in severe disability but no change in the 'less severe' categories. Fries (2003) also produced evidence suggestive of decreasing rates of chronic disability within the older American population. He suggests that disability has been decreasing at 2 per cent per year for the period 1982–1999, a larger decrease than 1 per cent annual decline in mortality. His thesis is supported by the work of Freedman *et al.* (2001). Fries (2003) suggests that a decrease in disability of 1.5 per cent per annum would be sufficient to contain health care expenditure within budgetary limits for at least 70 years. Fries (2003) suggests the causes of these declines are multifactoral and involve lifestyle, improved health interventions and other factors.

Healthy life expectancy

Another way of examining this issue is to use combinations of mortality and morbidity data to calculate measures of 'healthy' or 'disability-free' life expectancy. This approach has the merit of combining information about survival rates with data concerning the health status of survivors. There are several measures that can be used to describe this phenomenon. These include disability-free life expectancy, disability-adjusted life expectancy and healthy life expectancy. Despite the variation in the names of these measures and in the detail of the methods of calculation they all express a related, and rather fundamental, concept. How many years of the expected duration of life will be healthy or free from disability, dementia or dependency? Clearly two sets of data are required for the calculation of such measures: mortality and morbidity. We have already seen that Britain is well served by a comprehensive and robust mortality data. Measures of morbidity used to determine the expected likelihood of disability or dementia are rather less robust: we need to look carefully at the data upon which these measures are based before accepting their utility and accepting their arguments that healthy life expectancy has increased or decreased.

By combining overall life expectancy and 'healthy' life expectancy we can determine the number of years or percentage of the life span that individuals can expect to live, on average, free from disability. We can also use these measures to look at changes over time. For the United Kingdom, both life expectancy and 'healthy' life expectancy have increased. However, the rate of increase has been higher for life expectancy than 'healthy' life expectancy. Hence there has been a marginal increase in the percentage of life spent in poor health or disability (Kelly *et al.*, 2000). This analysis should be extended to determine if all sections of the population have benefited equally from this improvement. Given the evidence of previous sections, this seems rather unlikely.

Conclusion

In this chapter we have seen that health is a complex multidimensional phenomenon. Although it is a difficult concept to define and describe empirically there is little doubt about the centrality of health and illness to the quality of life of the individual whatever her/his age. Studies of older people have consistently shown that it is one of their major concerns. It is the loss of independence and autonomy, rather than the effects of illness itself, which is most prevalent among older people. The popular stereotype of old age is of universal ill health and a progressive, universal and inescapable decline in both physical and mental status. In this chapter we have confined our attention to physical health status. Our data refute this proposition as it was clearly demonstrated that, even among the very oldest age groups, physical ill health and disability are far from universal. We have shown that there is an increase in the prevalence of both acute and chronic conditions with age, but we must be wary of interpreting this as an intrinsic ageing effect. Without good longitudinal data it is impossible to ascertain how much of this increased prevalence of disability is due to biological ageing, how much is socially and environmentally produced and how much is a cohort effect resulting from the harsh conditions experienced by many now elderly people when they were in their youth. In particular we must be wary of interpreting age-related changes in health status as biologically determined 'facts'. The physical and social environment in which the older person lives will have a marked effect upon their health status and level of independence. The high steps up to buses may form a barrier to the mobility of older people. Low expectations of health in later life by older people may also influence their abilities. Classifying older people by their degree of dependency may facilitate efficient service planning but will have little positive effect upon the outlook of older people themselves.

The data upon which our analysis of the health status of older people has been based are largely cross-sectional in design. From this it is not possible to identify how much of the increased ill health found among older age groups is due to the effect of ageing per se. Rather it may well be that this is a manifestation of a cohort effect. The population who are now old experienced great privation during their formative years and few had access to medical treatment. With the establishment of the welfare state and socialised medicine, older people in the future may display much lower levels of ill health than the current generations of elders. Additionally changes in lifestyle such as the decreased prevalence of smoking may well have a very profound effect upon the health status of future generations of older people.

One of the key debates in gerontology is that concerning possible changes in the prevalence of ill health in later life. Exploration of this issue is methodologically complex, especially given our over-reliance upon cross-sectional survey data. The evidence presented concerning disability-free life expectancy, chronic illness and functional ability was inconsistent. No clear and consistent trend in either direction was evident. On the basis of current data there is no evidence to support the view that there will be massive changes in morbidity among older people in the near future, but within this broad generalisation we also need to examine the different subsets of the older population. It is entirely possible that different elements of the older population will benefit disproportionately from changes in overall patterns of morbidity. There was some evidence that, in Britain, women and those from higher social classes have gained most from improvements in both expectation of life and disability free life expectancy. Even if there is only a relatively small overall improvement in health status this may be differentially 'gained' by some groups at the expense of others. Indeed there is some evidence to suggest that it is the most 'advantaged' groups who are gaining from these changes and that differentials may be increasing rather than decreasing. This serves to emphasise that social and environmental factors continue to exert a major influence on the health resources available to older people.

6 Psychological health and well-being

Psychological health and well-being are important elements of the experience of later life and impact significantly upon the quality of life of individuals. This statement is probably true also of most other age groups within the population. For older people, issues of psychological and mental health and well-being are deemed to be especially important. It is, perhaps, in the domain of psychological and mental health that some of the most pervasive and pernicious stereotypes of old age persist. In particular there is an implicit link made between 'old age' and the clinical condition of dementia. 'Forgetfulness' and 'loss of memory' are seen by many as being part of 'normal ageing' and not as a manifestation of pathology or as a 'disease state'. Evidence of the widespread currency of such stereotypes is all around us and is frequently typified by 'joke' birthday cards and other forms of humour. However, there are many more equally negative stereotypes concerning mental health and psychological well-being in later life. These include the notion that 'the old cannot learn' and that with ageing, people become more conservative, less open to innovation and change, and experience negative changes in their personality. The extensive number of negative stereotypes of mental and psychological health in later life means that these are problems that are especially feared by older people. Furthermore older people, unlike most other age groups, have constantly to demonstrate and reinforce their psychological competence in order to maintain their independence and to 'prove' that they have not fallen prey to any of the above. Widespread acceptance of such stereotypes may also compromise the self-image of older people and thereby promote a 'downward spiral' and self-fulfilling prophecy. In this chapter we look at the key areas of psychological and mental health in later life and consider the degree to which the negative stereotypes of old age as a time of mental decline have any legitimacy.

Perceptions of ageing

Earlier we reintroduced the importance of images and stereotypes in influencing how we think about 'old age' as both individuals and in a more global sense. Images of ageing exist at two levels – the individual and the societal. In this chapter we shall examine both dimensions but focus predominantly upon the individual level. To fully understand the meaning of ageing requires an understanding of its impact upon the self-image of the individual. In addition, we need to know how the wider society perceives the place of older people and the relative status or stigma associated with old age. We also consider some of the more commonly held stereotypes about old age and consider how these views are formed and perpetuated. Stereotypes are an important element of the social context within which groups and individuals experience old age. Essentially a stereotype is a 'distorted' representation or set of ideas (or ideology) concerning a particular social group and as such may be either negative or positive. Some commonly held stereotypes are that English people are snobs, Irish people dull-witted and spectacle-wearers bright. Regardless of the group that is the recipient of the stereotype it is a source of partial or misinformation, which represents a set of ideas or beliefs (or ideology) about a group of people. There are many commonly held stereotypes about old age. Unlike the stereotypes concerning the positive intellectual benefits of wearing glasses, the stereotypes of older age and older people are, within the western context, almost universally negative.

Combining the many stereotypes and images of ageing leads to a very negative view of the experience of old age and the role and potential of older people. It is commonly believed that older people lead a rather gloomy existence characterised by social isolation, neglect from their family, beset with health problems and suffering considerable emotional stress. Retirement from paid employment is seen as leaving a vacuum which it is impossible to replace. In terms of intimate relationships older people are assumed to be neither capable of, nor interested in, an active sex life. Perhaps more pernicious and debilitating to older people is the presumed 'dependence' and passivity of older people. We have a stereotypical view of older people which represents them as incapable of running their own lives and which views older people as passive recipients of a range of services from food parcels to community service volunteers or to young offenders digging their gardens or redecorating their homes. Our images of later life contain the implicit assumption that, whatever their pre-old-age characteristics, older people are incapable of competent social functioning, devoid of critical faculties or intellect and incapable of exercising informed choice and control over their own lives. Perhaps the most obvious and prevalent manifestation of this perceived lack of independence and autonomy is the tendency to equate older people with children. The 'infantalisation' of older people is especially evident in institutional settings such as residential and nursing homes or hospitals.

Certainly older people are not unique in having a large number of stereotypes applied to them. Many oppressed or minority groups are the butts of stereotypes such as teenage mothers or young (black) males. At some levels stereotypes can be 'amusing' (or at least appear to be intended to be so), but for older people they are much more pernicious as they are evidence of a widespread ideology concerning older people and link into the notion of ageism. The term 'ageism' has been coined by gerontologists to describe pejorative images of older people. Ageism may be defined as systematic stereotyping and discrimination against people because they are of a particular age (see Bytheway, 1997). Most usually the term is used to describe negative discrimination against the 'old', but it could equally be applied to the 'young' where we could discriminate against 'young' people because of their perceived immaturity (and presumed irresponsibility). A good example of 'youth ageism' is the presumption that 'young' mothers are bad or inadequate mothers incapable of raising children 'properly' in comparison to the clearly responsible and competent 'older' mother. Ageism is similar to sexism or racism in that it is discrimination against all members of a particular group, in our case older people (however defined). Implicit within the term is the notion that the old (like minority community members, refugees or women) are in some way different from ourselves (and our future selves) or members of our family. As such they are not subject to the same wants, needs and desires as the rest of society and do not 'deserve' or 'merit' the same rights and privileges. Hence we make policy decisions not to include 'young' workers within benefit entitlements or young mothers to child benefit. Older carers may be denied carer benefits as it is 'natural' to undertake caring responsibilities in 'old age'; unlike sexism and racism, ageism is generally much more covert and subtle in its manifestation. The failure to provide renal dialysis or treatment in coronary care units to older people or stroke units or their exclusion from screening programmes simply because of their age are appraisals of the old which merit the term 'ageist'. It is extremely difficult in many instances to provide hard evidence of ageism although it is widely thought to exist, especially within the health and social care systems. Indeed the first standard of the National Service Framework for Older People is dedicated to combating ageism within the context of access to and quality of health services (Department of Health (DoH), 2001). Ageism is also implicated in the generation of negative stereotypes of later life. By seeing older people as different in some indefinable, but distinct, way from ourselves, that is by adopting ageist attitudes, society can conveniently ignore the real difficulties that this group may experience. Ageism is as ideology, which condones and sanctions the subordination and marginalisation of older people within society and legitimises (or at least ignores) poor quality care, neglect and social exclusion. Ageism links very well with the strictures of the disengagement theories: if older people do not disengage willingly then they can be made to do so by the application of social sanctions.

Ageism, it is argued, is not experienced equally by men and women for older women experience both ageism and sexism. They are discriminated against, or viewed negatively, because they are both old and female. This double disadvantage is reflected in what has been termed the double standard of ageing (Sontag, 1978; Arber and Ginn, 1995; Calasanti and Sleven, 2001). The notion that men and women differentially experience old age is not a new one: indeed it has a long historical pedigree. Hippocrates considered that old age started for men between the ages of 55 and 60 while for women old age started a decade earlier. In a similar vein Plato saw the prime of life as 30 years for man and 20 years for a woman. According to this widespread social view, old age for women starts earlier than for men and lasts for many more years. However, this discrepancy in the perceived onset of old age has no biological basis: life expectancy for a male is several years shorter than that of a female. Rather, this difference in the perceived onset of old age is socially defined, constructed, maintained and legitimised.

The differential negative stereotypes applied to older men and women is a product of this dual disadvantage. Growing older is, in the very broadest sense, seen as less problematic for a man because masculinity is associated with qualities such as competence, autonomy and self-control which withstand the ageing process much better than the qualities for which females are desired: beauty, physical attractiveness and childbearing. Ageing is seen as 'spoiling', 'corrupting' and stigmatising the identity of women much earlier and in a more comprehensive and corrosive way than for men. As Sontag (1978: 73) wrote 'Society is much more permissive about ageing in men.... Men are allowed to age, without penalty, in several ways that women are not.' This is clearly illustrated by our attitudes towards childbearing by post-menopausal women and the fathering of children by 'older' fathers. Those women who, through artificial methods, have borne children post-menopausally are viewed as selfish and highly negatively evaluated. Older fathers are thought of very differently, with the ability to father a child in (advanced) old age seen as a source of envy and a clear statement of their continued virility and engagement with life.

Although the realities of ageing do not fit the commonly held stereotypes, the myths about ageing continue to find common currency and expression in everyday life. Research has compared the perceptions of 'young' and 'old' as to the main 'problems' of ageing and later life. Public expectations about later life saw old age as a time of fear of crime, poverty, poor housing, inadequate medical care, poor health and lack of social interaction. Later life was seen as being a negative phase of the lifecycle, except that it was thought to have the freedom and lack of responsibility characteristic of adolescence. Older people consistently rated these features as much lesser problems than the non-elderly population. The discrepancies between the perceptions of the two groups as to the 'realities' of old age were enormous. For example, 60 per cent of the young thought that loneliness was a serious problem of old age compared with 12 per cent of older people. Interpretation of the meaning of these different perceptions is somewhat problematic. The low percentage of older people reporting loneliness as a problem may represent the influence of an overall expectation of loneliness in old age, i.e. an acceptance of the 'negative' stereotype, they may represent the reality of later life or be a public presentation that the older person thinks is acceptable to the researcher.

If these stereotypes are apparently so far from the feelings and perceptions of the realities of later life what function do they perform? Stereotypes about ageing, or any other group such as women or teenagers, are a shorthand method of communicating the particular social value of specific social groups and influence our social interaction with them by suggesting appropriate attitudes and behaviours. Current stereotypes about ageing teach us to ignore the old because they are essentially a non-productive group within a society, which places its strongest emphasis upon the roles of economic productivity and independence. As well as influencing our behaviour towards the target group, stereotypes communicate appropriate forms of behaviour to the group themselves. Modern stereotypes of ageing inform older members of the community that invisibility, passivity and disengagement best achieve successful ageing. Acceptance of this stereotype engenders an attitude of 'gratitude' and results in us (the younger age groups) expecting older people to be grateful for the pensions and benefits, which are given to them by the rest of society. Criticism of the levels at which these benefits and pensions are paid would be considered inappropriate and 'ungrateful'. Hence the antics of groups such as the HenCoop are very challenging to our image of older people as passive, sedate and grateful individuals. Although attitudes towards ageing and old age are highly negative, attitudes towards older people as a collectivity are somewhat different in that they are a 'worthy' group and often results in them being treated in a patronising way. Britain is characterised by a very negative evaluation of those who rely upon state welfare benefits for their income. Older people are generally seen as an exception to this general set of beliefs. They are seen as a group 'deserving' of support in the form of pensions and benefits as studies such as the British Social Attitudes Survey consistently demonstrate.

What are the sources of our stereotypes about ageing in general and older people in particular? Stereotypes about ageing (and obviously other groups) originate from two major sources – societal and the individual – and these are clearly interrelated. At the most fundamental level stereotypes are related to ideas about the social status and location within the system of social stratification of the group under consideration. Social status refers to a position in society which involves certain duties and privileges while social role involves the performance of these functions. Older people are, in most western industrial societies, ascribed a low-status social role which stresses old age as a dependent phase in the lifecycle where the individual lacks power, independence and autonomy. One of the most obvious sources of stereotypes is lack of information about the stereotyped group. Those who have the least knowledge about ageing probably hold the most negative views about later life. Despite the increase in the proportion of older people in contemporary western society, there is still a great lack of understanding about the realities of ageing among both the general population and those responsible for the development of health and social policies. Hence surveys of medical and nursing professionals consistently demonstrate incredibly negative (and inaccurate) ideas about old age. It is possible that some of the early British research undertaken by social gerontologists may have contributed to the creation and maintenance of these negative stereotypes of old age. Several early studies of ageing were based upon samples resident in institutions, rather than the wider community, thereby giving a very false image of the abilities and status of the older members of society.

Stereotypes assume an extra importance because they also influence the way the defined group perceive themselves. As noted earlier self-identity is, in part at least, influenced by both how we think about ourselves and how others see us. Given the overwhelming negative stereotype of old age, affluent and healthy older people perceive themselves as exceptions in a mass of poverty and ill health, rather than as evidence of the inapplicability of the stereotype. These are examples of upwards (or downwards) social comparisons. Similarly, active older people are seen, not as clear refutation of the myths about ageing, but again as exceptions from the norm of disability and infirmity. Hence the popular press focuses upon the 'exceptional' older person such as Fauja Singh, who ran the 2004 London Marathon at the age of 93. This ability to maintain the veracity of stereotypes in the face of contradictory evidence is termed 'pluralistic ignorance' and this describes the dissonance between our individual experience of our (great-) grandparents and older friends and relatives and the prevalent stereotypes. We are able to hold two apparently contradictory sets of views about, for example, the health of older people because our own experience of our grandparents as being predominantly fit and healthy is seen as exceptional. This strategy allows the maintenance of stereotypes in the face of overwhelmingly contradictory evidence. We may perceive all older people in a very negative fashion even though the older people with whom we are acquainted, our (great-) grandparents are active and independent and do not conform to the expectations suggested by our stereotypical beliefs.

(Old) age is a master status trait. This means that, as with labels such as black or homosexual, it becomes the major identifying characteristic of the individual. Hence I cease to be a person who has lived, for example, 70 years and become an 'old person' who is then presumed to possess the various other characteristics such as poor health or deteriorating mental abilities because of the application of this label to me. Adoption of the master status trait, in our case the label 'old', may influence the social world of older people by excluding them from activities such as paid employment or volunteering or social groups because of their age. These negative images may pervade the self-identity of the old and this is where the macro-analysis of social theory encounters the world of the individual older person. If older people, in the face of pervasive societal attitudes, accept the stereotype of age as a time of decline when they must relinquish normal activities they may then act in a way which makes the stereotype reality. Hence there is a negative downward spiral.

Why do older people accept these negative stereotypes? In the absence of detailed empirical research the answer to this question is inevitably speculative. We could argue that, because today's elders grew up in a time when 'old people' were sick and frail and disengaged from society, they might see the validity of the stereotype. Alternatively they may accept the pervasive youth and activity bias of society, and when they see evidence of 'bodily decline' become 'disaffected' and adopt the negative social role of 'old person'. Clearly the interaction between societal attitudes and individual identity construction and maintenance is complex. What is less conceptually problematic is the impact of negative social stereotypes upon the behaviour of individual elders. By accepting the negative stereotypes of ageing the older person may not seek help for a problem which he or she perceives as part of the ageing process but which, in fact, may be the early manifestation of disease. A feeling of tiredness may be viewed as part of normal ageing and not as a symptom of anaemia; painful joints may be disregarded as 'ageing' and not as symptoms of arthritis. Older people may not claim all the welfare benefits to which they are entitled because they perceive old age as a time of poverty or not engage in social activities because they see old age as a time of social isolation and loneliness and that 'disengagement' is the route to 'successful' ageing. It remains to be seen if future generations of elders will accept these labels and expectations or will generate a different response to the negative attitudes they will inevitably encounter.

Individual images of ageing

We each hold an 'image' of ourselves and this is linked with our notion of 'self' which is discussed later in this chapter. These images are important, for identity is based upon self-identity, how we think of others and how others actually see us. Our self-image is based upon a number of attributes, which we ascribe to ourselves such as intelligence, good looks, a caring nature or a short temper. This sense of self-image and identity is reinforced by interaction with others in our social environment and with the wider social context. Hence, if we function within a context that has predominantly a negative view of old age and older people, then such 'negative' views will rub off on us and thereby influence how we think, act and feel.

There are many aspects of 'self-image'. One important aspect of self-image is (subjective) age identity. Subjective age identity relates to how old a person feels and what broad age group, such as teenagers or the middle aged, an individual identifies with as opposed to his or her 'objective' or actual chronological age. Although the link between biological ageing and chronological age is far from perfect, we tend to use chronological age as a 'proxy' for biological status. However, people over these marker ages may reject labels such as 'old', perhaps because of the negativity and 'social redundancy' implicit within such terms; this is hardly surprising. 'I didn't feel old' is a refrain heard frequently from people of a 'certain age' and that people of advanced chronological age continue to define themselves as young or middle aged and the dissonance between chronological age and 'perceived' age seems to increase as people grow older. Given the widespread currency of the negative stereotypes of old age it is, perhaps, surprising that any survey respondents define themselves as old for this is to accept the stigma associated with what Goffman (1968) termed a 'spoilt identity'. More recent work by Kaufman and Elder (2002) suggests that, in the minds of the American population, 'old age' now starts at 74: this represents an increase of a decade from the pioneering study of Neugarten (1974). Hence 70 is the new 60! This serves to illustrate how the cultural and social meaning of particular chronological ages changes over time and are subject to almost constant reinterpretation and redefinition. Again, we can only speculate as to how age identity varies across the social classes, between men and women and, most fascinatingly between different minority groups (and cultures). Will this upward drift in the 'onset' of old age accelerate with the ageing of the baby boomers?

Kaufman and Elder (2002) looked at the link between age identity, chronological age, and the age respondents 'would like to be' (desired age). They report that most of their respondents felt 'younger' than their chronological age and 'desired' to be younger still. Interestingly these authors report that the strongest correlate of subjective age was the age 'other' people thought they were rather than chronological age. Although there is a potential degree of circularity in this argument it does provide an important link with the notion that how we see ourselves is greatly influenced by how others see us.

What conditions or circumstances influence people to adopt (or reject) a particular age identity? What factors precipitate the move from youth to middle age? What precipitates the dropping of the label 'middle aged' and the adoption of the identity of an older person? These may be broadly grouped into two sets of factors: physical health status (specific health problems, perceived physical and mental decline, illness of spouse) and changes in social role (retirement, bereavement, change in social contacts), dominate the definition of age identity and the transition from an identity of 'middle aged' to the acceptance of the label 'old'. Health, activity and changes in social roles appear to be the most important parameters defining age identity (Thompson *et al.*, 1990). Those in good health (or who perceive their health as good), or with high activity levels, continue to perceive themselves as middle aged. Often older people can identify a particular incident such as a fall, stroke or heart attack which made them feel that they were growing old and trigger the transition into another 'age-identity category'. However health problems need not be acute to bring about a feeling of ageing. Tiring easily, or difficulties in driving or walking, or untoward events such as falls may be frequent small reminders to people that they are not as young and fit as they once were. However, such observations are not exclusive to elders and may apply equally well to athletes who may observe such deterioration in 'fitness' in their thirties As we shall see in a later section, comparisons can be made with 'less fortunate' individuals or groups that make our 'downward' trend seem much less problematic.

Why is health linked to age identification? Two factors would seem to explain this interrelationship – body image and physical activity. First, health and body image are inextricably linked. Body image and appearance are in turn linked to images of youth and ageing. Appearance is obviously an important part of our personal identity. The manifestation of grey hair or wrinkles may be the first signs of ageing observed by an individual. Second, health is linked with physical activity. The inability to pursue what the individual perceives as normal activities may stimulate the development of a new sense of age identity that of an older person and the adoption of the roles and behaviour deemed 'appropriate' for an older person. The ability to perform daily activities, both physical and social, is seen as an important element of the lay definitions of 'health'. The tensions imposed upon self-identity have been termed the 'mask of ageing' (Featherstone and Hepworth, 1989, 1995; Hepworth, 1991). Over time the failing body becomes a trap from which a youth-identity cannot escape. This is another negative perspective which sees the maintenance of the body as the only way to liberate the young person trapped inside. Feminist scholars have started to develop these issues further by examining the role of gender within the context of notions of bodily decline and failure (Twigg, 2004).

Role changes such as retirement and widowhood are the second major group of factors linked to the adoption of the identity of 'old age'. Retirement is an unambiguous change of role, which indicates a shift of identity from economic independence and autonomy to financial dependence upon either the state or other forms of income provision. This is a crucial transition in a society, which is strongly influenced by notions of economic independence. Women who have not been formally employed in the labour market reject the label 'retired' as for them it has no real meaning. For this group of women, widowhood and other family events such as the arrival of grandchildren or great-grandchildren seem more important as markers of old age. Retirement and widowhood have some similarities in that they are both rites of passage, are suggestive of a change in status from independent to dependent, may be linked with an implied lack of fitness and declining health and often bring about a reduction in income. The most important aspects in the self-perception of ageing and changes in age identity are related to health, physical activity, chronological age, retirement and widowhood. At first sight these parameters seem to have little in common, but these factors all relate to implied changes in the individual's normal pattern of living. The onset of a disabling illness, retirement or the death of a spouse are all events which are suggestive of major changes in the lifestyle of the individual. The adjustment necessary to cope with these changes may stimulate the reassessment of subjective age identity and provoke the transition between age groups. This is an area of gerontological research where our evidence and empirical base is rather slim. It is clear that there is considerable scope for further research by looking at variations within the older age. It seems very unlikely that there is a homogeneous experience in this aspect of ageing and factors such as gender, class and ethnicity are undoubtedly important and define one of the most challenging research agendas for our developing subject.

Psychological perspectives on ageing and later life

Although there is some general agreement on the biological changes which accompany ageing and may be manifest in the 'post-mature' individual, such as decreased lung capacity, there is little agreement about the psychological and mental health dimensions of ageing. As with physical status the popular image of psychological health in old age is one of gradual, but inevitable and universal, decline. There is a very common assumption that, as one ages, we change and rarely are such changes seen as positive. Such psychological changes are usually conceptualised as being wholly negative. If we do change as we age then it is presumed that we will become cantankerous, unable to learn and with no capacity for personal positive development or growth. How valid are such assumptions?

In the very broadest terms psychology may be defined as the science of the mind and of human behaviour. The psychological perspective upon ageing has focused upon three main areas: first, cognitive function, intelligence and the impact of ageing upon these types of mental abilities, second, 'self' and personality studies, and third, issues of mental health where there is a clear link to the medical aspects of ageing. In this section we examine the evidence for these first two areas of interest. The mental health aspects of later life are dealt with in the later sections.

Cognitive function and ageing

Perhaps two of the most pervasive stereotypes of old age and later life are that as we age we become forgetful and lose our memory and that the old cannot learn. Indeed this presents both a very negative image for the old age that most of us will experience and, also, perhaps encapsulates our own individual fears as to what we are likely to experience in old age. The stereotype described earlier conflates two distinct but related aspects of cognitive function: learning and memory and these need to be differentiated, although in practice such distinctions are not always clear. Learning relates to the acquisition of new information or skills while memory relates to their retention for use in the future. Examining the impact of ageing upon these two aspects of intellectual functioning is challenging both in methodological and conceptual terms. Taken together these two dimensions link to cognitive functioning which may be most easily summarised as being concerned with 'problem solving' or as the mental capacity to function as a 'competent' individual within the social context. Such skills are clearly important as they link with the ability of the individual to maintain themselves in the community via the performance of key everyday tasks. Such abilities are, however, also constantly being challenged, for all of us, as society becomes more complex and requires new skills to cope with the demands and developments of everyday life.

Before considering the substantive findings in terms of cognition and ageing it is important to consider the methodological challenges which this particular area of gerontological study faces. There are clearly important issues concerned with study design that need to be examined before we consider the substantive evidence. The identification of age differences in intellectual function does not reflect, necessarily, the process of ageing as most of the data are based upon cross-sectional research designs. Cross-sectional studies, which show decreased intellectual functioning with age, may well just reflect differences in levels of education between different cohorts. In Britain older people were educated within a very different educational environment, the emphasis being upon basic literacy and numeracy; most people left school at the age of 14. As with other aspects of the study of ageing it is often difficult to distinguish age, period and cohort effects when considering cognition and ageing. Data from the Seattle Longitudinal Study of Aging (Schaie, 1996) offers an insight to just how important cohort effects may be to understanding apparent age-related declines in cognitive function. Using a variety of different measures of cognition, Schaie (1996) demonstrates marked positive increases in levels of functioning across cohorts in three types of tasks (inductive reasoning, verbal meaning and spatial orientation) while there are decreases for two other measures (number skills and word fluency). Regardless of issues of generalisability of the detailed findings to different cultures and populations these findings demonstrate the importance differences between cohorts will have upon apparently 'age-related' differences in cognitive function and ability. As such they illustrate the bundle of different skills and competencies included with the term 'cognitive function' and illustrate the enormous methodological difficulties experience when trying to undertake research in this area.

Some studies have shown a decreased performance in intelligence tests and psychomotor tests with age. The status of these kinds of finding remains highly contentious. This is a highly complex area of social investigation in which the methodology of the experiment used has great influence upon the resultant outcome. Identification of age-based differences in intelligence is rarely based on longitudinal studies. Evidence to support age-related decline in intelligence is often based on cross-sectional designs, so the influence of cohort effects of education levels cannot be discounted. It could be that intelligence itself does not change with age but that the skills and information held by older people has become obsolete and are not being tested accurately in the types of studies typically undertaken by psychologists. Similarly it may be that, although older people do not perform tasks which measure learning as well as younger subjects, their capacity to learn may be just as acute. We might speculate that in 'test' situations older people may sacrifice speed for accuracy, perhaps reflecting their general feelings of inadequacy and implicit adoption of negative stereotypes concerning their ability. The quality of the samples used in research, which has looked at changes in intellectual functioning with age, requires critical examination. Volunteer samples drawn from the wives of Oxford professors tell us little about the normal course of development of psychological functioning with age. We should also question very closely the relevance of findings from the laboratory and experiment environments when making inferences about psychological development or cognitive function in the 'real world'.

Given these important methodological caveats what do we know about the relationship between cognitive function and ageing? This statement implies that there is a single entity that we can loosely define as 'cognitive' function. This is, of course, a gross oversimplification. Cognitive function is a multidimensional concept that consists of numerous different components such as memory and verbal function. Baltes (1993) offers a model of how to overcome the seemingly impossible complexity of studying ageing and cognition by offering two broad categories of activities. He distinguishes between 'fluid' intelligence, which describes basic information processing processes such as reasoning, memory and attention, from 'crystallised' or 'pragmatic' intelligence, which describes the kind of knowledge accumulated across the lifecourse as a result of education, employment and 'life experience'. Baltes (1993) argues that 'fluid' intelligence starts to decline in early adulthood, although the precise age is subject to considerable debate (Schaie, 1996), while 'pragmatic' intelligence remains more stable and certainly appears to be stable until individuals are in their seventh decade. This offers some insight into the complexity of the entire area of cognition and ageing and leads us to be highly suspicious of apparently simple and unambiguous research findings that argue that cognitive function does/does not change as we age. Again we can see that, with age, some aspects of cognition may decline while others remain stable: it is clearly a highly complex area of research and we should be wary of oversimplified generalisations. It would seem likely that, within this area, there are also important variations with factors such as class, gender and ethnicity which have not yet been fully explored.

On selected measures of cognitive function older people do demonstrate lower levels of performance than younger people do. If we accept these 'deficits' as 'real' this provokes a further question of can such losses or deficits be reversed by intervention or are such declines inevitable? According to Marsiske *et al.* (1998) there is a remarkable degree of consistency across the research evidence which indicates that performance on certain cognitive function tasks can be improved with practice, training and a variety of different interventions. This is true also of other age groups. Children approaching various types of school exams are given practice for non-verbal reasoning papers for precisely this reason. Familiarity with the task improves performance and the observed gains can be maintained for fairly long periods of time. Hence 'improvements' in cognitive and psychological tasks observed in longitudinal studies may simple reflect the 'training' and experience of participants with the tests included in the studies. Similar improvements in the domain of memory have been documented although the benefits do not appear to be maintained for such long periods. Taken together these consistent patterns of results indicate that cognition is a much more 'plastic' concept and that declines or deficits, at least in certain tasks or activities, can be remedied by appropriate interventions. Current evidence indicates that ageing does not bring about inevitable and profound declines in mental ability. Older people can learn and improve their intellectual functioning given the right sort of educational programmes and stimulating settings or environments. Is it any wonder that older people show declines in cognition when they are removed from the labour market and other arenas of social stimulation and left to exist in a 'twilight' world heavily influenced by the remnants of disengagement theory. In particular, older people learn best in a non-threatening environment in which they can regain confidence in their own abilities. The increasing popularity of the University of the Third Age in a variety of countries testifies to the general high level of intellectual functioning and desire for education among many older people.

Given the best available evidence it seems clear that there is no single clear universal pattern to describe both intellectual performance in old age or changes to this with age. Furthermore it is clear that there are enormous differences between individuals and the subgroups within the older population. There is an extensive research agenda to be addressed considering how factors such as gender, class and ethnicity influence cognitive functioning in later life. It seems highly unlikely, given everything else that we know about later life, that the pattern of cognitive functioning is going to be universal and homogeneous experience across the older population. There are further sets of research questions that also require consideration and these relate to the link between cognitive function/change and the ability of older people to live within the community. Even when some degree of intellectual decline is found, the influence this has upon the ability of that person to exist in the community has rarely been explicitly established. How do declines in, for example, performance on specific tests of verbal reasoning translate into the ability of an older person (or indeed person from another age group) to reside successfully in the community and to undertake basic (and advanced) activities of daily living? How does cognitive function promote independence and how do cognitive changes compromise this (and what interventions might promote or restore independent living?). At what point in the 'cognitive decline' slope is the ability of the individual to live within the community and function appropriately compromised? These are issues which have been much more rarely addressed. Yet it seems self-evident that research into cognitive ability and ageing needs to be embedded and understood within the contexts within which people live their lives. Evidence presented earlier suggested that 'pragmatic' intelligence was maintained at a fairly high level at least up until the seventh decade. From this measure, which looks at experience, we might expect older people to continue to function well on everyday daily living tasks in which they have extensive experience. To try to tap this perhaps more relevant aspect of cognitive function measures of practical problem solving have been developed by psychologists. These seem to demonstrate the maintenance of high levels of functioning for many tasks but possible decreases for tasks which ask participants to respond to situations of change such as dealing with challenges arising from widowhood such as having to cook or change fuses and undertake minor tasks of domestic maintenance.

Overall the situation with regard to cognitive function and its relationship with age is far from clear and almost certainly demonstrates variation within the subgroups that make up the older population. Certainly we can be confident that the presumption of a universal, age-related and irreversible decrease in cognitive ability is an untrue stereotype and a gross oversimplification of a very complex set of relationships and interactions. The term 'cognitive function' is a portmanteau one that includes a multitude of different domains. In some areas older people do show lower levels of performance compared with younger people, especially in the area of 'fluid' intelligence while in the more experience-based elements such differences are much less evident. It is also very clear that there are very profound differences in intellectual function between different birth cohorts that reflect the differing educational and other societal experiences of differing groups. It also appears that, in some circumstances, where cognitive deficits or declines have been identified then this can be 'reversed' by appropriate interventions. Furthermore there is a need for much greater research looking at how cognitive ability links with the capacity of older people to remain active and independent within the community and to develop interventions to promote and enhance this.

Self, personality and 'successful' ageing

The study of notions of self and personality are central to the academic discipline of psychology and, as noted earlier, the conceptualisation of ourselves is a key component of 'social identity', but a detailed exploration of notions of self and personality and how they relate to ageing is beyond the scope of this book. Yet some limited consideration of these issues is required in order to consider the veracity of stereotypes that ageing 'changes' peoples' personality so that older people become 'set in their ways' and are in some very tangible way different from their 'younger selves' (and where the change is not a positive one of growth and development). Furthermore if we change as we age, what factors prompt such changes and could we develop interventions to promote positive rather than negative psychological changes.

Concepts of self and personality are difficult to define and conceptualisations of personality vary within the differing schools of psychological theories. At the most basic level the concept of personality may be considered as consisting of a variety of different traits. These are stable, long-term elements of personality that characterise a particular individual. The importance of particular traits in defining the personality of an individual is evident in popular discourse. Frequently we describe our friends, relatives and colleagues in terms of personality traits. How often do we remark, 'David is such a pessimist!' The precise traits that comprise personality are subject to considerable debate within the differing schools of psychology. This is not a debate that it is appropriate to enter here. Costa and McCrae (1988) argue that there are five major personality traits that have been consistently identified across a wide variety of tests, settings and participants. These are neuroticism, extraversion, openness, agreeableness and conscientiousness. We use the exemplar of conscientiousness to illustrate the debate about personality and ageing and to try to locate this within a broader social context. Each major personality trait is present within us to varying degrees. We may be highly conscientious, totally unconscientious or somewhere in between. Reflection upon the characteristics of our family, friends and colleagues demonstrates the varying degrees to which this personality trait is present. As we move across the lifecourse the domains within which these attributes are manifest may change. A school child or student may demonstrate the trait of conscientiousness in the way they approach their studies. An athlete may be a conscientious trainer, while an older person may demonstrate conscientiousness by providing reliable care for young grandchildren. This exercise demonstrates one of the important aspects of the concept of personality traits in that they are based upon the comparison between individuals. Labelling of someone as highly conscientious means that they are conscientious in comparison to others. There are few absolutes in psychology. The consensus of empirical psychology is that personality, as measured in terms of the major traits appears remarkably stable across the lifecourse, even given the changes in individual experience across the lifecourse. Hence, perhaps, the emphasis is upon the continuity of personality into later life. A grumpy young person may well turn into a grumpy old person! The notion of a fairly stable personality across the life course makes sense intuitively; if our traits were not fairly stable then they would not be good descriptors of our personalities.

Viewed from another perspective, this notion of essential personality stability can be a rather gloomy conclusion. If our traits are 'fixed and stable' this might imply that there is no potential for growth across the lifecourse and this is both a rather gloomy prospect and rather deterministic. Most psychologists recognise that, within a broad framework of a stable personality trait structure, individuals can and do change across the lifecourse. So, for example, the person with a high degree of conscientiousness can learn to become less so (and vice versa). Such changes usually reflect a process of learning and growth for, in order for such changes to be manifest, the individual must both recognise the nature of their own personality and be prepared to work towards modifying the particular dimension identified. As we grow older there are many factors that may well prompt modifications of our basic personality structure such as changes in our social or physical environment and the changes taking place to our own bodies. One of the major challenges of old age is the way that individuals respond to profound social and personal changes such as widowhood. How individuals react, or adapt, to such changes probably reflects how well they have adapted to changes experienced in earlier phases of the lifecycle. It is important not to forget that older people have a 'history' and this may well be highly influential in how they respond to the changes and challenges that may accompany ageing and later life.

'Ageing and the self'

The concept of 'the self' is central to the study of psychology. Embedded within this simple phrase is a concept of fearsome complexity, which is extremely difficult to define and study. At the most basic the notion of selfhood embraces the concept of 'who I am'. This is a manifestation of the integration of beliefs, behaviours and emotion; it is a representation of our (social) identity. There are, again, differing views as to notions of selfhood. It is now probably accepted that selfhood is a multidimensional concept and is most frequently conceptualised as a knowledge-based system in which our life experiences are organised. There are differing labels applied to these systems of knowledge organisation but they all contain the notions that they contain details of what we think and care about and what we spent time and energy upon and what domains are important to us (work, family, leisure, etc.). Personality is one element of the self but is probably the most widely researched. Hence personality characteristics are an element of selfhood (I am conscientious) alongside other factors such as demographic characteristics (I am a woman), social roles (I am a mother, I am a wife), work roles (I am a scholar), interests (I am a marathon runner) and political beliefs (I am a socialist) among other attributes. Selfhood contains notions of who we were (I was an international swimmer), our current self and potential future selves. It also contains functional aspects concerned with the organisation of experience, the regulation of experience and motivation.

Like personality the notion of self is both constant and dynamic. This apparent tautology may be best illustrated by thinking about how our notions of self may change in the future. Our potential future self (usually referred to as future selves) includes what we hope to incorporate into our lives (positive future selves) and negative or feared aspects of the self to come. For example, in the future we may hope to incorporate into our selfhood the roles of spouse, parent or grandparent or have fears such as widowhood, bereavement, ill health or financial insecurity. Another aspect of the changing notions of self, and one which is central to the notion of 'successful ageing', is that of flexible goal adjustment. In setting goals (or aspirations both positive and negative) for our future selves we may well influence current goals and behaviours. For example, if we 'aspire' or set as a goal a 'healthy' old age (or the avoidance of an 'unhealthy' old age) we may engage in current activities and behaviours orientated towards that objective such as not smoking, eating a balanced diet and taking regular exercise. Some social theorists have argued that as we age, we drop various goals or domains in which we are active (another manifestation of the notion of disengagement). Such reductions may be very depressing and achievable only if we reconceptualise their meaning (as in 'Oh well that really wasn't very important to me'). A rather more positive way of looking at goal readjustment across the lifecourse is the concept of flexible goal adjustment (also known as secondary control). This thesis argues that as we age we let go of some goals and redefine others. For example, an international swimmer is unlikely to remain at the elite level for more than a few years, but if swimming and competition remain important to the self-identity of the individual, this thesis suggests that the individual will specify new goals. Instead of 'I want to participate in the Olympic Games or I want to be the best butterfly swimmer in Britain' they may substitute 'I want to participate in Masters swimming competitions', 'I want to set a world record for my age group' or 'I still want to complete 200m butterfly without being disqualified for an illegal stroke!' Such modified goals enable older athletes to remain positive about their activity although objective performance, as measured by the stopwatch, has 'declined'. A similar type of proposition is that, as we age, we alter the standards with which we compare ourselves. We may make comparisons of either an upward or downward variety (i.e. to those who are better or worse off than ourselves). It has been suggested that older people are more likely to make 'downward' social comparisons in order to accentuate the limited 'positive' aspects of their social circumstances, rather than comparing themselves with those who are 'better off' in terms of health material and other types of resources. By such mechanisms, it is argued, the apparent contradiction of a 'stable self and personality' is maintained within a constantly changing social and physical context.

Well-being in later life: perceptions of health status

In Chapter 5 we considered the physical aspects of the health status of older people. In this section we consider how older people evaluate their own health status. This is often termed 'subjective' health status and 'subjective' health rating; however, the use of the term 'subjective' implicitly carries with it notions of inaccuracy and impressionism as compared with the 'objective rigour' of medical diagnosis and/or reliable/valid symptom or health status measures. How individuals feel about their own health status has a direct link with the illness model of health and offers another insight into the physical well-being of older people. There are a variety of different types of questions used to examine this aspect of health status and functional ability and such questions demonstrate aspects of both upward and downward comparisons.

Self-rated health status

Within many health surveys it is usual to find questions that ask respondents to evaluate their health as good, fair or poor in the last year (or a specified period before the interview) and, additionally, to compare themselves with other people of a similar age. These are two slightly different indices and invite both 'upward and downward' comparisons. The first is for an 'overall' global rating of health while the second is asking participants to compare their health with that of others of a similar age. Using data from the General Household Survey Table 6.1 indicates that, overall, about one-third of people aged 65+ rate their health as good, and the remaining two-thirds as

Table 6.1 Health rating in year prior to census, England and Wales, 2001 (%)

Age	Rating					
	Good health		Fairly good health		Not good health	
	M	F	M	F	M	F
65–74						
GHS	41	40	37	39	22	21
Census	42	39	39	38	19	23
75–84						
GHS	34	32	34	38	32	30
Census	32	30	43	44	25	26
85+						
GHS	22	26	47	38	31	36
Census	9	22	42	43	49	35

Source: ONS, 2003

fair or not good. Hence there is an approximate division into thirds. There is little gender variation in responses to these types of questions. Comparison of census and GHS data confirms the age-related decrease in health rating and the similarity of rating between the sources. This reflects the observation from Health Survey for England data that 52 per cent of those in care homes and 56 per cent of those in the community rate their health as very good or good and 11% of both groups rate it as poor. Given the profound differences in levels of chronic health and disability between these two groups, this is an intriguing observation. The group rating their health as 'fairly good' seems to remain fairly stable across the age groups; while there is a decrease in those rating their health as good, this is matched by an increase in those rating it as not good with increased age. Both GHS and HSE data suggest that there is an important class variation in responses to this question for older people living in the community. Health Survey for England reports differentials of 19 per cent for men and 13 per cent for women between manual and non-manual classes in the percentage rating their health as good.

Given the increased prevalence of chronic physical illness with age the increase in the percentage rating their health as poor with age is perhaps not surprising. Perhaps more surprising is that so few older people rate their health as not good in the face of the high incidence of chronic illness and impairments that afflict them. This anomaly probably reflects the highly subjective way we define and evaluate our own health status and reflects the influence of the group with whom we make comparisons for most people health does not mean the complete absence of symptoms or morbid conditions but rather that these do not significantly restrict social interaction or normal activity levels. Health status is very much seen as being able to fulfil social roles and functions. Additionally, health is relative to the expectations of the individual. A 'positive' evaluation of health may reflect the influence of downward comparisons of oneself with much less 'fortunate' people rather than 'upward' comparisons to a fit 20-something!

Comparing trends over time in how respondents answer such questions may offer some insight into the veracity of the compression of morbidity hypothesis. For those aged 65+ there seems to been remarkably little change in answers to this question (Table 6.2). In 1980 21 per cent of males and 26 per cent of females rated their health as not good compared with 25 per cent for both in 2001. For those rating their health as good the responses were 42 per cent males and 33 per cent females in 1980 and 38 per cent and 36 per cent respectively in 2001. Within this apparently broadly stable

Table 6.2 Trends in health rating of population aged 65+, Great Britain, 1980–2001 (%)

	Rating					
	Good health		Fairly good health		Not good health	
	M	F	M	F	M	F
1980	42	33	37	41	21	26
1985	44	38	35	37	21	25
1991	42	39	36	39	21	22
1998	42	37	37	38	21	25
2001	38	36	37	39	25	25

Source: Walker *et al.*, 2002

pattern, there may well be changes within specific groups. Over the period 1980–2001 women show evidence of having become more positive about their health status as illustrated by an increase in the percentage reporting their health as positive.

What factors may have brought about these intriguing changes that challenge our preconceptions that poor health is a universal and inevitable part of the experience of old age? Without further research interpretation of the changes noted above is problematic. The 'improvement' in the percentages rating their health as good may reflect a 'real improvement' in health status as more recent birth cohorts move into old age. For example, those aged 85+ in 1980 would have been born in 1895 (or earlier) compared with those aged 85+ in 2001 (born 1916 or earlier). This latter group have a very different life course compared with their Victorian predecessors, which may result in them experiencing a more healthy old age. Alternatively the 1916 cohort may have lower expectation of the likely health experience of later life (i.e. being satisfied with a lower level of health and making more downward comparisons when they respond to such questions) or indeed the observations noted in Table 6.2 may reflect some combination of both of these explanations and other factors. The complexities of the detailed changes noted above highlight some of the key issues that need to be addressed when considered the compression or expansion of morbidity hypotheses. The observation of detailed changes between people of different ages and sexes within an apparent pattern of no overall changes suggests that it is unlikely that either of these hypotheses would operate in a monolithic fashion. Rather it may well be the case that any benefits or disadvantages will be spread differentially across the distinct components of the older population thereby maintaining, and possibly accentuating, inequalities in health status characteristic of the younger age groups.

Another dimension of health status is concerned with expectations of health in old age. This relates to the evaluation of individuals as to whether their health status in later life has lived down (or up) to expectations and Bowling *et al.* (2002) have indicated that it is an important component of and predictor of quality of life in later life. Using data from a national survey we see that 31 per cent of elders report that their health was better than expected, 44 per cent that it met their expectations and for 27 per cent health in later life was worse than anticipated. There was no obvious relationship between either gender or age and 'health expectation'. However, this factor emerged as an independent vulnerability factor for the experience of loneliness in later life (Victor *et al.*, 2004). Clearly expectations of what old age (or other phases of the lifecycle) might be like will have an influence upon the quality of the experience and how this is evaluated by individuals.

Mental health in later life

As with any other age group within the population, older people suffer from a variety of different types of mental illnesses. While the gerontologist is keen to promote a 'positive' view of ageing and is often concerned with combating the most prevalent stereotypes and misconceptions of later life it would be foolish to argue that older people do not experience mental health problems. As with other groups within the population older people experience a range of mental health problems. Older people may experience a range of different types of mental health problems such as depression, anxiety or psychotic disorders such as schizophrenia. In experiencing these disorders the older population is little different from the younger age groups. Mental health problems such as depression or anxiety may represent a continuation of a previously established pattern of health problems or problems which present for the first time in later life. However, as the section on cognitive function indicated, there is a 'special' mental health issue that characterises the concern over mental well-being in later life and that is impaired cognitive function and dementing illnesses. Within the field of ageing and later life mental health problems, especially that of dementia, has been a major focus of research interest and activity and are a major source of concern for older people themselves (and their friends and relatives).

Dementia

Organic or biological disorders of the brain are often termed, rather pejoratively, 'senile dementia'. Organic states are often referred to as senility, a term which is both inaccurate and emotive and implies that progressive deterioration which accompanies the disorder is a normal part of ageing. It cannot be stressed too strongly that organic brain syndromes are not part of normal ageing but a specific disease process which, as yet, we cannot screen for or identify effectively, treat or reverse. This is a clear dimension of later life which is pathological and not a normal state that we can all expect to experience. Yet it is a prominent feature of the discourse of older people that memory loss is a part of 'normal' ageing. This is typified by comments such as 'what can you expect at my (his/her) age?' This group of disorders is chronic progressive degenerations of mental function due to vascular pathology (about 10–15 per cent), Alzheimer's disease (50 per cent) or some combination of the two (Kitwood, 1997). Although not exclusive to those aged 65+, especially with the recognition of AIDS-related dementia in younger people, these types of mental health problems are very much more common among older people (in a way which is not characteristic of conditions such as depression). Presenting symptoms for cognitive impairment include the 'classic' feature of 'memory loss/impairment' but also problems with language, motor functions, recognition and planning/organisation. So the concept of cognitive impairment is very much broader than 'simple' loss of memory. Indeed Kitwood (1997) would argue that some degree of memory loss/impairment, in the absence of the other symptoms, may be relatively benign. However, the combination of memory loss with other manifestations of the disease, such as language and ability to organise and plan is a major threat to the independence of older people and compromises their ability to live in the community.

The use of labels and diagnostic categories is clearly very important in any area of medicine. However, perhaps, in the area of categorising cognitive function it is of special importance. In proffering a diagnosis of dementia we are not simply labelling the 'brain' of the individual but categorising the individual and, by association, their carers, family and friends. The topic of cognitive impairment illustrates changes in the use of language to define and classify individuals. As noted above, until very recently, cognitive impairment was referred to as 'senile dementia'. However, in our more 'enlightened' times such terminology would be considered inappropriate, disrespectful and demeaning. The term 'cognitive function' has attracted less widespread use. Rather the discourse concerning dementia has, as Kitwood (1997), notes 'Alzheimerised'. Rather than refer to (senile) dementia, discourse is largely conducted in terms of Alzheimer's disease. Kitwood (1997) observes that this change can be seen in the growth of charitable or lobby groups dedicated to this issue and with the relabelling of dementia to Alzheimer's disease. This he suggests reflects a desire by clinicians to attract research funding: if an entity is labelled as a specific disease, this holds out the hope of a cure, however slim. He also suggests that the use of the term 'Alzheimer's disease' as a global term to refer to all dementias reflects, if not a desire to promote a more positive view of old age, then a desire to remove some of the more stigmatising consequences of cognitive impairment and to emphasise the pathological nature of this problem.

Diagnosing dementia in an individual is challenging whether one is using clinical judgement or the various psychological tests available or more recently established brain-scanning techniques. Given the difficulties inherent in reaching an individual diagnosis epidemiological work in this area is clearly complex. Researching the 'true' prevalence of cognitive impairment within the population is both methodologically and conceptually challenging. It is self-evident that cognitive functioning is best described as a continuum. Identifying the point along this 'line' that defines impairment is clearly problematic. Studies of dementia have produced widely varying prevalence estimates from 3 per cent to 60 per cent reflecting variations in the measurement method, the nature of the population studied, such as the inclusion of only those living in the community and the study response rates (cognitively impaired people being less likely to participate).

Dementia is an example of a disease with a low mortality and high morbidity profile. In 2001 in England and Wales there were 4792 deaths of people aged 65+ attributed directly to dementia – this represents less than 1 per cent of deaths in this age group. Hence if we took mortality as our key source of information then dementia and cognitive impairment would not be very significant health problems for the older population. Based upon a variety of studies there is a general consensus that about 3 per cent of the population aged 65+ suffer from clinically significant dementia (Fratiglioni *et al.*, 1999; Lobo *et al.*, 2000; Wimo *et al.*, 2003). This is very similar to the prevalence of 2 per cent reported by the Health Survey for England. Worldwide Wimo *et al.* (2003) estimate that there are approximately 25 million people with dementia, of whom 52 per cent are in the less developed regions, and this is projected to increase to 114 million in 2050. Fratiglioni *et al.* (1999) suggest, upon the basis of a meta-analysis, that the prevalence of dementia is remarkably consistent across different countries and, that where differences are observed, these are an artefact of methodological differences, rather than an indication of differences in the natural history of the disease. There is consistent evidence that the vast majority of dementia, in the age range sixties to seventies, is of the Alzheimer's disease type rather than vascular dementia. It is also suggested that vascular dementia may not show the same age-related increase of Alzheimer's disease. It is, however, much more difficult to establish the prevalence of mild impairment because of the difficulty of designing sufficiently sensitive and robust research tools to identify the condition. Indeed, if mild impairment does not disrupt social functioning and there is no cure for dementia, then there may be little point in pursuing this particular group.

The prevalence of dementia is one condition that varies considerably according to the population studied. In the community setting rates of dementia remain low but in the care setting the prevalence estimates are extremely high (given that cognitive impairment is a major reason for entry into care). Health Survey for England data suggest that, excluding those who could not participate, 33 per cent of care home residents had significant cognitive impairment while 17 per cent were borderline impairment. Perhaps more than any other aspect of the health status of older people, the population surveyed is a key influence upon the dementia prevalence estimates generated.

In addition to knowing how many individuals have the disease at a given point in time, we also need to establish the number of new cases or incidence of dementia. Clearly incidence and prevalence are linked in establishing the burden of any disease within a given population. For a given location and time period how many new cases are developing? Again, to some degree the answer to this question is highly influenced by the population studied and the methods used. Given the usual methodological caveats, Aronson *et al.* (1991) suggest that the 'all cause' dementia incidence rate is 3.4 per cent per annum and identified age-specific incidence rates ranging from 1.3% per year for those aged 75–79 to 6 per cent for those aged 85 years and over. These rates are very comparable to those suggested by Fratiglioni *et al.* (1999) of 0.4 to 0.8 per 1000 for those aged 60–64 to 49.8–135.7 per 1000 for those aged 95+.

Like most diseases dementia is not 'equally' distributed across the older population. Rather the disease shows a marked concentration among particular groups. Regardless of the population studied or the methodology used, prevalence is clearly age related and prevalence rates approximately double every five to six years (Victor, 1997). Among those 85 years and over, 15–20 per cent may experience some degree of organic brain failure. However, this may not necessarily be to such an extent that it impairs their ability to function normally in the community. Although dementia is clearly age related it is far from universal even in the very oldest age groups. Given the highly age-related nature of dementia simple demography means that there are more women than men who have dementia, but this just reflects the fact that there are more old women than old men. Are women more 'at risk' of dementia? Gender differences are minimal, when the effect of age is taken out. Kitwood (1997) notes that vascular pathology may be commoner in men and Alzheimer's in women. He also suggests that whereas the risk of developing Alzheimer's may 'peak' in the mid-eighties, the risk of developing vascular dementia continues to increase with age. The relationship with class is not entirely clear despite high-profile cases such as Iris Murdoch and Ronald Reagan.

Application of these data to the population of the United Kingdom serves to demonstrate the large number of people with this disease. If we use the consensus prevalence of 5 per cent of those aged 65+ based upon Health Survey for England data suggesting the prevalence of cognitive impairment at 3 per cent and 'borderline' impairment at 2 per cent then there are approximately 560,460 people with this condition in England and Wales. If we presume an annual incidence rate of 3 per cent then there will be 280,230 new cases annually.

Functional or affective disorders in later life

The study of mental (ill) health in later life shows a preoccupation with dementia and, more broadly, cognitive impairment. Such an emphasis reflects the devastating effects for individuals, families and society as a whole of this condition. However, this has, perhaps, been at the expense of a more broad-ranging and comprehensive examination of the mental health of older people and with a wider range of disorders which can have equally devastating impact upon the quality of life of individuals (and their families). Functional or affective disorders comprise a variety of states such as anxiety, depression and disturbances of mood and these have attracted much less attention from those concerned with the mental health of older people. Yet such disorders present significant problems, for both individuals and populations, and seriously compromise the quality of life and well-being of older people. Unlike dementia, however, these are conditions for which treatment, both pharmacological and behavioural, can bring positive benefits. Hence there is considerable benefit in being able to identify and treat older people with such conditions.

What is depression?

As with the other chronic physical conditions, disability and dementia the definition of depression remains a challenge, irrespective of the population/group that forms the focus of the investigation. Depression is a term that is regularly used in popular discourse to describe the characteristics of individuals. We regularly describe members of our families, ourselves and our friends as 'being depressed'. Over our life we all experience periods of sadness or upset that may make us feel 'depressed' but usually such episodes are short lived and resolved. How then do we distinguish 'normal' feelings of sadness from depression? Mann (2001) suggests that there are at least three possible categorisations of depression in later life (and this typology probably applies to those of other age groups). The most broad and wide ranging, inclusive definition of depression is concerned with depressive symptomatology. This state is defined by the possession by individuals of a variety of depressive symptoms such as worry or sleeplessness. Less inclusive and more restrictive is the concept of depressive syndrome. This is defined by the possession of a greater number of symptoms, experienced at a more severe level and for greater duration. This is the level at which Mann (2001) argues that quality of life and daily activity start to be compromised and is the threshold for treatment, although not necessarily with drugs. Major depression is the most extreme form of the condition and is made by clinical diagnosis based upon severity and duration of symptoms and treatment is almost always pharmacological.

As with other age groups, the prevalence of depression within the older age groups is contingent upon the definition used and the method used to operationalise this definition. Based upon studies in the Gospel Oak district of North London, Mann (2001) argues that up to 30–40 per cent of older people report the existence of depressive symptoms, while 12 per cent could be classified as having depressive syndrome and only a small minority, 1–2 per cent, 'major' depression. Marmot *et al.* (2003) report that approximately 25 per cent of the English Longitudinal Study of Ageing sample exhibit depressive symptoms. They also confirm that basic epidemiology of depression with increases in age and a higher prevalence among women. However, as with cognitive impairment, comparisons across studies are problematic because of the highly variable nature of the measures used and the case definition thresholds. Applying these prevalence rates to the 8.8 million people aged 65+ in the United Kingdom suggests that there are between 2.6 million and 3.5 million people with depressive symptoms, 1 million with depressive syndrome and 88,010 to 176,020 with major depression. Again, this is clearly a very significant public health issue and a major source of the 'disease burden' experience by older people.

Understanding the nature of depression in later life is problematic as, like many physical illnesses, we do not easily know from epidemiological studies whether this is a 'first' episode of depression or a recurrence/continuation of an illness experienced earlier in the lifecourse. When viewed from a lifecourse perspective Gatz *et al.* (1996) argue that depressive symptamology varies being highest in young or very late adulthood and decreasing in the middle years. It is not clear if severe or clinical depression follows this trajectory and when considering depression in later life we probably need to distinguish cases which represent a recurrence from earlier phases of life and new episodes of 'late-onset depression'. Furthermore, there are difficulties in diagnosing depression in older people because a considerable number of the diagnostic signs and symptoms such as weight loss, cognitive difficulties, negative mood or withdrawal may have plausible 'physical' explanations or reflect a response to losses such as bereavement (i.e. they constitute reactive or situational depression).

Given these caveats concerning definition and measurement, what is the patterning of depression within the older population and does it vary from that characteristic of younger ages? Furthermore does the prevalence of depression increase in old age? There seems to be a consensus among clinicians that clinically diagnosed depression does not increase in later life, although there is some evidence that more expansive definitions (such as depressive symptomatology) do increase as does secondary depression. Harris *et al.* (2003) report that the predictors of depression for older people are dominated by disability and health conditions. Those with poor physical health are at considerably elevated risk of experiencing depression. Adjusting for disability weakened the relationship with gender and eradicated the link with age. Hence it seems that it is not age per se that is linked with depression but the associated disability. Poor perception of social support and low socio-economic status were also linked with depression. Hence social factors can clearly mediate the experience of depression in later life.

Suicide in later life

One clear manifestation of psychological ill health is suicidal behaviour as manifested by both attempted suicide (parasuicide) and 'successful' suicide or intentional self-harm. The most obvious link with suicide or parasuicide is depression. Slater (1995) suggests that up to 70 per cent of suicides are committed by people with depression. Data upon the prevalence of parasuicide and its relationship with age are not readily available. Slater (1995) suggests that older people make fewer 'token' attempts at suicide and give fewer 'warnings' of their intentions and are more likely to be successful than younger people.

Mortality reports regularly publish details of deaths from intentional self-harm for all ages. However, these statistics must be interpreted with some caution for not all cases of death by self-harm include a category of intentional self-harm plus cases where the intent was unclear. In 2002, in England and Wales there were 3319 deaths from deliberate self-harm and 4773 cases where intent was unclear. Overall, 66 per cent of deaths from intentional self-harm are accounted for by those aged 65+. Older males account for 65 per cent of self-harm deaths in this age group. This predominance of males in the successful suicide category represents a combination of a pattern demonstrated by those of younger ages. Absolute levels of suicide among those aged 65+ are high in relative terms. Suicide among older people has declined over the period 1950–1998 (Gunnell *et al.*, 2003). In 1950 men aged 60+ had the highest rates of suicide at 41 per 1,000,000; by 1998 this had declined and men aged 25–34 had the highest overall rates. Similar decreases in suicide rates have been observed for older women. Gunnell *et al.* (2003) speculate that such decreases in suicide among older people may reflect improved living standards and better treatment for depression while we may speculate that the increase in suicide among younger people reflects an increase in social disengagement and attachment to society.

Psychosocial well-being

Another widely used measure of the general psychosocial well-being of older people is the General Health Questionnaire (GHQ). This comes in a variety of forms and is widely used in population-based surveys as it is deemed more 'acceptable' to study respondents than some of the more explicit depression measures. This measure does have its limitations because of the potential influence of physical health symptoms on respondents' answers to several of the questions. The distribution of this measure shows a similar pattern to that for depression. Overall 14 per cent of the general population illustrate poor psychological well-being compared with 26 per cent in care homes. Disability is the strongest predictor of GHQ score of poor psychological health with 5 per cent of those 'not disabled' having poor psychological health compared with 36 per cent of those with severe disability. It seems likely that the links between GHQ score and age/gender are largely 'artefacts' of the influence of disability. The availability of powerful data analysis packages means that we can now look critically at some of the links between age and gender and various aspects of later life. As with the case of depression and GHQ score gender-related patterns of social isolation and loneliness are removed when the confounding influence of widowhood and bereavement are taken into account (Victor *et al.*, 2004). Hence we may have to reconsider many of the previously gender-related aspects of later life.

Conclusion

In this chapter we have considered images of ageing at two levels of analysis: the individual and the societal. At the individual level each of us has an image of ourselves. One aspect of this is our subjective age identity, or how old we think we are as distinct from our actual chronological age. As we move through the life course our subjective age identity changes in response to changes in our social environment. Empirical studies indicate that the adoption of the age identity of 'old' is prompted by changes in physical health status or social role such as retirement or bereavement which result in people having to alter their lifestyle. However, other dimensions of self-image such as personality seem to remain remarkably constant over the lifecourse. Individuals who have been friendly and outgoing during their younger years will probably maintain these characteristics as they age. Thus we should not see later life as bringing about enormous changes in the self-image of people. Rather, old age should be seen as the continuation and culmination of characteristics displayed in younger life.

Older people (and of course other age groups) have an image of the way they feel others perceive them. Older people in Britain feel that they are well treated by the rest of society and cite provision of various services and benefits as evidence to support this view. However, they do comment that the levels at which these services are provided are inadequate and do not permit them to function as full members of society.

At a societal level we saw that there exist numerous highly negative stereotypes of old age. The personal attitudes of the old are very much more positive than the stereotypes held by other age groups and the representation of ageing that is often portrayed in the mass media. Such negative stereotypes are rooted in excessive fears of ageing based upon misinformation, or no information, combined with a social system which values ageing negatively and which reifies youth.

Dementia and cognitive impairment remain one of the spectres of old age for many people. Common discourse would suggest that the experience of dementia is almost universal in later life. While the prevalence and incidence increase with age, cognitive impairment is far from universal even in advanced old age. Apart from the strong relationship with age there are no consistent links with any other social factors such as class, gender or ethnicity. It remains a major threat to the independence and autonomy of older people as evidenced by the large numbers of residents in care homes who exhibit problems related to dementia and cognitive impairment. Depression is a much less recognised dimension of the mental health and well-being of older people. If we adopt an inclusive definition, there are more older people troubled with depression than dementia. Like the more inclusive concept of 'psychological well-being', depression is very strongly linked with disability. Again, in examining the health status of older people, there is a duality between physical and mental health. Social factors are linked to depression and well-being and this largely revolves around the perceived 'adequacy' of social support. Those older people who feel that they have access to a supportive network demonstrate better mental health than those who lack this attribute. This offers, in theory at least, the potential to intervene to embed older people within social fabric more firmly. The availability of more sophisticated data analysis facilities has enabled us to pass a more sophisticated and rigorous gaze upon many aspects of later life. Cherished presumptions of relationships between, for example, depression and age or gender, have been challenged by analysis strategies that enable us to take into account the effect of confounding (the inextricable link between age and gender for example). Such enterprises often challenge received wisdom and require us to reconsider accepted knowledge. These techniques also allow us to research the area of later life more thoroughly and greatly enhance our knowledge of the area. This illustrates how all scholars of gerontology must be prepared to reconsider cherished beliefs and accepted 'facts' in the face of new knowledge and understanding.

7 Family and social networks

The primary focus of this book is upon the social context within which both individuals and populations experience ageing. Perhaps the most influential and important of the social domains which shape the experience of ageing is that of family and wider social relationships. Over the lifecourse individuals belong to a variety of kinship and social groups, all of which bring interactions and relationships with family, friends and neighbours. They also provide us with many of our major social roles such as parent, child and spouse. The extent to which an older person is enmeshed within a social network of kin, friends and neighbours will greatly influence her/his experience of ageing. The availability of, and quality of, family and wider social relationships are very important factors in the quality of life experienced by older people and provide a major resource with which to negotiate the challenges which ageing and later life can pose. In this chapter we examine the extent to which older people are enmeshed within a network of kin and wider social relationships. This reflects the thesis of Phillipson *et al.* (2001) that the experience of growing older is not shaped solely by family and kinship groups but also encompasses wider social relationships such as friends and neighbours and other social activities and the proposal of Rowe and Kahn (1997) that social engagement is a prerequisite for 'successful ageing'. While we may not all accept the postulates of the successful ageing hypothesis, it is clear that engagement with the social context and social engagement generally is an important facet of quality of life in old age.

Jerrome (1993) suggests that five sets of factors have influenced the family relationships of older people. First, demographic changes have changed the 'distance' between generations and have fundamentally altered the size and age distribution of families. This change in the nature of family structures has been described as the 'beanpole' structure of long slim family structures created by increased longevity and decreased family sizes. This has resulted in the creation of family structures in which four or five generations are represented. Second, changes in employment have altered gender relationships within the family context. Third, legislative change, especially regarding divorce, has affected the structure and composition of families, especially in the creation of 'blended' families. Fourth, ideological change has altered the way that care is provided for dependent people and has resulted in changes within families in terms of expectations of marriage and parenthood. Finally, but perhaps more speculatively, rising levels of economic prosperity and the provision of welfare benefits has served to loosen the economic ties within families. In contemporary western societies older people are not, generally, directly economically dependent upon younger members of their families, although there are obvious financial co-dependencies across the generations. All of these factors combine to influence the family context within which older people experience old age. However, such changes are not unique to older people and such experiences are influencing all of us.

What is a family?

As with many such deceptively simple and uncomplex terms, defining precisely what does, and does not, constitute a family is a question which taxes policy makers, politicians and social commentators. Determining what type of living arrangements merit description and classification as a family is remarkably problematic. Are gay couples a family? Are children required to be present before the term 'family' can be applied to a living group? Clearly the way the 'family unit' is defined is, at least to some degree, an ideological construct. One way of defining what constitutes a family is by the characteristics of the individuals living within it. Some would argue that the term 'family' could be applied only to a heterosexual married couple with children – the stereotypical 'nuclear' family. Others would include single parents, cohabiting or gay couples within the term 'family'. Another way to define 'family' is by the number of generations included within it. A 'typical' nuclear family would constitute of two generations: parent(s) and children. The linking together of several nuclear groups by an extension of parent–child relationships, such as a married couple, their married offspring and grandchildren living together, produces the second major family type, the extended family. This is sometimes also known as a three-generational family, although examples of up to five generations living together have been enumerated. Whatever the definition used, we need to be aware of both the ideological underpinning of such definitions and their variability over time and across cultures. Like community care the term 'family' is one which remains constant but the precise meaning of which is fluid and is constantly subject to reinterpretation and definition.

A further distinction may be made between the term 'family' and the wider notion of the kinship group. De facto the term 'family' has become virtually synonymous with the concept of the nuclear family. Consequently Finch (1989a) suggests that the term 'kinship group' should be used when considering the web of wider blood relationships which extends beyond the immediate household (but which also includes them) while the term 'family' is restricted to groups of co-resident or immediate blood relatives. Again such definitions may be expanded to include the relationships resulting from the 'blending' of groups via (re)marriage, divorce and cohabitation. Regardless of how the concept is defined, families and kinship groups have been seen as being especially important for older people. Shanas (1979) proposed the primacy of the family for older people as the focus of their social world and as the primary and favoured source of support, both emotional and instrumental. Proponents of disengagement theory proposed that family relationships were more important for older people because of their loss (or disengagement) from other social spheres such as employment. More recently, notions such as 'successful' ageing continue to propose the centrality of social relationships and participation in maintaining, and potentially enhancing, quality of life in old age. Furthermore early gerontological research accepted at face value the highly gendered nature of family relationships and posited that women experienced ageing less problematically than men because of their more central location within family relationships and because of the enduring nature of these relationships. Throughout their adult lifecourse women are often defined by their 'caring' relationships such as mother, wife and grandmother rather than by occupational status. Such simplistic notions have been replaced but they have enduring implications because assumptions such as these influenced the type of research questions that have been asked about families and family relationships. Much of our knowledge of the family life and social relationships of older people is derived from studies concerned with 'caring' and the provision of care within families. Thane (1998) also notes that early gerontological studies were highly uncritical of the data they collected about intergenerational relationships and missed many of the potentially existing tensions. Despite this, Thane (1998) concludes that the family remains central to the experience of old age and later life and indeed other phases of the lifecycle and that this represents a continuation of the broad pattern established across a long historical perspective (see also Botelho and Thane, 2001).

Social and political commentators on the family, especially in its relationships with older people, have shown a rather narrow and pessimistic concentration upon the prediction of the demise of the family in modern industrial society and lament the neglect of older people by their family. Thane (1998) notes the surprise which social researchers expressed at the strong linkages identified between older people and their families. She argues that this illustrates how strongly such investigators had assimilated the notions that older people were marginalised by families and from society more generally because of spatial separation. However, gloomy forecasts of the disintegration of the family as a social institution have a long historical pedigree. Cicero, in his study of old age, lamented that families were not what they used to be, especially in the way that they cared for and respected their elders. As with many other social factors, such as the behaviour of children or relationships with older people, the extended family has been idealised and the nuclear family at best perceived negatively or at worst 'demonised' as a selfish and 'uncaring' form of family organisation. Social change is almost universally characterised as having a highly negative and damaging effect upon the social and family circumstances of older people. Hence the move towards nuclear families has been lamented without recognition that the family is a very flexible unit which demonstrates a pattern of almost continual adaptation to changing political, social and economic circumstances. When studying gerontology, as with other aspects of the social sciences, we need to avoid being drawn into ideologically based debates about families but rather reflect critically upon the evidence generated to determine the reality, which underpins many of these debates. Changes in family size or the increased prevalence of divorce can be well documented. The impact of such numerical changes upon older people is much less easy to be definite about and is a form of social change that probably has both negative and positive consequences.

What types of families did older people live in: an historical perspective

As with many other facets of the social world, it is difficult to reconstruct the different types of families in which older (or indeed other groups) lived at different historical time points. Thane (1998) notes this lack of empirical data and suggests that, in the absence of empirical evidence, there is an over-reliance upon anecdotal or highly localised material. The dearth of extensive empirical data means that pre-industrial times are often portrayed as the golden age of both the family and 'ageing', when older people were both respected and cared for by their own families with whom they lived. Wilson (2000) suggests that every age 'invents' its own 'golden age' as a response to the challenges and vulnerabilities posed by their own experiences. Two interrelated assumptions govern our predominant stereotypical and rather idealist historical view of family relationships. The first is that the extended family was the most common, indeed potentially universal, pattern of family organisation. The extended family constituted the 'social norm'. Second, this view assumes that because older people lived in the same dwelling as the rest of the family, they were cared for by the family and remained respected members of the kin network. How realistic are these two separate but clearly interrelated stereotypes?

This idealistic view of the past is highly simplistic and not supported by the available evidence. Historical research suggests that there is no single type of household or family unit that typifies pre-industrial society, as there are variations both over time and between different societies (Thane, 1998). This mirrors the current situation whereby the pattern of families in which older people varies considerable between countries and cultures and is constantly evolving in response to social change. Historically there is a marked diversity in the typical patterns of household formation ranging from simple nuclear families in Britain and northern Europe to the highly complex extended networks of southern Europe (Smith, 1998). The explanation for this diversity lies with the differing cultural, demographic and economic characteristics of these differing types of pre-industrial societies. Laslett (1989) argues that the nuclear family was probably the norm even in pre-industrial Britain because of the high mortality and fertility rates. He suggests that only about 11 per cent of households in pre-industrial Britain could be classified as extended family groups and probably only about 6 per cent of the population lived in three-generational households. For the vast majority of the population, perhaps 80 per cent, the two-generational nuclear family was the most common household type. The fertility and mortality patterns characteristic of pre-industrial Britain were those of high mortality and extended fertility with children continuing to be born late in the mother's life. Thus childbearing occupied a much longer phase of the lifecycle than it does at the present time – perhaps a span of twenty-five years (or slightly longer). This, combined with the shorter life expectancy, meant that older people were likely to be living in two-generational family groups simply because not all their children had yet left home to marry. For women the average life expectancy of about 50 years meant that few women lived to experience a significant period of life after the menopause. Additionally the high mortality characteristic of pre-industrial Britain meant that 30–40 per cent of older people had no surviving children with whom to co-reside (Smith, 1998). Furthermore the high mortality rates meant that older people, however defined, were a comparative rarity. In 1841 only 15 per cent of births would survive to age 75 and parishes rarely had more than 5–10 per cent of the population aged 60 or over (Smith, 1998). This, therefore, makes it very unlikely that the extended family, consisting of three-plus generations living together, could in any way be considered the normal or typical type of family arrangement for older people within pre-industrial Britain.

The second assumption implicit within the 'rose-tinted' perspective upon the past is that co-residence would ensure that older people were loved, cared for and respected. As we know with child and elder abuse evident in modern families' co-residence does not automatically and inevitably result in love, respect and care between or across generations. Hence for previous times in our history there is little direct evidence to support the assumption that co-residence with younger relatives necessarily guaranteed that older people would be well cared for. We can also develop the opposite argument in that the fact that different generations no longer live together does not preclude the development and maintenance of cross-generational caring relationships. This is parallel to the modern situation whereby Qureshi and Walker (1989) note that family care represents the extremes of quality, offering examples of the 'best' and 'worst' types of care. Furthermore the violent and abusive nature of the family environment is attested by the all too frequent cases of child abuse, domestic violence and elder abuse. It was fairly common practice in pre-industrial societies for older people and their children to draw up legal contracts and wills in which property was exchanged for care and maintenance in old age. This does not suggest a society dominated by a desire to venerate and serve the old. It could also equally well be argued that, because our ancestors had a much greater struggle just to survive, they would have little excess energy to spare upon the care of dependent older people, a point made by Smith (1998). When considering the family relationships of older people at previous points in our history, we need to try to distinguish reality from ideological wishful thinking and an uncritical reflection on the evidence presented.

Post-war changes

Whatever the situation in the past it is clear that the types of families and households in which current (and future) cohorts of older people live is highly dynamic and subject to considerable change. One way of tracking the evolving nature of types of families in which older people live is (and illustrating the highly dynamic nature of family organisation) to consider the changes which have taken place in the course of the twentieth century and to place these within a longer historical context where possible. Comparison of data from different sources, and for different time periods, can be used to illustrate how much the types of families in which older people experience ageing have changed (and to consider how much more it may change in the future). Although we are often using data from specific points in time it is very important to remember that families are dynamic and evolving structures: the use of cross-sectional data presents an overly stable and static perspective. Cross-sectional data do not entirely do justice to the fluidity and dynamic nature of household and living arrangements for older people.

One caveat needs to be drawn here. Thus far we have been concerned with the concept of the family. However in examining these temporal changes we have to use data about households and household composition. Although there is a considerable degree of overlap, households are concerned with the 'who lives with whom' component and do not have the wider social network or blood ties inferences of the term 'family'. Households are not necessarily synonymous with families (and vice versa). The majority of routinely available social data are concerned with households or living arrangements rather than families perhaps because of the difficulties of deciding how to define a family. The term 'living arrangements' is usually used to determine the number of people an older person lives with, the relationships between them, and the location of the household, i.e. community or institution. While such data are useful for illustrating changes over time or classifying and categorising current patterns they do not enable us to draw inferences and conclusions as to the relationships which take place within these structures and organisations.

Most older people live in the community; this proportion has remained constant over the past century at about 95 per cent. Even in the very oldest age groups, 85 years and over, the majority of people are resident in the community and experience ageing within this context; this has been a stable feature of the experience of old age within the British context. However potent the spectre of 'the workhouse', only a minority of older people ever experience old age within an institutional context. Again, as the generations who either remember the workhouse or were children of such people die off, then we may speculate that older people may review and reinterpret their perception of institutional or communal living. For the 'baby boomers', communal living may be viewed in a more positive light. Most older people live either with their spouse or on their own. Consequently, of the older people living in the community in 2001, 92 per cent live in single-generation households, living alone or with one or more other older person, usually either her/his spouse or more rarely a sibling. Two-generation households are where the older person lives with one or more people from the generation below them, usually their children (or children-in-law). Overall 3 per cent of older people are resident in two-generational households. A three-generation household is usually defined as one where the older person is living with both children and grandchildren. This type of household structure is much rarer with only about 1 per cent of elders living in this way. Table 7.1 shows that as early as 1945 the majority of older people lived in single-generation households and approximately 10 per cent lived in the 'classic' three-generation family. Considered from an alternate perspective Finch (1989b) reports that 5 per cent of those aged 45+ still live with their mothers but clearly the vast majority do not. Cultural and social factors, as well as financial and material circumstances, are an important influence upon cross-generational living arrangements. This is illustrated by the fact that, in Italy, 16 per cent of those aged 45+ still live with their mothers (Finch, 1989b). In Britain there is a growth in adult children returning to live with parents as a result of divorce, relationship break-up and the expense of entering the housing market in certain parts of the country. Such 'returning' adult children have been termed the 'boomerang children'.

The type of household in which older people live has shown much change since the mid-1940s (Table 7.2). It is important to remember

Table 7.1 Generational structure of households in which older people live, Great Britain (%)

	GB* 2001	Bethnal Green**		Wolverhampton**	
		1954–55	1995	1945	1995
One	92	58	75	49	86
Two	3	31	18	38	11
Three plus	—	10	8	13	2
Not known	5				

Sources: *Walker *et al.*, 2002: Table 3
**Phillipson *et al.*, 2001: Table 12

Notes: GHS data do not distinguish between two- and three-generational households. Bethnal Green and Wolverhampton are populations aged 60/65+. GB = 65+

Table 7.2 Comparison of the living arrangements of older people, Great Britain (%)

	GB* 2001	Bethnal Green**		Wolverhampton**	
		1954–55	1995	1945	1995
Lives alone	37	25	34	10	37
Lives with spouse	47	29	38	16	41
Lives with/out spouse and other relatives	10	58	25	51	20
Lives with siblings	1	4	2	8	1
Other	5	—	1	15	1

Sources: *Walker 2002: Table 3
** Phillipson *et al.*, 2001: Table 12.

that the households in which other subgroups within the population live have also changed. Social change does not just affect older people. For example, few newly married couples now start their married life living with their parents(-in-law), but this was common in the early 1950s. The emergence of the young single-person household and cohabitation prior to marriage are very recent social phenomena. Hence the factors that have influenced household and living arrangements of older people are society-wide trends that have influenced other age groups and are rarely specific to older people themselves. Using 'historical' data from key social surveys enables us to develop a temporal perspective, which illustrates just how much has changed in terms of the household circumstances, and living arrangements of older people. Two interlinked trends are illustrated in Table 7.2: the increase in living alone and the demise of the multigenerational household. Each of these trends is considered in more detail and placed where possible within an historical perspective (see also Harper, 2003; Tomassini *et al.*, 2004).

The rise of solo living in later life

At the 2001 Census there were approximately 21.6 million households in England and Wales of which 6.5 million (30 per cent) consisted of a single person. This contrasts sharply with the situation in 1951, when there were 14.5 million households of which single person households accounted for 11 per cent. Hence in four decades there has been both a huge relative and absolute growth in terms of this type of living arrangement. Of the 6.5 million single-person households, 48 per cent (3.1 million) were pensioner households (i.e. headed by a person aged 60/65+), thus in contemporary Britain the majority of single-person households are not headed by an 'older person'. The situation for older people generally mirrors this trend for the increased popularity of solo living. Investigating the extent of social change solely upon the basis of locally based surveys is problematic as we cannot be certain if the locality surveyed is representative of the total population. Examination of changes in the percentage of older people living alone illustrates the need to be cautious when generalising from locally based surveys. For example, Sheldon (1948) reported that 10 per cent of his sample lived alone compared with 37% in 1998. The percentage living alone in Bethnal Green in the 1950s was much larger at 25 per cent (see Table 7.2). Consequently using the Sheldon survey as our benchmark or baseline may overstate the change in the percentage of elders living alone in post-war Britain. Smith (1998) offers a longer historical perspective. He estimates that in pre-nineteenth-century rural England 8 per cent of people aged 65+ lived alone and that this was much greater for women (17 per cent) than men (2 per cent). Although there has been an increase in the percentage of older people living alone we need to be able to place this change in the appropriate temporal, spatial and cultural context.

Phillipson *et al.* (2001) repeated the classic surveys of Sheldon and Townsend; their results serve to emphasise the significant change in the living arrangements of older people (Tables 7.1 and 7.2). At the most simplistic in the immediate post-war period older people living alone represented a minority 'lifestyle' in comparison to the current situation. However, it did represent continuity with the 'established' historical pattern. The differential in the percentages of men and women living alone noted by Smith (1998) for Victorian Britain have persisted. The differential has narrowed from the eightfold difference noted for pre-1800 Britain to a twofold gender differential in favour of women for current cohorts of elders. What these data do not enable us to distinguish are those who enter old age always having lived alone and those for whom this is a new form of living arrangement. It is likely that the experience of living alone in later life will be very different for the new living-alone group as compared with those for whom this is a continuation of a previously well-established lifestyle. We may speculate that living alone in later life will be a very different experience for those for whom this is a new lifestyle arrangement as compared to those for whom it represents continuity, but this conceptual distinction is rarely discussed when we are examining this population subgroup. Such distinctions are, however, probably very important. For the 'new' living-alone group this represents a major reorientation of life given that such changes usually arise from bereavement, or more rarely, entry of a spouse or partner into long-term care. For those for whom living alone represents continuity with an established pattern of life, then the challenges may be rather different. Here the issue is maintaining an established life pattern rather than establishing a new one. It is clear that those living alone in later life represent a highly varied population and we should be wary of presuming an unproven homogeneity of circumstances and experiences.

While routine data enable us to document such changes, they do not enable us to determine what has caused the increase in living alone in later life. This could reflect more people entering old age having already established a 'solo living' arrangement (following divorce or because they have remained unpartnered) or an increase in those who establish this form of household following bereavement, death of a partner or sibling or entry of a co-household member into care. The group of older people classified as 'living alone' is often grouped as a single homogeneous group and are considered by some to be a 'risk group'. There are, conceptually, at least two groups within this category and for each of these the context within which they are experiencing ageing may well be very different. We might also speculate that the experience of living alone would be different according to class, gender and ethnicity, but researchers have yet to explore in depth the variety of experiences contained within the group classified for survey purposes as 'living alone'. Our tendency to treat all those 'living alone' as a single, homogeneous group illustrates the limited nature of the gaze that we have applied to this group. There is clearly a large research agenda to be developed in this aspect of the living arrangements of older people. We have yet to fully engage with the complexity encompassed by a simple category such as 'living alone'.

The change in the household circumstances of older people needs to be located within the broader social context. It is important to remember that the increase in older people living alone is part of a wider social trend. In 1951 'pensioner' households accounted for two-thirds of single-person households. In 2002 54 per cent of all single-person households comprise people under retirement age (Rickards *et al.*, 2004). Hence living in single person households is not something which is unique to older people. Rather the increase of solo living in later life is part of a wider social trend. As Table 7.3 shows, the percentage of the population aged 16+ living alone has almost doubled, from 9 to 16 per cent between 1973 and 2001. There has been only a marginal increase in the percentage aged 65–74 living alone (26 per cent to 27 per cent) but very big increases to those aged 25–44 (2 per cent to 12 per cent) and 45–64 (8 per cent to 15 per cent). Again it is important to determine the limits to the inferences that we can draw from these observed changes. We can certainly conclude that there has been a remarkable increase in the numbers of older people maintaining independent households in later life. However, we cannot use this as an indirect comment upon the family ties and social relationships enjoyed by older people. We cannot infer social isolation and family neglect from the increase in solo living. Sheldon (1948) noted with some surprise that older people who, for typological reasons, were classed as 'living alone' were in fact part of a complex, intimate, locality-based social network. Older people may construct the maintenance of an independent household in later life as a manifestation of autonomy and financial or economic independence in much the same way as younger people do. We must, for older people at least, be more critical of the easy assumption that living alone in later life is a 'bad thing' and inevitably an indication of social disengagement and failure. Indeed maintenance of an independent household may be a key indicator of successful ageing from the older person's perspective and it remains a key objective of government policy for older people. Neither, as noted earlier, should we treat this group as a single social category and we need to develop a more sophisticated analytical strategy for examining this group of older people.

Table 7.3 People living alone by age, Great Britain, 1973, 1991 and 2001 (%)

Age	1973	1991	2001
16–24	2	3	5
25–34	2	7	12
45–64	8	11	15
65–74	26	29	27
75+	40	50	49
All ages	9	14	16

Source: Rickards *et al.*, 2004: Table 3.3

Will living alone become the norm in later life?

This increase in living alone in later life is one of the most profound recent changes in the social context in which people experience old age (and indeed is an important feature of the social context for younger people). The data presented to date are all historical and retrospective: they enable us to document and review the changes which have taken place in the past. Perhaps of even greater interest is considering the likely living arrangements of future cohorts of elders. Evandrou and Falkingham (2000) suggest that the rise towards living alone will continue to gain pace. They argue that the cohort born in the 1960s has embarked upon a very different pattern of household formation compared with previous generations and that this will influence how this cohort 'experiences' old age and later life (and indeed other phases of the lifecycle). For those born in 1931 approximately 2.5 per cent lived alone at age 30 and about 15 per cent at age 65. For the 1964 cohort approximately 15 per cent were living alone at age 30. This increase reflects improved living standards, changes in patterns of long-term relationships and the greater availability of housing. Future projection of current trends suggest that 50 per cent of the 1960s cohort will be living alone at age 75 compared with 37 per cent for the 1916–1920 cohort and 41 per cent of the 1940s cohort (Evandrou and Falkingham, 2000). From these data we might speculate that living alone would indeed become the norm in later life. It is likely that a much greater percentage of people will, in the future, enter old age having lived alone at earlier phases in the lifecycle. We may well be seeing the re-emergence of the spinster as more women (and men?) opt for an unpartnered lifestyle. Although the implications of this change, taken in conjunction with changes in marital status and childbearing, are likely to profoundly influence the experience of old age in numerous dimensions in the future, the precise changes are not clear. It seems likely that future students of gerontology will have to adopt wider more flexible definitions of terms such as family and kin and that greater attention will be drawn to the roles played by non-kin in the lives of older people. Furthermore, we will need to place living arrangements in later life within a lifecourse/biographical context in order to enhance our understanding of these patterns and how they provide a context for older people's lives.

The decline of the multigenerational household

One area where the distinction between household/living arrangements and family is important is when discussing multigenerational matters. Co-residence between older people and their younger relatives (including both children and grandchildren) is becoming an increasingly rare feature of western society (Glaser, 1997). Sheldon (1948) reported in his study of Wolverhampton that 51 per cent of older people lived with their children or grandchildren and that this was the normative pattern of social organisation. Similarly Townsend (1957) in Bethnal Green reported that 41 per cent of those aged 60/65+ lived in two-plus generation families. Both locally and nationally, this form of living arrangement has declined markedly in the post-1945 period (Table 7.2). Recent general household survey data suggest that, at most, 10 per cent of people aged 65 and over live in multigenerational households and this percentage has halved since the early 1980s and may now be as low as 2 per cent. This national change is reflected in local areas. 'Resurveys' of Wolverhampton and Bethnal Green by Phillipson *et al.* (2001) demonstrate this succinctly as Wolverhampton now approximates to the national pattern and even in Bethnal Green, with its high concentration of migrants from the Asian subcontinent, only one-quarter of older people live in multigenerational households (see Table 7.2).

In the space of fifty years there has been a fundamental and profound change in the living arrangements of older people (and by extension other age groups as well). These data simply describe changes in the pattern of household organisation; we cannot use such data to infer that older people are not part of multigenerational families. Grundy *et al.* (1999) report that 75 per cent of those aged 60 and over are part of families which include three or more generations. Indeed, given greater life expectancy, it is not unusual for families to consist of four or five generations. People can be both grandparents and grandchildren simultaneously! Although there has been a spatial separation of families into separate living groups family ties are clearly being maintained and older people, like most of the rest of the population, consider themselves to be members of wider family groups. Again declines in co-residence cannot be used to make any inferences about the nature and quality of relationships between family members. Similarly we need to develop an analysis of family relationships which is more sophisticated than a simple 'proximity equals quality and intimacy' and 'distance mitigates against intimacy and support'.

Living with a spouse

In terms of the living arrangements of older people, most of the attention from policy makers and social commentators has been focused upon the two trends noted above: the rise in single-person households and the decline of the multigenerational co-resident households. This focus reflects a largely social policy-driven agenda, which reflects two commonly held assumptions. First, that older people living alone are a 'vulnerable' group neglected by family and friends alike and who, because of the presumed absence of a wider social network, will turn to the state in times of frailty and crisis. Second, multigenerational co-resident households are intrinsically warm, caring and supportive environments that will naturally care for any older family members who experience such problems, thereby decreasing calls upon the state. Hence there has been an ideological drive towards drawing attention to two social trends which appear to demonstrate the specific neglect of older people within families and a more general social comment about the uncaring nature of society towards perceived vulnerable groups.

By focusing upon these two household types we have tended to overlook the third and equally remarkable aspect of the changing living arrangements of older people and that is the increase in the number of married couples maintaining independent households from either children or siblings and other relatives. In the survey of Sheldon (1948) only 16 per cent of all respondents lived as a married couple alone and of those who were married only 35 per cent lived solely with their spouse. In contrast in 2001 47 per cent of those aged 65+ lived solely with their spouse and, of those who were married, 91 per cent lived with their spouse alone. Consequently it is evident that the decline in multigenerational households has not simply resulted in the increase in older people living alone but also in a rise of older couples living independently from their children or siblings (or both). This reflects a number of interrelated trends including the establishment of independent households by children and greater longevity for both men and women. A much less noted and remarked trend is that, because of the well-observed changes in mortality, that couples who marry or cohabit can expect to 'grow old together' and to live together in their own home in old age. This is in direct contrast to previous points in our history when marriages were ended by bereavement and few couples could expect to grow old together.

Explaining changes in the living arrangements of older people

Changes in the living arrangements of older people reflect the interaction of both general social changes and specific social policies aimed at older people. In terms of general social trends, important factors which have prompted the increase in older people living in independent households include a vastly increased stock of housing, the trend for young people to move away from the parental home to establish their own household upon marriage (or now even before marriage/establishing a cohabiting relationship) and changes in housing tenure. In addition the provision of state pension and occupational pensions and increase in owner occupation has provided many older people with the financial resources to maintain their own household in old age. Indeed the decrease in co-residence between adults of different generations reflects the huge preference expressed by older people (and all other adult age groups) for independent living. Such aspirations are not necessarily new. Rather more recent generations of elders, because of the greater availability of pensions, are able to achieve this aspiration. A survey by Shanas *et al.* (1968) revealed that for only 8 per cent of older people was living with the family the preferred mode of living. The vast majority, 83 per cent, preferred their own home and the much-valued commodity of independence. Moving in with offspring can result in a loss of independence for the older person and the reversal of roles between parent and child. Similarly Townsend (1957), in his study of Bethnal Green in London, reported that only 10 per cent of older people with children were in favour of sharing a house with them. More recently Thompson *et al.* (1990) noted the strength of the drive to preserve independence and autonomy in living arrangements. As one of their respondents noted, 'I'm not giving up my home for nobody' (Thompson *et al.*, 1990: 210). Indeed the whole thrust of current policy formulation for older people is towards maintenance of older people within their own homes and so, therefore, it is unsurprising that older people are indeed maintaining their own households into later life. Yet it remains a paradox that we continue to make negative comments about the success of older people in the achievement of this policy goal.

What factors influence living arrangements in later life?

The living arrangements of older people, as with other groups, are influenced by a number of factors including key demographic indicators and the health, financial and social resources available to the older person as well as cultural norms and values. However, it is not always easy to disentangle which are the most important factors as many of these aspects of later life are highly interrelated. The type of household in which an older person lives varies with key demographic factors, the most important of which are age, gender and marital status. The percentage living alone increases with age and is more common among women and the divorced/widowed/never married. Living arrangements in later life are not the result of a simple linear relationship with age or gender. Clearly the three variables of age, gender and civil status are strongly interrelated and it is not always clear as to whether age, gender or marital status is the key influence. The observation that the percentage living alone increases with age or is more common among women may, in fact, reflect the fact that older women are more likely to be widowed. Hence we must be wary of assuming that it is ageing per se which brings about the increase in solo living: rather it probably reflects the changes in household size resultant from widowhood. Other factors which are important for determining whether older people live alone in later life include the availability of other social resources such as the availability of children, health status, financial resources and cultural norms and attitudes. Independent of each other poor health and low income are associated with co-residence in multigenerational households (Glaser, 1997).

Understanding the living arrangements of older people is far more complex than simply noting an association with simple demographic factors such as age or gender. All the data presented to date derive from essentially cross-sectional surveys. They describe the living arrangements of older people at a single point in time and almost certainly oversimplify the complexity of the household arrangement of older people. In addition such analyses reveal nothing about the pathways which led to the current arrangements. The use of cross-sectional data often engenders a notion that living arrangements and household formation are static features of our social world when, in fact, they are dynamic and constantly evolving. This observation applies equally well across the age groups and is not confined to older people. The work of Pendry *et al.* (1999) and Evandrou *et al.* (2001), by using different types of longitudinal data, provide a more dynamic insight into the living arrangements of older people. Evandrou *et al.* (2001) report that there are eight major categories of household change. Over an eight-year follow-up period they report that the most stable forms of household arrangement were those living alone or in a couple: 92 per cent of those studied remained in the same type of living arrangement. The major 'drivers' of household change were bereavement and moves into long-term care. There is considerable complexity to the pattern of change, especially for those living in 'complex' households and again this work cautions against oversimplifying the extent of changes in living arrangements that characterise older people.

The kin and social networks of older people

The extent to which an older person is enmeshed within a series of kinship relations will obviously have an important effect upon the experience of ageing. For the social researcher, however, undertaking the apparently simple task of identifying the kinship and social networks is both methodologically and conceptually complex (Crow, 2004). We have already seen that most routine data are concerned with household or living arrangements rather than with establishing family, kin or social networks. In this analysis of the social networks of older people, we will confine our attention to the extent to which older people have access to the major kinship relationships of spouse, children and siblings. Excluded from the analysis are the more distant kin relationships. We must remember that such relationships may make an important contribution to the overall social networks of older people; Phillipson *et al.* (2001) argue that it is the immediate family (spouse, children, siblings) who play the largest role in the lives of older people, although the wider social network and context should not be neglected.

Social networks

Social networks are concerned with the mesh of relationships within which an older person is located. The concept of social network analysis has extended the approach used to the empirical and theoretical analysis of older people's social relationships because it is left up to the older person to determine who is (and is not) part of their network. Older people can include or exclude kin, friends and neighbours as appropriate. In Britain the work of Wenger (1984, 1994, 1996) exemplifies the use of social network analysis in understanding the experience of old age. There are a variety of different ways of measuring social networks; (Levin, 2000; Lubben and Gironda, 2004). Here we are not concerned with the methodology but rather with the conceptual distinctions which require articulation. We need to distinguish between social networks, which identify the web of relationships associated with a specific individual, and social support, which is the provision of financial, instrument or emotional support from a network member (Bowling, 1994). While not all members of the network may be called upon to provide support, it is highly unlikely that those outside of the network will be asked to do so. The social network circumscribes the maximum boundaries of support theoretically available to any one individual at a given point in time. We may speculate that perceived support of the greatest value to older people – it is not so much what is provided that is important but knowing that if the need arises help will be provided. Again our reliance upon cross-sectional data should not prevent us from recognising the dynamic changes underlying an apparently stable pattern of social network arrangements.

Phillipson *et al.* (2001) report that, for their samples, the average social network consisted of 9.3 people; women have larger networks than men (10.12 versus 8.18) but there was no obvious relationship with age. These patterns replicate those observed in North America by Antonucci and Akiyama (1987). For only 30 per cent of respondents did their network consist of five people (or fewer). This is very similar to the work of Wenger (1984) for North Wales who reported that 25 per cent of her respondents had a network consisting of five or fewer persons. Phillipson *et al.* (2001) classify their network types into four types based upon the composition: immediate family (approximately 60 per cent), other kin (16 per cent), non-kin (24 per cent) and care related (1 per cent). This serves to demonstrate the predominance of family-based and -centred networks. Such networks predominantly consist of same generation (49 per cent) or two-generational (34 per cent) relationships.

Research has consistently demonstrated that older people are part of a kinship network, which consists of combinations of spouses, siblings or children and grandchildren and that this is complemented by wider kin relationships and friends or neighbours. However, there are a minority of the current generation of elders, 6 per cent overall (8 per cent of women and 3 per cent of men) who have no children or siblings. A further 3 per cent of elders have never married, and had no children and no siblings. This mirrors data from the United States where about 4 per cent of the population aged 70–85 have no spouse, children or siblings. While this is very much a minority of older people, it does represent a potentially vulnerable group, although as old age represents a continuation of a pre-existing lifestyle this vulnerability may be more perceived than actual especially as friendships and wider patterns of social engagement may be 'substituted' for family networks. We must avoid the easy assumption that lack of family means lack of social engagement or the availability of a functional social network.

Spouse and marriage

The majority of people in the current cohorts of older people are married (or were married previously with the union terminated by divorce). At all ages above 65 years men are more likely to be married than women (Table 7.4). This reflects the interaction of two trends: the differential ages of men and women at marriage and the higher rates of male mortality. For women this results in one-third of them being widowed by the ages of 65–74 and almost three-quarters are widowed by the age of 80. In terms of the nature and context of ageing, for women they largely experience old age without the benefit of a spouse whereas for men the opposite is the case. This is not a new phenomenon. Smith (1998) reports that for pre-1800 Britain approximately 60 per cent of men aged 65+ were married compared with 40 per cent of women. This situation is not too dissimilar to the situation for contemporary Britain.

One issue which is not clear from routine statistics is how many of these marriages are second (or subsequent) marriages and whether the previous marriage ended because of divorce or widowhood. The 2001 Census, reflecting social change, collected data on whether marriages were first or second marriages and in the future we are likely to see an increasing number of people entering old age in a second or subsequent marriage. The emphasis upon 're-partnering' in later life has focused upon post-widowhood relationships, with post-

Table 7.4 Marital status of people aged 65+, England and Wales, 2001 (%)

	65–69		70–74		75–79		80–84		85–89		90+	
	M	*F*	*M*	*F*	*M*	*F*	*M*	*F*	*M*	*F*	*M*	*F*
Married (first)	65	54	64	45	60	33	53	20	42	10	27	4
Second or later marriage	11	7	9	5	8	4	8	3	7	2	6	—
Single	7	5	8	6	7	6	7	7	6	8	8	11
Widowed	7	24	12	37	21	53	29	67	43	78	57	83
Divorced/ separated	9	10	6	7	4	4	3	3	2	2	2	2

Source: ONS, 2003: Table S002

divorce relationships remaining relatively neglected. For future cohorts, the importance of divorce as a factor in remarriage will grow. Another notable absence from routine data is older people who are living in gay relationships. As such unions are not authorised, legitimised, sanctioned or counted by the state they are presumed not to exist. Clearly within the older age groups some apparently single people will, in fact, be living within an intimate relationship with a long-term same-sex partner. This invisibility means that such relationships remain largely unacknowledged by both the academic community and, perhaps more importantly, from policy makers and practitioners.

It seems likely that in the future social researchers will need to distinguish between first marriages, second marriages and de facto unions between homosexual and heterosexual partners, to incorporate the reasons for remarriage (i.e. divorce or widowhood) in order to develop a more sophisticated typology of marriage and marriage-like relationships in later life. It is, perhaps, instructive to incorporate an historical perspective into this analysis. Compared with the situation in 1851 the current cohort of older people are more likely to be married, although this differential appears to be greater for females than males. Assuming an average age of marriage in the 1850s of about twenty-two years and a life expectancy of 50 years we can see that the 'average' marriage would last, at most, twenty-eight years. This contrasts with the situation now of a slightly higher average age at first marriage of about 25 and a conservative life expectancy of 75 years, giving an average potential length of marriage of 50 years. The comparative rarity of golden (50 years) and diamond (60 years) wedding anniversaries has been replaced by their everyday occurrence. The ending of marriage now arises as much from divorce as widowhood. Compared with previous cohorts future generations of older people are more likely to include people who have been divorced (or who are on second marriages). There is a 'bulge' of people in the 45–54 age groups who are divorced; at 11 per cent this is much larger than that demonstrated by previous cohorts and this is reflected in the increasing percentage of older people classed as divorced or separated. The implications of this profound social change and, in particular, its impact upon the social and family network of older people remains unknown. It seems likely that future cohorts will enter old age with a much more complex web of intimate relationships, in terms of marital history, than previous generations of elders. The complexities brought by large family sizes may be replaced by the complexities resulting from creation of blended and reconstituted families and the need to negotiate a whole new set of social and marital relationships. The implications of this increasing complexity for the social world of older people remains a challenge for scholars of gerontology. It does illustrate how the nature and experience of ageing varies across the generations because of these changes in the social context.

Children

While almost every piece of social research collects data about the civil status of respondents (i.e. whether they are single, widowed, divorced or married) and their living arrangements, routine data and statistical sources rarely capture fuller details of the often complex family structures of older people. Apart from the spousal relationship the most dominant family tie is that of parent–child. McGlone *et al.* (2000) argue that this is a crucial relationship in terms of social contacts and as a mechanism for organising and delivering family support. Overall 72 per cent of the population disagree with the statement 'Once children have left home, they should no longer expect help from their parents'. It is important to remember that support can flow both ways across generational boundaries. Another novel feature of late-twentieth and early-twenty-first-century demography is the longevity of the parent–child relationship that has arisen because of overall decreases in mortality rates. Such relationships can now easily last upwards of sixty years. In October 2003 an American woman aged 114 died shortly after her 90-year-old daughter. Again this is a very new set of social relationships, and one in which both parent and child can be retired.

Grundy *et al.* (1999) and Shelton and Grundy (2000) provide one of the rare examples of national data investigating the availability of kin across a sample of the general adult population (aged 16 and over) of Britain. This survey revealed that 82 per cent of those aged 70 years and over had living children and that 18 per cent either had never had children or had children who had pre-deceased them. Confirmation of these data are provided by further data from the 2000 Omnibus (Victor *et al.*, 2004) survey which demonstrated that 85 per cent of those aged 65 and over had at least one living child. Again this is similar to the data for early-nineteenth-century Britain when Smith (1998) estimates that 80 per cent of elders would have children alive (and theoretically available to provide care and support). What has clearly changed is the number of children in older people's networks and their spatial proximity. In considering the social world of older people perhaps the first factor to consider is the spatial proximity of family members such as parents, children, siblings and (great) grandchildren. This statement is based upon the simple premise, which guided much early British work in these areas, that spatial proximity was a necessary and contingent factor in promoting social contact and by implication social and practical support. In Britain, of those with living children, 64 per cent live within five miles. Grundy *et al.* (1999) report that approximately half of those aged 50+ with non-resident children live within thirty minutes' travel. Nationally 65 per cent of the population live within one hour's journey of their mother (McGlone *et al.*, 2000), while Finch (1989b) reports that 32 per cent live within fifteen minutes' travel of their mother compared with 27 per cent in the United States, 37 per cent in Austria and 43 per cent in Hungary. In Britain for those elders with children, 29 per cent live within one mile and a further 35 per cent within five miles. This represents something of a change from the situation described by Sheldon (1948) where 30 per cent of his sample had children within five minutes' walk of their home. The simple fact that almost two-thirds of older people with children live within five miles of them challenges our assumptions of widespread geographical dispersal of families within contemporary Britain.

The majority of the current cohort of older people have at least one living child. Completed family size and numbers of surviving children are obviously key influences upon the extent to which the family can be a source of support. Those older people with either no surviving children or with small families have, all other things being equal, fewer opportunities for being involved in family networks than those with larger numbers of surviving children. Again it is likely that future cohorts of older people will illustrate three distinct trends with regard to the availability of children. First, average family sizes are decreasing so that, for those born in 1940, completed family size was 2.4 (these are the group who turned 60 in 2000) compared with 1.95 for the 1960 cohort (who will turn 60 in 2020). Second, increasing numbers of older people will be in families where they have step-(grand)children. The relationship with stepchildren (and step-grandchildren) and how this will affect the family context within which people age remains unclear and the subject for speculation in the absence of good empirical evidence. It seems likely that, as with 'natural' children, it is the quality of the relationship which is important and which will develop the ties of reciprocity across the generations. Third, assuming the continuation of current trends, there will be a significant increase in the numbers of people without children. Barring a late burst of fertility or a very rapid increase in post-menopause fertility then a much higher percentage of older people will be childless in the future. How this will influence the experience of old age remains an area for speculation but underlines the dynamic nature of the family context within which we will all experience later life.

Siblings

Siblings are an important aspect of the family network of older people. Less emphasis is usually given to the identification of sibling relationships in later life as research typically focuses upon the availability of primarily spouses and, to a lesser extent, children because of the emphasis on 'caring' relationships rather than understanding the social context of family networks. Siblings can be an important source of emotion and instrumental support in later life. Victor *et al.* (2004) indicate that 78 per cent of people aged 65 and over have surviving siblings, but not surprisingly, this decreases with age. The percentage of older people living with siblings is now about 1 per cent and has virtually died out as a form of household organisation. Given current changes in family sizes, future generations of elders are likely to experience old age with fewer siblings and hence with a less extensive but perhaps equally intensive primary kin network. As with children so the spatial proximity of siblings appears to have decreased in the post-war period. Sheldon (1948) reports that the majority had siblings living within five minutes' walk. In contemporary Britain of those older people with siblings, 20 per cent live within five miles and for 24 per cent the nearest sibling is over fifty miles away. Nationally, of those with adult siblings, 59 per cent live within one hour's journey. When considering such detail we need to acknowledge that notions of proximity have changed with mass access to cars, telephones and, increasingly, to email, video conferencing, instant messaging and voice mail (using a computer as a telephone).

Contact with family members

The structure of an older person's family, such as the existence of children and siblings, and their geographical proximity influence the frequency of direct contact between them as do other important factors such as income and health status. The way in which social contact takes place between family members has changed markedly since the classic social research of Peter Townsend and his contemporaries. Social contact can be achieved by other methods such as telephone calls, letters or now via electronic means. Thus geographical separation does not necessarily imply neglect or lack of contact between the older person and the family. This increase in the ways that social contacts can take place means that we need to reconsider some of the simple assumptions underlying much research, which presumes that 'direct' face-to-face contacts are the most favoured and highly rated form of social contact. While this assumption may be justified for current cohorts, it may not hold true for future generations brought up on telephones, mobiles, text messaging, email and other newly emerging forms of electronic communication.

Overall, levels of interaction are generally high between older people and their children/siblings and family generally. Victor *et al.* (2004) indicates that three-quarters of older people (77 per cent) saw relatives at least weekly, with approximately 10 per cent seeing relatives less than once or twice a year; phone contact levels were higher although there is little evidence of extensive use of email yet. Women report higher levels of contact with family and friends. This may reflect the greater number of older women living alone, who turn for social contact outside the immediate household, or women's role as 'kin keepers' (or some combination of the two). Family contact seems to remain largely constant with age and there does not seem to be a clear class or income link. The nature of the contact may change with older people making the transition from visitor to visitor as they age.

Friendship in late life

Gerontological researchers have largely marginalised non-kin-based social relationships. The assertion by Shanas (1979) of the primacy of the family in determining the social context of ageing resulted in many investigators ignoring the role and importance of non-kin-based social relationships. The initial focus upon kin relationships meant that the potential complexity of the social worlds of older people was downplayed. Clearly friends are also important for older people, as they are for people of other ages. Friendships, especially those of long-standing, can provide continuity across the lifecourse. It is interesting to note that, overall, McGlone *et al.* (2000) found that 59 per cent of the population report that they would rather spend time with family than friends. Phillipson *et al.* (2001) have clearly demonstrated the importance of friendship networks and non-blood relationships in later life, especially for urban middle-class couples. Jerrome has also demonstrated the importance and value of friends to older women. These data may lend support to the argument of Pahl and Spencer (1997; Pahl, 2000), that is in some circumstances friends may be becoming the 'families of choice', especially for future generations of elders, who will be less likely to have either children or siblings (or possibly a spouse). For future generations it will be even more important to capture the 'personal communities' within which older people will be enmeshed. This proposition is supported by the empirical work of Phillipson *et al.* (2001), who report that for those elders without children 39 per cent of networks included friends compared with 20 per cent of those with children. There is some evidence of the substitution of family with friends. Levels of direct and indirect contact with friends are high with approximately 70 per cent of people seeing their friends weekly, and similar percentages being in weekly phone contact; only 6 per cent reported that they had not seen friends in the previous twelve months. Contact by letter or email was less frequent. Only 5 per cent had been in email contact with friends or family and 10 per cent wrote or received letters from friends weekly. However, we may speculate that in the future social relationships may well see the development of 'e-relationships' in the same way that past decades saw the development of telephone relationships. The form of the 'contact' that underpins relationships between older people and their families has diversified since the early 1960s to include telephones and other forms such as email and this trend for ever more diverse and creative forms of social contact seems likely to continue.

It is not just the amount of social contact that is important but the value that social actions ascribe to the relationship. One important dimension of this is the closeness or confiding nature of relationships. The presence of a close confiding relationship is of importance to people, irrespective of age. The vast majority of older people (99 per cent) report that they have such a relationship. For approximately 10 per cent of people their confidant does live 'close by', but it is not clear if spatial proximity is an absolute requirement for such relationships.

Wider social engagement

A variety of different pieces of evidence indicate that the older population of Britain is socially active. Recent data from a survey of those aged 65+ and living at home (Victor *et al.*, 2004) indicated that overall 81 per cent of those aged 65+ reported that they voted in the last local election and 74 per cent had been on holidays and outings in the previous twelve months. Only 3 per cent had not been out of the house in the previous week. Participation rates for activities in the last month such as attending local organisations (42 per cent), church (29 per cent), the theatre or cinema (29 per cent), voluntary work (16 per cent) or sporting activities (22 per cent) were high.

Has social contact with family and friends increased or decreased?

Using cross-sectional data makes it difficult to examine social contact and relationships across the lifecourse. It also makes it difficult to consider if there have been temporal variations in the level of social contact between older people and their family and friends. Data from the General Household Survey can cast some light upon this topic. The percentage of older people having weekly contact with friends or relatives appears to be fairly stable across the two decades that the GHS has collected data on this topic. There are some fluctuations over time but no consistent pattern of increase or decrease. A similar pattern is evident for contact with neighbours (Table 7.5). These data, taken in conjunction with the work of Phillipson *et al.* (2001), suggest that levels of contact between older people and their families or friends have remained fairly frequent, although the forms of contact are now much more diverse than in the immediate post-war period. Furthermore there is no one single pattern of social networks and contact in later life. Rather there are a variety of different patterns, which demonstrate variations in the balance between kin and

Table 7.5 Weekly direct contact with relatives or friends, Great Britain, 1980 and 2001

	65–69		70–74		75–79		80–84		85+		All	
	1980	*2001*	*1980*	*2001*	*1980*	*2001*	*1980*	*2001*	*1980*	*2001*	*1980*	*2001*
Male	87	78	83	79	83	71	76	73	71	79	84	77
Female	89	84	88	81	83	81	79	78	80	77	86	81

Source: Victor, 1994; Walker *et al.*, 2002

non-kin relationships, and these variations reflect important social factors such as class, gender and ethnicity as well as geographical distance. In the absence of good empirical data, we must be wary of presuming that one mode of social engagement is more valuable than other types.

Social support in later life

Clearly contemporary older people are both socially engaged with the wider community and embedded within a network of family and friendship relations. Research has, however, consistently shown that it is not quantity of relationships that is important but the nature of the relationship. For older people a feeling of 'social support' is positively correlated with both physical and mental health. Those older people without such relationships report poorer physical and mental health and poor quality of life. Data from the Health Survey for England suggest that 19 per cent of men and 11 per cent of women can be classified as having 'low' levels of social support. Although this does not seem to vary with age or class, levels of 'fragile' social support are higher for men and women living in care environments – 28 per cent and 21 per cent respectively and for those classed as severely disabled. Given the nature of the data, while we can observe a link between social support and health we cannot be certain as to which is cause and which is effect or if both are linked to some unknown or confounding variable.

Loneliness and social isolation

Family and friends constitute an important component of the social context within which we experience ageing. Overall, levels of contact between older people and their family/friends remain high and older people are embedded within extensive social networks. Researchers, from Sheldon (1948) onwards, have shown interest in two 'pathological' extreme aspects of social relationships: loneliness and social isolation.

The changed roles experienced with ageing, from employed to retired and from provider to dependant, it is argued, render older people particularly prone to these experiences. Loneliness as a concept is both theoretically and conceptually complex (see Victor *et al.*, 2000; Jong Gierveld, 1998). At the most straightforward level, loneliness is concerned with how individuals evaluate their overall level of social interaction. Loneliness describes the state in which there is a deficit between the individuals actual and desired level of social engagement. As such loneliness needs to be distinguished from three related, but not coterminous, concepts. These are being alone (time spent alone), living alone (simply a description of the household arrangements) and social isolation, which refers to the level of integration of individuals (and groups) into the wider social environment.

Clearly these four different concepts share some commonality although the precise degree of overlap is unclear and the terms should not be used interchangeably (Victor *et al.*, 2000). The lack of consistency of conceptualisation is reflected in the varying ways that loneliness is defined and measured. Social isolation has been seen as a more quantitative, empirical measurement of social engagement. This ranges from the simple tallying of social contacts in a given reference frame to more sophisticated conceptualisations incorporating contacts and spatial proximity, etc.

There are at least four perspectives to the investigation of loneliness in later life (Andersson, 1998) – peer group, generation contrast, 'age related' and preceding cohort – and, by extension, social isolation. The most common approach is the examination of 'peer group' patterns of loneliness and isolation. This approach concentrates upon describing the prevalence and distribution of loneliness among older people (but this perspective could of course be applied to other age groups) and seeks to identify vulnerable or at risk groups. Peer group studies of loneliness dominate the research literature, especially for older people and later life. This is, however, a very static perspective upon what may be a very fluid and dynamic concept and the focus in age-related studies is to compare and contrast the experience of loneliness in later life with that experienced at other phases of the life-cycle. Generation-contrasted studies draw direct comparisons between the experience of loneliness between people of different ages. For example we can enumerate the extent of loneliness among young, mid-life and older people and draw comparisons between them. Preceding cohort studies attempt to compare patterns of loneliness and social engagement among current cohorts of older people with those demonstrated by preceding generations of elders.

In considering peer group patterns of loneliness and isolation within the older age groups a set of classic 'risk factors' has been identified. These include socio-demographic factors (living alone, being female, not having any surviving children, being aged 75 years and over), material circumstances (poverty and low income), health status (including disability, self-assessed health, mental health and depression) and life events (recent bereavement and admission of a relative or spouse into care). Subsequent research has verified the association of these factors with the descriptive epidemiology of loneliness in later life (Victor *et al.*, 2001) and isolation.

The perceived problem of the social isolation of older people has been a key component of many research studies of later life. This concern is indicated by the way that studies have attempted to summarise the levels of social contact among older people rather than just describing the networks (Townsend, 1957). Social isolation is a rather nebulous concept consisting of both an objective and subjective component (Victor *et al.*, 2004). Objective measures of social isolation relate to the extent of social contacts. This is usually achieved by summing the number of contacts the older person had in a defined period with household members, family, friends and 'official' visitors, and attendance at social clubs and other gatherings. There are several conceptual problems inherent in this type of mathematical exercise. It is often difficult to differentiate between a prearranged social contact and the casual exchange of greeting between neighbours or acquaintances in the street. How long does a social interaction have to be for it to be valued by participants? The scoring systems used are often highly arbitrary and based upon a set of unsubstantiated assumptions. Despite the lack of good empirical data, a higher priority and weighting is usually given to contacts with family members as opposed to friends. Direct contacts are presumed to be more valued than indirect forms of contact. Again this is an assumption that is not supported by research evidence and does not reflect the increasing diversity of the forms within which older people (and indeed other age groups) engage in social participation. Furthermore, such researchers are usually, but not always, studies undertaken at a single point in time and do not locate current patterns of social participation within a biographical or lifecourse perspective (Wenger and Burholt, 2004).

Using the quantitative 'tallying' methodology Townsend (1957) reported that 3 per cent of those aged 65+ were 'severely' isolated and 29 per cent as partly isolated. In her North Wales studies, Wenger (1984) reported that 6 per cent of her sample were very isolated and 29 per cent as partly isolated. Application of this methodology to a contemporary sample of elders, and using the same threshold of twenty-one contacts a week, then 75 per cent of elders were defined as isolated. Victor *et al.* (2002), using a slightly different methodology, report that 17 per cent of their national sample were not in weekly contact, either directly or by phone, with family and friends.

If we define isolation as those who have less than monthly contact with friends or family then 11 per cent of those aged 65+ in contemporary Britain can be so categorised. This is somewhat less than 20 per cent reported by Scharf and Smith (2004) for older people living in deprived urban neighbourhoods.

The subjective component of social isolation is loneliness. Loneliness among older people has been an aspect of ageing that has received a great deal of attention and has contributed greatly to the negative stereotype of old age. Studies of loneliness in later life have tended to be lacking in either theoretical or conceptual sophistication and have largely taken a simple 'social problem' type approach (Victor *et al.*, 2000). Several British studies have used variation upon the question developed by Sheldon (1948) which asks responders to rate how often they feel lonely and, generally speaking, the older people involved in these investigations have seemed to understand the concepts underlying the question. Consistently a variety of social surveys from the pioneering work of Sheldon (1948) in Wolverhampton have suggested that about 5–10 per cent of older people perceive themselves as being lonely all, or most of, the time (Victor *et al.*, 2001, 2002). The similarity of these results suggests that the prevalence of loneliness among older people has remained stable and not increased as is often suggested. Because researchers have largely perceived loneliness as a problem of old age, this type of question has rarely been asked of younger populations. Thus it is difficult to establish if older people feel more (or less) lonely than the rest of the population. This again illustrates how our preconceptions about specific groups influence the research agenda. Furthermore, with few exceptions (Wenger and Burholt, 2004) such studies fail to put such study responses within a longitudinal perspective. Victor *et al.* (2004) propose a typology of loneliness that distinguishes the primary (or lifelong) lonely group from those where loneliness is a secondary result of a major social change such as bereavement or ill health. The pathways (or trajectories) for these two different types of loneliness are very different and may well call for different types of interventions aimed at alleviating the problem.

The classic risk factors for loneliness and isolation may be grouped into four main domains: socio-demographic, material resources, health resources, and social resources and social network. Only the network/contact variables fail to demonstrate a link with loneliness and for isolation. These dimensions are clearly interrelated and when such linkages are taken into account four major factors, independent of each other, place older people at excess risk of reporting loneliness. These are marital status, with all groups vulnerable when compared with married elders, time alone, reported increases in loneliness and a high GHQ score, an indirect indicator of poor mental health. Two factors appear 'protective' against loneliness – advanced age and possession of educational qualifications (Victor *et al.*, 2004).

Although isolation and loneliness share a number of common risk factors, they do not vary consistently with each other. Those who are most socially isolated do not, necessarily, express the highest rates of perceived loneliness and vice versa. Andersson (1999) suggests a fourfold typology to describe the interrelationships between loneliness and isolation: the lonely and isolated, the lonely, the isolated and those who are neither lonely nor isolated. Defining isolation as those without weekly direct contact with family, friends or neighbours (17 per cent), there is a small minority who are both lonely and isolated (2 per cent) and then two independent groups of lonely and isolated elders.

The dynamics of family relationships

The previous sections have indicated that older people are members of kinship groups based upon blood (and marriage) ties and that there is extensive contact between older people and their families. Simply counting the number of kin or size of the social networks of older people does not shed much light on how and why family relationships endure nor on the social roles which older people play within these groups. Documenting the social network does not tell us much about the mechanism by which support is transferred between family members. Family relationships and their meaning are very difficult to research. Such work offers both conceptual and methodological challenges and there are many intriguing questions about how and why families work. In understanding the social roles that older people play within families we first have to explore the broad set of social rules within which families operate. Family relationships are, like so many other spheres of life, believed to be governed by a set of social rules or norms. Various explanations of the nature of kin relationships have been proposed. Some argue that kin relationships are essentially 'moral' in nature (we help our family because they are our family with no thought of personal gain) while others argue that kin relationships are simply based upon economic and material interests of the individuals concerned (Finch and Mason, 1993). Finch (1989a) proposes a more fluid concept of kinship relationships based upon a set of guidelines rather than fixed social rules. However conceptualised, it must be acknowledged that the nature of kin relationships varies between relationships and between membership of different social groups (e.g. by class or ethnicity) and can be specific to individual family or kinship groups investigated. It is important to remember that social guidelines within which families operate will vary over time and between varying social, cultural and spatial contexts and may, not necessarily, be generalisable to the wider social context. Collecting empirical data, which look at issues such as the provision of support, is difficult to undertake. Most of the research undertaken into the reasons underpinning support use attitude statements to determine 'cultural' norms and hypothetical questions concerning expectations of support. Such questions do at least offer some insight into where people think they would turn for help in times of crisis.

There are several key organising principles, which help us to understand the nature of family and kin relationships. The major and most enduring social norms providing the framework for social relations are the concepts of independence, reciprocity and obligation. These form the backdrop against which we consider issues on intra- and intergeneration exchange. The twin issues of dependence and independence are at the heart of understanding and analysing family and kin group relationships. Children are dependent upon their parents while spouses usually exhibit mutually supporting dependencies. It is the strongly ingrained cultural norm of independence, which prompts older adults to live independently and autonomously of their adult children (and vice versa). The notions of obligation and reciprocity operate within a normative context of the maintenance of individual independence and autonomy.

Central to much of the literature concerning kin relationships are the notions of obligation and filial piety. Much is written from a theoretical and conceptual perspective in the area. It is argued that it is level of obligation that distinguishes family relationships from friendship. To put this most crudely in terms of need or crisis, families are supposed to respond whereas friends are under no such 'obligation', although friends may well choose to respond positively to a crisis situation. As part of our family roles we all have rights but along with these come responsibilities. It is argued by some that kinship ties based upon obligation have become looser with ties based around voluntary fulfilment of duties (Hareven, 1995). Clearly the rights and obligations we experience vary according to our status within the kinship network. The obligations of mutual care and support, which characterise the marital relationship, are not necessarily the same as those of siblings. The relationship between adult children and parents is qualitatively different from more distant kin relationships. Phillipson *et al.* (2001) provide extensive empirical material which demonstrate how filial and family obligation manifest themselves in the everyday lives of older people to provide a predominantly supportive family and social environment.

Reciprocity is a key organising principle of family and kinship groups (and indeed the world of wider social relationships). Reciprocity is concerned with mutual assistance and transfers support (financial, physical or emotional) towards those family members who need it on the understanding that it will be 'repaid', in some form, at a future date (or where the help being provided is 'repayment' for support given previously). Antonucci (1985) describes reciprocity as a support bank – 'deposits' are made in the expectation of withdrawal at a later date. This is a difficult area to study using cross-sectional techniques as it is an essentially dynamic process using a very long time frame. Intergenerational transfers of love, affection and material/social support are at the heart of family relationships. Gerontologists have tended to concentrate upon studying the role played by younger family members in caring for the older generation. There has been much less study of aid given by the old to the young. It is clear that flows of help between the older person and the family are not unidirectional and that there is a considerable degree of reciprocity within and between the generations (Finch, 1989a; Phillipson *et al.*, 2001). Where such reciprocity has not been built up across the generations, for example where parents have been abusive or neglectful of their children, then there are negative consequences of neglect when the parents become older. This is illustrated by the classic study of Issacs *et al.* (1972) in Glasgow. Careful investigation of the older people apparently 'wilfully neglected' by their families revealed a history of poor relationships with children when the parents were younger, hence they did not have the 'bank' of reciprocity and mutual support to call upon in times of need. Although Thane (1998) provides examples of where family care is provided in spite of poor relationships between parents and children, there is less certainty about such transfers of support and less 'moral' sanction if it is not provided.

It is presumed, perhaps in an unstated way, by policy makers and planners (and numerous social commentators) that there is a consensus concerning the responsibilities of families towards each other in terms of parent–child relationships and the role of families in caring for dependent relatives. McGlone *et al.* (2000) demonstrate the primacy of the family as a source of help in a crisis. The family was reported as the primary source of help for household jobs (79 per cent), help while ill (88 per cent), marital problems (53 per cent), financial problems (51 per cent) and depression (68 per cent). Finch and Mason (1993) provide one of the few empirical examples of work testing this widely held social belief with reference to the responsibilities of families towards their older relatives. They undertook a quantitative study in the north-west of England to examine whether there is any social consensus about family obligations and responsibilities across the age range. They report that the responses to the questions about helping older relatives indicate that it was difficult to establish that a consensus existed. Participants in the survey were asked to respond to hypothetical questions and hence may give a very different answer if asked about their own family members. Finch and Mason (1993) argue that responses to these questions about family responsibilities show the complexity of these issues. They argue that factors such as the 'deservingness' of the cases and the perceived limitation of the commitment are important and can be suggested as 'procedural' guidelines operating within a framework of reciprocity. Additionally some issues such as dealing with dementia or incontinence may be seen by family members as being in the 'domain of professionals'. Hence the whole rubric of family responsibilities is far more complicated than simply a moral duty imposed by the simple existence of a blood tie. They make the important point that simply knowing that a person has thirteen siblings or ten cousins does not enable us to predict (with any accuracy) that he will be looked after if ill or lent money in a financial crisis. Rather the provision of help and support across the generations is mediated by a whole variety of factors including the nature of the relationship, the quality of the relationship, the nature of the problem and the perceived duration and complexity of the problem. This is clearly a very complex area, which requires considerable further research if we are to understand how modern families 'work' and to consider how the increasingly complex family structures of the future might operate.

Social roles in families

Within families older people experience a number of different social roles. In this section we focus upon three key social roles – spouse, grandparent and widow(er) – and consider how these influence the quality of the experience of ageing and shape the social context within which it is experienced.

Marital relationships

Expectations of marital relationships in later life are complex. Most married couples who enter old age together have been married for a considerable time, while some marriages, if they are second or third partnerships, may be of more recent duration. Men expect to be married until they die and do not expect to have to 'care' for their wife or that their wife will predecease them; women expect to be widowed. The majority of couples who enter old age as married expect to maintain their own household until either the death or entry into an institution of one partner. How older couples experience marriage in later life largely represents a continuation of pre-existing patterns. Those who have had a good relationship in pre-old age are likely to maintain this into later life. The quality of the marital relationship is certainly an important factor in maintaining quality of life in old age (and probably other phases of the life-cycle). Old age can pose some special challenges such as reduced income, retirement and health problems. All of these may force couples to renegotiate previously stable patterns of gender-specific roles (Wilson, 1995). Regardless of the pattern of internal organisa-tion, the long-term marital relationship is a major source of identity, support (both physical and emotional) and intimacy in later life (Jerrome, 1993). There is clearly a large research agenda investigat-ing different types of marital experience in later life. Again, it is easy to presume that the experience is one of uniformity and homogene-ity, but this seems unlikely to be the case. There are clear research issues in terms of long-term cohabiting relationships, same-sex relationships, re-partnering and the meaning of such relationships in later life.

Grandparenting

One of the most common social roles available to older people in families is that of grandparenthood and, increasingly, great-grand-parenthood. The great majority of people with children eventually become grandparents, but given current profound changes in fertility, this observation may not hold for future generations. The British context for grandparenting is influenced by three sets of factors: the spatial separation of generations makes the grandparent more 'remote', the relationship is one that is voluntary and is not set within a rigid framework of rights and responsibilities, and the interests of grandparents are seen as secondary to the conjugal or immediate family. In thinking about the role of grandparent we need to disentan-gle the stereotype and myths, of grandparents as kindly, indulgent and caring, from the reality. Perhaps the first myth that requires re-exami-nation is the linkage of grandparenthood with old age. Changes in childbearing and the closer spacing of children have made grandpar-enthood a more 'youthful' experience. Becoming a grandparent is not, necessarily, synonymous with old age and later life. Increased life expectancies, coupled with shorter periods of child-rearing, have exposed many people to the role of grandparenthood at an earlier age than for previous cohorts. The Olympic 100-metre champion of 1996, Linford Christie, became a grandfather at 36, but this is an atypical example. Grundy *et al.* (1999) report that 35 per cent of adults in Britain are grandparents at the age of 50 and 80 per cent by the age of 60, and that approximately 10 per cent of those aged 60–69 are great-grandparents. It seems that grandparenthood has become an integral part of middle age while, perhaps, great-grand-parenthood is the role associated with later life. The reduction in mor-tality rates also means that most grandparents survive well past their grandchildren's adolescence; indeed most children can expect to have several grandparents surviving into their adulthood. Again, the fact that most children have grandparents is a fairly novel aspect of society – for children born a hundred years ago there was no such certainty.

  Grandparenthood is a role that is seen as being open to most older people and is one which is almost universally welcomed, but we must remember that it is usually a secondary role. Thus the individual may be an employee, a wife and a grandmother. It seems unlikely that for any single grandparent the role will remain constant over time.

Rather it develops in response to changes in both grandparent and grandchild. We also need to note that grandparents are a highly diverse group and the age range encompasses a 70+ year range (32 to 100+). The more complex set of family structures that characterise modern Britain (and other countries such as the United States) and the growth in the numbers of step-grandchildren enhances this diversity. This is a relationship which has been subject to much less academic scrutiny. Reported contact levels with grandchildren are generally high, seem to be fairly consistent over time, but decrease with the age of the older person and are higher for daughters' as compared with sons' children. Grundy *et al.* (1999) report that 50 per cent of those aged 50–59 with grandchildren see them weekly. This decreases to about 35 per cent for those aged 70–79 and reflects the fact that contact is more likely when grandchildren are young and living at home with their parents. Clarke *et al.* (2004) suggest that 60 per cent of grandparents see their grandchildren weekly. Despite this generally high level of contact, 46 per cent would have liked to see more of their grandchildren (Grundy *et al.*, 1999). The usual reasons for reduced contact were either the distance that they lived from the grandchild, indeed approximately 50 per cent of those aged 50+ with grandchildren report that they live more than 30 minutes' journey time away (Grundy *et al.*, 1999), or their own infirmity. However, the complexities of contemporary family breakdown mean that grandparent ties are rendered more fragile.

What do grandparents do? What are the rights and responsibilities of this role? Given the fairly recent emergence of substantial numbers of people living long enough to become grandparents it is, perhaps, not surprising that there are fewer established social norms governing the role of grandparents and great-grandparents within the family. Grandparenthood is seen by many as a rather symbolic role which links past, present and future (see also Thompson *et al.*, 1990) and which offers continuity across the generations. The varying styles of grandparenthood may be classified as passive, active and detached. Passive grandparenting involves providing support by assisting with childcare, giving presents and babysitting, but not taking over the role of the parent – it is seen as secondary to that of the parent. Active grandparenting involves becoming a surrogate parent. This is most often the role played by a grandmother caring for a child while the mother works or when grandparents are required to replace the parents. A survey of the family life of older people in the East End of London revealed that two-thirds of older women with grandchildren performed some regular service for them such as fetching them from school, giving them meals, looking after them while their parents were at work or looking after them in the evening (Townsend, 1957). Grandfathers were much less active in this role than grandmothers, with only one-fifth performing a regular childcare function. A recent national survey (Victor *et al.*, 2004) revealed that 24 per cent of all those aged 65+ had undertaken 'babysitting' childcare activities in the previous month. Expressed as a percentage of those with grandchildren, it seems that the levels of activity by grandparents are not far short of the levels recorded by Townsend (1957). Detached grandparenting, as the names implies, is a distant relationship characterised by involvement on holidays and special occasions but otherwise out of contact. There is a considerable research agenda to investigate in the developing area of (great-) grandparenthood, especially examining class, gender and ethnic variations and the longitudinal dynamics of the relationship.

Widowhood

At some time, married couples, especially older couples, have to face the possibility of their own death or the death of their spouse. There are gender differences in how this is approached as men, overall, do not expect to outlive their wives because of the age differential between spouses. One recent change in the social context of ageing has been the concentration of the experience of widowhood almost exclusively into later life, rather than being characteristic of all phases of the lifecycle. For example, in 1851 one-third of women were widowed while they were aged 55–64; this percentage is now reached a decade later.

Marriage is important because of its intrinsic value and the links it provides to social networks and activities. A marriage relationship can provide companionship, intimacy, affection and a sense of belonging, and provide evidence to the wider world of social competence as well as being a 'legitimate' context for sexual activity. All these are lost upon widowhood. This is, perhaps, one of the key transitions that accompanies later life and is highly stressful. Upon widowhood not only is the relationship with the spouse lost but also all sorts of other factors change including relationships with family and friends, the domestic division of labour, and the identity, sense of personal worth and financial circumstances. Widowhood has strong negative consequences as it is linked with high rates of mortality, morbidity and self-reported ill health. It is not clear if these factors are directly linked to widowhood or reflect the influence of an intervening, or confounding, variable such as low income or age. Furthermore, many of these associations are based upon cross-sectional data and may not be so marked when studied within a longitudinal framework.

Widowhood is predominantly a female experience. It is, to a large extent, a normative or expected experience. By the age of 75–79 years 56 per cent of women are widowed (21 per cent of men) and of those women aged 80+ 71 per cent are widowed and only 16 per cent are still married. For women, however, widowhood increasingly becomes the norm with age and thus may be a less socially disruptive experience. Indeed for very elderly women marriage may be perceived as the deviant status rather than widowhood. While most widowed persons attain acceptable adjustment levels to their bereavement, this process of adaptation seems to take some time. Studies from the United States indicate that two-thirds of widows take at least a year to come to terms with their new status, to learn to be alone and to be independent. Widowhood disrupts, at least in the short term, established patterns of social relationships. At such times the widow usually turns to her family for help in coping with immediate problems and establishing a new life. In particular, children are a first line of support. Typically daughters provide emotional help while sons provide financial help. However, widows seem much less inclined than widowers to move in with their children after their bereavement. This reflects the adherence to the powerful social norm of independence. Again, our understanding of the impact of widowhood in later life is based upon studies of 'traditional' married couples. There is less literature examining the impact of bereavement upon those in gay or cohabiting relationships or those who have lived with siblings or friends. Hence, our understanding of bereavement and widowhood does not reflect the diversity of the living arrangement demonstrated by current (and future) generations of elders.

Conclusion

In this chapter we have demonstrated that the popular myths of the 'golden age' of older people when they lived in large family groups loved and venerated by all is an inaccurate and simplistic view which does not do justice to the complexities of the past. Although most older people live in households confined to members of their own generation, this seems to be an expression of their desire and ability to maintain independent living. This should not be seen as evidence of a demonstration of neglect by their family. Indeed it is the prime objective of government policy for older people to maintain them in their own homes and living independently in the community. It is a paradox that those who espouse this policy objective interpret it very negatively when musing on the family and support networks of older people. Those who extol the importance of co-residence are ignoring the wishes of older people and are denying them an independent and autonomous existence. This is both patronising and a misplaced reading of the social changes that have characterised living arrangements in contemporary British society. It seems highly unlikely that younger people would embrace exhortations to maintain co-residence with their parents (and grandparents) with any degree of enthusiasm.

Social engagements and participation is suggested by Rowe and Kahn (1997) as one of the three key elements of 'successful ageing'. Irrespective of the acceptance of notion of successful ageing this does serve to emphasise the importance of social participation for the well-being of older people (and indeed other age groups). The majority of older people are enmeshed in a complicated family network consisting of family, friends and neighbours. We have seen that where they are part of a kin network, older people demonstrate high rates of social contact, which seem to bring a large amount of satisfaction to them. Older people are also active in the wider social world and few conform to the stereotype of isolated and lonely lives. There is an extensive research and policy agenda to be addressed in terms of our understanding of social engagement in later life and in developing interventions to promote and enhance this. Some older people, either because they never married or have no children, have far fewer kin within their networks. This may have a profound effect upon the ageing experience because it may limit their sources of support. Lack of an extensive kin network may also restrict the opportunities for the older person to make a positive contribution. Such individuals may have developed strategies to compensate for loss of this by developing other sorts of equally valuable relationships. We must be careful not to presume that the only types of relationships which matter are kin based. It seems likely that increasing numbers of elders will experience later life within 'families of choice' – friendship- rather than kinship-based relationships. The implications in both policy and practice terms of such changes remain unclear. It seems highly likely that policy makers will need to be more flexible in responding to such changes.

The family, and its much more easily measured relative the

household, is not a static entity. Rather it is a social institution, which is subject to almost continuous change. In the future, changes within society will inevitably affect the experience of ageing. The 'shape' of the family in changing from the classic tree shape to the beanpole structure of long thin family lines which may involve the 'blending' of family units via divorce and remarriage. In addition, future cohorts of elders may well enter 'old age' with a much greater diversity of domestic circumstances than previous generations. In coming decades we will see the ageing of the generations that have had several marriages, cohabiting relationships and the re-emergence of the unmarried spinster as a new generation of women opt for an unpartnered and childless lifestyle. It remains the subject for speculation as to how these changes will influence the kin and wider social context within older people's experience of ageing. This increasing complexity and diversity of our social location reasserts an increase in the social roles that older people will play. We will see an increase in 'great' and 'great-great' family linkages as well as new emerging roles of step-grandchildren to complement the existing role of grandparent. Clearly the experience of these differing roles will vary with structural factors such as class, gender and ethnicity. The social relationships and modes of participation for future generations of elders are likely to exhibit increasing diversity. However, it seems unlikely that the importance of such relationships for quality of life in old age will be supplanted. The challenge for researchers is to be able to reflect the complexity and diversity obscured by the application of social category labels such as living alone, to record the dynamic nature of household and social relationships and to be able to integrate factors of age, class and gender. For policy makers and practitioners the challenge is to be able to integrate such complexity into everyday decisions concerning the care and well-being of older people and to develop interventions that can enhance and support family and social relationships to enhance quality of life in old age.

8 Material resources in later life

Clearly a key element of well-being in later life, and one that is highly influential in setting the social context within which later life is experienced, is that of material resources. Included within this broad aspect are housing, issues of income maintenance and of more expansive measures of economic well-being such as access to consumer goods, etc. In this chapter we start our analysis with an examination of work and retirement issues. Work, retirement and access to material resources are all interrelated concepts. Following from that we examine the access that older people have to the broader material resources and wider consumer culture as indicated by factors such as income, housing and the 'consumer durables' that provide the framework for the lives of other members of the population, especially now that we inhabit a consumption-based economy where the emphasis is upon services rather than manufacturing and production in the 'classic' Fordist model of capitalist economy.

Work and retirement

Within western 'Protestant' societies the work ethic is an important organising principle. However, in most discussions of work and retirement the focus is confined to the domain of paid employment and the formal labour market. The narrowness of the conceptualisation of 'work' and therefore of the related notion of 'retirement' must be borne in mind when discussing factors such as declining rates of labour force participation. Such debates are framed within a very limited and partial summary of the 'work' that is undertaken within a given society. Excluded from this narrow focus is all 'non-paid' labour such as family-based childcare and the substantial 'black' or 'cash' economy. Many of the debates about the impending crisis of old age are based upon the calculation of dependency ratios, and similarly, statistics takes a very narrow view of economic activity and a rather expansive view of dependency. Not surprisingly, women are then marginalised in debates about work and retirement because of their often interrupted relationship with the formal labour market (Ginn *et al.*, 2001; Ginn, 2003). Given the changing role of women within the labour market, this is clearly going to change in the future and can contribute to the development of a whole new female-based exploration of the meaning and experience of retirement. A related and similarly neglected aspect of the preoccupation with paid, formal labour market participation is that studies of retirement are entirely limited to this arena. For those who have had only limited contact with the formal labour market, the concept of 'retirement' may be both inappropriate and meaningless. Can one retire from being a housewife or homemaker? It is a presumption of much popular literature that retirement is a major social transition in the life of an individual. However, it is self-evident that this can be true only if the individual has something to retire from. Our research focus upon retirement may mean that we have failed to note some other major transitions characteristic of later life and, perhaps more crucially, failed to note the continuities that may well characterise the lives of many older people. Again we have focused upon 'role loss' for a minority of elders to the exclusion of considering continuities among, speculatively, the majority. We have focused upon the individual rather than looking more expansively at couples (Fairhurst, 2004).

Work and employment

The view that retirement results in a fundamental crisis of identity for the individual is widespread in both popular discourse and more academic arenas. This perspective assumes that (paid) work or employment is both central to the life of the individual and that it is the major or central characteristic defining personal identity, self-esteem, social status and self-worth. However, this is a very narrow and limited view as to how we determine the 'worth' of both ourselves and others. Gilleard (1996) and Gilleard and Higgs (2000) argue that consumption and patterns of participation in the consumer culture of contemporary society are now a more important and relevant dimension of differentiation in a post-modern world. Identity is based upon consumption rather than production. While there are critiques that can be made of the argument of Gilleard and Higgs (2000), these commentators are important because they have extended our thinking about the issues of the nature and scope of material resources in later life and how these may be linked to identity in later life. Despite these theoretical developments it remains the case that work is certainly an important part of our own (and others') sense of our 'social worth'. We are not yet an entirely consumption- and lifestyle-dominated society. In the United Kingdom at least, social introductions swiftly and almost inevitably include the phrase 'and what do you do?' (i.e. what is your occupation). Information about an individual occupation can tell us indirectly about the income, education and 'social standing' of individuals. This simple social convention (or norm) enables us to locate individuals (very roughly) in terms of their income, education, social status and 'social value', but it has limited currency, for many within contemporary Britain are 'outside' this classificatory system and it is culturally and temporally specific.

To look at the relevance of this stereotype and to understand the impact of retirement, for the individual and the wider society, we must first look at the role that paid work and formal employment plays in contemporary society. In a post-modern, post-industrial economy what is the role of work and how is 'work' to be defined? Sociologists have identified four main functions that work performs in the lives of individuals: the provision of a wage, the regulation of time, the provision of social status and the provision of social relationships. Such meanings are inevitably socially and culturally specific, which suggests that perception of work (and by inference retirement) may change for future cohorts of older people. Attitudes and norms towards the role and function of work (and retirement) are therefore fluid and dynamic and are likely to be very different in the future; we may also 'rediscover' that the opportunities for work and retirement, and the way that they are experienced, will vary within the older age groups and it will almost certainly not be a homogeneous experience across age, gender, class and ethnic divides.

To fully understand the impact and meaning of retirement from the formal labour market, we must examine its effects upon each of the functions noted above; these functions may not be of equal importance to different types of workers, for different types of occupations and for different types of people. The importance ascribed to the major broad functions of work almost certainly vary with the social profile of the individual, such as gender or class, and the degree to which such opportunities are available elsewhere. The first, and perhaps most obvious, function of a job in a post-industrial society is to provide an income and other financial reward to the worker in exchange for their labour, skills or expertise. For those no longer in the formal labour market, alternative forms of income are required and we return to this issue for older people in a later section. The provision of a wage is not the only important function of formal work, as the continued employment of lottery winners attests! A second, and very important, function of work is as a regulatory activity and a temporal framework around which other aspects of life such as leisure, hobbies or social relationships are organised. Work provides a sense of identity for the individual and also serves as a status-organising concept. In Britain the complex concept of social class is often conceptualised, operationalised and measured with respect to occupation, hence the notion of 'occupational class'. Thus paid work is an important component contributing to the social standing of the individual in the community. Those without work, because of unemployment, retirement or family and/or caring responsibilities, are usually accorded a lower social status than those currently in employment; women who are not gainfully employed are often accorded the status of their husbands. There are instances within a UK context where individuals without an obvious paid employment are accorded very high status, as in the case of the Royal Family. Finally, work also serves as an important basis for social relationships of varying degrees of intimacy. It is a major source of social contacts and a primary reference point. Much of the research concerned with the individual impact of retirement has focused upon the 'social losses' associated with retirement and with subsequent negative consequences for the individuals concerned. Work was seen as occupying perhaps the central role in the social lives of individuals and retirement as creating a 'social void' that could not be filled. Retirement, from this perspective, is always problematic as it is conceptualised as a constant search for activities to 'replace' work because it creates discontinuities and disjunctures in both the internal and external world of individuals. From this perspective the key to a successful retirement is the 'substitution' of new activities such as volunteering, golf or gardening for the gap created by work – a clear echo of the strictures of activity theories. The above perspectives all paint a rather rosy view of employment and the labour market from, perhaps, a rather 'middle-class' perspective. It does not incorporate some of the negative aspects of the work arena evident in some manual and repetitive occupation such as shift-work, monotonous jobs and lack of control over the work pattern or work environment. Again, the importance of these different aspects of work may vary between jobs and people (and indeed may vary in importance for the same individual across his or her employment career). We may speculate that the importance of work may vary between men and women as well as class or ethnicity and with age. If we accept the premise that the meaning of work varies within the population then it follows logically that the meaning of retirement will also vary within the different segments of the population. The 'retirement literature' has yet to catch up with the diversity of experience and multiplicity of meanings that can be attributed to an apparently simple and single concept as retirement.

Our understanding of retirement is, as Fairhurst (2004) notes, strongly influenced by our understanding of work. The entry of significant numbers of women into the workforce is likely to help us reconsider and develop our ideas about retirement and its meaning. Much work in the field of retirement has presumed a male-orientated model of working life (Bernard and Meade, 1993; Fairhurst, 2004). This model of the working life has an implicit presumption of a separation of home and family life and retirement from paid employment at a 'fixed' age with the reward for fifty years' participation in the labour market, often in the same job or with the same employer, of a state- or employer-provided pension. Such a model was also based upon a relatively short post-retirement lifespan. Changes in the nature of the labour market, the development of multiple and fragmented careers, the increased participation of women and the development of pensions have all combined to change the nature of retirement. Individuals can now take a variety of routes into retirement and, increasingly given the role of women in the workforce, retirement is becoming a 'couple' experience. The retirement experience is becoming more fragmented and diverse in character. As yet, however, our conceptual and theoretical thinking about retirement has not kept pace with these changes nor developed sufficiently to include the diversity of ethnic, class and gender diversities and how such diversities intersect.

Participation in the labour market

The labour market is a diverse entity consisting of the formal labour market, about which we have data, and the 'black' economy of unregulated employment outside the formal structures plus the informal care economy of parents or neighbours and families providing services for children and others, or 'domestic maintenance' services on a reciprocal basis. Within this the formal labour market is a dynamic and constantly changing entity and the study of older people's participation in it, and their subsequent withdrawal on retirement, have been major areas of activity within gerontological research. There is clearly a constantly changing relationship between the demand for, and supply of, labour. Furthermore the types of labour required are also constantly evolving. In post-war Britain there has been a marked decline in the requirement for manual labour and increases in demand for people with new information technology (IT) skills as we have moved from a manufacturing to a service-based type of economy. Full-time jobs are increasingly being replaced by part-time jobs and 'women's' jobs are replacing 'men's' jobs. The formal labour market is becoming increasingly globalised as service-based call centre jobs move from Britain to India, and Britain recruits health care professionals from Australia and the Far East. Our understanding of the role that older people play within the labour market has to be located within this highly dynamic context and within the context of more widespread economic changes. Disentangling the various factors underlying changes in labour force participation by older workers is a major methodological challenge.

There is clear, incontrovertible empirical evidence that older people have, over the course of the twentieth century, gradually withdrawn from participation in the labour market as the practice of formal retirement has gained widespread acceptance. In 1900 approximately 80 per cent of males aged 65+ were employed. By 1931 this had decreased to 50 per cent while the 2001 Census indicated that of males aged 65 years and over, 7 per cent formally defined themselves as economically active. There are a variety of different methods of calculating engagement with the labour force. The Census identifies those who self-report that they are economically active – this includes both those in work and those who are unemployed and looking for work. However, regardless of the precise method of calculation used, labour force participation by older males has declined markedly so that at age 60–64, half of men indicate that they are economically active. This contrasts with the situation in 1971, when 82 per cent of this age group were economically active. The twentieth century has seen, for men, decreasing labour force participation rates trickle down the age groups.

Only a small minority of women aged 65+ (3 per cent) are defined as economically active and, at all ages, women have lower economic activity rates than men. Especially for women, labour market participation is strongly linked to birth cohorts. For example approximately 60 per cent of the 1957–1962 cohort of women are in paid employment at age 30 compared with a little over 40 per cent for women born a decade earlier. As extensive and sustained female labour market participation is a fairly recent phenomenon, the likely pattern of older women's participation in the labour market remains the subject of speculation. As yet it is not clear whether older women will opt for 'early exit' or will remain in employment for as long as possible and this may be influenced by their partnership arrangements. However, the pattern of women's employment differs from men's in that it is still predominantly part-time in nature. This has consequences for the financial circumstances of older women. Ginn (2003) argues that the financial impoverishment experienced by many women in later life is a direct consequence of their restricted engagement with the formal labour market. When examining the participation of older workers in the labour market, two contradictory trends are evident. The decrease in male economic activity rates coexist with an increase in economic participation by women. These trends are not unique to Britain: rather similar trends may be observed across the developed countries.

Explanations for the decline in formal labour market participation of older males have been advanced at both the micro- and macro-levels of analysis. At the individual level a variety of explanations have been advanced to account for the dramatic decline in employment rates among older men. These explanations range in the degree of 'coercion' experienced by the older worker in making the 'decision' to withdraw from the formal labour market. At one extreme there is the notion of the 'truly voluntary' withdrawal from the labour market. At the opposite extreme is the notion of compulsory or forced exit via retirement or compulsory redundancy. Intermediate between the extremes are notions of 'constrained choices' resulting from involuntary labour supply changes, the availability of occupational pensions benefits, a shift in demand away from the skills provided by older workers and age discrimination. Clearly there is an interrelationship between these differing factors as they are not independent of each other and disentangling these linkages is problematic. Much of the decline in male employment probably reflect changes in labour demands, older male workers being concentrated in industries where there has been a decrease in demand for skills and that much of the decline is the result of 'constrained choices' rather than 'truly voluntary' choice to retire early. In the face of contracting demands for their skills older workers, if offered an appropriate 'incentive package', may opt for early retirement rather than wait for compulsory redundancy with reduced benefits. With the changes in the nature of the economic base, both nationally and locally, such workers may not then be able to find alternative sources of employment and the worker can slide into retirement.

There are also macro-economic and policy concerns underlying the explanatory frameworks for the reduction in male employment. As a method of reducing unemployment, especially among younger people, early retirement commands almost universal approval despite its obvious ageist premise. In times of limited demand for labour it is often uncritically accepted that an older worker is less deserving of a job than a younger worker. Early retirement has been justified upon social grounds. For example trade unions have consistently argued that retirement at the age of 65 years discriminates against manual workers, who are often in poorer health than those in non-manual occupations and who have fewer years in the post-work phase of life (and will experience retirement in poorer health than their counterparts from professional occupations). The second major impetus behind the development of early retirement is wider labour market and political concerns. These include the use of early retirement to disguise long-term unemployment among older males, release jobs for younger people and reduce the labour force without recourse to redundancies. Early retirement schemes have thus been used to remove from the labour force the workers perceived as least productive, such as the long-term sick, or the 'old' who are presumed to be inefficient, unable to adapt to change and expendable. To a large degree these arguments mirror many of those advanced to support the original notion of retirement and exemplifies the types of arguments advance by Phillipson (1982) of the use of retirement to manage wider labour market problems. Older workers, like women, can be conceptualised as a 'reserve' labour supply to be called upon in times of labour shortage and excluded in times of labour 'oversupply'.

The widespread acceptance of retirement at specific ages, and the widespread decline in employment for those in the 'pre-retirement' decade, have important consequences for those older workers remaining within the labour force. Older workers, that are those in the years immediately preceding mandatory retirement age, often suffer from the consequences of commonly held beliefs or stereotypes concerning their abilities. Examples of such beliefs are that older workers are less productive, have higher absenteeism rates and are unable to learn new skills. Not surprisingly most of these presumptions have been refuted (Atchley, 1999). In Britain, older workers, those aged 65+, are over-represented in the primary industries (mining, farming, fishing, etc.) with 9 per cent employed in these occupations compared with 3 per cent nationally. However, it remains the case that approximately 35 per cent of those aged 65+ who are still employed are in the managerial and professional occupation groups and this approximates to the distribution for all male workers.

Given the widespread prejudices about the capabilities of older workers, it is hardly surprising to find that unemployment is also high among this age group, especially in a time of economic recession. Changes in the methods of defining unemployment often make it difficult to state precisely the unemployment levels among older workers. In addition it is argued that in times of recession and high unemployment, the transition from work to retirement becomes increasingly complex and it becomes more difficult to categorise older people in terms of their attachment to the formal labour force. Determining unemployment rates among older workers continues to be complex as it is highly subject to the changes in definitions and classification of 'formal' unemployment. However, whether they are retired or unemployed, there are substantial numbers of older men who are not formally employed. This mirrors the situation for older women where the majority is not in formal employment. For many of these women this represents a continuity, rather than discontinuity, with earlier phases of the lifecycle, when they may have withdrawn from the labour market for family reasons and never returned. This is unlikely to be the case for future generations of women, who are much more likely to have been working full-time in the labour market across the life course and who may not have experienced the 'traditional' female pattern of interrupted and part-time working fitted around childbearing and childcaring responsibilities.

The development of retirement

Retirement is usually defined as the formal withdrawal from the labour market and gainful economic activity at a specified chronological age usually associated with the age at which benefits and pensions are made available. In Britain this is more usually associated with eligibility for the state retirement pension. A ruling by the European Court has deemed that it is illegal to discriminate between men and women in terms of the age of retirement and hence the differential ages at which men and women became eligible for the state retirement pension, 65 years and 60 years respectively, are being phased out so that in 2010 this will have been abolished. Indeed Britain was one of only a few countries, including Italy, Switzerland and Belgium, that maintained differential retirement ages. The reasoning behind the establishment of the differential retirement age in Britain was that women 'aged' earlier than men and that they had 'two jobs', that of worker and housewife. The National Spinsters Association campaigned for women to retire at 55. The pension age was reduced to 65 for both sexes in 1925 and for women to 60 in 1940. Eligibility for such benefits is, however, dependent upon withdrawal from the formal labour market. Retirement may be seen, therefore, as a legal, economic and socially defined construct. It is not a 'natural' concept although we often presume that it is! Here is an important role for the gerontologist in casting a critical gaze upon aspects of later life that have become taken for granted.

The emergence of retirement

As a social institution the concept of 'retirement' or withdrawal from the labour market at a pre-specified chronological age is fairly recent, although it is one that is now well established. The presumption that for those who are involved in the labour market, they will have a period of 'free time' towards the end of the lifecycle is now expected by all workers, although it is rooted in a traditional male experience of work and the labour market. Such have been the changes in life expectancy that for many of us the post-retirement phase of life can be extensive. Expectation of life at age 65 is about fifteen to twenty years. This is significantly different from 1908, when the 'old age' pension was introduced. Then at age 70, the age of entitlement, the average man could expect to live for another five to eight years. The establishment of 'retirement' or 'post-work' phase of the lifecycle is predominantly a concept derived from the second half of the twentieth century. Given the changing demographic and economic profiles of contemporary society, it is unclear that fixed age retirement will be sustained in the twenty-first century and that more flexible transitions into the post-work phase of life will develop as a response to the changing labour needs of the increasingly globalised British economy.

As a social construct and phase in the lifecycle, retirement was almost unheard of in pre-industrial times and is rarely observed in developing nations. In pre-industrial economies older people expected to continue working until they were physically incapable of doing so any longer (Midwinter, 1997). This reflects the way that all members of the family group or household were engaged in economic activities to sustain themselves, as the example of some of the world's subsistence-based economies still demonstrate. Mirroring the growth of 'retirement' is the development of childhood as a period of education rather than employment. Both segmentations of the life-course are difficult to sustain outwith a modern, developed manufacturing or service-based economy. One result of the growth of fixed age retirement has been the twinning of the onset of old age, at least in policy terms, with the concept of retirement. The result has been the popular expectation that old age starts at a definite chronological age (Thane, 2000).

What has brought about the growth of retirement such that it is now seen as a 'normal' phase of life? The growth and institutionalisation of fixed age retirement in western industrial countries was a largely twentieth-century phenomenon and its emergence is linked with the growth of pensions in a way which is complex and difficult to disentangle. Clearly retirement is not a viable concept without the provision of pensions and benefits to those precluded from earning a living in the formal labour market. According to Midwinter (1997) the first recorded publicly funded post-work pension was paid in 1684 to an employee of the Port of London. From the early eighteenth century, British civil servants benefited from a variety of superannuation or pension schemes. They became the first occupational group for whom a fixed retirement age with a pension attached was available when, in 1859, they became eligible for a pension at the age of 65. The selection of 65 years as the retirement age was based upon impressionistic notions rather than empirical data. We can see from this example that from its inception in Britain, retirement was an essentially middle-class concept. The Northcote-Trevelyan report of 1857 on the efficiency of the civil service first promoted the idea of retirement and argued that the efficiency of the civil service would be enhanced by removing older workers and providing them with pensions. Such a system would enable the smooth introduction of younger workers into the civil service by an 'orderly' exit of older workers. This is a clear articulation of the ideas of intergenerational transfers of power expressed by the 'disengagement' theorists almost a century later. In Britain at least, retirement has been seen as a way of improving the economic efficiency rather than as a reflection of concern for the well-being of the workforce. Furthermore, the initial civil service schemes established a template that subsequently trickled down the occupational hierarchy. A more flexible strategy of a decade of retirement was rejected on grounds of administrative complexity and the pattern of fixed age retirement was the one that became the norm (Thane, 2000). However, changing social attitudes and economic circumstances may result in a rather belated adoption of the notion of a 'decade' of retirement initially rejected in the 1850s!

Proponents of fixed retirement argue that it creates employment opportunities for the young. This approach argues that without compulsory retirement, the workforce would become 'clogged up' with inefficient older workers. There would be fewer opportunities for new people to join the labour market; younger people would be confined to unemployment, and new practices and procedures would not be adopted because of the inflexible characteristics of older workers. We can see clearly that these arguments illustrate many of the negative stereotypes held about older people more generally. This argument is, of course, predicated upon the assumption that the number of jobs within the labour market is finite, an assumption that is as yet unproven and is of questionable veracity. Such arguments derive from an essentially functionalist perspective whereby retirement is seen as a key regulatory mechanism of the labour market which facilitates the smooth entry of new workers into the system by the regimented exit of older workers. Introducing younger workers into the system in an orderly fashion is seen as a major contribution to the maintenance of broader issues of social order. Retirement is presented as a 'reward' for the individual's contribution and one that has benefits for both the individual and the wider society. Implicit within this line of argument there are clear echoes of the disengagement theorists – withdrawal from productive and gainful employment is one stage in the process of the wider act of disengagement and the facilitating of transitions across generational boundaries. Additionally this is an essentially ageist perspective upon the rights of different age groups to employment. This suggests that in a choice between young and old, it is the old who should suffer exclusion from employment and, in times of high unemployment such as the interwar depression, older workers are at risk from pressures to 'make way' for younger workers. This is now an assertion which is being openly debated and where, in the United States, there is legislation against 'ageist' practices in recruitment and other aspects of employment. European countries are now examining the issue of ageism within the workplace and re-evaluating the value of older workers. Indeed it is now commonly being asserted that 'younger' workers will have to work well into their seventies – perhaps the golden age of retirement is passing?

Fixed age retirement is often justified because older workers are seen as less desirable than the young, being perceived as less efficient and less well educated, with declining physical and mental capacities. However, all the evidence suggests that older workers are more reliable than younger workers and are just as capable in timed tasks; older workers often have skills lacked by the young. Thus by forcing them to retire at a fixed age it could equally well be argued that we are decreasing the overall efficiency of the economy. Retirement is often justified because pensions, both state and occupational, provide income opportunities not available to the young. This again is an essentially ageist position because pensions rarely match earnings from employment. By making retirement mandatory, we are forcing large groups of people into lower living standards just because of their age. Again there has been little formal debate about whether it is socially desirable to force large sectors of the population to accept a decrease in their living standards simply upon the basis of age. Its proponents argue that mandatory retirement makes planning easier for workers and employers by having a fixed age at which retirement must take place. However, people change jobs or retire early through ill health, and companies can adjust to these circumstances. Flexible retirement with a statutory period of notice from the employee would seem to be a viable solution especially with the increasing availability of computerised record keeping and there is considerable support for the notion of a flexible 'decade of retirement' in a time of perceived skill shortages and concerns about income maintenance in later life.

Canon Blackley suggested the first national state pensions policy in 1878 and Charles Booth produced the first costed plan for a state-funded pensions scheme in 1891. These schemes were based upon the concept of insurance with workers contributing to the pension scheme and receiving their 'reward' upon retirement. It was not until 1908 that the Liberal government of Lloyd George introduced non-contributory means-tested old age pensions. All those over the age of 70 were entitled to apply for this pension, which amounted to five shillings (twenty-five pence) a week. In order to receive this pension, people had to pass a means test to ensure that they had an income of less than £21 a year and that they were nationals who had been resident for at least twenty years. A moral test also had to be passed before the pension was paid out. To gain a pension individuals had to prove themselves as 'deserving' and to demonstrate that they had not been idle, feckless or work-shy. This maintains the well-established tradition within British social policy of a fundamental distinction between the deserving and undeserving recipients of state support which we still see played out in contemporary discussions concerning social policy.

In Britain from the initial (very narrow) occupational group of civil servants in the 1850s, the notion of retirement developed so that by the time of the 1891 Census there was a separate category for those officially retired from the labour market. The decennial census of that year found that 35 per cent of males over the age of 65 could be so defined. The categories used in the decennial census can be used as barometers to chart the emergence of particular concepts and social issues and their adoption within the broad social and policy context. What are the economic and social conditions required to facilitate the creation and maintenance of the concept of retirement? The creation of the concept of retirement is linked to four distinct features of a given society: economic productivity, organisational sophistication, social attitudes and social conditions. As observation of the organisation of many less developed countries indicates, retirement is a viable concept only where the economy has a sufficient surplus to enable the 'non-productive' segment of the population to be supported. Retirement (or childhood) are not options within the constraints of a subsistence-based agricultural economy.

In addition to the existence of an 'economic surplus' there has to be an organised set of bureaucratic and administrative arrangements to facilitate the distribution of some (or all) of the surplus to the retired or other non-productive groups. There needs to be an established system of pensions and benefits to support the retired and therefore there is a very intimate link between pensions and retirement. Unless there is some form of provision for income support for the 'non-employed' then there is little incentive to leave the labour market. The idea of pensions payable at a specified chronological age was first suggested by Daniel Defoe in 1690, who thought that all people over the age of 50 should receive a pension. It was not until the late nineteenth century that popular opinion began to favour the provision of both state and occupational pensions. For all its failings late Victorian England was characterised by a more sophisticated understanding of poverty and its causes. Increasingly it was recognised that even the most thrifty and temperate of working people experienced poverty in old age because their working wages had not been adequate to allow them to save for it. Older people came to be seen as a special group, distinct from the 'feckless or work-shy', who had particular social needs requiring specifically formulated social policies to deal with them. Older people were differentiated from other groups in 'poverty' and were accorded special status. According to Midwinter (1997) from 1890 onwards, people aged 60 and over who were looking for support from the Poor Law authorities were not to be classified as 'able bodied' and therefore, they were not seen as being able to work. According to Midwinter (1997) this provides an early example of the 'institutionalising' of old age: the association of old age with a specific chronological age rather than in terms of declining functional ability or health status. Ever since the Poor Law Act 1601 there had been a 'state policy' in Britain for the relief of poverty. Older people, who were unable to work because of infirmity or other reasons, were recipients of support from this scheme. These 'aged paupers' received regular, if meagre, support from the state, but dependence on the Poor Law was seen as 'stigmatising' and divisive. Hence the pressure for universal state-financed pensions to alleviate the problems of poverty in old age and to which all older people would be entitled. There was also substantial agitation from organised labour for the provision of state pensions. This was a concession which governments felt that they could justifiably meet in order to reduce labour unrest at a time of considerable social tension.

It would be naive to view the development of the concepts of retirement and pensions as deriving from altruistic concerns of policy makers for the 'poor' or as a way of ensuring that social unrest did not take hold. Wider labour market and economic concerns have had a profound influence upon the development of retirement. There have also been labour market or 'supply side' pressures upon the development and emergence of retirement as both a social concept and phase of the lifecycle. The increased social consensus for the concept of pensions and retirement was not, however, wholly philanthropic. There were also wider labour market concerns. We have already noted the linkage of the concept of retirement with 'economic efficiency'. In addition there was the widespread discrimination against older workers in the labour market. In late-nineteenth-century Britain older workers were threatened by changes in work practices and the obsolescence of their skills as was reflected in the high rates of unemployment among older workers. This was a time of economic depression and great international economic competition with the other nations of Europe, particularly Germany. Older workers were caught in a situation of shrinking job opportunities and a decrease in demand for their particular skills. Pensions, both occupational and state financed, were seen as a legitimate way of excluding older workers from the job market and thereby decreasing the demand for employment.

There has always been a very intimate link with the economy in general and, more specifically, changes in the labour market. Part of the growth of retirement has also arisen in response to changes in the now increasingly global characteristics of the labour market. Decreased opportunities for employment were, therefore, an important set of pressures leading to the institutionalisation of fixed age retirement. In addition there were increased demands for efficiency with the older worker perceived, rightly or wrongly, as being inefficient. Older workers were threatened by the perceived obsolescence of their skills. It is important to remember that labour market policies change over time and are dynamic. One function that 'retired' older workers can fulfil is as a reserve army of labour to be called upon in times of economic growth. This is a thesis advanced by Phillipson (1982), who argues that retirement is largely determined by the labour requirements of a capitalist economy. In times of 'surplus' labour, retirement is encouraged while in times of full employment and labour shortage, it is discouraged. Another example of the notion of the reserve army of labour is the contribution made by women to the economy during the Second World War. Once peace was restored, women were supposed to return to the domestic sphere leaving participation in the formal labour market to men. During the full employment of the 1950s there was considerable enthusiasm for employing older workers because of labour shortages and pessimistic fears about demographic balance between productive and unproductive workers. Beveridge (1942) questioned the inevitability of excluding older workers from employment and felt that older people should be encouraged to defer claiming their pension and carry on working. His argument anticipates many more recent debates as to whether we can, as a society, 'afford' widespread retirement as a social process. Hence during the 1950s there was less enthusiasm among policy makers for policies designed to support the concept of retirement, although it is not clear if the workforce shared these reservations. Conversely during the economic slump of the 1980s, the concept of early retirement was embraced wholeheartedly. This was seen as a way of offering workers an honourable exit route from the labour and achieved the wider macro-economic goal of reducing the 'oversupply' of labour. A whole variety of incentives and schemes were developed to help workers leave the labour market. From a labour market perspective retirement offers a means of shedding unwanted labour from a saturated job market; in times of labour shortage the opposite case is advanced. The immediate post-war period in Britain was characterised by the reversal of the trend towards retirement by encouraging older workers to stay in the job market and delay the time at which they would become dependent and non-productive. The period of full employment was short-lived and the exhortations to older people to delay their retirement ceased in the early 1960s. The current concerns of labour market analysts are very much preoccupied with potential future labour shortages and the unsupportable burden of maintaining future 'pensioners'. In combination we are likely to see the abolition of fixed age retirement and encouragement for us to carry on working at least into our seventies.

Two further conditions accompany both the need for an economic surplus and the means to distribute it to the population before retirement could be established as an accepted social entity. These both relate to social conditions. First, in a culture that was very heavily linked to the Protestant work ethic, positive social attitudes towards the concept of retirement must be present. Retirement as a social construct would not have gained such popularity if it was not seen as being a social legitimised state. To help promote such positive evaluations, policy debates clearly distinguish between the 'deservingly non-productive' (such as the retired) and the 'non-deserving' (for example lone teenage mothers or the 'work-shy'). This is illustrated by the condition in the Lloyd George pension plan that those who had habitually failed to work were not entitled to the benefit. Pensions were not to be seen as a 'reward' for a lifetime of indolence. One reflection of this 'positive' attitude towards retirement has been the development of the 'retiree lifestyle' as illustrated by the number of specialist magazines and services for those in the post-work phase of life and the growth of a consumption rather than work-based identity. Finally, social conditions need to be such that average life expectancy should be sufficiently long to enable workers to have 'contributed for long enough' to 'deserve' support in retirement (and to have accumulated sufficient financial credits to pay for their pensions, etc.). The current increase in longevity means that the average person can expect to experience at least two decades of retirement.

Retirement as a social process

Thus far we have largely been concerned with retirement as a macro-economic concept. However, (early) retirement can be approached from the perspective of the individual as well as from the societal level. For those who have been active in the labour market, retirement and the changes in the social context of people's lives that it brings is an important social process. Sociologists define certain events such as weddings or starting work as rites of passage. These are events which alter the status of the individual in the eyes of society and bring about changes in social role and the broader social context within which we are all located. Retirement, like entry into the labour market, is very clearly an important rite of passage and a clear marker of a significant social transition but only for that segment of the population for whom it is relevant.

Older male workers have increasingly withdrawn from the labour market, and retirement at a fixed age of 65 (or even earlier) has become the 'social' norm. Indeed, such has been the extent of social change that most working people now expect and want to retire at a specific age with a reasonable standard of living, at least sufficient for them to participate in society. Furthermore the 'post-retirement' phase of the lifecycle can represent a significant percentage of an individual's lifespan. The twin trends of later entry into the job market, as a result of an extended period of education, and earlier exit have combined to challenge the initial view of retirement as a fairly short phase at the end of a long (fifty or more years) working life. Stanley Parker (1980) in his classic study of older workers reported that 59 per cent of men and 53 per cent of women were looking forward to retirement; only 8 per cent and 15 per cent respectively were unhappy at the prospect of retiring. It seems unlikely that responses to these types of questions would be very different for a contemporary cohort of workers. Retirement was thought to pose a period of change and adjustment, with 35 per cent of women and 27 per cent of men reporting that they thought it would be difficult to 'settle down' when they retired. We must be somewhat cautious in how to interpret responses to these types of surveys apparently indicating widespread support for the concept of retirement. Clearly the responses given to such questions are influenced by the economic, social and political context as well as the specific circumstances of the individuals interviewed. Apparently widespread support for the notion of retirement at a pre-specified age may simply reflect individuals 'accepting the inevitable' and making the best of it. Furthermore negative attitudes towards retirement, with widespread debate about the 'burden' of older people and the potential for 'intergenerational conflict' over welfare resources, mean that it would be of little surprise if attitudes towards retirement became rather less positive. Attitudes are not fixed and stable but rather develop and modify in response to the changing social context; older people are as influenced by these as other groups. Again we may also find that attitudes vary within the older age groups.

The predominant conceptualisation of retirement in much gerontological work has been framed by the notions of loss and these have very strongly influenced the nature of the research undertaken concerning retirement. Retirement, through the loss of regular employment which provides income, social status and a social focus, has been largely seen as a threatening transition for individuals and a challenge to their 'social identity' and well-being. However, the focus upon the perceived 'negative' aspects of retirement means that there remain large aspects of the retirement process about which we know very little, such as the transition from employed to retired and how responses to this important social transition vary between social groups. It seems unlikely, given the highly stratified nature of the British labour market, that the experience of retirement will be uniform. We would expect issues such as class and gender (and perhaps ethnicity) to exert an influence upon the nature of the retirement experience. One of the major constraints upon knowledge of this important social process is that many studies are cross-sectional rather than longitudinal in design. The observation that those who retire early are in worse (or better) health than those still in employment may simply reflect pre-existing differences and have little to do with the process of retirement. Studies of retirement have often focused upon specific occupational groups such as steelworkers or miners. This clearly limits the generalisability of the results as does the widespread exclusion of women from such studies.

At the most simplistic, 'retirement' has been defined as withdrawal from the formal paid labour market into a publicly funded pension scheme and as such describes a dichotomy between the waged and the pensioner. As we have seen this distinction between 'workers' and (old age) pensioners has become less distinct by the early exit of considerable numbers of (male) workers from the labour market. The pathways which individuals may follow before they define themselves (or are defined by the benefits system or others) as 'retired' have become increasingly complex and blurred (Phillipson, 1993). Phillipson argues that old models of the pathway from work into retirement are now redundant because of the diversity and fragmentation of the labour market. The model underpinning much early research was based upon a context of full employment, lifelong continuity in employment and a desire by workers to remain in employment until retirement age. Phillipson (1993) suggests that the transition into retirement is much more complex and can include some (or all) of the following: labour market factors such as forced or voluntary early retirement, redundancy (voluntary or compulsory), labour supply issues (unemployment) and personal factors (ill health, caring responsibilities, availability of retirement benefits). There are factors pushing workers from the labour force and attracting them towards retirement and these are mediated by personal factors such as health.

For any individual several different pathways may be interrelated. The development of a more complex set of routes from employment to retirement has several important implications. Much of our research concerning transitions and adjustment to retirement is based upon the old simple model, thus its relevance to current circumstances is questionable. Related to this, these more complex exit routes proffer an extensive research agenda for gerontologists or social scientists interested in the work–retirement transition. These different pathways for exiting from the labour market still, however, resonate with Phillipson's (1982) threefold typology of approaches towards retirement.

Retirement is a complex phenomenon and it is probably far too simplistic to divide people into the retired and non-retired. Rather adoption of the new social role of 'retired person' is a complex social process, which may be divided into a series of phases in a clear implied parallel with the stages of bereavement: again another linkage of the notion of retirement as a major loss in the life of the individual. The role of 'retired person' includes both rights and obligations. The major 'right' associated with the role is that of economic support without employment but without the stigma of other non-deserving 'welfare-dependent' groups. The 'obligations' of the retired are, perhaps, less well defined but include not seeking 'formal' paid work and, in a society imbued with the 'work ethic', to keep busy. The phases of adaptation to retirement constitute an ideal type and not every experience of retirement will encompass them all. Rather these phases serve to stress the variety of experience covered by the term 'retirement' and, perhaps, offer a conceptual framework for thinking about the diversity of this experience and trying to provide an organising framework for the collection and analysis of empirical material. They also offer the potential for looking at the increasingly fragmented nature of the entry into and experience of retirement. It may well be that models such as these fit only a limited range of male-centred retirement experiences and there is a heavy emphasis in this model of the individual adapting or coming to terms with the pervasive losses seen to be inevitably resulting from the retirement experience. Such work is heavily imbued with the ethos of the disengagement theory approach to the study of ageing and, again, we can see that there is considerable potential to expand the research base by looking at different occupational groups and the response of women to retirement. Fairhurst (2003) in her analysis challenges us to examine and to investigate the new 'lifestyles' which are now emerging in retirement with all the complexity that this can bring.

The effects of retirement

The literature on retirement has focused upon the negative consequences with a distinct emphasis upon the problematic, losses associated with retirement and examination of how individuals can compensate or adjust for such losses. At both individual and societal level there has been a bias towards the challenging and negative sequelae of this social process. Most research seems to have focused upon the negative aspects of retirement as if expressing a subconscious expectation by the researcher that retirement ought to be an unsatisfactory experience. It may be that retirement remains unsatisfactory because of the conditions which accompany it such as low income or poor health, rather than retirement per se. In both Britain and North America only a minority of old people want to work and then only for financial reasons. The aspects of work that people missed related to income and interaction rather than the work itself. Studies of retirement often carry the inbuilt assumption that the loss of the work role creates a void in the social world of the individual that cannot be filled by various substitutes and that retirement constitutes a vain attempt to search for a valid replacement. Thus it seems possible that the problems of retirement arise because of the lack of suitable alternatives to the activity and social interaction provided by work. Although work is clearly an important aspect of our social identity, it is not the only one and it certainly does not apply to the entire population. If paid employment were our only means of attributing social worth, then entire segments of the population would be denied any form of social identity. Post-modernist approaches question the importance of work and retirement in ways that older people construct their late life identities. Gilleard and Higgs (2000) suggest that consumption remains an important vehicle for post-work citizens to maintain and reinforce their identity. In a post-modern world we are defined by what we consume and our engagement with culture and society more than by what we produce or what we did for a living while employed. This perspective is stimulating in that it challenges to see how far older people are engaging with society or being excluded from it (Scharf and Smith, 2004).

One stereotype concerning retirement is the notion that retirement 'causes' bad health or death. We have all heard stories of the dedicated worker who drops dead within a short time of retirement. It is certainly true that when comparing the retired and non-retired, the former have worse health than the latter. Clearly, with cross-sectional data, it is impossible to determine if people retired because they were sick or whether they are sick because they retired. There are age-related increases in morbidity but these are not 'caused' by retirement. Indeed we may speculate that for those who retire because of ill health that their health may improve (or at least deteriorate more slowly) in retirement. The continuation of the myth that 'retirement is bad for your health', in the face of substantial empirical evidence to the contrary, probably relates to the influence of two factors. First, retirement is clearly a major life event and is seen as having equivalence with other major life changes such as widowhood which have a 'folk link' with poor health status. Such major life events are seen as 'stressful' and as having major health consequences, but the analysis of the linkage between life events and poor health outcomes rarely examines the relationship in sufficient detail to demonstrate the spuriousness of the association or to identify any potentially confounding factors, and positive life events show no real link with health outcomes. Second, we might speculate that by stating the 'perils' of retirement we are reinforcing the importance of work and the work ethic within the wider social context, thus there is an ideological underpinning to the debate which requires formal articulation and acknowledgement.

One aspect of retirement that has received attention is the consideration of feelings of usefulness among the retired. Western society values usefulness and contribution, especially in the 'formal' labour market from its participating members. Consequently we might speculate that the retired occupy a limbo position. If we are not in paid employment then we should be 'busy'. Atchley (1999) suggests that for retired people, the 'busy ethic' replaces the 'work ethic' as a source of self-esteem and self-respect. 'Work' is redefined in terms of the effort expended by the retired person towards achieving their specified goals, such as being a grandparent or helping children to read in school, rather than in terms of economic productivity. There seems to be little good evidence that the retired do not feel that they are not contributing to the wider social good or have not contributed in the past. Indeed in studies of the contribution of volunteers and of childcare and other related activities, retired people are always major contributors. At the most basic level the ability to maintain oneself and one's home, and to continue living independently in the community, provide sufficient evidence of social worth and keeping busy in retirement. Some studies have demonstrated an increase in feelings of uselessness following retirement. Only about one-fifth of the change was attributable to retirement itself, the rest related to other profound changes in circumstances such as loss of a spouse or the onset of a disabling illness which occurred at the same time as retirement. Again this serves to emphasise the importance of distinguishing the effects of retirement from the other events and changes that may be taking place within an individual's life. Many of the negative expectations of retirement relate to the association of retirement with ill health and a decrease in physical activity. If the compression of morbidity thesis is correct, more of us will enter the post-work phase of life in better health than previous generations of elders and hence may illustrate much more positive evaluations of this period.

Another important aspect of retirement is that of social status. We have already argued that one of the important methods of maintaining self and general esteem in retirement is by being 'busy'. How does retirement link with perhaps the major dimension of social stratification in Britain, that of social class, which is strongly allied to occupational status? There is a tendency among many social researchers to perceive the retired population as a homogeneous mass isolated from the major status-giving trait, employment. It is all too easy to assume that notions of class and the importance of class are negated once the individual has left the workforce, but this is far too simplistic a view. Class retains an importance to both individuals and in a wider social context. Among the retired themselves there is a very strong tendency to retain identification with their former occupation. Thus retired people may describe themselves as retired teachers (or whatever their former job had been) rather than just as retired. A university professor may be given an emeritus title and continue to go to 'work', write papers and books, supervise students and attend conferences. Retired people may continue to retain links with their former occupation by work-based groups (e.g. the Shell pensioners' group) or with their specific occupation or union. Occupational affiliations may be maintained in very advanced old age with the development of residential or nursing homes associated with particular occupational groups such as actors or publicans. However, class has a wider impact upon the retirement experience. First, the retired, especially those who reach 'state retirement age', represent the 'survivors' of their birth cohort. Phillipson (1993) reports that those from social class 5, the unskilled occupation groups, have a much higher rate of premature mortality and are two-and-a-half times more likely to die before retirement age than their contemporaries in social class 1, the professional and managerial occupation groups. Victor (1991) shows that, once retired, there are marked differences in health status. Those from unskilled or semi-skilled occupations are less likely to reach retirement age and, for those who do, are more likely to start retirement in poor health than their more privileged contemporaries. Overlaying these 'simple' class distinctions are issues of gender and ethnicity. We tend to analyse one dimension at a time. For older people the retirement experience is largely shaped by the inter-relationships between these factors, but it is clearly evident that social class exerts an important influence over the retirement experience, although researchers and policy makers have often ignored the importance of this. We need to embed this within other structural factors such as gender and ethnicity.

Theorising retirement

The development of, and experience of, retirement has been a major area of activity for gerontologists. We have studied both the historical development of the notion of retirement (Thane, 2000), the 'adaptation' of individuals to retirement and the development of the concept of 'early retirement' and the emergence of more complex routes into retirement. As well as the different types of research perspectives taken towards the notion of retirement, a variety of different theoretical frameworks have been applied to this area. Retirement studies illustrate better than many areas of gerontological endeavour the explicit (and implicit) influence of social theory upon the types of research undertaken and the explanations for the empirical material gathered. Again the topic illustrates the types of retirement issues that have been viewed as unproblematic by researchers and consequently not subject to the critical gaze of investigation. Examples include topics such as women and retirement, or the experience of retirement as a couple.

Both functionalism and disengagement theory have been highly influential in the study of retirement. Studies from a functionalist perspective have focused upon the adaptive qualities of retirement as an institution and a social process. Retirement is seen as a mechanism for ensuring the smooth transfer of work between the generations. Functionalist research has concentrated upon three main research questions – adjustment to retirement, financial aspects of retirement and the development (and evaluation) of strategies providing 'positive' retirement.

Disengagement theorists conceptualise retirement as the start of a more general process of withdrawal from the social world. Given the presumed importance of work in providing social contacts, retirement could be seen as being highly disruptive to the social network of the individual. This perspective has generated an extensive body of work investigating the continuity or discontinuity in the social world of the retired. Activity theory has stimulated a plethora of research looking at how 'active' people are in retirement and advance the thesis that successful adaptation to retirement requires extensive engagement in activities. A version of this on the individual basis is continuity theory and the notion of the busy ethic. This, like activity theory, argues for the moral imperative of engagement in retirement and sees the successful retirement as one that is 'busy'. Within the British context we can see evidence of how the 'old age as a social problem' perspective has influenced research with a focus upon the difficulties and losses for the individual and for the wider societal impact of retirement. Finally, thinking about retirement at a macrolevel has been heavily influenced by the 'political economy' school of thinking about old age. Conflict theorists, such as political economists, argue that retirement is part of the broader struggles between labour and capital in which retirement marginalises and stigmatises older people. Such perspectives question whose interest retirement serves. They also argue that gender and ethnic differences greatly influence the experience of retirement with inequality forming the heart of the political economy research agenda. More recently new approaches to retirement are being investigated. Gilleard and Higgs (2000) raise the issue of post-work lives and the creation of identity in terms of consumption rather than production and the importance of wider cultural factors in the creation and maintenance of identity. The diversity of the theories that have been applied to the study of retirement in many ways mirrors the development of theory in gerontology. It also illustrates how the (partial) nature of the questions asked provides only partial answers. Retirement was regarded as non-problematic for women because it was presumed that women derived their primary source of identity from their roles as wives and mothers and hence the topic of women and retirement was deemed unworthy of research.

Retirement in the future

The post-war period saw the development in the United Kingdom of retirement as a mass social experience. However, since the early 1980s the nature of both work and retirement has changed. The notion of a continuous period of employment from 16 to 65, often with a single employer, with retirement on a state-provided pension at a fixed age, now seems rather unrealistic in the diverse working world that we inhabit. The period in employment is reducing and many of us will experience much more varied working lives with multiple careers, multiple employers and, perhaps, multiple ways of working (part-time, full-time, home-working, etc.) with the resultant 'blended' work history. There are now many more complex exit routes from the labour market into retirement and it is probable that the experience of retirement will be much more fragmented for future cohorts. Researchers need to incorporate this greater degree of complexity into our research agenda and policy makers need to recognise this in their thinking about retirement. The debate about retirement needs to incorporate the increasing female participation in the labour market and the influences of factors such as class and ethnicity into the debate to consider questions as to whether the benefits or disadvantages characteristic of the working life are sustained into retirement.

Financial resources

The growth of retirement as a socially defined state and accepted phase of life has, as we noted earlier, been facilitated and paralleled by the growth of pensions. In Britain there are two main categories of pension, the state-provided sector and those paid by a former employer (subsequently referred to as occupational pensions). These two systems for financial support have developed separately but have both played important roles in the development of retirement and the quality of the experience of retirement. The systems for the provision of income in retirement do not, however, exist in isolation – rather they meet at the interface between employment and labour market issues and the wider social security context.

State pension provision

In Britain there has been a state-organised response to the problems of 'poverty' since the time of Queen Elizabeth I. Despite various reforms and changes, the basic outline of arrangements for social welfare provision in Britain stems from the 1942 Beveridge report on social insurance. Old age, unemployment, industrial injury and widowhood were seen as the main 'causes' of poverty and to combat these Beveridge proposed a two-tier system of benefits. As Ginn (2003) notes the system of welfare support was modelled upon the gendered assumptions of full-time employment for a male working life of about fifty years and the confinement of women's economic role to the pre-marriage, pre-childbearing years. As we have seen, many of these assumptions have been challenged by the changing demographic, cultural and social profile of twenty-first-century society.

Although the system of social welfare provision in Britain is termed 'National Insurance' the pension component is, in fact, a 'pay as you go' scheme. This means that present-day workers, via their taxes and National Insurance contributions, are paying the pensions of current elders. It is this link that underpins many of the debates about the 'affordability' of pensions (and indeed other benefits) in the future and concerns about intergenerational conflict. With demographic trends suggesting that there will be fewer classic 'workers' (unless there is either a dramatic change in fertility or extensive in-migration) it is argued that the support of retired people via pensions will be an unfair burden upon future generations. In the contemporary British context the first component of income support consists of a series of benefits paid out of general taxation and eligibility for which was defined by contributions made via the compulsory system of National Insurance paid by all those in employment. These types of benefits are 'universal' in that they are paid to all who meet the stated eligibility criteria. For older people this element of income maintenance is the state retirement pension, colloquially known as the 'old age' pension. The second arm of state welfare support consists of a set of means-tested additional benefits. To receive such additional benefits, claimants must undergo a 'means test' and demonstrate that they have an income below the required threshold. Such benefits are justified by reference to the notion of targeting. Additional state support is being 'targeted' at those most 'in need'. Despite various modifications, and numerous changes of name, this system, based upon a mix of universal and means-tested benefits, lies at the heart of state support for those in retirement in the United Kingdom.

In Britain state 'old age' pensions were based upon the presumption of a contribution into the post-work phase of life of a standard of living that was predominantly subsistence in nature. The basic philosophy underlying the level at which the pension was originally set was that it should provide the minimum acceptable income in old age and not one which equalled that which individuals had received during their working life and to enable them to engage in surplus consumption. Therefore from its inception the state retirement pension has been inadequate for anything but the very lowest standard of living and, furthermore, was never designed or conceptualised as doing anything else. While the architects of the welfare state were keen to alleviate 'poverty' in old age, there was never any sense that they wished to promote an affluent, or even modest, lifestyle in 'old age'. Rather benefits were defined as being paid at a level required to maintain a minimal lifestyle, which has implications for the wider inclusion (or exclusion) of older people within society. It is difficult to participate or engage with society when one only has a minimal disposable income.

The provision of universal pension constitutes a significant element of the overall social welfare and public expenditure budget in the United Kingdom. The health and social welfare budget, and public sector spending more generally, was subjected to intense scrutiny by the Conservative administrations in power between 1979 and 1997 (headed by Margaret Thatcher for the period 1979–1990). For the 'right-wing' Thatcher administration (and the US neo-liberal administration headed by President Ronald Reagan) public spending was seen as 'a bad thing' for both society as a whole and the individual. For society, extensive public spending, of which welfare was a major element, was seen as a 'burden' in that it required the raising of taxes that were seen as deterring enterprise both individual and societal. Taking taxes from individuals is conceptualised as stifling individual enterprise and removing responsibility from individuals to organise their own retirement pensions. Raising taxes for the provision of social welfare benefits was seen as part of the 'nanny state' which disempowered individuals. Universal pensions were increasingly seen as a 'burden' that threatened the living standards of the rest of society, especially given the 'apocalyptic' scenario of an increasingly 'ageing' population (see McDonald, 2000, for a discussion of this issue within the Canadian context). Neo-liberals advance the argument that population ageing will overtake the accepted systems of pension provision and create an 'unfair' burden on those of working age (World Bank, 1994). Continuing support for public pension provision is 'problematised' in the context of an apocalyptic demographic crisis that will see older people swamping the world – a kind of demographic domination. One manifestation of this concern was in the issue of 'intergenerational conflict' where different generations were seen as being in dispute over (finite) social welfare resources (Thompson *et al.*, 1990). This proposition argues that younger generations will be 'impoverished' in order to keep older people in 'luxury' without them 'contributing' to the economic development. This thesis conceptualises the needs of the different age groups as in competition for welfare (and other) economic resources.

No such disbenefits are seen as arising from private systems of pension provision. Like many other propositions this argument is based upon a series of assumptions. This intergenerational conflict model presumes (a) the widespread affluence of older people, (b) an effective 'political' pensioner lobby to influence welfare decisions, (c) failure to increase productivity. There is little empirical evidence to support the first two propositions and, while it is always difficult to predict the future, a scenario of 'no increases' in economic productivity seems unrealistic. Furthermore the intergenerational conflict position takes a very narrow view of 'generational accounting' in that it is almost exclusively concerned with taxes and public sector expenditure and is restricted to a single point in time (Arber and Attias-Donfut, 2000). This obsession with the rising numbers and perceived burden of older people (especially the very old) and the notions of intergenerational conflict are examples of the use of population ageing as a moral 'panic', perhaps to divert attention away from other pressing social issues (Jefferys, 1983).

Private pension provision

In Britain non-state pensions were initially limited to specific occupational groups and hence were initially referred to as occupational pensions. The term 'private pensions' now includes both occupationally based pension schemes and a whole raft of other forms of non-state-organised pension arrangements. As we have seen, the first pensions paid in Britain were occupationally based rather than state provided as the examples of civil servants, the police and teachers all illustrate. In their initial manifestation these types of pensions were used as a method of attracting and retaining staff in occupations for which a lengthy training was required. They could also have a less positive aspect in that they could be used as a means of 'ridding' the workplace of older workers who were seen as being inefficient. Typically these types of pensions are based upon a combination of duration of service and level of earnings and as such these types of provision preserve the inequalities in living standards characteristic of the working life into old age. Women, part-time workers and those in lower paid jobs, inevitably fared worse than other groups (Ginn *et al.*, 2001; Arber and Ginn, 2004). Occupationally based pension schemes are, like the notion of retirement itself, largely based upon an idealised model of male labour force participation. While other types of private pension are not linked to occupational inequalities, they do rely upon sufficient surplus income to make regular contributions. As such they suffer from the same structural inequalities as the occupational pensions.

There were a number of conceptual limitations of the system of occupational pensions, most notably their inflexibility. If employees changed jobs then they could not transfer pensions. This was seen as reducing the efficiency of the labour market by acting as a disincentive to mobility. Inequities in access to such schemes were not seen as problematic. In response to and as a means of 'privatising' the welfare system the 1979–1997 series of British Conservative governments encouraged the development of occupational and 'portable' private pensions. Significant levels of tax relief were offered to 'encourage' individuals to develop private pension portfolios. Private pension arrangements were advanced as being more efficient than state schemes; coverage of such schemes is, however, far from universal.

As yet occupational pension schemes do not cover all of the working population (Table 8.1). Approximately two-thirds of male and female full-time employees are members of occupational pension schemes, but those working part-time are much less likely to belong to such schemes. There are also socio-economic differentials in scheme membership. Of those in full-time professional and managerial jobs, 80 per cent of women and 81 per cent of men are members of an occupational pension; for those in unskilled jobs the equivalent membership rates are 41 per cent and 56 per cent respectively. Nor are all the population covered by personal pension schemes. In the public sector most full-time employees are part of an occupational pension scheme, but in the private sector coverage is more variable. Approximately two-thirds of workers are covered by an occupational pension and about 20 per cent have a 'personal' pension (Midwinter, 1997). Access to such schemes is differentiated between men and women and between full- and part-time employees. Male full-time workers have the highest levels of occupational personal pension provision and female part-time workers the lowest. This differential is, according to Ginn *et al.* (2001), not encouraging for the post-work incomes and financial position of future cohorts of older women. It is not simply gender that differentiates access to private pensions; issues of class and education are also important. Although women, en masse, are less likely to have access to private pension income, this does vary with occupation, education and class (and possibly ethnicity). Future cohorts of elders are going to be strongly differentiated between those who have recourse only to the state pension and those who have an additional pension from a previous employer or a

Table 8.1 Membership of employer pension scheme, Great Britain, 1983, 1991 and 2001 (%)

	1983	1991	2001
Male full-time	62	61	54
Female full-time	55	55	58
Female part-time	13	17	33

Source: Walker *et al.*, 2003: Table 6.3

personal pension scheme (or both of these for some). Such differentials will reflect the complex interplay between age, gender, class and ethnicity.

For the individual reliance on state benefits for old age, or indeed other social vicissitudes, were similarly seen as decreasing initiative and developing a culture of dependency. This is a philosophical approach to social welfare that sees universal, state-sponsored collective provision as vastly inferior to individually arranged and managed 'private' provision. Such arrangements are seen as promoting the independence and freedom of citizens by giving them control over their own lives. From this perspective state-organised and -provided services were seen as monolithic, inflexible, inefficient and unresponsive to the needs of individuals. As noted above, social factors such as class and gender clearly constrain the choices available to individuals across their working lives and these are then translated into the retirement experience when there is a reliance upon privately organised schemes. By reinforcing the differentials in income characteristic of working life, reliance upon occupational and private pensions will inevitably result in the creation of two nations in old age: the consumers of the Gilleard and Higgs (2000) post-modern consumption-based society and the socially excluded and marginalised.

How has the move towards private pensions influenced older people's access to different sources of income? Not surprisingly, older people who are retired from the labour market are dependent upon the state for the bulk of their income and this has been the case since the early 1960s. The state still provides 50 per cent of the income for pensioners; reliance upon the state for income is greatest among older pensioners, women and those over 75. Davies *et al.* (2003) show that single pensioners aged 75+ receive 68 per cent of their income from the state compared with 37 per cent for recently retired pensioner couples, but reliance upon the state for income

Table 8.2 Source of pensioners' total gross incomes, Great Britain, 1951–2001 (%)

	1951	1961	1984	1986	2001
All state benefits	42	48	55	59	51
Occupational pensions	15	16	15	20	29
Earnings	27	22	17	7	9
Savings	15	15	13	14	11

Sources: Johnson and Falkingham, 1992; Davies *et al.*, 2003

support in later life is decreasing. In 1980 Victor (1986) estimated that 53 per cent of older people had no sources of income other than that provided by the state compared with 9 per cent in 2001–2002 (Davies *et al.*, 2003). Table 8.2 indicates that older people are less reliant upon the state for their income than previously and that pensioners increasingly have access to non-state income sources. Women, single pensioners and those aged 75+ show greatest reliance upon the state, demonstrating a cohort effect for these groups with least access to non-state income sources. Arber and Ginn (2004) continue to point to the gendered experience of income access in later life: women rely upon the state for 66 per cent of their income compared with 54 per cent for men.

Affluence and poverty in later life

In Britain 'old age' pensions were introduced approximately 100 years ago. At this time the labouring classes, who comprised the bulk of the population, existed at little more than subsistence level. There was little opportunity for either the employed or the retired to participate in the 'consumer economy'. In trying to evaluate the current financial and economic position of older people we need to examine their income and ability to engage with the consumption culture of post-modern Britain.

Clearly in absolute terms older people have higher incomes than ever before, but we need to consider what our reference group is (or should be) when evaluating the financial position of older people. Should we undertake historical comparisons and look at the position of present-day elders in comparison to previous generations? Should we compare them with other 'welfare dependent' groups or should we compare their incomes to those of people in employment? Comparing the incomes of older people and the rest of the population, or historically, is methodologically challenging. Clearly such calculations need to take into account household and housing costs as well as considering issues of gross and net (i.e. income after deductions such as taxation) income and household size. The method of summarising either mean or median incomes is also important as it may accentuate or minimise differentials. One illustrative way of doing this is to consider the overall income distribution and divide it into fifths (or quartiles) and then calculate the percentage of pensioners in each quartile. According to Davies *et al.* (2003), after allowing for housing costs, 46 per cent of pensioners were in the bottom income quintile in 1979 compared with 27 per cent in 2001–2002 with a further 30 per cent in the next quintile so that 57 per cent of pensioners are in the bottom 40 per cent of the national income distribution. Only 12 per cent of pensioners were in the top 20 per cent of the income distribution. While the overall financial position of older people shows some improvement, progress has hardly been dramatic and pensioners remain concentrated in the two lowest income quartiles. The difference between those in the top and bottom ends of the income distribution is access to non-state sources of income. Those in the bottom quintile were reliant upon the state for 90 per cent of their income as compared with 20–30 per cent of those different types of pensioner groups in the top income quintile. Arber and Ginn (2004) note that about 20 per cent of all pensioners are 'in poverty' compared to 17 per cent for the total population. Although it is clear that in absolute terms pensioners are better off now than in previous points in history, it is easy to exaggerate the levels of affluence and to fail to appreciate the increasingly heterogeneous nature of the post-work segment of the population. Gender, class and, increasingly, ethnicity are likely to exert a significant influence upon income in retirement. The financial status of older people depends very much upon who they are compared with. While older people have shared in the property of society, they have fared better than other groups on welfare but not as well as those in employment.

A key argument advanced by neo-liberals against state pensions in general relates to the level at which benefits are paid and is a development of the 'social burden' thesis. This argues that pensions are more generous than we can afford and considerably more than pensioners need to maintain an independent household. This insidious argument is based upon the premise that older people are now relatively affluent and the level at which pensions are paid should be set so that we are not 'over-providing' for old age. This line of thinking clearly links to the 'minimalist' aspirations of the original pension reformers and the philosophy underpinning the determination of the levels at which pensions were paid in the post-war period. Pensions should be paid only at a subsistence level – sufficient to stave off 'poverty' but not provide a level of income comparable with those in employment.

Income data analysed by Davies *et al.* (2003) indicate that there are marked variations in levels of income among the older population. This, perhaps, does represent something of a change from earlier periods when the vast majority of older people would have experienced poverty or low income in later life. Clearly some segments of the older population are more affluent than others. For a minority, their living standards greatly exceed those of the general population. Largely the income differentials observed among older people reflect that characteristic of the earlier phases of the lifecycle. Davies *et al.* (2003) demonstrate that younger, newly retired pensioners are more affluent than those longer established retirees. Couples are more affluent than single pensioners, the under-75s are better off than the older pensioners, and men are better off than women. Ginn *et al.* (2001) demonstrate empirically the disadvantaged financial status of older women both in the United Kingdom and elsewhere. While gender is important in understanding the distribution of income among older people, there are other influential factors such as class (Midwinter, 1997), age and potentially ethnicity.

To a large degree these income inequalities are explained by the issue of access to different types of income to pensioners at different points in the income distribution. Taking the example of pensioner couples in 1979, state benefits represented 93 per cent of the income of those in the bottom quintile of the income distribution and 24 per cent for those in the top quintile. The situation for 2001–2002 is very similar. It is clear that it is those who are largely reliant upon the state for their income that are concentrated among the low income sectors. The more affluent element of the older population has access to significant additional (i.e. non-state) means of financial support. For most older people the experience of later life is one of restricted incomes. Compared with other low income groups largely reliant upon the state for support, such as unemployed people or lone parents, older people are somewhat better off, but compared with those in employment the chasm in income remains as wide as ever. When considering their financial position, do older people refer down to the less affluent groups below them or look up to those above them?

The other element of living standards analysis concerns patterns of consumption and participation in the 'consumer culture' of the early-twenty-first century. Gilleard and Higgs (2000) argue that older people have increasingly engaged in the consumption-based economy, as manifest by the 'third age' recently retired individuals. We can look at the issue of consumption in two distinct but inter-related ways: patterns of expenditure and the access of older people to consumption goods. In terms of expenditure patterns older people spend more of their income on housing, food and fuel, items considered essential to life, than the rest of the population. Conversely they spend relatively less upon 'luxury' items such as tobacco, alcoholic drink, transport and consumer durables. This largely reflects the lower incomes on which older people exist. For the majority of older people their level of income leaves little for luxury items once the essentials of life have been paid for.

Another aspect of living standards relates to the possession of consumer durable items, such as washing machines, freezers and refrigerators. These are items now considered by many as essentials rather than luxuries. Table 8.3 shows how the access of older people to these goods has increased. For example access to white goods such as freezers and washing machines is now almost universal, which was

Table 8.3 Access of people aged 65+ to consumer goods, Great Britain, 1980–2001 (%)

Consumer good	1980	1985	1991	1994	1998	2001
Television (colour or black and white)	96	97	98	99	99	99
Satellite/cable/digital	—	—	—	—	14	23
Video recorder	—	—	35	49	66	75
CD player	—	—	7	17	34	51
Home computer	—	—	4	5	11	18
Access to internet at home	—	—	—	—	—	14
Microwave oven	—	—	31	47	66	77
Refrigerator	88	93	—	—	—	—
Deep freezer/fridge freezer	—	48	71	61	89	93
Washing machine	59	65	75	80	85	87
Tumble drier	—	17	27	31	39	41
Dishwasher	—	—	—	9	13	16
Telephone (fixed or mobile)	61	78	89	93	97	97
Mobile phone	—	—	—	—	—	36
Car	36	40	43	46	52	53

Source: Walker *et al.*, 2002

certainly not the situation in the early 1980s. Table 8.3 also reflects the development of consumer goods in terms of the data collected, such as the inclusion of home computers, access to the internet and satellite, cable and digital television. It remains the case that it is the 'oldest' old who have least access to these goods, which reflects the complex interaction between age and generation and the circumstances in which people enter the post-work phase of life.

Housing

Housing is an important aspect of the quality of life of older people and can enhance (or constrain) some of the social, physical or financial aspects of ageing. In Britain, where the predominant mode of tenure is for home ownership, housing represents a substantial financial asset for older people (and indeed other social groups). Indeed for most of the population their house is their largest financial asset and their largest single financial transaction.

The housing circumstances of the current generation of elders largely reflect the housing decisions taken earlier in the life course. Table 8.4 shows the changes in the housing market in the post-1945 era – the promotion of home ownership (including the purchase of previously publicly owned accommodation) and the demise of

Table 8.4 Housing tenure for older people, Great Britain, 1980–2001 (%)

	1980	1985	1991	1994	1998	2001
Tenure						
Owner occupied, owned outright, or with mortgage	47	50	58	64	68	67
Rented from council or housing association	41	40	36	30	26	28
Rented privately	12	10	6	6	5	5
Age of accommodation						
Before 1919	27	22	20	19	17	17
1919–1944	30	27	22	24	19	19
1945–1964	25	26	30	29	28	29
1965 or later	18	25	28	29	35	34
Central heating						
Has central heating	47	63	76	82	88	91
Has no central heating	53	37	24	18	12	9

Source: Walker *et al.*, 2002

private renting. Some two-thirds of older people now own their own homes, which represents a very different situation from 1980 when this was under a half. We can also see from Table 8.4 that the housing occupied by older people is of more recent construction and has access to better heating than that of previous generations. As was the situation for other types of consumer assets, it is the 'oldest old' who are more likely to be in the 'worst' housing and are less likely to own their own home. Sheltered housing, where older people live in a 'supported' environment, is used by only a small minority of elders (approximately 5 per cent). The development of private-sector sheltered housing was one of the boom segments of the housing market in the 1980s and 1990s but it still remains a niche sector of the housing market. Clearly the housing occupied by older people represents a significant financial asset; policy makers and others clearly see a potential for these assets to be 'unlocked' in order to pay for the care that older people may require or to supplement their income. However, there is little evidence of this happening to any large degree.

Conclusion

Older people are, predominantly, inactive in the formal labour market. This reflects the interaction of two interrelated twentieth-century social phenomena – the construction of 'retirement' as a legitimate stage of life and the development of pensions as a way of guaranteeing income to those in the post-work phase of life. These two trends are clearly interrelated and unpicking the links between them is virtually impossible. There are a variety of different perspectives upon retirement, each of which has some validity. The conflict-based political economists see the creation of retirement as a way for capitalism to 'manage' variations in the supply and demand for labour. The structuralists equally saw retirement as a way of managing labour but in a way that emphasised the smooth transition of opportunities across the generations. More recently, the development of ideas concerning the third age has seen retirement downgraded as a status transition and emphasis placed upon social engagement and consumption as a method of creating and maintaining post-work identities.

It is evident from the analysis of UK data that the nature of the population entering the post-work phase of life is very different from the experience of the immediate post-war generation. The current generation of elders has better housing, greater access to material goods and a higher absolute income than those retiring at previous points in history. However, one aspect of these changes has been to accentuate and reinforce work-based inequalities. It is clear that the post-work population is considerably more heterogeneous than it was in, for example, 1945, as comparison of current circumstances with those reported by Townsend (1957) and Sheldon (1948) indicate. Issues of age, gender and class are being maintained and re-inforced. Older people, women and those from unskilled and insecure occupation groups are disadvantaged in terms of access to all major assets. Rather than poverty in old age being a universal experience, it is being disproportionately experienced by specific groups, especially women. Current policies, which are downgrading the role of the state in income maintenance in later life and emphasising 'private' pension arrangements, are likely to reinforce such inequalities and create 'two nations' in old age. We may well see the emergence of a small consumption-based post-work lifestyle and the development of the grey market, but given current arrangements for the provision of pensions and levels of payments, this seems unlikely to be a mass experience.

9 Caring networks

Although not all older people are frail or disabled it remains the case that older people present significant needs for health and social care. For the gerontologist there is a delicate balance to be struck between combating the myth that 'all old people are ill' and understating the very real needs for care and services presented by physically and mentally frail older people. For those older people who need care in later life, there are two major resource domains available, in theory at least, to meet these needs: the formal services provided by statutory or voluntary agencies and informal networks. In this chapter we are concerned with the 'informal' network. We consider how this presents a framework within which care for older people is organised and describe the wider historical context, although the detailed social policy dimensions of this issue are considered in Chapter 10, which deals with formal care services and the relationship between 'formal' and 'informal' services. Although the two resource domains are presented as separate and distinct, this rigid division is somewhat artificial. We need to remember that 'caring work' takes place in both public and private spheres and that to draw too rigid a distinction between them is somewhat artificial.

Why the interest in family care?

Two interrelated factors, the rise of feminism and concerns about the 'demographic time bomb', seemed to underpin the 'rediscovery' of informal care and caring for older people (and other groups) in the 1980s and 1990s. The development of interest in the field of research classified as 'caregiving' is a key feature of the academic and policy development of gerontology in 1980s and 1990s. It shows how the interplay between theoretically and policy related research combined to develop a specific area of research. Examination of many of the early British gerontological textbooks and research papers does not reveal the presence of terms such as informal care or caregiving. Clearly in the studies by Sheldon (1948) and Townsend (1957) there is much material describing the family lives of older people and the whole area of intergenerational exchanges. However, these activities are not referred to as 'caring' and these inter- and intra-generational patterns of exchange are neither problematised nor defined as deviant or 'abnormal' family relationships. Remarkably little comment is made about the involvement of family members in the domestic lives of older people. There is a legitimate question to ask in terms of the factors that prompted activities within families to be rebranded as 'caring' and for such relationships to be defined as outside the normal pattern expected within families.

Although it is not clear which came first, feminism or policy makers' and politicians' concerns about the impact of demographic and family change upon the 'availability' of (potential) family carers, these combined to stimulate interest in this broad field of research. In the 1980s a feminist critique of community care and the assumptions upon which it was based was articulated (see, for example, Finch and Groves, 1980, 1983; Ungerson, 1987; Dalley, 1988). This critique argued that this was a policy based upon implicit (sexist) assumptions. These were that caring was (almost) exclusively and 'naturally' a task undertaken by women who were usually daughters (-in-law) caring for their parents (-in-law) or wives caring for husbands, and that women were 'natural' carers. The continued availability of such a pool of carers was presumed by government policy developments that emphasised maintaining people at home rather than in institutions and with 'state' services seen as being deployed in the last resort. The prime responsibility for maintaining older people in the community was firmly located with 'the community'. Current demographic trends, especially the reduction in family size and the increased labour market participation of women, 'threatened' the availability of a pool of family members available to take care of those experiencing physical or mental frailty and dependency. Hence the 1980s and 1990s saw the rise of interest in 'informal care' (caregiving in North America). Initially this sphere of interest was confined to the domain of those assisting or living with an older person experiencing cognitive impairment (Martin-Matthews, 2000). The terms are now used much more broadly to describe almost every form of intra-family assistance, especially that which crosses generational boundaries.

How many older people need care?

Earlier we explored the health status of older people and considered some aspects of the difficulties faced by older people with disability and infirmity. How does the prevalence of disease and disability translate into a 'need for care' by older people (or indeed other groups?). This is not a straightforward question to answer as there is no algorithm or protocol that translates the prevalence of arthritis, dementia or disability into a direct need for care. Clearly measures of mortality offer us little help here. There would seem to be two main approaches to the consideration of the need for care by older people within a community context. These relate to trying to enumerate (or quantify) the need for help with specific tasks expressed by older people and then building scales which reflect 'need'. An alternate approach is to develop models of need for care based upon the time intervals for which people need help. This second approach, while identifying levels of severity, does not directly relate to specific types of needs.

A key strand of British gerontological work, from the pioneering work of Sheldon (1948) onwards, has concentrated upon investigating the difficulties that older people experience with specific activities of daily living. Such activities may relate to personal care needs (e.g. washing), instrumental activities (such as shopping or housework) and mobility problems. Earlier there was some initial discussion as to the issues concerning activities of daily living. Table 9.1 describes the percentages of older people living in the community unable to undertake selected key activities of daily living. The first point evident from Table 9.1, and stated earlier, is that at any particular point in time the majority of older people do not need care (although this does not necessarily mean that they are not receiving care!). The percentages of older people requiring help with these activities are not especially large. These range from 5 per cent who are unable to prepare and cook a hot meal to the 30 per cent unable to cut their toenails. Although there are age-related increases even in the oldest age groups, only a minority of people report difficulties with these activities. Even a small percentage of a large absolute population group can represent a significant number of older people experiencing difficulties and who, by implication, may need help to remain living in their own homes. For example, the 5 per cent unable to cook a meal translates into almost half a million people unable to perform this activity, representing a considerable number of people who are vulnerable and who may well need assistance with cooking (and

Table 9.1 Population aged 65+ unable to perform selected activities of daily living, Great Britain

	Unable to perform (%)	Estimated number in UK*
Cut own toenails	30	2,787,600
Wash all over or bathe	7	650,440
Go up and down stairs	9	836,280
Do heavy housework	10	929,200
Shop or carry heavy bags	14	1,300,880
Prepare and cook a hot meal	5	464,600
Reach an overhead shelf	6	557,520
Tie a good knot in a piece of string	5	464,600

Source: Walker *et al.*, 2002

Note: *Assumed to be 9,292,000

related preparatory activities) to remain at home. This scale of 'need' is unlikely to be met by statutory or voluntary agencies. As Askham (2003) observes the 'meaning' of many of these activities to older people themselves is rather presumed by researchers. It remains unclear as to whether the items in such lists reflect the major barriers to older people remaining independently at home or represent the key areas where they would welcome assistance. Much more work is required to consider the key problems to remaining at home for older people and to elucidate their main concerns and areas where they would deem a service response appropriate.

We could argue that, of themselves, each of these individual questions is subject to error because of lack of scientific evidence as to their validity and reliability, and potential problems resultant from differential interpretation by men and women. Hence any estimates of need for care based upon a response to a single question may be subject to bias and imprecision, demonstrating very wide confidence intervals. An alternative approach is to group the items into a scale and use this to determine need for care. McGee *et al.* (1998) have used the Townsend disability score (Meltzer *et al.*, 1999) in their study of cognitive function and ageing. This measure has been widely used and is simple to administer. Responses to the nine items in the scale are used to classify respondents into four categories: no disability, some disability, appreciable disability and severe disability. This last category may be considered as representing a significant need for care and support because such respondents will have reported a need for help with two of the nine index activities and have difficulties with the rest. Using this index McGee *et al.*, (1998) report that 15.7 per cent of those aged 65+ are so classified; this represents approximately 800,000 people of whom 82 per cent live in the community. These authors also developed a further typology of needs (Meltzer *et al.*, 1999), which relates to those older people with physical disability only, cognitive impairment only and both. This revealed that there were approximately 244,000 elders with cognitive impairment (83 per cent living in the community), 234,000 with both (47 per cent in the community) and 971,780 with physical problems only (70 per cent of whom lived in the community). While these estimates vary from the 'simple' disability approach they are within the same 'ballpark'. This illustrates how different methods will produce varying levels of disability and impairment, there is no 'right' answer to the number of disabled people in the community and how the bulk of care for those people who do have difficulties is provided within the community. This reinforces the point made earlier that institutional care such as nursing and residential homes meets only a minority of the care needs of older people.

It is problematic to translate these measures of performance of activities of daily living and other methods of classifying physical and mental impairment into an unambiguous need for care. In addition it is not clear how well such measures reflect the views of older people themselves (Askham, 2003). As these measures refer to single points in time it is difficult to consider how such needs develop in a dynamic context. We may also speculate that the importance of different daily activities may vary across generations and between elders of different classes and genders. An easy assumption is that these problems are all equally relevant to all older people, but such homogeneity seems unlikely. For all their limitations, such measures represent probably our 'best' currently available population level needs for care by older people. In the rest of this chapter we examine the role of kin and friendship networks in the support and care of older people. In Chapter 10 we consider the role of the state in meeting care needs. Again we need to reiterate the slightly artificial nature of this dichotomy made by drawing a sharp distinction between the location of the caring work (public or private spheres) and the identity of the care provider (family or professional worker).

Social networks and support networks

As we saw earlier, ageing takes place, for the vast majority of the population, within the context of a multiplicity of social and kin relationships. These networks of kin and non-kin relationships provide many of the resources with which older people (and indeed younger people) turn when faced with the vicissitudes of life such as illness, infirmity, frailty, emotional distress and financial or material problems. As part of a web of social obligations and relationships, it is important to remember that older people are also providers of help and support as well as being recipients of help. Flows of assistance within families and kin networks are not unidirectional. The existence of such social networks, whether solely kin based or more expansively defined, are conceptualised as a resource for 'successful' ageing. The family and wider social network clearly plays an important role in the lives of older people, as it does with people from other age groups. In this sense the experience of old age represents a continuation of previous patterns of social and family relationships.

We saw that there is a complex mixture of social obligations and rules, which govern the provision and receipt of care and assistance within and between family members. Help may be provided during times of illness, and money or gifts given in times of hardship. These flows of help occur both between generations, between siblings for example, and across (several) generations as between grandparent and grandchildren. Such flows of help and support between and across generations are complex and highly dynamic. Such dynamism is often lost from the social research perspective because our studies of family relationships and, in particular, the provision of help in times of 'need', are far too often cross-sectional in nature. They describe the fabric of social relationships at a single point in time and cannot present for us how this pattern of social linkages has been arrived at and how it may (or may not) change in the future. While the true complexity of family and social relationships is rarely captured in the researcher's gaze, we can be fairly certain that the stereotype that portrays older people as the 'receivers' and the younger generations as the 'providers' of help is far too simplistic. For example perhaps 10 per cent of older people are grandparents acting as 'surrogate' parents and at least 24 per cent of those aged 65+ are actively involved in childcare and babysitting.

We need to distinguish social support and care networks (Phillipson, 2004). The focus earlier was upon examining the broadly based social networks of older people. Enumerating and quantifying the number of individuals within a specific social network clearly provide the context or opportunities for the development of active support networks. We may define the support network as a more limited entity in that it is directed at a specific purpose such as helping an older person remain at home by providing various forms of assistance. Social and support networks are clearly interrelated but not necessarily coterminus entities. We cannot presume that those people in an individual's social network will be available to provide support, in either emotional or instrumental terms, although we can be fairly certain that those outside an individual's social network are unlikely to provide this unless as part of a professional–client relationship. Access to care and networks may vary geographically (Wenger, 1984, 1994). Although theoretical and conceptually plausible, it is unlikely that people from outside a network would be available to provide care and support unless they were from voluntary or statutory agencies. We cannot, however, presume that the existence of a social network translates into the actual provision of care and support. The social network frames, outlines and contextualises the potentially available resources but the mechanisms and frameworks by which a social network is translated into a support network remain opaque. Furthermore we cannot take for granted that care and support, which may be available, is necessarily beneficial. Support and help can provide active care or may also bring about dependency and compromise independence. The focus in support network research has predominantly been upon the role of kin and friendship networks. It is rare that support network analysis and investigation integrate the role and contribution of both informal and formal or voluntary sectors. For the most part the groups of literature concerning the roles and functions of these three different sectors have remained separate, although there are clear linkages between these dimensions of support and care. Investigation of such linkages could usefully inform our understanding of how the different elements of a caring and support network interrelate.

According to Nolan *et al.* (1996) the study of social and support networks can be approached from three major theoretical perspectives each of which has a specific focus. Human ecology theory is concerned with understanding the impact of social systems upon human development; social support and social network theory is concerned with understanding relationships between different social units and help seeking or giving perspectives focus upon the interdependencies between carers and dependants and the mechanisms for seeking or providing care. Furthermore they argue that there are four major roles of the support network that need to be defined and con-textualised. These are providing care, providing a 'buffer' for the provider of care, referring the individual to services when appropri-ate and transmitting cultural values as to the provision of care and support across and between generations. Each approach defines 'carers' slightly differently, asks different types of research questions and provides different types of answers. When evaluating 'carer' research we need to examine the theoretical perspectives and assump-tions underpinning the research. This serves to emphasise the fact that there is no single approach to the study of social networks (or indeed other facets of later life); rather there are a variety of complementary theoretical approaches that we may take towards the investigation of this subject. We then need to be able to integrate and synthesise the results of such diverse studies in order to develop a more sophisticated framework for the analysis of caregiving to older people (and other groups).

In order to consider the issue of provision of care to older people we need to examine the contributions made by the differing sectors and attempt to integrate the contributions of these differing sectors. In this chapter, where we are addressing the provision of care to older people by families and friends, we need to consider at least three different dimensions. The first relates to the provision of care and assistance between generations, the second to the provision of assistance across generations and the third to temporal or historical variations in care and assistance across time. We shall start with the third topic. These data provide the context within which to consider the other two perspectives and also to consider the role of more formal health and social welfare agencies.

Social and family networks and caring: an historical perspective

The provision of care, in either the public or private spheres, takes place within historical, cultural, geographical and temporal contexts. We clearly need to understand 'caring' within dynamic frames of ref-erence. This relates both to individual relationships within each 'caring dynamic' and the need to incorporate an historical perspect-ive to our understanding of the 'caring relationship'. Although there was a reawakening in the 1980s as to the importance of family in the care of older people (and indeed other 'dependent' groups) family care was not 'invented' in the 1980s. Thane (2000) notes how Sheldon (1948), Townsend (1957) and Young and Willmott (1957) were all surprised by the extensive involvement of families in the care of their older relatives. She argues that this was because these investigators had readily absorbed, like the wider social world, the stereotype that families neglected older people and that extended family ties had disappeared. Hence they did not expect to find the considerable level of involvement evident of the family in the lives of older people (and vice versa). The empirical data collected by these investigators and the more recent contemporary surveys contradict the popular stereotype of the old as being neglected by their families. Consistently research has demonstrated the very high degree of involvement of the family in the lives of older people and the importance of older people within families. Sheldon (1948) notes that of those older people who need help with domestic matters, only 10 per cent was provided for outside of the immediate family. Yet we continue to be surprised and amazed as each new generation of social researchers rediscovers 'the family' and its importance in the lives of older people and vice versa. Following on from this is another popular image of the family as making little, or no, contribution towards the care of older people (and a more implicit but related idea that older people do not contribute to the well-being of other family members). This stereotypical attitude was clearly articulated in Britain in the 1950s in the wake of the establishment of the post-war welfare state, where policy makers and practitioners were convinced that children would not be prepared to care for their elderly parents following the establishment of the welfare state (Means and Smith, 1998). Indeed concerns about the perceived 'negative' effect of welfare provision upon the willingness of families shaped both the development of services and the nature of these services (Means and Smith, 1998). Initially levels of service development were limited so as not to 'undermine' families and services were provided within institutional settings: the development of domiciliary services was initially seen as too threatening of family 'responsibility'. Rather services were provided in impersonal institutional settings to stop families from shirking their responsibilities. It is only comparatively recently that a more sophisticated view of the relationship between the family and the person receiving care has developed and there is a recognition that by providing help within a community context support networks can be enhanced and strengthened and enabled to function for longer. There is little evidence that the provision of formal support decreases the provision of informal care.

Yet contemporary investigators should not have been surprised when their empirical data contradicted their beliefs, attitudes and stereotypes. As a resource for responding to the social, material and health challenges experienced by individuals as they age (or indeed for other groups), the family has always been the main focus of response. This expectation was enshrined in the Poor Law Act 1930 which stated:

> It should be the duty of the father, grandfather, mother, grandmother, husband or child of a poor, old, blind, lame or impotent person, or other poor person, not able to work, if possessed of sufficient means, to relieve and maintain that person not able to work.
>
> (quoted in Means and Smith, 1998: 19)

Thane (2000) illustrates graphically, using a variety of sources, the interdependence of older people and their families over a very long historical perspective. However, such research has almost exclusively focused upon the support links provided between families and older people and rarely acknowledged the potential for help to flow in the opposite direction. Such studies were rarely designed or conceptualised to include non-family-based supportive or caring relationships. In the future it is likely, if current trends continue, that these types of caring situations will increase as friends and 'families of choice' become part of the caring network.

These questions and stereotypes remain in popular currency. Indeed, every historical epoch tends to look back at a 'golden age' of family care and contrast it with current circumstances. Empirical data suggest that this perception of the family as refusing to accept the care of their older members (or indeed other age groups who have either chronic or acute problems) is a myth totally without foundation. Consistently a stream of research reports from the 1950s onwards has demonstrated that it is the family which provides the bulk of the care required by older people resident in the community (and indeed for other groups with care needs such as disabled children). In terms of contemporary and more distant historical times, there is an enduring and consistent pattern of support for older people within families. For all the very profound changes in family composition discussed earlier, the provision of family care to dependent members remains fairly consistent within the western context.

Brody (1990) considers that our continued emphasis upon documenting the extent of family care, and our subsequent surprise that it is still 'alive and well', means that we have failed to ask the really fundamental question. She argues that our focus upon the continual 'rediscovery' of family care means that we have singularly failed to ask why people continue to provide extensive care to their older relatives, often at some personal cost. For her one of the key questions is, if caring is so hard and extracts such a high personal cost, why do we do it? What are the mechanisms which mean that we continue to support and care for our frail and infirm family members? Identification of the factors that 'promote' caring could also be helpful in policy terms by identifying potential strategies for prevention. We may develop this argument by identifying a further important but neglected question. There has been an emphasis upon the identification and enumeration of the negative aspects of caring. There are copious measures of care or caregiver burden and numerous studies of the problems and difficulties faced by carers. Yet again we have failed to ask, in the face of such apparently pervasive negative consequences, why do people continue to care? Furthermore policy makers and practitioners have not then considered the issue of what societal interventions can we promote to encourage and reinforce family care in order to ensure the continuation of this resource. Rather there has been a bias towards documenting 'carer strain' rather than identifying the factors that might promote and enhance caregiving. This reflects the dominant focus in UK health and social welfare policy of curing or solving problems once they have appeared rather than trying to prevent them in the first place.

Defining carers and caring

Before we can examine issues of care and support across and between generations we need to define the topic under consideration. The first questions that require examination in undertaking our analysis of family care, regardless of context, are ones of definition. What is the informal care sector? Who is a carer? What is caring? How are carers and caring distinguished from other social roles and functions? There are still no easy answers to Gubrium's deceptively simple question 'what is this thing some call caregiving?' (Gubrium, 1991: 268). Similarly Bulmer (1987) observes that the meaning of care and, by inference, the identity of a carer, may be intuitively obvious but difficult to define, operationalise and measure within a social research context. At a basic level of analysis, informal caring, the most usual UK term for the American term 'caregiving', may be defined as care provided by family, friends and neighbours which is not organised via a statutory or voluntary agency. Such care and assistance are not provided directly for money but rather stem from the complex relationships of responsibilities and obligations which arise within families or from long-term friendships. Informal care is largely provided by untrained people and may be best characterised as 'doing what comes naturally'. In contrast 'formal care' is based upon the presentation of an assessment of need. Interventions with a planned goal are selected from an evidence base and delivered by trained workers. Viewed in this light there is a sharp distinction to be drawn between the two spheres. However, we should be wary of such an idealised dichotomy.

Although perhaps hidden from view in the early days of the British welfare state the informal sector has always been the main provider of help to older people, especially with the non-professional, 'non-specialist' personal and household tasks which are required to maintain frail and dependent people in the community. As we shall see later in this chapter this statement is applicable to the contemporary period, contradicting the powerful popular myth that older people are neglected by their family and that the main burden of caring for older people falls upon the state. The importance of the informal sector in maintaining older people in the community (and indeed other groups with long-term care needs) is now an accepted and acknowledged part of community care policy and carers are seen as a 'resource' by statutory or voluntary agencies.

Having established the broad context of the concept of informal or family care, we need to be more specific in our definitions of the tasks and people involved. In particular from a policy perspective, especially one driven by the 'demographic imperative', there has been a concern to define and quantify the numbers of carers and describe what carers do in order that the state can consider the kinds of support functions it may be required to provide to future generations of elders. There have been several approaches to the definition of carers and caring and not all of them reflect the instrumentalist task-related focus of work informed, implicitly or explicitly, by the focus upon 'apocalyptic' demography.

One common approach has been to define caring by the tasks and functions undertaken by carers. Parker (1981) draws out the distinction between caring about and caring for. 'Caring about' is conceptualised as being concerned about an individual and could include such tasks as providing emotional support, while 'caring for' is usually taken as being concerned with more direct 'hands on' help and can also be conceptualised as 'tending'. A carer could be performing either (or both) of these activities plus other functions. As Nolan *et al.* (1996) argue, although an interesting conceptualisation, this is a highly instrumental definition of caring as it is concerned with 'what is being done' although it does distinguish a task-orientated definition from the more emotional element. The links between these two different conceptualisations are not really explored. Is it necessary to 'care about' before one can tend or 'care for' an individual?

The notion of tending or caring for is the conceptualisation implicit in the national surveys of caring (Rowlands and Parker, 1998) and the typologies devised by Parker and Lawton (1994) based upon the reanalysis and classification of the national carer survey data (Maher and Green, 2002). This classification offers the theoretical and conceptual possibility of developing a more sophisticated typology of caring, perhaps based upon combinations of activities and relationships. However, to date the typology has largely limited itself to the types and combinations of activities performed. Qureshi and Walker (1989) and Pearlin *et al.* (2001) have proposed very similar typologies and definitions of carers and caring that attempt to distinguish the affective dimension from the caregiving. There remains a very heavy focus upon the tasks performed in a highly instrumental way within the caring relationships analysed. Typically these approaches towards defining caregiving are highly task orientated, almost providing an 'audit' of tasks that would need to be taken over by the state or voluntary bodies if families were not providing them.

Arber and Ginn (1995) have developed a notion of caring that is defined by the performance of three different sets of activities which are a further sophistication and refinement of the tending–caring dichotomy. They distinguish between physical labour, emotional labour and managerial or organisational labour. Echoing the way feminists attempted to redefine childcare and domestic tasks as work or labour, Arber and Ginn (1995) have used this analogy in the field of caring. The relationships between the affective and caregiving dimensions of caring have rarely been studied in depth. Does one need to 'care about' an individual before one can care for (or tend) them? This remains one of the many unanswered questions on the caregiving research agenda. The notion of organisational or managerial care is an interesting development and expansion of the definition of caregiving. Arber and Ginn (1995) argue that, for the instrumental and affective elements of caregiving to be delivered, there is an important managerial or organisational workload that needs to be completed. Routines have to be established and regimes adhered to. This is a largely neglected element of the caregiving role but Arber and Ginn (1995) argue that it the organisational and emotional aspects of caring that contribute most to the quality of life experienced by the care recipient. This is a proposition that requires considerably more research to establish its veracity. It seems likely that the organisational aspects of caregiving have been neglected within the private domain. In contrast 'care organisation' is a key aspect of the provision of care within the public arena. Arber and Ginn (1995) may well be right in their assertion and are clearly correct in drawing our attention to a hidden aspect of the provision of care within the private dimension.

Others have attempted to define carers and caring by developing a typology of carers based upon the nature of the caring relationship rather than upon the delivery of physical activities or other types of tasks. These approaches focus upon the identity of the carer rather than the tasks performed. This is a more conceptual or theoretical approach than the more instrumental approaches described earlier. Lewis and Meredith (1989) and Twigg and Aitkin (1994) sought to categorise carers based upon the relationship between carers and the recipient of care. Lewis and Meredith (1989) in their study of daughters caring for elderly mothers argue that the caregiving relationship can be conceptualised in two distinct ways. The first is as a 'linear' or continuum concept or service-orientated model of caring as compared to the complex or 'mosaic' model of caring. Lewis and Meredith (1989) note that caring constitutes both an activity and a source of identity. Lewis and Meredith (1989) and Twigg and Aitkin (1994) have sought to move beyond a fixation with the components of care to develop typologies of caregiving that link identity and relationships. Lewis and Meredith (1989) propose a threefold typology of carers: the 'balanced' carer who integrates caring within a framework of other social roles, the 'integrated' carer where caring provides both a sense of purpose and satisfaction and the 'immersed' carer where there is both a heavy commitment to caregiving and it becomes the focus of the carer's identity. These categories resonate with those proposed by Twigg and Aitkin (1994), who distinguish between the 'balanced' carer where the carer can set boundaries and develop a balanced life, the 'symbiotic' carer who constructs caring within a relationship from which the carer develops positive benefits and the 'engulfed' carer who subordinates his or her needs and life to that of the person being cared for. The experience of caring and the effect it has is clearly most problematic for the immersed and engulfed categories of relationship. Such typologies offer new insights into thinking about caring by raising issues of the dynamics of the relationship and (implicitly) what happens when the caring role stops.

In broad terms the definition of carers and caring remains contentious and problematic. There are many different ways that researchers and policy makers have approached the definition and conceptualisation of this group. Given the lack of consensus among policy makers and researchers, how do members of the general population understand the term 'carers' which is used so widely in academic and policy discourse? There are remarkably few studies investigating 'lay' understanding and definitions of carers and caregiving. In a survey of the general adult population by the Carers' National Association (CNA, 1996), only 5 per cent thought a carer was someone who looks after a family member or friend who cannot look after themselves because of frailty, disability or illness. The vast majority of the people included in this survey thought that a carer was 'a caring person' (79 per cent: CNA, 1996). The other main definitions of a 'carer' identified in the CNA (1996) survey were someone with a *paid* job involving caring or working for social services sources (31 per cent) or a voluntary worker (7 per cent) (the remaining respondents didn't know). There are clearly considerable issues of definition for academics, policy makers and the wider population. While such discrepancies in definition exist, creating a common discourse between policy makers and 'carers' is going to be problematic. Such differences of semantics take on real importance if they mean that people fail to claim benefits or other welfare supports to which they are entitled because they do not define themselves (or other people within their family) as carers. It also shows the difficulties experienced when the state attempts to define and legislate for aspects of 'normal' family relationships.

It is clear that there are a number of ways to approach the definition of carers and the work of caring. Broadly speaking we may distinguish the approaches which focus upon the performance of physical tasks, wider instrumental definitions that include the organisational and managerial elements of task performance and emotional tasks, and those definitions based upon the nature of the relationships between carer and cared for. When evaluating statements about the number of carers within a given population, we clearly need to consider the nature of the definition used.

Who cares?

It seems likely, given the complexities discussed above, that there is no simple definition of either carers or caring. The search for a simple definition that distinguishes 'carers' from 'non-carers' is probably futile. Indeed it seems likely that caring, like chronic disease and disability, forms a continuum of relationships between an individual and the family or social network, and where the line is drawn along this is largely arbitrary. Attempting to distinguish 'normal' from 'abnormal' family relationships is clearly going to be problematic. Most of the definitions of caring ignore the nature of the relationship. It seems probable that there are differing definitions and thresholds of caring contingent upon the relationship context. It is likely that spouses caring for each other may define caring very differently from adults caring for their parents (-in-law). Finch (1995) suggests that different sets of social 'rules' govern the reasons why individuals become the carers of their spouse, mother or father (or parents-in-law). We return to this point in a later section. Despite these conceptual difficulties in determining what caring is and who carers are, there are numerous examples of attempts to develop an operational definition of caring (Nolan *et al.*, 1996). Such measures have usually been used in a quantitative setting to try to count the number of carers and quantify what they do. Indeed the 2001 Census held in the United Kingdom in April 2001 included a question about caring. This highlights the importance ascribed by policy makers and governments in trying to determine the number of current carers and, by implication, to consider how demographic change may affect the pool of potential future carers. This is another manifestation of the concern with the impending 'caregiving' crisis resultant from the family changes noted previously.

Counting carers

The survey of carers included as part of the 1985 General Household Survey (Rowlands and Parker, 1998) was the first attempt in Britain to undertake a large scale nationally representative prevalence type survey of the provision of informal care and was repeated in 1990, 1995 and 2000 (Maher and Green, 2002). The definition used in these studies, which asked about extra responsibilities resulting from the care of someone who was elderly (or sick or handicapped), was also included in the 2001 Census. In context it is similar to the definitions used by other quantitative researchers (see Nolan *et al.*, 1996 for a summary) and focuses upon the instrumental facet of caring by examining what is being done, by whom and who is receiving the care provided. This concentration upon the tending and physical care dimension of caring suggests that, from a policy perspective, the response to physical dependency is seen as the 'essence' of caring as this is the arena that the government is concerned that it will have to replace if families or friends stop caring (or are no longer available as a result of demographic change). The policy premise underpinning these studies is that of 'apocalyptic' thinking which emphasises two scenarios. These are the increasing likelihood of being faced with caregiving as a result of demographic or family change and the perceived likelihood that an older person needing care will not have a family member available to provide this (Martin-Matthews, 2000).

As well as the limited focus upon the physical responses to dependency driven by an acceptance of the apocalyptic demographic change thesis, the definitions used to enumerate caregiving are highly relative. They require respondents to compare what they do against some hypothetical norm of family and friendship relationships and define it as 'abnormal' or outside of normal family and friendship roles and functions. Clearly it is up to respondents to define what they are providing for their dependant as abnormal (or even deviant) and outside of 'normal' spouse, sibling or filial (or other relationship) roles. Concerns have been raised about this definition in that specific subgroups may systematically over- or under-report their family responsibilities as caring. For example, it has been proposed that this definition is 'gender biased': women will under-report what they do as caring while for men the opposite case may hold. There may well be biases in how this question is answered in terms of age, class or ethnicity, although these aspects have been less well investigated.

It is, perhaps, fruitless for the reasons already outlined to try to determine the 'correct' number of carers providing support to their dependants or family members or friends at any specific point in time. Arguments aimed at identifying the 'correct' number of carers are very similar to medieval theological debates as to how many angels could dance on the head of a pin. Indeed Martin-Matthews (2000) notes how, in a Canadian survey of caregiving, they had wildly overestimated the 'true' prevalence of what they term 'eldercare' by having a very inclusive definition of this concept (i.e. help with any of a range of eighteen tasks in the previous six months). Martin-Matthews (2000) rather convincingly argues that this highly inclusive definition overstated the extent of caring and defined as deviant or pathological perfectly 'normal' intra- and intergenerational exchanges within a family context. Given the definitional and conceptual caveats noted above, in 1985 14 per cent of the adult population self-defined themselves as carers compared with 15 per cent in 1990, 13 per cent in 1995 and 16 per cent in 2000 (Table 9.2). A survey undertaken by the Carers' National Association

Table 9.2 Prevalence of caring, Great Britain, 1985–2001 (%)

	1985	1990	1995	2000	2001 Census
Male	12	13	11	14	11
Female	15	17	14	18	14
16–29	7	8	6	8	
30–44	14	15	10	13	
45–64	20	24	20	24	20
65+	13	13	13	13	12
Married	16	18	15	19	
Single	9	10	8	10	
Widowed/divorced	12	13	9	12	
Same household	4	4	4	5	
Other household	10	12	8	11	
All	14	15	13	16	13
Total numbers (million)	6.0	6.8	5.7		

Source: Rowlands and Parker, 1998: Part one, Tables 1, 4, 5

(CAN, 1996) provides some face validity for the GHS results. Using the definition of a carer as 'someone who looks after a family member or friend who cannot look after themselves because of frailty, disability or illness', 12 per cent of the adult population (11 per cent males and 13 per cent females) rated themselves as carers. The most recent 2001 Census data suggest that 11 per cent of the total population and 13 per cent of those aged 16+ provide unpaid care. Hence this type of question appears to generate an approximately consistent rate of positive response. If we translate these percentages into absolute numbers, using the 2001 estimate, there are 5.2 million carers in England and Wales. For the reasons outlined above, this could be subject to error and is likely to be either an under- or overestimate. Whichever way the bias is influencing the results, there are many people within the population who self-define their caring 'responsibilities' within their family or social network as 'abnormal' or not part of 'normal' family or social relationships. Again results such as these provide the starting point for developing a whole research agenda. One obvious area for research is determining how people determine what are (and are not) 'normal' family relationships. When does 'normal' intergenerational exchange become caring? When does a 'normal' marital relationship of mutual help transform into a 'caring' relationship? These are really intriguing questions which we have hardly started to address. While there are obvious conceptual difficulties with these definitions, the large sample sizes included within these surveys offer the potential for applying some of the other types of definitions of carers and to examine issues of cross- and intergenerational exchanges.

There is one further caveat that applies to the national surveys of caring and that needs to be acknowledged before undertaking further analysis of these data. All of the data presented from the GHS and Census are derived from the perspective of the carer. These data do not take into account the perspective of the person receiving care. We can only speculate as to whether cared-for people see themselves as being a 'dependant' and whether they identify the carer as a 'carer' and not as a spouse, daughter or friend. There are (at least) two sides to the caring relationship and, in most of the data that follow, we must acknowledge that this is generated largely from the perspective of the carer. Clearly there is a large research agenda to be addressed in terms of understanding and evaluating the caring relationship from the perspective of the 'dependent' person.

Who are carers?

Given this important caveat, who are these people who self-define themselves as carers and what are their characteristics? Within the British context who are these people who define their activities as outside the 'norm' of 'ordinary' family transactions and relationships? What are the main characteristics of those who define themselves as carers or are 'carers' generally representative of the adult population? One of the key challenges already noted is that of defining the relationships, activities and behaviours that characterise caregiving. We can look at this in two ways: what is the 'prevalence' of caring across different socio-demographic groups and what are the socio-demographic characteristics of the population who self-define themselves as 'carers'. For Britain the most extensive data set is the four surveys of carers and informal care provision undertaken as part of the General Household Survey. Examination of these empirical data reveals that carers, like many other subsets of the general population, are a heterogeneous group encompassing variation in terms of age, gender and relationships. This heterogeneity was less obvious in small-scale qualitative research where the focus was upon specific types of carers and caring relationships, such as Lewis and Meredith's (1989) survey of daughters who care or Ungerson's (1987) study of caring for a disabled spouse. Hence the variation within the 'caring population' only really emerged as a result of undertaking large-scale empirical studies where the sample size was sufficient to encompass the diversity of this population. Consequently for all its conceptual limitations in how caring has been defined and measured, the GHS caring surveys have made an important contribution to our understanding of caring by highlighting the diversity and complexity of this population, a diversity which is not always recognised in policy discourse or service development.

The prevalence of caring

In each of the GHS carer surveys and the 2001 Census a higher percentage of women than men have defined themselves as carers, although the differential is not especially large (see Table 9.2). For example, in 2001, 11 per cent of men and 14 per cent of women defined themselves as a carer. One criticism levelled at the GHS carer definition (as noted earlier), is that it is understood differently by men and women. It is argued that women see caring as part of their 'normal' responsibilities and hence do not define themselves as a carer. The comparatively small percentage difference in the prevalence of caring among men and women may be an artefact resulting from an increased willingness of women to see caring as part of 'normal' family life and being less willing to define themselves as a carer. Men, it is argued in contrast, adopt the opposite perspective and are more willing to define what they do as outside of normal family responsibilities. This interpretation is, perhaps, disingenuous to men and seems to downplay the contribution of men. As this comment hints at, one of the more challenging findings from the GHS surveys has been the 'discovery' of male carers (Arber and Gilbert, 1989; Davidson *et al.*, 2000; Calasanti, 2003) as much of the initial work conducted in this field derived from the feminist paradigm and the feminist critique of community care and related social policies. Approximately 11 per cent of adult males defined themselves as carers. Consequently the role of the male carer is now acknowledged and discussed (Wilson, 1995). This discovery has served to highlight the centrality of gender in gerontological research. However, as Martin-Matthews (2000) observes, the function of investigating male carers has largely been to offer a comparison and contrast with female carers, still seen as the norm, rather than considering the different types of men (and women) involved in the provision of family care.

The percentage of the population defining themselves as a carer does not show a linear or neat relationship with age. Rather the 45–64 age group demonstrates the highest percentage of carers at 20 per cent, but it is important to note that 13 per cent of those aged 65+ define themselves as carers. This starkly contradicts the popular stereotype of older people as a dependent group making little contribution to the well-being of the nation as a whole. Disregarding any other contribution they may make to family life (such as the care of grandchildren and great-grandchildren) older people are clearly important contributors to the care of other older people (and indeed other groups within the population). Furthermore the involvement in 'informal' care of the younger age groups suggests that caring is not the sole prerogative of the middle-aged plus group. It also hints that the age and care requirements of the people receiving care may vary. We may speculate that receiving care is not an activity solely confined to older people. This age spread of the caring population again serves to highlight the diversity of the population and the complexity of the interrelationships we are trying to describe and understand and indicates that care is being provided within and between generations within a variety of different age bands.

Examination of the marital status of the caring population is probably of little utility, unless this is being used with other variables to try to determine the number of carers who are undertaking multiple roles (the classic 'women in the middle' group to which we return later). Arber and Ginn (1991) consider that an important conceptual distinction needs to be made between those carers who live with the person they are caring for (co-resident carers) and those looking after someone in a different household (extra-resident carers). The percentage of co-resident carers has remained stable at about 4 per cent of the adult population, while the highest prevalence group are the extra-resident carers, this represents two-thirds of the caring population (4.27 million people). Conceptually, these are two distinct types of relationships, caring for different types of person and raising different types of problems.

The alternative perspective is to examine the socio-demographic characteristics of the population self-defined as carers. This demonstrates a preponderance of women (60 per cent) and a concentration in the 45–64 age group (48 per cent) and, perhaps, conforms more to our expectation as to what the composition of the caring population is really like, but 20 per cent of carers are aged 65+, indicating that caring is not the sole prerogative of the young. One-third of carers are looking after someone in the same household. Of those aged

16–64 identified as carers in the 1995 GHS, 10 per cent reported that they were working full-time and 14 per cent worked part-time (Rowlands and Parker, 1998). There was no variation in the percentage reporting themselves as carers between manual (14 per cent) and non-manual workers (14 per cent). Indeed there were very little socio-economic status variations between different types of carers. One variable, which has been lacking in this analysis, is that of ethnicity. We know very little about the extent and nature of informal care provision within Britain's ethnic minority populations. Blakemore and Boneham (1994) draw attention to our stereotypical view of minority elders being embedded within a close knit and caring family. This fails to take account of variations between different minority communities (e.g. treating members of Chinese, African-Caribbean and Asian communities as if they were a single group – clearly an error of judgement) and the fact that because these individuals are mostly migrants, they may have dislocated or very small family networks in the United Kingdom. With the 'ageing' of UK minority communities, this is going to become a topic of considerable policy relevance and one which researchers should start to examine seriously.

Who is being cared for?

Who is being cared for and what are their characteristics? There are two major groups of people being cared for: parents (-in-law) who represent 43 per cent of this group and spouses (although not necessarily elderly ones!) who account for 19 per cent of 'dependants' (Table 9.3). The predominance of these two groups in the dependent population has remained stable over the four surveys in the series. Overall 24 per cent of those being cared for are 'other relatives' (14 per cent) and neighbours (14 per cent). This indicates that, in the vast majority of cases, the person being cared for is a close relative or spouse (72 per cent). Caring is predominately a family activity with comparatively few instances of caring being provided to non-family members. This suggests that 'caring' outside of a close family relationship is comparatively unusual and, by inference, suggests that it will be difficult to develop a pattern of caring outwith the family relationship. However, these may change as the generations with more constricted kin networks start to age. Understanding friendship-based caring systems is a key research challenge. We have little idea as to how such friendship-based caring relationships are established or what the necessary conditions for their establishment

Table 9.3 Who is being cared for? Great Britain (%)

Dependant	In same household	In another household
Spouse	55	0
Child	20	2
Parent (-in-law)	27	65
Other relative	9	27
Neighbour	4	29
Male	50	28
Under 16	9	1
16–44	17	6
45–74	30	10
75–84	16	41
85+	9	24

Source: Maher and Green, 2002

and maintenance are. What conditions are required to move from feeding the cat while a friend is on holiday to the provision of domestic and personal care for a sustained period of time?

Caring across and between generations

Routine survey data provide only indirect information concerning intra- and intergenerational caring relationships. This distinction is not especially novel as Sheldon (1948) noted the role of both intra- and intergenerational help in the provision of domestic care for older people. Table 9.3 provides hints as to the issue of caring across and between generations, although the information is provided in terms of household relationships. As we can see, where the cared-for person is being cared for in the same household as the carer, half of the dependants are spouses. We can infer that, in at least half of cases, co-residence of carers illustrates intra-generational caring relationships and this is confirmed by the fact that 45 per cent of dependants were aged 65+ (Rowlands and Parker, 1998). Where the carer lives in a different household, the caring relationship is predominantly intergenerational as is indicated by the fact that 85 per cent of dependants were aged 65+. While it is only a crude approximation, we can use household relationship as an approximation for intra- and intergenerational patterns of caring and this distinction is used to consider the type of help being provided by carers.

The analyses of intra- and intergenerational care illustrate the complexity of the gender differences in informal caring. Where care is being provided to someone in the same household, carers are almost equally divided between men and women (54 per cent of such carers are female) but in cross-generational care, the majority of carers are women (69 per cent in 1985, 62 per cent in 1990 and 63 per cent in 1995: Rowlands and Parker, 1998). Although male carers are important they are usually confined to a specific caring situation, that of a co-resident, intra-generational carer usually looking after their elderly spouse. Arber and Ginn (1995) argue that for women (but not men) marriage defines them as the (potential) carer of anyone within the household; men are seen as having only limited caring responsibilities beyond their spouse or, possibly, mother.

What care is being provided?

Parker and Lawton (1994) have developed a typology based upon the activities of caring. This defines carers on the basis of what they do rather than who they are, whom they help or the number of other carers involved in caring. It is, perhaps, more useful from a policy development and community care perspective to discuss caring from the perspective of what is being done. Although knowing who carers are and how many others are involved is clearly useful, it is not possible to develop services which support carers if the types of caring being provided is unknown. Without such information we might be developing gardening services while carers are busy cutting their dependants' toenails (or vice versa). The typology developed by Parker and Lawton (1994) is based upon the eight caring tasks included in the GHS survey. This of course curtails the development of their theoretical model, as they are limited to the topics covered in the survey. Some caring tasks such as practical help (shopping, preparing meals) and surveillance activities such as 'keeping an eye on' were much more common than other tasks such as physical care or giving medicines (Table 9.4). It is useful to reiterate the point raised by Martin-Matthews (2000) that in casting activities such as 'surveillance' tasks and help with paperwork as 'caring', are we pathologising aspects of normal family relationships? These patterns of help seem to have been consistent since the late 1980s. While we may all agree that tasks such as giving personal care are indicative of a 'caring' relationship, it is difficult to ascribe such a status to activities such as helping with paperwork, taking out or keeping company. Martin-Matthews (2000) developed a similar argument for her Canadian data set, but in the absence of the families' perspectives we are limited in how far we can develop this critical analysis. Also we should be wary of entirely

Table 9.4 Type of help given by carers, Great Britain, 1985–2000 (%)

	1985	1990	1995	2000
Personal care	24	22	31	26
Giving medicine	22	16	27	22
Physical help	22	21	36	35
Paper work/finance	40	45	43	39
Other practical	82	79	73	71
Keeping company	66	69	59	55
Taking out	49	55	53	52
Keeping an eye on				60

Source: Rowlands and Parker, 1998: Part two, Table 2

dismissing the importance of the less obvious 'caring' tasks. While they may not constitute 'caring' in the strict sense of the term, they may be crucial to the quality of life of older people.

Clearly there is some overlap between the tasks and there is clearly an implicit hierarchy of caring activities. Parker and Lawton (1994) developed a sixfold typology. Overall the most common forms of caring comprised the provision of practical help, provided by 38 per cent of carers, while the provision of personal care, indicative of a significant degree of dependency, was provided by 23 per cent of carers. This broad pattern of caring activities again has been broadly stable over time and vary with the nature of the caring relationship. Same-generational caring relationships, as indicated by co-residence of carer and dependant, are characterised by high levels of provision of personal care but, of course, some intergenerational caring situations are included within this category (Table 9.5). This is further reinforced by the differences in the amount of time spent in 'caring'. Arber and Ginn (1991) analysed data from the 1985 carers' survey and report that, on average, co-resident carers spent fifty-three hours a week of care compared with nine hours for extra-resident carers. In 1990 over 50 per cent of co-resident carers spent thirty-five hours a week or more caring (Arber and Ginn, 1995). Clearly co-resident carers are providing a different level of care and support and represent different needs for support from the formal sector than do those who are extra-resident carers. We may speculate that it is those who are receiving intensive informal care who are the ones who are 'at risk' of admission to nursing or residential care and that this population is most likely to be found living with their carer. There does not seem to be much support for the suggestion of Pickard (2002) that intensive intergenerational care is decreasing.

Table 9.5 Provision of care by household type (%), Great Britain

	Co-resident	Extra-resident
Giving personal care	51	15
Giving physical help	57	25
Caring 20+ hours	63	10
Sole carer	56	22
Caring for 5+ years	52	41

Source: Rowlands and Parker, 1998: Part one, Tables 17, 21

A network of informal care?

Evandrou (1992) in her analysis has concentrated upon the carer's level of responsibility for the dependant as a method of distinguishing and defining different types of carers. She identifies three different types of carers: sole carers, joint carers (where the caring responsibility is borne jointly with another person) and peripheral carers (where there are more than two people providing care). This latter category may be conceptualised as approximating to the network of informal care that is so consistently implied by government policy statements concerned with the provision of community care (Victor, 1997). The majority of carers in the four GHS surveys (between 50 and 60 per cent) were classified as sole carers, approximately 10 per cent were joint carers and about 33 per cent were peripheral carers (Table 9.6). For the majority of dependants (whatever their age) there is only a very limited network of people involved in their care. While the contribution of the informal sector is hugely significant, most of it is being provided by a sole carer and sole carers are concentrated within the co-resident carer category. This concentration of caring responsibilities upon a single individual serves to reinforce the tenuous nature of the link between social network and caring network. It also serves to make us reconsider our stereotype of older people being enmeshed within a network of care.

Women in the middle

The work by Brody (1981, 1990) has been of special significance in that it emphasised the importance of 'women in the middle' in the provision of care of older relatives. These women, also sometimes referred to as the 'sandwich generation', are largely middle aged who, as well as discharging childcare responsibilities, are then faced

Table 9.6 Levels of caring responsibility, Great Britain, 1985–2000 (%)

	1985	1990	1995	2000
Sole or main carer	52	48	62	65
Joint carer	11	15	8	8
Peripheral carer	37	37	29	37

Source: Rowlands and Parker, 1998: Part two, Table 4

with accepting responsibility for the care of an aged parent (-in-law). While this is a concept that has gained widespread acceptance and popularity, how extensive is this suggested phenomenon? It is certainly not 'new': Sheldon (1948) described, but did not really comment upon, the numerous support roles of the daughters in his sample. Evandrou and Glaser (2002) and Agree *et al.* (2002) report that the 'multiple role' phenomenon is not frequently observed among contemporary cohorts. For women born between 1941–1945 only 11 per cent occupied the roles of parent, worker and carer at age 45–49 and this is broadly in line with work from North America (Rosenthal *et al.*, 1996; Penning, 1998).

Why do people care?

Considerable research effort has been expended on quantifying the extent, type and negative consequences of providing informal care. As we noted earlier in this chapter, much less attention has been given to considering the question 'why do people care?' and what, if any, positive benefits flow from this role? The provision of care in the informal or family situation is clearly a result of the interrelationship between several sets of factors. Caring takes place within a relationship between the carer and his/her dependant which has developed over a number of years and which is embedded within a web of family and community responsibilities. Parker (1981) distinguished between caring (as in being concerned about someone) and tending (i.e. performing tasks to look after him or her). In the debate about informal care the focus has been upon tending (doing things for people that they cannot do for themselves). Interpretation of caring and distinguishing where caring starts and the 'normal' family pattern of tending stops is problematic, but it seems likely that the label 'care' is one which is externally applied and derives from policy makers and professionals: it probably is not a label that individuals apply to each other.

Finch (1995) has undertaken one of the few studies examining the nature of obligations and responsibilities within families concentrating upon the adult child–parent relationship rather than marital relationships. Finch (1989a) has argued that there is, within the family context, a hierarchy of caring obligations and relationships that cross the generations and would be invoked in times of 'crisis' not just to cope with 'old age'. Hence the provision of care to older people by their families is contextualised by the same sets of factors that would see parents responding to the difficulties faced by their adult children. She suggests that informal care be organised around four central relationships:

- The marital relationship is of primary importance so that the spouse is the first source of care for married people.
- The parent–child relationship is the second source of obligation. Children become a principal source of care for elderly parents, while parents are the main source of care for disabled children.
- Those who share a household are major care providers; the child who shares the parental home is more likely to provide care than siblings living away from home.
- Where there is a 'choice' between male and female relatives as to who becomes the carer, then it is the female relative who usually does so.

While there are some examples of people feeling 'pressured' into becoming a carer, it seems that the majority of carers become so willingly and that the reasons given for the adoption of the role resonated with the hierarchy of relationships described by Finch (1989a). Finch (1995) argues that the spouse and child–parent caring relationships are arrived at by differing routes and require differing perspectives in order to understand them.

The marital relationship is qualitatively different from that of parents and children. Marriage is a legally contracted relationship, based upon a promise of mutual care and support and the establishment of a shared household. As such becoming the carer of a disabled spouse may be perceived as an integral part of the relationship, echoing the promises in the (religious) marriage ceremony of 'in sickness and in health'. However, the expectations of couples, especially men, as to whether they will ever be called upon to enact this obligation may be very different. This was typified by such comments as 'the person I care for is my husband', 'because she's my wife' and 'as it was my husband, who had the stroke, I became the carer – if it had been the other way about he'd have been the carer'. These quotations seem to fit with the model proposed by Finch (1995) that caring for a spouse is seen as part of the obligations of the roles of husband and wife. There is clearly more scope for looking at the meaning of long-term marriage: the relationships between the partners and their expectations regarding the provision or receipt of care in old age (and earlier) in the life course require further research (Askham, 1995; Wilson, 1995). Will such expectations arise in (longstanding) cohabiting relationships or where spouses are in a second or sub-sequent marriage? Marital obligations and expectations are not con-stant but, again, are fluid and reflect social norms. The expectations of future generations of elders concerning their 'responsibilities' towards their spouse may be very different from current (or previous) generations.

Finch (1995) argues that filial responsibilities are not based upon fixed obligations but upon commitments and reciprocal relationships developed over time between parents (-in-law) and their adult chil-dren. Thus perceived responsibilities for caring for their parents will depend very much upon the relationships within the family across the lifecourse and not just at a single point in time. The notion of reciprocity is central to the initiation and maintenance of cross-gener-ational caring relationships. Nolan *et al.* (1996) note the importance of both altruism and reciprocity in such relationships. They stress that most caring partnerships are based upon a longstanding bond where 'caring' is 'repayment' for past services received or simply the result of long-term 'loving' relationships.

This would suggest that the provision of informal care outside the family and kinship obligations identified above would be compara-tively rare and confined to less 'personal' tasks. We have already seen that most care is indeed received by close family members (i.e. spouse or parent (-in-law)). Although 22 per cent of caregivers are looking after a friend or neighbour, this represents only 7 per cent of total time caring as compared with 81 per cent for close family members (30 per cent for spouse, 40 per cent for parent and 11 per cent for a parent-in-law) (Arber and Ginn, 1991). However, this pattern may well change in the future if friendships are 'substituted' for kin rela-tionships. Again this raises the interesting research question of what is required to translate a friendship, which encompasses elements of mutual support, into a caring relationship?

The dynamics of caring

Most literature concerned with estimating the extent and nature of the provision of informal care has been cross-sectional studies conducted at a single point in time (a point prevalence study). As such, these types of studies do not give any indication of the incidence of caring (i.e. how many 'new' carers take on the role in a given time period), over-represent those who have been caring for extensive periods of time and tell us little about ex-carers (i.e. those who, for whatever reason, have given up their caring responsibility). As yet there are no large-scale longitudinal studies which study the relevant history of the informal carer from the start of the commitment until its end, but some data are available about some of these issues, notably the incidence of caring and becoming an 'ex-carer'.

The incidence of caring

Data from the GHS survey indicate that 19 per cent of carers had been caring for less than one year, i.e. 18 per cent of co-resident carers and 20 per cent of extra resident carers. Applying this estimate to the general British population, of the 6 million carers estimated from the GHS 780,000 are 'new' carers, i.e. they had become a carer within the past year. Taking the much more restricted definition of a carer as someone who is a co-resident carer, which represents about 1.2 million adults, then 18 per cent (216,000) will have become carers in the past year. Hence the caring population is fairly dynamic in nature with an ever-changing membership. Such dynamism is rarely reflected in policy discourse and is clearly an area where more research is required. Such data do not, of course, identify those who have 'stopped' caring.

Stopping caring: becoming an ex-carer

Just as new carers are coming into the provision of informal care, so some carers are becoming ex-carers. The main reason that carers had stopped caring is, not surprisingly, the death of their dependant or admission of their dependant into a residential or nursing home.

Once the role of carer is accepted, this is a long-term responsibility which is discharged only when the dependant dies or is admitted to long-term care. How does the loss of the caring role affect the carer? Problems reported after 'giving up' caring include loneliness, depression, loss of income, loss of friends and difficulties of getting paid work. Not surprisingly, those caring for a spouse are the most likely to report problems, such as loneliness and depression, but these may reflect bereavement rather than the loss of the caring role. When almost two-thirds of carers give up this role because of bereavement it is a challenge to disentangle the effects of the two different but related events. Such surveys typically do not include any questions about how the loss of the caring role may have positively influenced their lives and we do not know if there are any positive aspects to the change of role or how different types of carers may be differentially affected.

McLaughlin and Ritchie (1994) followed up 157 ex-carers who had been receiving a carer benefit, and also undertook qualitative in-depth interviews with a small sample of carers. These authors adopted the typology of caring roles proposed by Lewis and Meredith (1989) and categorised their carers into three groups – balanced, integrated and immersed. Those who had 'immersed' themselves in caring such that it provided their main sense of identity found the consequences of becoming an ex-carer more problematic than the other two categories, especially with reference to the social and psychological after-effects. There is a clear need for more research which looks at the consequences for people of giving up caring and to disentangle the various factors involved, including the nature and quality of the relationship with the dependent person.

The consequences of caring

How does the role of carer affect the lives of those who undertake this service? This is a difficult area to research because ideally a long-term or lifecourse perspective is needed to identify the financial, employment, health and social consequences of becoming a carer. As such data are unavailable, we have to use cross-sectional studies which compare the characteristics of carers with non-carers (or indeed we can compare non-carers with ex-carers), but the methodological limitations of this approach need to be borne in mind. For example, a person with few qualifications and limited employment prospects may be more likely to become a carer than someone with better qualifications and prospects. However, to draw the inference that it was 'caring' which was the 'cause' of their poor employment prospects would be erroneous. This highlights the problems involved in this type of analysis. If we show differences in, for example, the financial circumstances of non-carers, ex-carers and carers, we must be very cautious in attributing any identified differences to the effect of caring. The relationship is probably much more complex than one of simple cause and effect. There is an extensive body of work indicating that carers experience problems with employment, decreased finances, poorer health and lower quality of life, but attributing these relationships to the impact of caring is problematic because of the issues noted above.

The benefits of caring

We have already documented the extensive nature and commitment which characterise the role of informal carer and have indicated that people undertake this role because of the strength of their relationship to the dependant. There are some negative consequences which result from undertaking this role, but it is also important to determine the benefits and rewards of undertaking this task.

Nolan *et al.* (1996) report that satisfaction levels among carers typically range from 55 to 90 per cent. It would be very easy for respondents to give what they thought was the correct, socially accepted response, although such consistent high levels of satisfaction would reflect either large-scale denial by the populations surveyed or 'real' levels of satisfaction. Grant and Nolan (1993) identified three main sources of satisfaction among carers: first, satisfaction deriving from the relationship between carer and dependant. This was the largest group of comments and related to the satisfaction gained by carers from caring for their dependant and includes such things as altruism, reciprocity and the obligations deriving from marriage: 'What little I am able to do is for the love and vows I took with my wife, with no sense of duty' and 'For better or worse I fully believe in this' (Grant and Nolan, 1993: 153). Second, satisfaction is derived by the carer, such as the development of a positive role, feeling useful and responding to new challenges: 'Compliments from friends and relatives' (Nolan *et al.*, 1996: 89). Third, satisfaction is derived from the avoidance of negative consequences for the dependant. This is a rather perverse category which describes the satisfaction that carers feel from avoiding the entry into care of their dependant or the pride gained in offering higher quality or more tailored (or personalised) care than could be hoped for from the statutory sector. This also included the promotion of positive consequences: 'I am determined that she is not to go into a nursing home' (Nolan *et al.*, 1996: 93).

Grant and Nolan (1993) report that satisfaction with the caring role did not vary between men or women or with level of dependency but was highest among those caring for close family members (children, spouses and parents) rather than more distant relationships. Consequently they argue that satisfaction with the role of carer is related to the quality of the relationship between carer and dependant rather than more objective measures such as the level of disability of the person being cared for. This suggests that interventions aimed at maintaining the quality of the relationship between carer and dependant could be effective in supporting the role of informal carers. Clearly there is scope for more research looking at the motivations of carers and the evaluation of interventions designed to promote and strengthen informal care. If it is the quality of the relationship that promotes caring and carer satisfaction, then there is no fundamental reason why friends and neighbours cannot become carers and that in the future 'families of choice' may be equally as involved in caring as kinship based families are in contemporary society.

Conclusion

The research base concerned with issues of family care is largely rooted in the 'social problem and political arithmetic' approach to the study of ageing. There is a concentration in the literature with enumerating the 'true involvement' of family and friends in the care of older people, describing their characteristics, describing who is 'cared for', what type of care is provided and how much care is provided. This emphasis reflects the policy concerns of successive governments who are troubled by the implications of family reconfigurations for the 'supply' of informal care. There is less concern with the dynamic aspects of this issue. Our research base is limited in that it has been far more concerned with investigating the care received by older people (rather than care given by this group) and has predominantly been characterised by a cross-sectional perspective. Hence it is difficult to examine the 'dynamics' of caring and temporal patterns of care and assistance within families. There is a vast research agenda that requires attention. We have only just started to recognise the diversity represented by the carer population by recognising both male and female carers, but we have not yet paid sufficient attention to issues such as race and class. We also need to develop a research and policy agenda that can reflect the changing family context within which future generations of elders will experience old age.

10 Services for older people

Arber and Ginn (1991) argue that the experience of ageing and later life is shaped and contextualised by three sets of factors: health resources, social resources and material resources. We would argue that we need to add, if not another dimension, then another aspect of the 'social resource' dimension, which relates to the provision of services by the 'formal' sector for older people. As a society, Britain has developed a variety of services in response to the perceived needs and problems of older people. In this chapter we consider the wider issues of state responses to the issues of ageing in terms of services designed for or used by older people and the wider issues of the ageing population. Clearly these are two different aspects of the 'state' response to both the ageing of populations and the ageing of individuals. At the level of providing services to individuals, there is a strong humanitarian tradition in British policy development. This chapter represents a change in perspective from the rest of this book. Previous chapters have sought to get away from the stereotyped emphasis upon ageing as a problem both for the individual and the wider society. As we are examining issues concerned with service needs, delivery and use, in this chapter the problem-orientated approach to the issue of individual or population ageing will figure more prominently. At both the individual and societal level, old age is seen by policy makers (and often policy deliverers) as a tragedy which requires a response. Here the focus is upon the responses concerned with the problems presented by older individuals. All elements of service provision and development are located within the broader macro-context of how governments understand and respond to the issue of population ageing. We start by offering a brief history of the development of health and social welfare services for older people. This historical context forms the backdrop against which to examine the patterns of utilisation of these services and current policy debates.

State responses to the issue of ageing

Within the British social welfare context it is only fairly recently that 'the elderly' have been identified as a specific 'social problem' group separate from the general mass of the indolent, the poor and the destitute. It was in the Victorian period (mid- to late nineteenth century) that the problems of 'aged paupers' were distinguished and, with the establishment of a system of pensions, separate provision made by the state to respond to these problems. Older people were considered to be one of the 'deserving' groups of poor people and arrangements were put in place to respond to their basic needs. Old age was, for the pauper at least, conceptualised by the Victorians as a 'personal tragedy' to which measured responses were required. The generosity of the response was not overwhelming, although it does mark a change in thinking about older people. Before this, older people were predominantly the responsibility of the family, but in the late Victorian period, older people were identified as a separate social group with distinct 'problems' that required addressing. With the development of the post-war welfare state in the late 1940s and early 1950s, older people have had access to a wide range of health and social welfare services, but comparatively few such services were designed specifically for older people per se. Instead, older people utilise the generic provision encompassed within the broad structure of the welfare state. Older people were conceptualised as being both 'needy' and 'deserving' (again this distinction between the deserving and undeserving poor). They are presented as being lonely, isolated, neglected by their family, in poor mental and physical health, poorly housed and poor. Unlike the United States, there are no specific Acts concerned with older people. Britain does not have the equivalent of the Older Americans Act (passed in 1965) that created the Administration on Ageing, an agency in the US Department of Health and Human Services. Consequently services have developed in different ways but it is still possible to identify within Britain the 'ageing enterprise' proposed by Estes (1979). The ageing enterprise consists of the myriad of professional and voluntary organisations, special programmes and projects involved in the care of older people. Estes (1979) argues that all of these enterprises have a vested interest in the maintenance of the 'separateness' of older people and in perpetuating stereotypes of a universal set of needs that can be met by a uniform set of policy responses. One important distinction between Britain and the United States is in the entry criteria for services. In the United States entitlement to programmes such as Medicare is based upon chronological age; that is entitlement to support derives from an individual having achieved a specified age. In Britain the entitlement to health and social welfare is based more upon need than age, although chronological age may frame how those needs are met. For example, patients above a minimum age may be treated in a speciality concerned with the medicine of old age rather than be treated under the care of a general physician.

Within the broad British social policy context, the state response to the perceived problems of old age and older people may be categorised in several different ways. These largely reflect wider debates within social welfare in Britain and relate how best to organise effective service delivery to those 'in need'. These debates relate to three major issues: the type of care needs presented, who provides care and where is the care provided?

Defining care needs

First, there is an important policy and provision 'demarcation' in the distinction between the types of needs (or problems) presented by the older person (or indeed any other age group as this does not apply simply to older people). There is an important distinction made by policy makers between those services concerned with the provision of health care from those concerned with the provision of social care. At the heart of the post-1945 British welfare state is a dichotomy that presumes that individuals seeking help will be easily classified into those with 'social care' needs and those with 'health care' needs. This duality of approach reflects the two arms of the post-1945 welfare state, which was premised upon the differentiation of health services (designed to cater for those with health problems), and social care services (designed to deal with those who had non-health problems such as personal or house care needs). This distinction between the two aspects of the welfare state has had a strong influence upon the development of services for older people and indeed social welfare more generally. It has served as the framework within which individual services have been delivered and had a key influence upon many of the debates surrounding the successive post-1945 reforms to services.

Given older people's complex needs, it is often problematic to draw this distinction between health care needs and social care needs (Twigg, 2000; 2004). This point was made almost from the inception of the system, when concerns were expressed about those who would fall between the remits of the different services, or whose complex needs would mean that they would become the contested responsibility of both parties (Means and Smith, 1998). This requirement for services to categorise needs into 'social' or 'health' is not simply an issue of interest to academics and policy makers. Rather, it is important for individual service users because the different arms of the welfare state had differing philosophies, structures and eligibility criteria which could have important consequences for older people and their families. Health care in Britain is provided free of charge at the point of consumption and is funded largely out of general taxation. The 'mission statement' of the National Health Service (NHS) established in 1948 includes an ideology of social and spatial equity of access to care of equal quality. Clinical need is the criterion for the provision of services and a commitment to social and spatial equity by providing users with equal access to care of equal quality. Older people should, in theory at least, have access to services of equal quality regardless of where they live in Britain or their social and economic background, and services for older people should be of the same quality as those provided to other age groups. If an older person has 'health' needs, these are met free. In contrast social services were, until very recently, designed to respond to 'local needs'. Variation in levels and types of services was positively encouraged and it was not felt appropriate that social services provision should be the same across the United Kingdom. This diversity of approach included charging for services. Although not always exercised by local authorities, there has always been the potential for social services departments to charge for their services, such as home or residential care. Needs that are defined as falling within the remit of 'social care' may require users to pay, thus those who entered long-stay care because of health problems received this free, whereas those who had social care needs had to contribute to the costs (if they had sufficient means). This anomaly resulted in a Royal Commission on Long-Stay Care, which concluded that while the 'nursing' element of long-term care should be free, other components such as personal care should not be. This remains the position in England, but as a result of devolution the Scottish Assembly has determined that *all* long-stay care for older people in Scotland should be free. This perceived inequity in how older people with apparently similar needs could be responded to between different parts of the United Kingdom and different components of the social welfare system illustrates how such 'demarcation' disputes can have a profound impact upon the experience of care. It also highlights one of the consequences of devolved government that enables different parts of the United

Kingdom to develop services in directions that do not necessarily mesh with the policies of the Westminster Parliament.

Who provides care?

A second perspective upon the classification debate relates to who provides the care. Three main providers of 'care services' outwith the family are the state, the private sector and voluntary agencies. Just as there have been debates as to the optimal location for providing care, there are parallel debates as to the most appropriate agencies to provide care. Furthermore, within the state and voluntary sector, there are further layers to this debate. Within medicine in particular there has been a persistent concern as to the most appropriate model of care for older people. Should services be 'age based' and arrange for care to people above a threshold age to be provided by specialist services (the name of which varies, including medicine for old age, health care for older people and so on) or are older people best served by the generic services? This specialist versus generic care debate is not exclusive to older people as it can be seen in other areas such as the treatment of strokes or HIV/AIDS, and remains one of the major issues within the NHS. Should particular groups like asylum seekers or refugees be treated within the NHS or in 'specialist' services? Those in favour of the integrated model argue that the general service should be able to cater for all needs, no matter how complex, while those favouring the specialist care model note the problems of responding to complex care needs within the mainstream. Neglect and poor care are suggested as the result of mainstream services not being able to cope with the complexity of an older person's needs while marginalisation and stigmatisation are advanced as the down-side of the specialist care model. Perhaps it is within the realm of the specialist services for older people that we can see elements of the ageing enterprise thesis advanced by Estes (1979). Are older people's needs best met by services where age is the criterion for entry or do such services serve to detach older people from the mainstream and thereby isolate and stigmatise them? In the absence of rigorous evaluation data upon which to compare outcomes, it is difficult to come to a firm conclusion as to the best model of care. In addition to developing a programme of work within the NHS to evaluate the 'best' models of care delivery, we also need to critically reflect upon the ideologies and assumptions underpinning our views as to the most appropriate models of care for older people.

Within the framework of the current configuration of the welfare state, there are a variety of different agencies involved in the provision of care to older people. Within the health service both primary and secondary care services are heavily involved. In addition there are other direct care providers or organisers such as local authorities. Independent contractors provide both domiciliary and institutional care, while voluntary agencies are also heavily involved in providing support services for older people. There is a plethora of other agencies involved such as housing. So, even considering only the most basic aspects of the service response to ageing, it is obvious that a variety of agencies are involved, all of whom have varying professional objectives and differing modes of working. Almost from the inception of the post-war welfare state there have been concerns expressed about the co-ordination of care, especially for those groups with often-complex needs such as older people, which have resulted in several administrative reorganisations within the health and social care agencies. Specific transition points such as admission and discharging older people from hospital back into the community (or into a long-term care facility) are exemplars of the organisational problems that beset the care of those groups who move between different sectors of the caring services (Healy *et al.*, 1999). The complications involved become ever more complex when we include the 'informal' care sector in the equation.

Where is care provided?

We can distinguish between the location where services for older people are provided, either in a group or institutional setting or in 'the community'. This is not an issue exclusive to older people but one that influences their experience of the receipt of care. Perhaps the most influential and important debate within the post-war British welfare state has revolved around the issue of the location of care and the debate about institutional versus community-based responses to needs of groups such as older people, those with learning difficulties and those with physical disabilities.

The idea of caring for older people in group or institutional setting is neither novel nor recent, but has been an enduring component of the development of services for older people in Britain (Means and Smith, 1998). We may identify two distinct perspectives upon the development of institutional or communal responses to the problems of old age. The idea of an institutional or custodial care setting as the correct response to the problems of older people has a long historical pedigree. As early as the third or fourth century AD, Christian groups developed institutions called *gerontochia* to care for older people and, in Britain, there were ad hoc local developments; for example, during the medieval period in Britain, 'hospitals' run by the monasteries contributed greatly to the care of older people. These institutional responses may be conceptualised as both humane and caring and as a manifestation of a wider 'Christian' duty to care for the vulnerable members of society. As with income maintenance, the initial state responses to the issue of the aged were not distinguished from the more general problem of pauperism or poverty. Older people were encompassed within schemes of relief that were designed to provide minimal support to 'genuine paupers' and to deter the 'idle poor' from 'scrounging' support from the state (or parish). Hence policies for poverty developed from a concern with discouraging claims for support except from those in the most desperate circumstances. The first systematic response to poverty in general was the Poor Relief Act 1601, the culmination of a series of statutes passed in Tudor England which laid the responsibility for the relief of what were termed impotent and able-bodied poor upon the parish. In turn, the parish could raise a rate (or tax upon residents or property) to pay for this. Under these laws social casualties such as the poor, sick and the aged were to be cared for in custodial institutions known as houses of correction, which were established in every city and county. However, this legislation did not differentiate between the different categories of pauper, nor did it really consider different types of needs presented by poor people, especially those who were reduced to poverty because of old age. Frailty, disability and sickness were not differentiated from indolence or idleness. When this system was revised in 1834, the punitive element became more evident with the suspension of outdoor relief payable to the able-bodied poor and the development of a system of workhouses. The prime objective was to ensure that the support available to society casualties was so harsh that only the most destitute would accept the regime and thereby to act as a deterrent against 'scroungers', a constant preoccupation of the British social welfare system. The first workhouses appeared in Britain in 1594 but they did not develop substantially until the passing of the Reform Act 1834. The ideology underlying this reform was that conditions inside the workhouse were to be harsh in order to deter 'scroungers' from claiming support. For aged people without family or friends to support them, the only means of maintenance was the workhouse and its spectre has cast a long shadow over the lives of many older people. Although this has entered the folk memories of many within Britain, it is one that resonated with a particular cohort of older people and will become less potent as those old enough to remember the workhouse die out.

The publication of the Royal Commission reports into the Poor Law at the start of the twentieth century marked a change in the prevailing social attitude towards the care of the older people. In combination with the passing of the Pensions Act 1908 these reports did much to convince the public that 'the old' were a group who merited special treatment and should be differentiated from other groups in poverty. As well as being important as an indication of a more sophisticated understanding of the causes and nature of poverty, these reports represent the first manifestations of a wider policy concern with the problems of old age. They expressed concern about the wholesale consignment of older people to the workhouse and the failure of such institutions to provide adequate nursing and medical care for those who were frail or infirm. In addition to observing the 'therapeutic' limitations of such warehousing approaches to the problems of older people and the 'inhumanity' of the regimes, the report was also concerned with the fiscal implications of such policy responses. In many ways this is a precursor of more recent reports and policy developments that have questioned the 'institutional' response to the issues of old age in humanitarian, therapeutic and fiscal terms. The solution proposed in the early Royal Commission also predates more recent statements by suggesting that community-based social and health services might be a better response to the care of 'elderly poor' whose only 'crime' had been that economic forces, family problems or ill health, rather than personal failings, had meant that their old age was a time of illness and financial hardship.

It was argued that, by developing domiciliary services to bring care to old people living at home, either on their own or with their families, admission to the workhouse could be 'prevented'. Such sentiments evoke more recent policy developments such as the Kent community care schemes, which were developed to prevent admission of older people to long-stay care, or 'hospital at home' schemes, which are intended to prevent hospital admissions. Much of the subsequent policy development specifically related to older people has followed on from the Royal Commission in that they have been designed to 'prevent' specific adverse outcomes such as hospital admission, hospital readmission or admission to nursing or residential homes. Few developments have been phrased in positive terms. Policy makers rather than older people define the 'adverse' outcomes which innovations have tried to 'avoid'. For example, we might speculate that older people might prefer to be treated in hospital rather than at home because of the greater support available in the hospital setting. These policies are attempting to prevent the negative rather than promote the positive, and are being 'reactive' in trying to (usually) contain costs rather than promoting more positive outcomes (either for older people themselves or society more generally).

The workhouse system has been rightly condemned for its harshness and naive assumptions about the causes and victims of poverty, but it did provide a 'statutory right' to assistance in times of need which was unique throughout Europe at the time. Older people in other countries had no such recourse. Although much criticised, the workhouses remained a feature of the British social welfare system until the development of the welfare state in the immediate post-war years. The National Assistance Act 1948, section III, laid a duty on local authorities to provide residential accommodation for all persons who because of age, infirmity or other reasons are in need of care and attention which is not otherwise available to them. Because this statutory duty was laid down in section III of the Act, local authority residential homes were often referred to as 'Part III Homes'. In the immediate post-war period, little money was available to build the new small homes envisaged by the Act and the local authority homes sector developed around the basis of the old public assistance institutions or workhouses. This piece of rebranding, changing the name from workhouse to residential home, was almost entirely cosmetic. The NHS 'inherited' the 'chronic sick' wards from the pre-existing hospital system and this gave rise to the long-stay beds that were found within the acute hospital sector up until the 1990s. Again these two sectors were, in theory at least, catering for different populations: the NHS cared for those with 'health needs' and the residential sector for those who were 'frail' but not sick. The difficulties of making such rigid distinctions is one that has been well articulated within the research literature, as has the generally poor quality of long-stay care within the welfare state.

The second area of policy development in the domain concerned with the location of care has focused upon the provision of care within community settings. Although these are often presented as two distinct strands of policy development, these two types of service response are inextricably interrelated. Debates as to the relative merits of these two different models of service provision continue to shape current patterns of provision of services to older people (and indeed other groups such as those with disabilities). Townsend (1964), in his book *The Last Refuge*, strongly attacked the quality of residential care provided for older people in post-war Britain. He drew attention to the use of inappropriate buildings (usually old workhouses), inadequate facilities, low standards of care and a quality of life for the residents which was regimented, and with little personalisation. He wrote: 'communal homes of the kind which exist in England and Wales today do not adequately meet the physical, psychological and social needs of the elderly living in them . . . alternative services and living arrangements should quickly take their place' (Townsend, 1964: 222). These empirical data meshed with the theoretically informed writings of Goffman (1968), who noted the inhuman, depersonalising and all pervasive timetabled nature of life within an institutional setting where regimes were often organised for the benefit or convenience of staff and were not linked to the needs and wishes of individual residents. The theoretical sociological notion of the 'total institution' resonated with the careful 'social arithmetic' critique proffered by Townsend (1964). This combination of academic research and sociological theory combined with the revelation of systematic and sustained abuse in various British long-stay hospitals, such as Ely in Cardiff, combined to create a powerful perception that institutional care was inherently a 'bad thing'. Irrespective of the resources and funds involved, institutional care solutions were seen as being inherently therapeutically ineffective and inhumane. Hence community care, in its conceptualisation, is identified by both positive attributes (the cosy and comforting image of the 'caring community' as personified by fictional villages such as Ambridge from the BBC radio programme *The Archers*) and important negative ones (i.e. it is not institutional care!).

Clearly there was a significant 'humanitarian' dimension to the alacrity with which 'community care' as a broad policy objective was adopted, but the ready acceptance of the 'pro-community–anti-institution' arguments might probably not have been so rapid if it had not resonated with the concerns of policy makers about the financial implication of institutionally based responses to the problems of old age within the context of an ageing population. It was in the 1950s that concerns first began to be raised about the 'ageing' of the population and the impossible financial burden that this would place upon society in terms of the provision of care (and pensions). Clearly there was a significant, but probably implicit, assumption that community care would be not only more effective than institutional forms of provision but also cheaper (and hence be more cost effective). The presumed financial advantage of community-based care solutions has remained, although academics and researchers have consistently argued that community care is 'cheaper' than institutional care only if the contributions of family or friends are 'uncosted' and that fully resourced community-based care solutions are as expensive, if not more so, than institutional solutions. Townsend reiterated the thesis first advanced in the Poor Law Royal Commission that community-based models of care would be more humane, therapeutically effective and fiscally prudent. He argued strongly that the community was the right and proper place to care for older people. Since this date, the policy for the care of older people has concentrated almost exclusively upon community care with the explicitly stated goal of policy being to maintain older people at home for as long as possible. The supremacy of the notion of community care has remained largely unchallenged. However, the nature of the concept encompassed by this term has undergone radical transformation since the early 1950s.

Community care

There was no single factor involved in stimulating the development of community-based care for older people. Rather there was a combination of different factors including the social upheaval and family dislocation created by the Second World War and the discredited image of the institutional or communal care sector. The large and impersonal nature of many of the existing institutions increasingly became a topic of social concern and disapproval and the impact of Peter Townsend's (1964) book should not be underestimated in changing the climate of opinion concerning long-stay care provision for older people. There was also an economic element in the discrediting of institutions as the 'appropriate' policy response to the needs of older people. Policy makers felt that it was expensive to care for older people in institutions, especially given the widespread pessimism about the projected numbers of (frail) elders whom the institutional sector would have to cater for in the future. Almost from its inception, community care has been perceived by policy makers as a cheap option in comparison to institutional forms of provision. Academic commentators have, to their credit, consistently pointed out that this is not the case and noted that much community care policy is based upon a false premise (i.e. the assumption that it is a cheaper way to provide care). Providing good quality care in the community may be just as expensive, if not more so, than providing care within group settings such as nursing or residential homes – however timely acknowledged.

Community care remains the favoured policy goal for the care of the older people. There is insufficient space here to consider, in detail, all aspects of the development of community care policy since the early 1950s (Means and Smith, 1998). However, some key points merit brief articulation. The analysis of community care policy requires both an understanding of the techniques of policy analysis and an acquaintance with socio-linguistics. Although the details of the organisational and administrative arrangements have changed, the term 'community care' has remained constant and has been a common objective of governments with wildly different philosophies on the role of the state. Detailed analysis of key policy statements indicates that, while the term 'community care' has remained constant since the early 1950s, the meaning, substance and operationalisation of the term has undergone a subtle transformation. As far as older people are concerned, at the outset community care meant the provision of state services of various types such as nursing, meals and home care to them at home with the aim of preventing admission to an institution of some sort. Increasingly, however, this concept of (state-provided) care in the community has been superseded by the notion of care by the community. This manifestation envisages the state playing a minimal role in supporting older people with the family and community assuming the main responsibility for support and care. State-sponsored services are seen as being employed only in the 'last resort'. Hence a semantic, but fundamental, distinction may be drawn between care in the community and care by the community. Care in the community is best defined as the provision of care by the placing of professional and specialist personnel in the community to provide services to clients in their own home. Care by the community stresses the provision of care by lay or non-specialists on a voluntary or semi-organised basis. Since the early 1990s, it is the concept of care by the community which has become the organising principle for the provision of services to older people (and other groups such as mentally ill people or those with learning difficulties).

This is a very different configuration of care from that conceived by the original proponents of community care. In our acceptance of the posited expensiveness of institutional care, its inherent inhumanity and presumed therapeutic ineffectiveness we have not always examined community care with the critical (in the sense of reflective and questioning) gaze that such major policy goals deserve. We have already noted the questionable nature of the presumed financial advantage of community-based solutions and the way that community care has consistently been redefined. However, there has been less attention paid to questioning the inherent advantages of community-based solution in terms of therapeutic effectiveness and humanity.

There are comparatively few studies that have compared community versus 'institutional' forms of provision for those with long-term care needs. Clearly there are schemes that have been 'effective' in terms of preventing or delaying entry to long-term care and others where, for example, community-based physiotherapy is compared with group provision such as that available in day hospitals. There are also effective 'hospital at home' schemes, but these are not entirely comparable with the types of people and services that would be found in the institutional sector. Overall the research evidence indicates that community-based solutions can be as effective as those provided in institutional settings such as hospitals, day hospitals or nursing and residential homes, but the cost of achieving these outcomes is more contentious. It remains a subject for debate as to whether community-based solutions are cheaper than institutional services. The answer almost certainly reflects what is included within the cost calculation. If 'informal' help is not counted then community solutions may well be cheaper, but if we cost in the roles played by informal carers then the benefits of community-based solutions are less evident. This enthusiasm for community-based solutions could very easily look like attempts by formal services and the state to 'cost shift' care. Less interest has been expressed in looking at the presumed 'humanitarian' advantage of the community-based solutions. Researchers have rarely examined if community-based caring solutions for very frail people may reproduce some of the classic institutional features such as lack of control and autonomy and a routinised timetabled lifestyle which fails to respond to the needs and wishes of the individual – a key advantage advanced for community-based solutions. This is an example where, perhaps, researchers have failed to look critically at the supposed advantages of a particular policy formulation.

Providing services or assessing needs?

As originally organised, the welfare state established a series of health and social care services. The health services were based upon a pyramid-type structure of primary care, secondary hospital services and tertiary hospitals dealing with the most specialised services. Access to health services was to be based upon a clearly identified clinical need. The value of domiciliary services such as district nursing and domestic services was recognised and these were incorporated within the welfare state. The result was that the initial fabric of domiciliary or community-based services was 'service' rather than needs based and came to be typified by two services, home helps and meals on wheels, both of which were extensively used by older people. Why were these services identified and how appropriate were they for meeting older people's needs and in achieving the wider policy objective of maintaining older people in the community?

The two social care services, which for many years were seen as the two major support services for older people, provided by the social care agencies, had origins which suggested that they were not the best ways of achieving the government policy agenda and meeting the needs and wishes of older people. Meals on wheels services evolved from the provision of meals to those who had had their homes destroyed during the Second World War, while home helps developed from the provision of domestic help to new mothers in the early 1900s. There is an extensive literature examining the many limitations of these services, and evaluating and cataloguing 'extensions', and recording developments to these services, but up until the NHS and Community Care Act 1990, the emphasis was upon fitting people to the services provided; we did not consider the needs and wishes of the older people themselves. However, more recent policy developments have attempted to overcome these fundamental limitations by developing a needs-led service based upon comprehensive assessment and the design of an appropriate 'care package'. Although the philosophy has changed, it is not yet clear as to whether service delivery has become more innovative with this change in emphasis. Indeed, work by Healy *et al.* (1999) suggests that the care package delivered reflects the professional origin of the assessor as much as the needs of the individual, thus a nurse undertaking the assessment is more likely to suggest a nurse-based 'needs response' package than a physiotherapist. In terms of data collection, routine statistics still collate information about home care services, while routine surveys such as the GHS continue to ask questions about the receipt of 'traditional' services such as home help, mobile meals, district nursing and health visiting.

What should be provided?

What services should we provide and in what quantities? Health and welfare services for older people have developed in a piecemeal and pragmatic fashion over the past 100 years. For many years central government was reluctant to formulate any detailed norms of provision or models of care for which service providers (local, voluntary or health authorities) should aim and which would inform public expectations. Indeed within the social care field, where services were provided by local authorities, no national norms were specified so that local governments could design services that 'responded' to local needs. Such policies contributed to marked variations in levels and quality of provision, so there is now an overt aim to decrease variations and offer British subjects more equitable levels and quality of care. Although the NHS was, at least notionally, committed to a vision of equal access to services of equal quality for all subjects, the reality is that the NHS is characterised by wide variations in access to care, quality of care and care outcomes. Via the development of national service frameworks (NSF), such as the one for older people, the current Labour government is trying to establish the basic element of a modern health service and to address the inequalities in access and quality of care. While the NSF for older people is very explicit about processes and targets, it is rather more coy on the resources required to deliver such care. Service provision guidelines such as those articulated by the British Geriatrics Society, which are stated in terms of minimum levels of staff and facilities required, seem rather outdated and do not fit easily with the new rhetoric of needs-led rather than service-led arrangements. However, this approach does demonstrate the resources required to deliver services and enables judgements to be made about the quantity if not the quality of the provision.

Use of services

We shall look at the use made by older people of the different components of the welfare state services in terms of three categories of service: long-term care, hospital services and community services. Where possible we shall try to examine questions concerning levels of provision, access to care and the relationship between supply and need.

Long-term institutional care

In Britain those older people unable to live independently in the community, the prime objective of government policy, may reside in a variety of 'long-term' care institutions. Despite a very strong ideological antithesis to the concept of institutional care this remains an important element of the state response to the problems of ageing. As we saw earlier the long-stay services provided by both the NHS and the local authority have links with the old and much despised Poor

Law workhouses. The shape of provision within the long-stay sector has changed remarkably since the early 1970s. Until the 1990s there were two main types of long-stay provision, both largely provided by the public sector: long-stay hospital beds (including psycho-geriatric beds) and residential homes. In theory, the residential sector catered for those who, though frail, need only care and attention while the hospital sector cared for those with medical needs. This reflects the duality of provision at the heart of the welfare state. In practice this distinction has often been blurred, although it remains at the heart of the system for providing long-stay care, especially for determining who 'pays' for the care provided. If an older person requires long-term care because of 'health needs', this is funded by the NHS but if it is for social care needs then the individual has to pay part (or all) of the cost depending upon their circumstances. The recent report into the funding of long-term care (Royal Commission on Long-Term Care, 1999) addressed this inequity and concluded that older people should still contribute to the costs of residential care. However, Scotland has opted to provide free long-stay care for all.

The current arrangements have seen the NHS withdraw almost totally from direct long-stay provision. Indeed long-stay hospital beds were a relic of the 'chronic sick' wards of public and Poor Law institutions inherited with the creation of the NHS. Britain was unique in being the only country which had hospital beds for which the length of stay was, in principle at least, indefinite. The withdrawal of the hospital sector from direct long-stay provision is a reflection of the way that the NHS has sought to define hospital care ever more tightly in terms of acute care. The ethos of the hospital service is orientated towards acute medical problems which can be 'cured' and the patient then discharged. The existence of beds for long-stay patients, with virtually no realistic chance of discharge home, does not conform to this philosophy. The type of regime characteristic of hospitals is, perhaps, more likely to foster dependence than independence and the quality of care provided has also sometimes been less than optimal. Hospitals probably are not the best place to care for those with long-term needs. The distinction is still drawn between residential and nursing homes catering for the different types of needs noted above, although the provision of places is now largely in the hands of the private sector and the state has largely withdrawn from direct care provision, while remaining very active in the regulation, inspection and funding of such care.

Residential care was conceptualised as catering for the physically frail older person who did not present nursing or health care needs.

Initially, residential care provision was undertaken by the local authority, supplemented by a small independent (or private) sector and voluntary sector, but the landscape of provision has changed markedly. In 1980 it was estimated that the private and voluntary sector provided approximately 18 per cent of long-stay places compared with 85 per cent in 2001. The expansion of private sector care, in both institutional and community environments, has been encouraged by an ideological debate about the provision of welfare that preoccupied Britain in the 1980s and 1990s. The philosophy of the 'new right', as manifest in 1980s Britain and the United States, was one rooted in the primacy of individual responsibility, a belief in the efficiency of the market as a method of organising the distributions of goods and services and a repudiation of state-provided welfare services as inefficient, mediocre in standards and unresponsive to the needs and wants of consumers. The development of private care solutions has been justified by reference to six major themes. These are as follows: meeting existing, but unsatisfied, demand for care, expanding the choices and autonomy of older people (and their relatives), decreasing the power of professionals and 'experts', reducing inequality in old age by extending the available choice, improving quality by developing private care providers, giving older people the freedom to move if they are dissatisfied with the standard of care provided and the comparative failure of the public sector to respond to the changing nature of the older population and their needs and wants. Although there have been several changes of government in Britain since the first articulation of this policy, there has been little enthusiasm for the regeneration of state-provided long-term care. Indeed current policies still favour largely private sector solutions and emphasise the role of 'choice' in driving up standards across the caring spectrum in combination with a more rigorous inspection regime. The local authority is conceptualised as an organiser rather than direct provider of care.

As of 31 March 2001 there were 341,200 residential home places in England, provided in 24,100 homes and 186,800 registered beds in 5700 nursing homes and private hospitals. There were 142,500 places for older people in nursing homes and 236,700 in residential homes giving a total of 379,200 places. Nationally there are 304 older person residential places per 10,000 population aged 65+ and 183 nursing beds per 10,000 aged 65+. If we assume a conservative 80 per cent bed occupancy rate, as compared with the 83 per cent for residential homes and 89 per cent reported for nursing homes by the Health Survey for England, then there were 303,360 people aged 65+

in long-term care of whom 68 per cent (204,879) were funded, wholly or in part, by the local authority. This approximates to the returns from the 2001 Census, which reported that, for England and Wales, there were 384,970 people, aged 65+ living in residential or nursing homes of whom 92 per cent were in 'private' homes.

It is, despite the wealth of available data, worth reiterating the nature and characteristics of older people resident in residential and nursing homes. The socio-demographic profile of care home residents is that they are predominantly women (75 per cent in the health survey for England) and old, with an average age of about 84 years. The predominance of widows among women in these establishments (76 per cent of female residents) is established, as is the large percentage of single never-married men (25 per cent). Levels of disability and dependence among the care home population are significant. The Health Survey for England reports that 91 per cent of those in nursing homes and 70 per cent of those in residential homes were severely disabled (compared with 15 per cent in the community). Confining the analysis to 'personal' care problems indicates that about 80 per cent of those in nursing homes had problems with personal care and about 30 per cent in residential homes, compared with about 3 per cent in the community. The scale and nature of the difficulties experienced by those living in residential and nursing homes should not be underestimated. Exclusion of such people from surveys will inevitably result in underestimates of the true nature and extent of disability and dependency within the older age groups.

How many people are admitted to home annually? This is a difficult question to answer definitively given the limited nature of our data sources which are largely concerned with places or beds rather than people. Using the British Household Panel Survey, Scott *et al.* (2001) suggest an annual admission rate of 0.95 per cent per annum and this increases with age. Turnover in these homes is significant: in the Health Survey for England about 30 per cent of residents had been there for less than a year and the median length of stay was between one and two years for men and two to three years for women. However, they also note that about 20 per cent of residents had been there for five years or more. Admission to residential or nursing homes is a major transition in the life of an older person and his or her family and often happens at a time of crisis. The Health Survey for England data show that 60 per cent of admissions are from the older person's own home. In contrast to the PSSRU survey (Personal Social Services Research Unit: Challis and Hughes, 2003) the percentage of admissions from hospital was lower at 15 per cent compared with 30 per cent which may suggest that there have been changes in policy and practice with more older people able to go back to the community after a spell in hospital (or this change could be the result of an increase in the admission threshold!). Scott *et al.* (2001) have developed our thinking in this area by developing a theoretical model that takes into account a variety of factors, including the need for care, availability of care within the household and costs of care. Initial application of this model indicated that measures of 'need', age and health status were the biggest predictors of admission, while service and economic factors had little impact. They also noted a decline in admission rates for the period 1995–1998 compared with 1992–1994, which may reflect the impact of changes in care provision policies.

There have been negative observations about the poor care standards and quality of life experienced by those elders living in communal settings. The Health Survey for England provides some nationally representative data about the extent of social participation in these environments. The HSE notes the correlation between decreased activity and increased frailty, and also notes that those in care homes have lower rates of weekly contact with family and friends than those in the community: 64 per cent compared with 81 per cent, increased rates of isolation (6 per cent having no family contact compared with 2 per cent in the community) and lower rates of 'perceived' social support (74 per cent compared with 86 per cent). While we do not know why contact rates are lower, there is clearly a 'detachment' of care homes from the wider social world. Engagement, where it takes place, is internal rather than external and there is clearly a potential for enmeshing such care environments more closely within the wider social fabric to the benefit of both residents and (probably) staff. One result of the detachment of care homes from the wider world is that it can lead to the institutionalisation of 'poor practice' – one obvious mechanism for improving the quality of care and, perhaps, improving the 'image' of care homes would be to make them more open systems and actively encourage and facilitate interaction with the wider social environment.

It is unfashionable to argue for the importance of care homes as part of the spectrum of care for older people. There are many negative images of such environments, but we need to examine critically both the potential of communal care settings and the currently more favoured community-based approaches. Is it really better to care for people at home or in communal settings? Could care homes, if sufficient money and care were invested, present a more positive environment? Even if the compression of morbidity thesis is found to be correct, there will still be significant numbers of elders in the future who will have severe problems of disability and dependency. Future generations of elders may present care networks that are less supportive, hence as a society we need to carefully evaluate the best methods for caring for older people with dependencies. This may mean re-evaluating and rehabilitating the notion of the care home and asking more 'critical' questions of community-based solutions. What are required are appropriate responses to the problems faced by dependent elders, not predetermined ideologically based positions on the supposed merits or disadvantages of specific types of care solution.

Acute hospital services and community health

We can examine the use made by older people of health and social services in two distinct but complementary ways. These relate to investigating older people as a part of all users of health care, while the second approach relates to examining what percentage of all older people use health services. Both perspectives are adopted here as appropriate. Each perspective is informative as to the analysis of resources provided in response to the 'problems' of old age. We then consider the relative balance of care between the formal and informal caring sectors.

The health service is traditionally divided into primary and secondary care sectors. In the British system most members of the population are registered with a general practitioner, who acts as the gatekeeper for accessing other health (and social) care services. Routine data record hospital activity in terms of finished consultant episodes (FCEs), which relate to a discrete period of care under a specific consultant. These do not neatly equate to a hospital episode as they may include several individual 'consultant' episodes. However, the 'consultant' episode is the basic unit of measurement for hospital activity. These data enable us to consider what part of the hospital workload older people account for. In 2001–2002 there were 12,357,360 FCEs in England, of which 14.2 per cent were for those aged 65–74, 13.8 for those aged 75–84 and 6.3 per cent for those aged 85+. Hence those aged 65+ account for 34.38 per cent of FCEs. Although the system for monitoring the use of hospital-based services has changed over time, the utilisation pattern for older people has remained remarkably consistent. For example, data for 1969 indicate that 34 per cent of hospital episodes were accounted for by those aged 65 years and over (Victor, 1997). Older people are consistently demonstrated as being the major user group for most branches of hospital medicine, with the exception of paediatrics and obstetrics.

Utilisation not only consists of admission but also relates to the length of time individuals spend in hospital. The length of stay of older people is something that both policy makers and the medical profession have been concerned about almost from the inception of the NHS. In particular, concerns have been consistently expressed about the 'blocking' of acute hospital beds by older people, who are medically fit for discharge, but cannot leave hospital because the required care arrangements are not available. These are pejoratively referred to as 'bed-blockers'. While not all 'bed-blockers' are older patients, they do dominate this group. Length of stay in hospital increases with age, while stays in hospital have decreased significantly. In the 1970s the average length of hospital stay for a person aged 65–74 was approximately eighteen days (twenty-one days for those aged 75–84 and thirty days for those aged 85+; this had been sixty days in about 1950). Currently the approximate average length of stay for a hospital admission for a person aged 85+ is sixteen days (thirteen for those aged 75–84 and nine days for those aged 65–74).

The other way to look at service use is to consider what 'percentage' of the target population, in this case older people, uses different types of services. Overall approximately 15 per cent of older people are admitted to hospital annually and about 10 per cent as a day patient and these self-reported percentages are approximately stable across studies (Table 10.1), with those living in care homes reporting higher levels of hospital inpatient stays than their community-dwelling contemporaries. There is some suggestion from Table 10.2

Table 10.1 Self-reported use of health services in previous year: a comparison of GHS (Great Britain) and Health Survey for England

	HSE care homes		HSE community		GHS 2001	
	M	F	M	F	M	F
Outpatient	39	31	44	43	26	22
Day patient	9	7	12	8	9	8
Inpatient	27	22	17	14	17	13
Visit to GP in previous 14 days	29	26	20	21	20	22

Source: Walker *et al.*, 2002; Hirani and Malbot, 2002

that increasing percentages of older people are being admitted to hospital as both in- and day patients, especially for the population aged 75 years and older. Indeed other utilisation data suggest increasing admission rates for older people as the benefits of offering treatment to this group have been recognised. Primary care use is also important for older people, with approximately 20 per cent reporting a GP consultation in the previous fourteen days. Levels of reported utilisation are, again, higher among those resident in care home environments (Table 10.1). This is almost certainly an underestimate and there is some suggestion of an 'upward' trend in consultations for those aged 65–74 (Table 10.2). These increases in utilisation rates for the key health services could reflect a number of different trends including increased awareness of health problems by older people and the expansion of the type treatments available to them. From the GHS data it has been estimated that each older person makes five or six GP consultations per year. Levels of contact between older people and the primary care service is, in fact higher than this, because these

Table 10.2 Trends in health service use in the year before interview, Great Britain, 1982–2002 (%)

	1982	1991	2001
Inpatient stay			
65–74	10	12	11
75+	13	18	17
Day patient			
65–74		4	8
75+		3	9
Outpatient			
65–74	15	18	21
75+	15	21	26
GP use			
65–75	15	18	18
75+	19	19	21
Mean consultations per person per year			
65–74	4	6	5
75+	6	6	6

Source: Walker *et al.*, 2003: Tables 7.18, 7.19, 7.29, 7.30, 7.32, 7.33

Table 10.3 Utilisation of community services in previous month, Great Britain, 2001 (%)

Source	65–69	70–74	75–79	80–84	85+	Lives alone
Private home help	5	6	10	17	28	17
Home help (local authority)	1	2	3	7	18	7
Meals on wheels	0	0	1	4	7	3
District nurse	2	3	5	10	19	8

Source: Walker *et al.*, 2003: Tables 59, 60

data exclude contacts with nurses and contacts resulting from routine repeat prescriptions.

For district nurses older people (aged 65+) represent 57 per cent of all new contacts for 2002–2003 and this percentage has been constant since the early 1990s. Older people, therefore, account for approximately two-thirds of the district nursing workload. Community-based services are similarly received by only a minority of the population aged 65 years and over (Table 10.3). Service utilisation rates show some relationship with 'need' in that the very old and those who live alone (Table 10.4) demonstrate higher levels of utilisation. However, even for the very oldest, only a minority receives services. For example, of those aged 85+ just 28 per cent are in receipt of home help. Although in absolute terms the numbers of older people receiving community-based services has increased, Table 10.4 shows that the percentages receiving services have remained fairly static, with the exception where home helps have decreased and been replaced by 'private' sector providers.

We can examine the link between needs and supply in more detail by considering (a) how many older people require help with key self and instrumental care tasks, (b) how many of these receive state care and (c) how does state care compare with the levels of care provided

Table 10.4 Utilisation of key services by age, Great Britain, 1980 and 2001 (%)

Source	65–69		70–74		75–79		80+	
Home help	2	1	5	2	11	3	22	12
Meals on wheels	0	0	0	0	3	1	9	6
District nurse	2	2	2	3	4	5	14	14

Sources: Victor, 1984: Tables 12.7 and 12.9; Walker *et al.*, 2003: Table 59

Table 10.5 Usual sources of help for those able to undertake tasks only with help, Great Britain, 1998 (%)

Source	Cutting toenails	Bath/ showering	Domestic tasks	Personal affairs	Cooking	Shopping
Spouse or partner	12	45	42	55	74	45
Other household	3	10	9	11	9	11
Other relative	5	13	25	27	6	29
Friends or neighbours	—	2	5	3	2	6
State	2	25	4	2	1	5
Private help	77	5	14	1	1	3
Other	1	1	2	1	3	2

Source: Bridgwood *et al.*, 2000: Table 43

by the informal sector. Table 10.5 indicates that, for the key self-care and other tasks, only a minority of older people who need help to undertake these tasks receive this from the state. We can see that, where help is provided, it is predominantly provided by the family, with the exception of cutting toenails, where most help is provided by professional chiropodists. While direct comparisons are problematic because of changing definitions, this general pattern represents a very similar one to that described by Townsend (1957) and Sheldon (1948). In his study of Wolverhampton, which predates the establishment of the welfare state, Sheldon (1948) reported that 'paid help' accounted for 10–12 per cent of help received with domestic tasks, a result not so very dissimilar to that for current generations of elders. The services provided by GPs and hospitals are usually highly specialised and not easily substituted for by other forms of provision. For the apparently less specialist tasks of responding to disability and dependency in activities of daily living then we can see very readily that state services may be substituted by informal arrangements.

The relationship between state and 'informal services'

Throughout Chapters 9 and 10 we have maintained a distinction between the public provision of care to older people and that provided within the 'private' domain within a welfare system where the onus is upon the family to be the main provider with the state occupying a residual position. However, we have not yet examined the relationship between these two sectors. As Ward-Griffin and Marshall (2003) note, policy makers and academics have yet to decide whether 'formal' care, provided by paid professionals, complements, parallels, substitutes or 'competes' with the care provided by the 'informal' sector. The relationship between the two sectors sees informal carers variously conceptualised as unpaid resources, as co-workers, co-clients, or as superseded carers. Each of these theorised relationships requires a different type of response from the 'formal' sector.

There are several models of the linkage between formal and informal sectors (Ward-Griffin and Marshall, 2003). The compensatory model posits a hierarchy of or ordering of sources of care, with older people turning to the formal sector only when help from the informal sector has been exhausted. The family, and the wider caring network, is seen as being the 'first choice' for the provision of caring tasks. The 'substitution' approach suggests that formal and kin services are interchangeable although there is little empirical evidence to support this proposition. A third model argues that in meeting the needs of older people, the formal and informal sectors are selected according to the nature of the task, rather than older people's preferences. The final theoretical model is that formal care and informal care are complementary in that they compensate for and supplement each other. There are challenges, which can be laid down against these theorised models. There is little empirical evidence to support many of them. Perhaps more fundamental is that they largely derive from the perspective of the professional worker, not from either the carers or dependants. Furthermore the models are based upon a presumed sharp dichotomy between the care sources. This rather simplistic assumption ignores the similarities between the types of tasks undertaken by the different sectors, especially when services are delivered within the domestic environment by a largely female workforce. Feminists in particular have argued against this dichotomy, arguing that the activities and relationships undertaken in these different spheres have more in common than the 'public–private' split would indicate. Predominantly those undertaking 'caring' work within the domestic sphere are women. Ward-Griffin and Marshall (2003) from the basis of their empirical study of both carers and workers in Canada argue for the need to incorporate the temporal dimension into our thinking about the relationship between formal and informal carers. They demonstrate how the relationship is dynamic and can move through different stages of these models. They also note the dynamic linkage between the two styles of care and how 'work', in terms of caring duties and tasks, is transferred between them.

Conclusion

Formal services provided by the welfare state represent a major resource for responding to the vicissitudes of 'old age'. The 'strict' distinction between health and social care needs, presumed at the inception of the welfare state, still lies at the heart of how formal services for older people are organised. While such a distinction may hold for younger service users, it is an intensely problematic dichotomy to maintain for older people. Services have developed in response to a variety of concerns expressed by policy makers including disenchantment with institutionalised care, the expense of providing such care, fears about the numbers of older people who might want such care and a perception that community care is a 'cheap' option compared with institutional provision. Perhaps the most interesting feature of the development of policy is the way that it has evolved in a highly pragmatic fashion with little reference to the needs and wants of the consumers of care (of any age). Policy developments are characterised more by the needs of professional groups than the expressed wishes of the older people. The power of the vested interests of professional groups remains a powerful influence upon policy development. In particular there is still a tendency to deny the autonomy of older people and to provide them with the sorts of services we think are good for them, rather than responding to their expressed wishes. Perhaps here we can see echoes of the 'ageing enterprise' of Estes (1979) where providers and policy makers concentrate on maintaining their own 'power base' and autonomy with little acknowledgement of the needs and wishes of service users.

For older people there is a persistent and as yet unresolved debate, as to the most appropriate method of service organisation which is exemplified by the issue of the role of geriatric medicine. The defining features of geriatric medicine are concerned with the assessment, diagnosis rehabilitation and continuing care of older adults. However, there remains a debate as to whether geriatric medicine is a true medical specially. Are there principles of care that are unique to the clinical management of the older adult? Can a speciality based upon 'age' as a key defining criterion really exist? Paediatrics does not seem to have similar problems justifying its existence, except perhaps at the adolescent end of the age spectrum. Two main models of care are operated. In the 'specialist' model, departments of geriatric medicine treat all patients, acutely or chronically ill, above a defined age while in the 'generic' model the geriatric and general (internal) medical services are integrated, with certain consultants having a special interest in the care of older people. At the inception of the NHS, Amulree (1955) recommended the evaluation of the effectiveness of both the NHS and its newly created departments of geriatric medicine. Despite this very forward-looking statement that anticipates the recent development of 'evidence-based' health care, there has been little research which has looked at the effectiveness of hospital treatment of the old and the effectiveness of different models of care. The absence of conclusive evaluation data makes it difficult to be definitive as to the best (i.e. most effective) model of care. To some degree the referred model of care reflects current fashion and thinking as to the relative merits of generic or specialist services within the NHS more broadly. Currently the integrated care model appears to be in the ascendancy, but this may change in the future.

'Formal' services, catering for 'social' needs or responding to problems of remaining at home in the community are received by only a minority of those older people 'in need'. With the exception of key specialist health tasks, the vast bulk of care received by older people is provided by the informal care network of family and friends. Formal responses either from the state or provider care agencies contribute only at the margins. Even for 'high-risk' groups such as those living alone or the very old, the formal service sector demonstrates only limited involvement. Despite the creation of a welfare state, it seems that it is still the family that represents older people's major resource and recourse in maintaining an independent life within the community. This contribution is not fully recognised nor integrated into the debate concerning how best to enable older people to live independently in the community. Formal services remain unclear as to how to relate to the informal sector. This is a potentially fruitful area for further research. We certainly need to develop a more sophisticated understanding of how these two sectors relate to each other. What the pattern of formal service provision for older people will look like in the future remains a subject for speculation. However, it seems unlikely that there will be a massive expansion of state services and that future generation of elders, to substitute for the 'lack' of family to act as carers, will increasingly turn to the private sector with the state providing an ever more residual role.

11 The future of old age

In this volume we have examined the diversity characteristic of the experience of old age in contemporary Britain. We have demonstrated how the social and environmental context and factors such as age, gender and social class influence later life and the resources that older people bring to later life. It is clear that those from professional occupations experience better health and higher levels of material resources than those from less privileged backgrounds. Such class-based differences are overlaid by gender and, increasingly in the future, ethnic differences. So, although we have often examined each parameter of social differentiation separately, in reality these all interact and are interrelated and there is an extensive research agenda to be addressed in looking at these linkages (Arber, 2004). Gender and age, rather than class overtly, were more important in determining access to both social resources and formal state services. Hence there are some domains of later life where social class may exert less influence than others. In this final chapter we shall consider some of the main issues which now confront the position and status of older people. We shall conclude with an examination of the politics of ageing in the United Kingdom.

The nature of old age in the future

It is very easy to look at the current population of elders and use these characteristics as the template for the profile of older people in future decades. However, as has been evident from earlier chapters in this book, 'old age' and the nature of old age is a dynamic and shifting entity. From a historical perspective we can see that the lifecourse has become increasingly differentiated into a larger number of entities as longevity has increased. This is illustrated by the emergence of both childhood and later life as discrete phases of life and with the emergence of new phases such as 'empty nesters' or the 'fourth age'. These examples serve to illustrate the essentially socially constructed nature of the lifecourse and of the stage we are interested in here – later life. At the most basic level, old age is a social construct that is both defined and given meaning by the historical and cultural context. Consequently it seems highly unlikely that, by the mid-2050s, we will be using the same definition and construction of old age, given current demographic trends. Furthermore, given the increasingly fluid notions of identity developing in post-modern society, it may well be that the notion of a segmented, linear life-course no longer fits with the complexity and fragmented nature of an individual lifecourse. Chronological age may have less utility as a staging post across life and less relevance as a mechanism for the allocation of social roles.

We will almost certainly see a change in the nature of old age in response to the changing characteristics of this segment of the population. If current trends continue, always a key assumption when thinking about the future, then the socio-demographic profile of future generations of elders are going to be very different from those described in this book. Clearly the growth of the older population is set to continue, especially for those in the very old categories. Older people are going to be more visible not only within British society but also in many other western industrial nations. Population ageing is a global phenomenon. We will see an increasing number of men surviving into old age. We have largely presumed that old age is a female experience, but the predominance of women within this population looks set to decrease in response to improvements in male survival rates and increasing adoption by women of negative lifestyle habits. The older population will inevitably start to develop ethnic diversity. Within contemporary Britain old age is predominantly a 'white' experience, except within a few small geographically limited locations. In the future we will see the ageing of the population of migrants who moved to Britain in the post-war periods. This will certainly pose a challenge for service providers, who presume a common cultural heritage for all older people who require services. In addition to growing ethnic and religious diversity, there are other parameters to consider. The nature of families, in terms of size, complexity and roles played by members, is a major source of change. Lower fertility means that future generations of elders will have smaller families. These families may be spatially distant, although not socially or emotionally. How will increased labour market participation by women influence women's roles within families or how they themselves approach old age? Future generations will enter old age with a very different pattern of intimate relationships. How will a pattern of marriage, divorce and remarriage affect family relationships in later life? We also have the emergence of a new generation of women entering old age unpartnered and childless. There is a variety of forms of relationships such as companionship, same-sex relationships and cohabiting which will increase the diversity of the domestic arrangements and social networks of future generations of elders. We know remarkably little about such relationships and how they influence the nature of the ageing experience. As researchers we often focus upon marriage and widowhood but there are many other types of relationships illustrated by older people and we need to widen our gaze upon the social relationships of older people.

A key area where change seems likely to be manifest is in terms of health status. We have noted the two competing paradigms between those who argue for delayed and decreased morbidity in later life and those who suggest that it will increase. Evidence to date is ambiguous with data to support both propositions, but we can see that most morbidity is concentrated among the 'oldest old' with less distinct differentiation in health status between the middle-aged and the young old. It is not clear how lifestyle practices and developments in health and medical care will influence the health status of future generations. Current reading of the evidence, perhaps, offers limited support for the notions of delayed or deferred morbidity. If there are improvements taking place, it seems highly unlikely within the British context that these will be equally shared across the different social groups. It would seem almost inevitable that if there are health gains in the future, it is the most privileged who will benefit most. Hence it is an entirely plausible scenario for Britain that there will be an overall decrease (or at least no increase) in levels of morbidity and disability but that there will be much greater variation in health status between elders from different social class and ethnic groups.

If life expectancy continues to increase, we shall start to redefine the start of old age and to develop finer distinctions of the later phases of the life course. In Britain in 1900 with an average life expectancy of about 50, and about 1.6 million people aged 65+ and 120 centenarians, then there was, perhaps, little point in developing fine distinctions between this population group as most were in the 65–74 age range. Contrast this to the situation forecast for 2050, when there will be 35,000 centenarians. It clearly makes very little sense to treat these as a single social category. We may well develop and refine the ideas of Laslett (1989) where there is a normative period of good health in the post-retirement period in which activity, largely good health and social engagement are seen as 'the norm' with disability and dependence characteristically confined to a later stage, say post-85.

Responses to old age

We have demonstrated that, in a continuation of a largely constant historical theme, the major sources of care for older people derive from their family and, potentially, their wider social network. It is only within the domain of health care that the professional contribution assumes dominance and then it is largely integrated within a broader social context with the family supporting the professions once an acute episode is over. The involvement of the state in terms of pension and care provision for older people is, in the scale of human development, very recent and novel. Old age has been only recently identified as both a distinct phase of the lifecourse and one which merits special attention from the state. Old people have been differentiated from the broader group of vulnerable members of society and deemed 'worthy' of support by the wider society. This 'compassionate ageism' stereotypes older people as lonely, isolated, badly housed, poor and in ill health (both physical and mental). Parallels between this conceptualisation of older people may be drawn with the 'old age as a humanitarian social problem' approach characteristic of many of the immediate post-war social surveys of older people undertaken by Townsend (1957) and Tunstall (1966) widespread acceptance of these stereotypes influenced the development of policies for older people that conceptualised them as a homogeneous and undifferentiated social group. However, in Britain policies to respond to old age, with the exception of pensions, have been needs based rather than age based in terms of eligibility criteria. As such Britain does demonstrate the plethora of age-related programmes illustrated by the United States and which Estes (1979) described as the ageing enterprise. We can see some of the issues she raised with regard to specific services such as age-related health care where it can be argued that such solutions are socially divisive that stigmatise and isolate older people from the wider (health care) context.

Older people, within contemporary Britain, largely retain their image as a social group worthy of support. There are debates about the future role of the state in providing for old age, especially in the pensions and health and social care arenas. The neo-liberal critique of the welfare state argues that the 'greying' of the welfare budget, as a result of the well-established increase in the number of older people, is an issue which has profound political implications and which could effectively bankrupt the state and generate conflict between generations over access to scarce welfare (and other) resources. Clearly the argument about the affordability (or otherwise) of pensions and health care provision is highly dependent upon the assumptions used to generate the models. Welfare expenditure, especially that concerned with health and social care, may not be problematic if the compression of morbidity hypothesis is proved correct. Hence in thinking about the potential future demands upon welfare provision we need to be clear as to the assumptions being used to inform our modelling and debate.

One topic area of debate concerning the future of old age is concerned with notions of intergenerational conflict – the idea that there will be conflict between generations (young and old) for the distribution of scarce government welfare resources. This notion of intergenerational conflict first arose in the late 1960s and is especially associated with the 'ageing' of the baby boomer generation. It is argued that this generation has exercised control over welfare resources across their lifecourse, as they grow older they will come into conflict with less numerous younger cohorts for control of welfare resources. Although this has been a topic about which there has been much debate and speculation, there is remarkably little empirical evidence to support the ideas encompassed within the ideas of intergenerational conflict. At the heart of the debate are notions of both age identity and the development of an age-based narrowly defined group interest. Such an approach presumes that older voters will develop a solidarity based exclusively upon age and will vote for policies which directly benefit them and not for those beneficial to younger people (extra expenditure on education) or where they may not live long enough to reap the benefits such as environmental improvements. Everything that we have considered in this book suggests that older people do not express a group, age-based identity. Rather class, gender and other factors determine identity. Although older people are more likely to vote than other age groups, there is little evidence that they vote as a gerontocracy. Furthermore, in contemporary Britain, there is a lack of formal political organisation for older people and the main political parties do not always actively engage with the politics of old age. In addition there are barriers to political activity such as disability, poverty and ill health. In addition the notion of inter-cohort conflict presumes a lack of reciprocity across generations yet we have demonstrated that there is considerable reciprocity between generations within family settings. Why should this not exist at the macrolevel? The intergeneration conflict notion portrays older people as 'greedy geezers' who are exploiting the welfare state at the expense of other groups, but there seems to be remarkably little evidence to support such notions. While we may observe that childhood poverty has increased and poverty among older people may have increased, we cannot presume a causal relationship between these two events. When thinking about changes in patterns of welfare provision between and across groups we must not assume causal relationships for phenomena that may not be linked.

The final issue relates to the access to care by older people. The National Service Framework for Older People has taken up the battle against 'ageism' and 'age discrimination' as its first challenge. This a complex issue with several different elements, including entitlement to care (should we use age to ration care?), 'simple' access to services (can older people get the care they need?), and the quality of care (are older people treated to the same quality of care as other groups)? Furthermore we need to distinguish between three interrelated but subtly different concepts: ageism (negative attitudes towards older people and similar to the concepts of sexism or racism), age discrimination (positive or negative discrimination in terms of service access on the basis of age, e.g. free prescriptions for those aged 60+ or no access to dialysis to those aged 70+) and age-based rationing (access to health denied solely on basis of age). The debate is further complicated by differences in how the varying subgroups of the older population are treated. Are older men more likely to receive care than older women are? Do issues of class and race matter? Clearly, the whole debate around ageism and age discrimination is highly complex, especially when the primary and secondary care distinction is included. Additionally these different factors can operate at a variety of levels ranging from societal, strategic (e.g. the NHS) to decisions made by individual clinicians and can either be explicit or implicit.

There are many stereotypes in existence concerning the nature and characteristics of older people. Stereotypes are simply a distorted representation of a specific social group and may be positive but are usually negative. There are many stereotypes concerning old age including (a) all older people are lonely, (b) older people cannot learn, (c) all older people are in poor health, (d) old people are a 'dependent' group incapable of exercising self-determination (a common analogy is made with children via the notion of 'the second childhood') and (e) all old people are alike. This last stereotype is important for the development and delivery of services in that it suggests that there are a single set of needs that can be met by a universalist response. Older people, like the rest of the population, are differentiated in terms of gender, class and (probably) ethnicity. Consistently research has demonstrated significant variation in access to health, material and social resources in terms of class and gender and these dimensions intersect. The most privileged, in terms of resources, are men from the professional and managerial classes. Least privileged, in terms of access to these types of resources, are women from manual occupations. Hence the social inequalities in health (and other factors) that characterise modern British society are maintained into old age. Negative stereotypes are also applied to ageing populations, which helps explain the concerns expressed about population ageing. The stereotypes are important because they can influence the availability of and quality of care provided to older people as many health and social care professionals (along with policy makers and the general population) hold very negative views of old age and the potential of older people. They are also important because they may influence the (health) behaviour of older people. Older people may not consult because they attribute their shortness of breath or knee pain to 'ageing' rather than disease (eg. chronic obstructive pulmonary disease and arthritis). We may treat people simply on the basis of their age and not look at the wider social context or quality of life.

The notion that society, as a whole, is generally prejudiced against older people is encapsulated by the concept of 'ageism'. This is the idea that older people are systematically discriminated against (either implicitly or explicitly). Ageism, of course, may also be exerted against other groups, most notably teenage men, but this is not usually as pernicious as the ageism experienced by older people. Ageism is rife in health care: there are numerous examples of the negative attitudes held by staff about older people and this may influence the quality of care received by older people. Ageism may take place on a variety of levels from the overt or covert decisions of an individual clinician, through the ways various specific programmes such as screening operate to the strategic and macrolevel societal.

There are essentially two positions in terms of the attitudes towards age-based rationing of health care and the relative entitlement or claims of different groups within the population to care. Williams (1997) argues for the 'fair innings' thesis, in that once a certain age has been achieved then priority for treatment should be given to other age groups. Consequently, above a certain age there should be no 'entitlement' or 'claim' to care, and societal debate would determine where this boundary should be drawn. In this scenario, the older person's previous contribution to society does not bring with it an open-ended claim to (limited) health care resources. This position gives priority to the care of the young; by denying services to the old we give the young the opportunity to reach old age! For example, we could determine that no 'acute' interventions such as dialysis or pacemakers should be prescribed to people aged 80+, or that those above a certain age should not be resuscitated in the event of a collapse. Overt ageism with specific age bars to services such as cardiology are less evident but covert ageism is more difficult to identify (Bowling, 1999). The Department of Health (2002) reports that forty-one health service areas have age-related policies (some of which positively discriminate in favour of older people). There is clear evidence that older people experience discrimination in accessing care and in the quality of care provided, and those differing groups within the older age groups are differentially treated. The Department of Health report acknowledges the lack of clarity concerning terms such as age discrimination and the widespread nature of implicit age discrimination. Most of the debate about age-based rationing has been conducted in terms of access to acute care. Would we also ration access to primary, preventive or community care on the basis of chronological age?

Grimley Evans (1997) supports the view that age is a very imprecise mechanism by which to allocate care and that we should treat older people individually according to their needs. This view suggests that, irrespective of chronological age, older people have a legitimate claim to care rooted in 'past contributions' to society and the intergenerational contract. Clearly this is the view accepted by the NHS and the first standard of the National Service Framework is concerned with eradicating age discrimination and negative attitudes towards older people.

Given the potentially increasing diversity of the older population, we might speculate that there is as much scope for conflict between the 'haves' and 'have nots' of an increasingly polarised population as there is between generations. The ethos of the welfare state in Britain was to diminish, if not eradicate, the class-based inequalities which pervade British society. Access to health care was to be determined by clinical need rather than ability to pay and pensions provided to provide financial security in later life. In reality it is the articulate middle class who have fared best in the state allocation of welfare. Provision of health care largely follows the 'inverse care law' first proposed by Julian Tudor Hart (1971) and class-based health inequalities have been little altered by the creation of the welfare state. The centrality of social class to the understanding of modern British society is evident by its inclusion as a key variable in most social investigations, with the exception, until recently, of those concerned with older people. We clearly need to examine in more detail the variations in health and social care needs within the older population and establish the equity or otherwise that different social groups have to services of equal quality. A key feature of any such investigation would relate to the issue of gender and access to health and social care. A variety of authors have argued that community care is merely a euphemism for care by women because of gender inequalities in caring roles, although the discovery of the 'male carer' was uncomfortable for many feminists.

In forecasting the future shape of the ageing experience we have already noted the changing nature of the family structures that future generations of elders will display. Even with the potential deferral of disability, there will be a proportion of elders who experience problems of disability and dependency. Given that there may be fewer family to care for such individuals is it time to reconsider our uncritical acceptance of 'community-based' care solutions and reconsider if the 'institutional' form of provision could not, in theory at least, be rehabilitated. It is quite clear that many old-style forms of institutional or communal care were dire. Is the communal solution inevitably 'bad' or could such solutions be made to work if sufficient resources and quality of staff were invested in such facilities? It is certainly worth reviewing our prejudices and biases for particular forms of provision, especially if future generations of elders express a positive choice for these types of care solutions.

Much of the current ideological debate about service provision centres upon the issues of private versus public sector care. Within the contemporary British welfare state the private sector is now a large provider of community and communal care, although the private sector still plays only a residual role in health care. The key to the ideological debate seems to be the notion of 'freedom of choice' allied with feelings that private services are inherently better than public services because the consumer has the ability to withdraw from unsatisfactory arrangements. However, often the notion of freedom of choice is more illusory than real. The 'free market' is an insecure place for vulnerable people who may lack power in the decision-making process. The idea that a free market will necessarily bring high standards of care, either domiciliary or residential, is both naive and dangerous when one outcome of the free market – business failure and bankruptcy – carries important implications for the residents of private homes and those reliant upon private care to maintain themselves at home.

Conclusion

The experience of ageing within contemporary society is richly diverse. Structural factors such as age, sex and social class contribute to make the older population as heterogeneous and socially differentiated as the rest of the population. The popular negative stereotypes of later life are clearly inappropriate and later life is best seen as a continuation of earlier phases of life. Older people are, however, a group which is under threat. The widespread fears about the 'greying' of the population and the welfare budget have brought about a sharp attack upon the living standards of a group who are, in comparison with the rest of society, already deprived. The persistence of inappropriate negative stereotypes about later life results in both discrimination and prejudice against the old. Society consistently displays ageist attitudes that demonstrate a marked lack of concern about its older members. It is not only the elderly who lose out because of the existence of ageist attitudes. Only by changing attitudes across society will we be able to ensure that future generations of elders experience old age as fully participating members of society, instead of as observers confined to the margins. To achieve this end we must stress the common interests between age groups instead of seeing old people (or any other marginal group) as fundamentally different from ourselves. The main goal for an ageing society must be to replace notions of independence and dependence with a social framework which emphasises interdependence and reciprocity across and between generations.

References

Abbott, R. D. (1997) Cross-sectional and longitudinal changes in total and high density lipoprotein cholesterol levels over a 20-year period in elderly men: the Honolulu Heart Programme. *Annals of Epidemiology*, 7, 6, 417–424.

Achenbaum, A. and Bengston, V. (1994) Recognising the disengagement theory of aging. *The Gerontologist*, 34(b), 756–763.

Agree, E., Blissett, B. and Rendell, M. S. (2002) Simultaneous care for parents and care for children among mid-life British women and men. *Population Trends*, 110, 29–35.

Aldwin, C. M. and Gilmer, D. F. (2004) *Health, Illness and Optimal Aging*. Sage, Thousand Oaks, CA.

Amulree, Lord. (1955) Modern hospital treatment and the pensioner. *Lancet*, 17 September, 571–575.

Andersson, L. (1998) Loneliness research and interventions: a review of the literature. *Ageing and Mental Health*, 2, 4, 264–274.

Antonucci, T. C. (1985) Personal characteristics, social support and social behaviour. In Binstock, R. and Shanas, E. (eds) *Handbook of Aging and the Social Sciences*. Van Nostrand Reinhold, New York.

Antonucci, T. C. and Akiyama, H. (1987) Social relations in adult life. *Journal of Gerontology*, 4, 517–527.

Arber, S. (2004) Gender, marital status and ageing. *Journal of Aging Studies*, 18, 91–108.

Arber, S. and Attias-Donfut, C. (eds) (2000) *The Myth of Generational Conflict*. Routledge, London.

Arber, S. and Gilbert, N. (1989) Men: the forgotten carers. *Sociology*, 23, 1, 111–118.

Arber, S. and Ginn, J. (1991) *Gender and Later Life*. Sage, London.

Arber, S. and Ginn, J. (1995) Gender differences in informal care. *Health and Social Care in the Community*, 3, 19–31.

Arber, S. and Ginn, J. (2004) Ageing and gender. In Summerfield, C. and Babb, P. (eds) *Social Trends 2004*. The Stationery Office, London.

Arber, S., Davidson, K. and Ginn, J. (eds) (2003) *Gender and Ageing*. Open University Press, Maidenhead.

Aroni, R. and Minichiello, V. (1992) Sociological aspects of ageing. In

Minichiello, V., Alexander, L. and Jones, D. (eds) *Gerontology: A Multidisciplinary Approach*. Prentice Hall, Sydney.

Aronson, M. K., Ooi, W. L., Geva, D. L. *et al.* (1991) Dementia: age dependent incidence, prevalence and mortality in the oldest old. *Archives of Internal Medicine*, 151, 5, 989–992.

Askham, J. (1995) The married lives of older people. In Arber, S. and Ginn, J. (eds) *Connecting Gender and Ageing*. Open University Press, Buckingham.

Askham, J. (2003) Interpreting measures of activities of daily living. In Bytheway, W. (ed.) *Every Day Living in Later Life*. Centre for Policy on Ageing, London.

Askham, J., Barry, C., Grundy, E. *et al.* (1992) *Life after 60*, Age Concern Institute of Gerontology, King's College, London.

Atchley, R. C. (1999) *Continuity and Adaption in Old Age*. Johns Hopkins University Press, Baltimore, MD.

Baltes, P. (1993) The aging mind. *The Gerontologist*, 33, 580–594.

Barker, D. J. P. (1998) *Mothers and Babies and Health in Later Life*, 2nd edn. Churchill Livingstone, Edinburgh.

Bengtson, V., Rice, C. J. and Johnson, M. L. (1999) Are theories of aging important? In Bengtson, V. and Schaie, K. (eds) *Handbook of Theories of Aging*. Springer, New York.

Berger, P. L. and Berger, J. (1976) *Sociology and Biographical Approach*. Penguin, Harmondsworth, Middx.

Bernard, M. (2000) *Promoting Health in Old Age*. Open University Press, Buckingham.

Bernard, M. and Meade, K. (eds) (1993) *Women Come of Age: Perspectives on the Lives of Older Women*. Edward Arnold, London.

Beveridge Report (1942) *Social Insurance and Allied Services*. HMSO, London.

Biggs, S. (1993) *Understanding Ageing*. Open University Press, Buckingham.

Biggs, S. (1999) *The Mature Imagination*. Open University Press, Buckingham.

Blaikie, A. and Hepworth, M. (1997) Representations of old age in paintings and photography. In Jamieson, A., Harper, S. and Victor, C. (eds) *Critical Approaches to Ageing and Later Life*. Open University Press, Milton Keynes, Bucks: 132–142.

Blakemore, K. and Boneham, M. (1994) *Age, Race and Ethnicity*. Open University Press, Buckingham.

Blau, Z. A. (1973) *Old Age in a Changing Society*. Franklin Watts, New York.

Bond, J. and Carstairs, V. (1982) *The Elderly in Clackmannan*. Scottish Health Services Studies, No. 42, Scottish Home and Health Department, Edinburgh.

Bond, J., Coleman, P. and Peace, S. (1993) *Ageing in Society*, 2nd edn. Sage, London.

Bone, M., Bebbington, A., Jagger, C. *et al.* (1995) *Health Expectancy and its Uses*. HMSO, London.

Boothby, H., Blizard, R., Livingston, G. *et al.* (1994) The Gospel Oak Study Stage III: the incidence of dementia. *Psychological Medicine*, 24, 1, 89–95.

Bornat, J. (2002) Doing life history research. In Jamieson, A. and Victor, C. R. (eds) *Researching ageing and Later Life*. Open University Press, Buckingham.

Botelho, L. and Thane, P. (eds) (2001) *Women and Ageing in British Society since 1500*. Longman, Harlow.

Bowling, A. (1994) Social networks and social support among older people and implications for emotional well-being and psychological well-being. *International Review of Psychiatry*, 6, 41–58.

Bowling, A. (1999) Ageism in cardiology. *British Medical Journal*. 319, 1353–1355.

Bowling, A. (2002) *Research Methods in Health Services*, 2nd edn. Open University Press, Buckingham.

Bowling, A. and Grundy. E. (1997) Changes in functional ability in three samples of elderly. *Ageing and Society*, 26, 107–114.

Bowling, A., Banister, D., Sutton, S. *et al.* (2002) A multidimensional model of the quality of life in older age. *Aging and Mental Health*, 6, 4, 355–371.

Breeze, M., Sloggett, A. and Fletcher, A. (1999) Socio-economic status and transitions in status in old age in relation to limiting longstanding illness measured at the 1991 Census. *European Journal of Public Health*, 9, 4, 205–240.

Breeze, E., Fletcher, A., Leon, D. *et al.* (2001) Do socio-economic disadvantages persist into old age?. *American Journal of Public Health*, 91, 92, 277–283.

Bridgwood, A. (2000) *People Aged 65 Years and Older*. Office for National Statistics, London.

Brody, E. (1981) Women in the middle. *The Gerontologist*, 21, 5, 471–479.

Brody, E. M. (1990) *Women in the Middle: Their Parent Care Years*. Springer, New York.

Brown, W. S., Bryson, L., Byles, J. E. *et al.* (1998) Women's health Australia: recruitment for a national cohort study. *Women Health*, 28, 1, 23–40.

Bulmer, M. (1987) *The Social Basis of Community Care*. Unwin Hyman, London.

Bury, M. and Holme, A. (1991) *Life after Ninety*. Routledge, London.

Byrd, M. and Bruess, T, (1992) Perceptions of sociological and psychological age norms by young, middle aged and elderly New Zealanders. *International Journal of Aging and Human Development*, 34, 2, 145–153.

Bytheway, W. (1995) *Ageism*. Open University Press, Buckingham.

Bytheway, W. (1997) Talking about age: the theoretical basis of social gerontology. In Jamieson, A., Harper, S. and Victor, C. (eds) *Critical Approaches to Ageing and Later Life*. Open University Press, Milton Keynes, Bucks: 7–15.

Bytheway, W. (ed) (2003) *Every Day Living in Later Life*. Centre for Policy on Ageing, London.

Calasanti, T. M. (2003) Masculinities and care work in old age. In Arber, S., Davidson, K. and Ginn, J. (eds) *Gender and Ageing*. Open University Press, Maidenhead.

Calasanti, T. M. and Sleven, K. F. (2001) *Gender, Social Inequalities and Aging*. AltaMira Press, Walnut Creek, CA.

Carers' National Association (CNA) (1996) *Who Cares? Perceptions of Caring and Carers*. CNA, London.

Challis, D. and Hughes, J. (2003) Residential and nursing home care – issues of balance and quality of care. *International Journal of Geriatric Psychiatry*, 18, 3, 201–204.

Clarke, L. and Roberts, C. (2004) The meaning of grandparenthood and its contribution to the quality of life of older people. In Walker, A. and Hennessey, C. (eds) *Growing Older*. Open University Press, Maidenhead, Berks: 188–209.

Coleman, P. (2002) Doing case study research in psychology. In Jamieson, A. and Victor C. R. (eds) *Researching Ageing and Later Life*. Open University Press, Milton Keynes, Bucks: 135–155.

Cornwell, J. (1984) *Hard Earned Lives*. Tavistock, London.

Costa, P. T. and McCrae, R. R. (1988) Personality in adulthood. *Journal of Personality and Social Psychology*. 54, 853–863.

Cowgill, D. O. and Holmes, L. D. (eds) (1972) *Aging and Modernisation*. Appleton, New York.

Crow, G. (2004) Social networks and social exclusion: an overview of the debate. In Phillipson, C., Allan, G. and Morgan, D. (eds) *Social Networks and Social Exclusion*. Ashgate, Aldershot.

Culyer, A. J. (1981) *Health Indicators*. University of York, York.

Cumming, E. and Henry, W. E. (1961) *Growing Old*, Basic Books, New York.

Daatland, S. (2002) Time to pay back? Is there something for psychology and sociology in gerontology. In Andersson, L. (ed.) *Cultural Gerontology*. Auburn House, Westport, CT.

Dalley, G. (1988) *Ideologies of Caring*. Macmillan Education, London.

Davidson, K., Arber, S. and Ginn, J. (2000) Gendered meanings of care work within late life marital relationships. *Canadian Journal of Aging*, 19, 4, 536–553.

Davidson, K., Daly, T. and Arber, S. (2003) Exploring the social worlds of older men. In Arber, S., Davidson, K. and Ginn, J. (eds) *Gender and Ageing*. Open University Press, Maidenhead.

Davis, I., Leigh, S., Parry, S., Kent, C. and Nicholls, M. (2003) *The Pensioners' Income Series 2001/2*. Office for National Statistics, London. Available from http://www.dwp.gov.uk.

Department of Health (DoH) (2001) *National Service Framework for Older People*. The Stationery Office, London. Available from http://www.doh.gov.uk/nsf/olderpeople.htm.

Department of Health. (2002) *National Service Framework for Older People: Interim Report on Age Discrimination*. Available only from http://www.doh.gov.uk/nsf/olderpeople.htm.

Dunnel, K. (2001) *Policy responses to population ageing and population decline in the UK*. Population Trends, 103, 47–52.

Ebrahim, S. and Kalache, A. (1996) *The Epidemiology of Ageing*. BMJ Books, London.

Engel, G. L. (1977) A need for a new medical model: a challenge for biomedicine. *Science*, 196, 129–136.

Estes, C. L. (1979) *The Aging Enterprise*. Jossey-Bass, San Francisco, CA.

Estes, C. (2001) *Social Policy and Aging*. Sage, Thousand Oaks, CA.

Estes, C and Associates (2001) *Social Policy and Aging*. Sage, Thousand Oaks, CA.

Estes, C. and Binney, E. A. (1989) The bio-medicalisation of aging. *The Gerontologist*, 29, 5, 587–596.

Estes, C., Swan, J. and Gerard, L. (1982) Dominant and competing paradigms in gerontology. In Minkler, M. A. and Estes, C. (eds) *Readings in the Political Economy of Aging*. Baywood, Farmingdale, NY.

Estes, C., Binney, E. A. and Culbertson, R. A. (1992) The gerontological imagination: social influences on the development of gerontology. *International Journal of Aging and Human Development*, 35, 1, 49–63.

Estes, C., Biggs, S. and Phillipson, C. (2004) *Social Theory, Social Policy and Ageing*. Open University Press, Maidenhead.

Evandrou, M. (1992) Challenging the invisibility of carers. In Laczko, F. and Victor, C. R. (eds) *Social Policy on Older People*. Gower, Aldershot.

Evandrou, M. (ed.) (1997) *The Baby Boomers? Ageing in the 21st Century*. Age Concern England, London.

Evandrou, M. (2000) Ethnic inequalities in health in later life. *Health Statistics Quarterly*, 8, 20–28.

Evandrou, M. and Falkingham, J. (2000) Looking back to look forward: lessons from four birth cohorts for ageing in the 21st century. *Population Trends*, 99, 27–36.

Evandrou, M. and Glaser, K. (2002) Changing economic and social roles: the experience of four cohorts of mid-life individuals in Britain, 1985–2000. *Population Trends*, 110, 19–29.

Evandrou, M., Falkingham, J., Rake, K. and Scott, A (2001) *The Dynamics of Living Arrangements in Later Life*. SAGE discussion paper no. 4, London School of Economics, London.

Fairhurst, E. (2003) New identities in ageing. In Arber, S., Davidson, K. and Ginn, J. (eds) *Gender and Ageing*. Open University Press, Maidenhead.

Falkingham, J. (1997) Who are the baby boomers? In Evandrou, M. (ed.) *The babyboomers: ageing in the 21st Century*. Age Concern England, London.

Falkingham, J. and Victor, C. R. (1991) The myth of the Woopie. *Ageing Society*, 11, 4, 471–493.

Featherstone, M. and Hepworth, M. (1989) Ageing and old age: reflections on the post-modern lifecourse. In Bytheway, W. (ed.) *Becoming and Being Old*. Sage, London.

Featherstone, M. and Hepworth, M. (1995) Images of positive ageing. In Featherstone, M. and Wernick, A. (eds) *Images of Ageing*. Routledge, London.

Finch, J. (1989a) *Family Obligations and Social Change*. Polity Press, Cambridge.

Finch, J. (1989b) Kinship and friendship. In Jowell, R., Witherspoon, S. and

Brook, L. (eds) *British Social Attitudes: Special International Report.* Gower, Aldershot.

Finch, J. (1995) Responsibilities, obligations and commitment. In Allen, I. and Perkins, E. (eds) *The Future of Family Care for Older People.* HMSO, London.

Finch, J. and Groves, D. (1980) Community care for the elderly: a case for equal opportunities. *Journal of Social Policy*, 9, 4, 487–514.

Finch, J. and Groves, D. (eds) (1983) *A Labour of Love: Women, Work and Caring.* Routledge and Kegan Paul, London.

Finch, J. and Mason, D. (1993) *Negotiating Family Responsibilities.* Routledge, London.

Fisher, D. H. (1978) *Growing Old in America.*Oxford University Press, New York.

Ford, G. (1985) Illness behaviour in old age. In Dean, K, Hickey, T. and Holstein, B. (eds) *Self Care in Old Age.* Croom Helm, London.

Fratiglioni, L., De Ronchi, D. and Aguero-Torres, H. (1999) Worldwide prevalence and incidence of dementia. *Drugs and Aging*, 15, 5, 365–375.

Fratiglioni, L., Launer, L. J., Andersen, K. *et al.* (2000) Incidence of dementia and major subtypes in Europe. *Neurology*, 54, 5, S10–S15.

Freedman, V., Martin, L. and Schoeni, R. (2001) Recent trends in disability and functioning among older adults in the United States: a systematic review. *Journal of the American Medical Association*, 288, 24, 3137–3146.

Fries, J. F. (1980) Aging, natural death and the compression of morbidity. *New England Journal of Medicine*, 303, 130–135.

Fries, J. F. (2003) Measuring and monitoring success in compressing morbidity. *Annals of Internal Medicine*, 139, 5, 455–463.

Gatz, M., Kasl-Godley, J. E. and Karel, M. J. (1996) Aging and mental disorders. In Birren, J. and Schaie, K. W. (eds) *Handbook of the Psychology of Ageing.* Van Nostrand Reinhold, New York.

Gilleard, C. (1996) Consumption and identity in later life. *Ageing and Society*, 16, 489–98.

Gilleard, C. and Higgs, P. (2000) *Cultures of Consumption.* Prentice Hall, London.

Ginn, J. (2003) *Gender, Pensions and the Lifecourse.* Policy Press, Bristol.

Ginn, J., Street, D. and Arber, S. (eds) (2001) *Women, Work and Pensions.* Open University Press, Buckingham.

Glaser, K. (1997) The living arrangements of elderly people. *Reviews in Clinical Gerontology*, 7, 63–72.

Glaser, K., Murphy, M. and Grundy, E. (1997) Limiting long-term illness and household structure among people aged 45 years and over: Great Britain 1991. *Ageing and Society*, 17, 3–19.

Glenn, N. (1974) Aging and conservatism. *Annals of the American Association of Political and Social Science*, 415, 176–180.

Goffman, E. (1968) *Asylums.* Penguin, Harmondsworth.

Grant, G. and Nolan, M. (1993) Informal carers – sources and concomitant of satisfaction. *Health and Social Care in the Community*, 1, 147–159.

Grimley Evans, J. (1997) The rationing debate: rationing health care by age: the case against. *British Medical Journal*, 314, 822.

Gruenberg, E. M. (1977) The failures of success. *Millbank Memorial Foundation Quarterly*, 55, 3–24.

Grundy, E. M. (1997) The health and health care of older adults in England and Wales, 1841–1994. In Charlton, J. and Murphy, M. (eds) *The Health of Adult Britain 1841–1994, vol. 2.* The Stationery Office, London.

Grundy, E. and Glaser, K. (1998) Migration and household change in the population aged 65 and over, 1971–1991. *International Journal of Population Geography*, 4, 323–329.

Grundy, E., Murphy, M. and Shelton, N. (1999) Looking beyond the household: intergenerational perspectives on living kin and contacts with kin in Great Britain. *Population Trends*, 97, 19–27.

Gubrium, J. and Holstein, (2000) *Aging and Everyday Life.* Blackwell, Malden, MA.

Gunnell, D., Middleton, N., Whitley, E. *et al.* (2003) Why are suicide rates rising in young men but falling in the elderly? *Social Science and Medicine*, 57, 4, 595–611.

Hareven, T. K. (ed.) (1996) *Aging and Generational Relations.* Aldine de Gruyter, New York.

Harper, S. (2003) *Changing Families as Societies Age.* Research report no. RR103, Institute of Ageing, University of Oxford.

Harris, T., Cook, D. G., Victor, C. R. *et al.* (2000) Predictors of depressive symptoms in older people. *Age and Ageing*, 32, 5, 510–518.

Hattersley, L. (1997) Expectation of life by social class. In Whitehead, M. and Driver, F. (eds) *Health Inequalities.* The Stationery Office, London.

Havighurst, R. (1963) Successful aging. In Williams, R. H., Tibbits, C. and Donahue, W. (eds) *Processes of Aging, vol. 1.*, University of Chicago Press, Chicago.

Hayflick, L. (1996) *How and Why We Age.* Ballantine, New York.

Health Advisory Service (1982) *The Rising Tide: Developing services for mental illness in old age.* HMSO, London.

Healy, J., Thomas, A., Seargent, J. and Victor, C. R. (1999) *Coming Up for Care.* Policy Studies Institute, London.

Hepworth, M. (1991) Positive ageing and the mask of age. *Journal of Educational Gerontology*, 6, 2, 93–101.

Herzlich, C. (1973) *Health and Illness.* Academic Press, London.

Hessler, R. M., Erikson, B., Dey, D. *et al.* (2003) The compression of morbidity debate in aging: an empirical test using the gerontological and geriatric population studies in Goteborg, Sweden. *Archives of Gerontology and Geriatrics*, 37, 213–222.

Hirani, V. and Malbot, K. (2002) *Disability among Older People.* Health Survey for England, The Stationery Office, London.

Hockey, L. and James, J. (1993) *Growing Up and Growing Old.* Sage, London.

Isaacs, B., Livingstone, M. and Neville, Y. (1972) *Survival of the Unfittest.* Routledge and Kegan Paul, London.

Jamieson, A. and Victor, C. R. (eds) (2002) *Researching Ageing and Later Life*. Open University Press, Buckingham.

Jefferys, M. (1983) The over eighties in Britain: the social construction of a moral panic. *Journal of Public Health Policy*, 4, 367–372.

Jerrome, D. (1993) Initimate relationships. In Bond, J., Coleman, P. and Peace, S. (eds) *Ageing in Society*, 2nd edn. Sage, London.

Johnson, M. (1978) That was your life: a biographical approach to later life. In Carver, V. and Liddiard, P. (eds) *An Ageing Population*. Hodder & Stoughton, Sevenoaks: 99–115.

Johnson, J. and Bytheway, W. (1997) Illustrating care: images of care relationships with older people. In Jamieson, A., Harper, S. and Victor, C. (eds) *Critical Approaches to Ageing and Later Life*. Open University Press, Buckingham: 132–142.

Johnson, P., Conrad, C. and Thomson, D. (eds) (1990) *Workers versus Pensioners*. Manchester University Press, Manchester.

Johnson, P. and Falkingham, J. (1992) *Ageing and Economic Welfare*. Sage, London.

Jong Gierveld, J. de (1998) A review of loneliness: concepts and definitions, causes and consequences. *Reviews in Clinical Gerontology*, 8, 73–80.

Kaufman, G. and Elder, G. H. (2002) Revisiting age identity. *Journal of Aging Studies*, 16, 2, 169–176.

Kelly, S., Baker, A. and Gupta, S. (2000) Healthy life expectancy in Great Britain 1980-1996. *Health Statistics Quarterly*, 7, 16–24

Khaw, K. T. (1997) Healthy ageing, *British Medical Journal*, 315, 1090–1096.

Khaw, K. T. (1999a) How many, how old, how soon? *British Medical Journal*, 319, 1350–52.

Khaw, K. T. (1999b) Inequalities and health: older people. In Gordon, D., Shaw, M., Dorling, D. and Davey-Smith, G. (eds) *Inequalities in Health: The Evidence*. Policy Press, Bristol.

Kirkwood, T. (1999) *The Time of our Lives.* Weidenfeld and Nicolson, London.

Kitwood, T. (1997) *Dementia Reconsidered*. Open University Press, Buckingham.

Kramer, M. (1980) The rising pandemic of mental disorders and associated chronic diseases and disabilities. *Acta Psychiatrica Scandinavica*. 62 (supp. 285), 282–297.

Lamping, D., Constantinovici, N., Roderick, P. *et al.* (2000) Clinical outcomes, costs and quality of life from the North Thames study of elderly people on dialysis. *Lancet*, 356, 1543–1550.

Laslett, P. (1989). *A Fresh Map of Life: The Emergence of the Third Age*. Weidenfeld and Nicolson, London.

Latimer, J. (2000) *The Conduct of Care*. Blackwell, Oxford.

Lawton, M. P. and Herzog, A. (eds) (1989) *Special Research Methods in Gerontology*. Baywood, New York.

Lee, I. and Paffenbarger, R. (1995) Longevity and exercise intensity in men. *Journal of the American Medical Association*. 19, 273, 1179–84.

Levin, C. (2000) Social function. In Kane, R. L., and Kane, R. A. (eds) *Assessing Older Persons.* Oxford University Press, Oxford.

Lewis, J. and Meredith, B. (1989) *Daughters who care.* Routledge, London.

Lobo, L. A., Launer, L. J., Fratiglioni, L. *et al.* (2000) Prevalence of dementia and major sub-types in Europe. *Neurology,* 54, 11, S4–9.

Lubben, J. and Gironda, M. (2004) Measuring social networks and assessing their benefits. In Phillipson, C., Allan, G. and Morgan, D. (eds) *Social Networks and Social Exclusion.* Ashgate, Aldershot.

McDonald, L. (2000) Alarmist economics and women's pensions. In Gee, E. and Gutman, G. (eds) *The Overselling of Population Ageing.* Oxford University Press, Ontario

McGee, M., Johnson, A. L. and Kay, D. N. K. (1998) The description of activities of daily living in five centres in England and Wales. *Age and Ageing,* 27, 605–613.

McGlone, F., Park, A. and Roberts, C. (2000) Relative values: kinship and friendship. In Jowell, R., Curtice, J., Park, A., Brook, L. and Thompson, K. (eds) *British Social Attitudes: the 13th Report.* Dartmouth, Aldershot.

MacIntyre, S. (1977) Old age as a social problem. In Dingwall, R., Heath, C., Reid, M. and Stacey, M. (eds) *Health Care and Health Knowledge.* Croom Helm, London.

McKeown, T. (1979) *The Role of Medicine.* Blackwell, Oxford.

McLaughlin, E. and Ritchie, J. (1994) Legacies of caring: the experiences and circumstances of ex-carers. *Health and Social Care,* 2, 241–253.

Mann, A. (2001) Depression in the elderly. *Maturitas,* 38, 1, 53–58.

Mannheim, K. (1997) The problem of generations. In Hardy, M. A. (ed.) *Studying Aging and Social Change.* Thousand Oaks, CA.

Manton, K. (1991) New biotechnologies and limits to life expectancy. In Lutz, W. (ed.) *Future Demographic Trends in Europe and North America.* Academic Press, New York.

Manton, K. and Gu, X. (2001) Changes in the prevalence of chronic disability in the United States black and non-black population above age 65 from 1982 to 1999. *Proceedings National Academy of Science USA,* 98, 6354–6359.

Manton, K., Corder, L. and Stallard, E. (1997) Chronic disability trends in elderly United States populations: 1982–1984. *Proceedings National Academy of Science USA,* 94, 2593–2598.

Marmot, M. (2004) *Status Syndrome.* Bloomsbury, London.

Marmot, M. and Shipley, M. (1996) Do socio-economic differences in mortality persist after retirement? *British Medical Journal,* 313, 1177–1180.

Marmot, M., Banks, J. Blundell, R. *et al.* (eds) (2003) *Health, Wealth and Lifestyles of the Older Population in England.* Institute of Fiscal Studies, London.

Marsiske, M., Franks, M. A. and Mast, M. T. (1998). Psychological perspectives upon aging. In Morgan, L. and Kunkel, S. (eds) *Aging: The Social Context.* Pine Forge Press, Thousand Oaks, CA.

Martin, J., Meltzer, H. and Elliot, D. (1988) *The Prevalence of Disability among Adults.* HMSO, London.

Martin-Matthews, A. (2000) Intergenerational caregiving. In Gee, E. and Gutman, G. (eds) *The Overselling of Population Ageing*. Oxford University Press, Ontario.

Mauss, M. (1954) *The Gift*. Free Press, Glencoe, NY.

Mayer, J. and Green, H. (2002) *Carers 2000*. The Stationery Office, London.

Mead, G. (ed.) (1956) *Mind, Self and Society*. University of Chicago Press, Chicago, IL.

Means, R. and Smith, R. (1998) *From Poor Law to Community Care*. Policy Press, Bristol.

Meltzer, D., McWilliams, B., Brayne, C. *et al.* (1999) Profile of disability in elderly people: estimates from a longitudinal study. *British Medical Journal*, 318, 1108–1111.

Meltzer, D., McWilliams, B., Brayne, C. *et al.* (2000) Socio-economic status and the expectation of disability in old age: estimates for England. *Journal of Epidemiology and Community Health*, 54, 286–292.

Midwinter, E. (1997) *Pensioned Off*. Open University Press, Buckingham.

Morgan, K. (1998) The Nottingham Longitudinal Study of Activity and Ageing: a methodological overview. *Ageing and Society*, 27 53, 5–11.

Myles, J. (1984) *Old Age in the Welfare State*. Little, Brown, Boston, MA.

Neugarten, B. L. (1974) Age groups in American society. *Annals of the American Academy of Political and Social Science*, 415, 187–198.

Nolan, M., Grant, G. and Keady, M. (1996) *Understanding Family Care*. Open University Press, Buckingham.

Office for National Statistics (ONS) (2003) *Census 2001: National Report for England and Wales*. The Stationery Office, London. Available from http://www.statistics.gov.uk/census 2001/default.asp?

Office for National Statistics (2004a) Annual update: 2002 Mortality Statistics. *Health Statistics Quarterly*, 21, 70–72.

Office for National Statistics (2004b) *Birth Statistics*, series FM1 no. 31. ONS, London.

Office of Population Censuses and Surveys (OPCS) (1992) *Mortality Statistics: Serial Tables*, Series DH1 no. 25. HMSO, London.

Olshansky, S. J. and Carnes, B. A. (2001) *The Quest for Immortality*. H. H. Norton, New York.

Olshansky, S. J. and Rudberg, M. A. (1997) Postponing disability: identifying points of decline and potential intervention. In Mickey, T., Speers, M. and Protraska, T. (eds). *Public Health and Aging*. Johns Hopkins University Press, Baltimore, MD.

Olshansky, S. J., Carnes, B. and Cassel, C. (1990) In search of Methuselah: estimating the upper limits to human longevity. *Science*, 250, 634–40.

Olshansky, S. J., Rudberg, M. A., Cassel, B. A. and Brady, J. A. (1991) Trading off longer life for worsening health: the expansion of morbidity hypothesis. *Journal of Aging and Health*, 312, 194–216.

Olson, L. (1982) *The Political Economy of Aging*. Columbia University Press, New York.

Pahl, R. (2000) *On Friendship*. Polity Press, Cambridge.

Pahl, R. and Spencer, L. (1997) Friends and neighbours. *New Society*, 26 September, 36–37.

Pampel, F. (1998) *Aging, Social Inequality or Public Policy*. Pine Forge Press, Thousand Oaks, CA.

Parker, G. R. (1981) Teaching and social policy. In Goldberg, G. M. with Hatch, S. (eds). *A New Look at the Personal Social Services*. Policy Studies Institute, London.

Parker, G. and Lawton, D. (1994) *Different Types of Care, Different Types of Carers*. HMSO, London.

Parker, S. (1980) *Older Workers and Retirement*. HMSO, London.

Parsons, T. K. (1951) *The Social System*. Routledge & Kegan Paul, London.

Peace, S. M. (ed.) (1990). *Researching social gerontology*. Sage, London.

Pearce, D. (1999) Changes in fertility and family size in Europe. *Population Trends*, Spring, 95, 33–40.

Pearlin, L., Pioli, M. F. and McLaughlin, E. (2001) Caregiving by adult children: involvement, role disruption and health. In Binstock, R. H. and George, L. K. (eds) *Handbook of Aging and the Social Sciences*, 5th edn. Academic Press, London: 238–254.

Pendry, E., Barrett, G. and Victor, C. R. (1999) Changes in household composition among the over sixties. *Health and Social Care in the Community*, 7, 2, 109–119

Penning, M. (1998) In the middle: parental caregiving in the context of other roles. *Journal of Gerontology: Social Sciences*, 53, S188–197.

Phillipson, C. (1982) *Capitalism and the Construction of Old Age*. Macmillan, London.

Phillipson, C. (1993) The sociology of retirement. In Bond, J., Coleman, P. and Peace, S. (eds) *Ageing in Society, 2nd edn*. Sage, London.

Phillipson, C. (1998) *Reconstructing Old Age*. Sage, London.

Phillipson, C. (2004) Social networks and social support in later life. In Phillipson, C., Allen, G. and Morgan, D. (eds) *Social Networks and Social Exclusion*. Ashgate, Aldershot: 35–49.

Phillipson, C., Bernard, M., Phillips, J. and Ogg, J. (2001) *The Family and Community Life of Old People*. Routledge, London.

Pickard, L. (2002) The decline of intensive intergenerational care of older people in Great Britain, 1985–1995. *Population Trends*, 110, 31–41.

Pilcher, J. (1995) *Age and Generation in Modern Britain*. Oxford University Press, Oxford.

Quadagno, J. and Reid, J. (1999) The political economy perspective of aging. In Bengtson, V. and Schaie, K. W. (eds) *Handbook of Theories of Aging*. Springer, New York.

Qureshi, H. and Walker, A. (1989) *The Caring relationship*. Macmillan, London.

Rickards, L., Fox, K., Roberts, C. *et al.* (2004) *Living in Britain, Number 31. Results from the 2002 General Household Survey*. The Stationery Office, London.

Riley, M. W. (1971) Social gerontology and the age stratification of society. *The Gerontologist*, 11, 79–87.

Riley, M. W. (1987) On the significance of age in society. *American Sociological Review*, 52, 1–14.

Riley, M. W. and Riley, J. (1994a) Age integration and the lives of older people. *The Gerontologist*, 34, 110–115.

Riley, M. W. and Riley, J. (1994b) Structural lag. In Riley, M. W., Kahn, R. L. and Foner, A. (eds) *Age and Structural Lag*. John Wiley, New York.

Riley, M. W., Johnson, M. and Foner, A. (1973) *Aging and Society: A Sociology of Age Stratification*. Russell Sage Foundation, New York.

Riley, M. W., Foner, A. and Riley, J. W. (1999) The aging and society paradigm. In Bengtson, V. and Schaie, K. W. (eds) *Handbook of Theories of Aging*. Springer, New York.

Robine, J. M., Mathers, C. and Brooard, N. (1996) Trends and differentials in disability free life expectancy, concepts, methods and findings. In Caselli, G. and Lopez, A. D. (eds) *Health and Mortality among elderly populations* Clarendon Press, Oxford.

Rosenthal, C., Martin-Matthews, A. and Matthews, S. (1996) Caught in the middle? Occupancy in multiple roles and help to parents in a national probability sample of Canadian adults. *Journal of Gerontology and Social Sciences*, 51, S274–83.

Rowe, J. W. and Kahn, R. L. (1997) Successful aging. *The Gerontologist*, 37, 4, 433–40.

Rowe, J. W. and Kahn, R. L. (1999) *Successful aging*. Pantheon Random House, New York.

Rowlands, O. and Parker, G. (1998) *Informal Carers*. ONS and the Stationery Office, London.

Royal Commission on Long-Term Care (1999) *With Respect to Old Age: Long-Term care – rights and responsibilities* (The Sutherland Report). The Stationery Office, London.

Royal Commission on Population (1949) *Royal Commission on Population: Report*. HMSO, London.

Russell, C. (1990) A multi-discipinary course in gerontology. *Educational Gerontology*, 16, 151–63.

Ryder, N. (1997) The cohort as a conception: the study of social change. In Hardy, M. A. (ed.) *Studying Aging and Social Change*. Sage, Thousand Oaks, CA.

Schaie, K. W. (1967) Age changes and age differences. *The Gerontologist*, 7, 128–132.

Schaie, K. W. (1977) Quasi-experimental research designs in the psychology of ageing. In Birren, J. and Schaie, K. W. (eds) *Handbook of the Psychology of Ageing*. Van Nostrand Reinhold, New York.

Schaie, K. W. (1993) The optimization of cognitive functioning in old age: predictions based on cohort-sequential and longitudinal data. In Baltes, P. B. and Baltes, M. E. (eds) *Successful Aging*. Cambridge University Press, Cambridge.

Schaie, K. W. (1996) *Intellectual development in Adulthood: The Seattle Longitudinal Study*. Cambridge University Press, Cambridge and New York.

Schaie, K. W. and Hoferson, N. (2001) Longitudinal studies in aging research. In Birren, J. W. and Schaie, K. W. (eds) *Handbook of the Psychology of Aging*. Academic Press, San Diego, CA.

Scharf, T. and Smith, A. (2004) Older people in urban neighbourhoods. In Phillipson, C., Allan, G. and Morgan, D. (eds) *Social Networks and Social Exclusion*. Ashgate, Aldershot.

Scott, A., Evandrou, M., Falkingham, J. *et al.* (2001) *Going into Residential Care*. Sage discussion paper no. 5. London School of Economics, London.

Seeman, T. E., Berkman, L. F., Charpentier, P. A. *et al.* (1995) Behavioural and psychosocial predictors of physical performance: the MacArthur studies of success for ageing. *Journal of Gerontology*, 50, 4, M177–83.

Settersten, R. A. and Hagestad, G. O. (1996a) What's the latest? Cultural age deadlines for family transitions. *The Gerontologist*, 36, 2, 178–188.

Settersten, R. A. and Hagestad, G. O. (1996b) What's the latest – 2? Cultural age deadlines for education and work transitions. *The Gerontologist*, 36, 5, 602–613.

Shah, S. and Cook, D.G. (2001) Inequalities in control and treatment of hypertension. *Journal of Hypertension*, 19, 1333–1340.

Shah, S., Harris, T., Rink, E. *et al.* (2001) Do income questions and seeking consent to link medical records reduce survey response rates? *British Journal of General Practice*, 51, 223–225.

Shanas, E. (1979) The family as a support system in old age. *The Gerontologist*, 19, 169–174.

Shanas, E., Townsend, P., Wedderburn, D. *et al.* (eds). (1968) *Old People in Three Industrial Societies*. Routledge & Kegan Paul, London.

Shaw, C. (2001) United Kingdom population trends in the 21st century. *Population Trends*, 103, 37–46.

Shaw, C. (2004) 2002 based national population projections for the United Kingdom and constituent countries. *Population Trends*, 115, 6–15.

Sheldon, J. H. (1948) *The Social Medicine of Old Age*, Oxford University Press, Oxford.

Shelton, N. and Grundy, E. (2000) Proximity of adult children to their parents in Great Britain. *International Journal of Population Geography*, 6, 3, 181–195.

Shkolnikov, V., McKee, M. and Leon, D. (2001) Changes in life expectancy in Russia in the mid 1990s. *Lancet*, 357, 917–21.

Sidell, M. (1995) *Health in Old Age*. Open University Press, Buckingham.

Slater, R. (1995) *The Psychology of Growing Old*. Open University Press, Buckingham.

Smeeth, L., Fletcher, A., Stirling, S. *et al.* (2001) A randomised controlled trial of three methods of administering a screening questionnaire to elderly people. *British Medical Journal*, 323, 1–7

Smith, J. and Harding, S. (1997) Mortality of men and women using alternative social classifications. In Drever, F. and Whitehead, M. (eds) *Health Inequalities: Decennial supplement*. ONS Series DS No. 15. The Stationery Office, London: 168–182.

Smith, R. (1998) Ageing and well-being in early modern England. In Johnson, P. and Thane P. (eds) *Old Age from Antiquity to Post Modernity*. Routledge, London.

Snowdon, D. (2001) *Aging with Grace*. Fourth Estate, London.

Sontag, S. (1978) The double standard of aging. In Carver, V. and Liddiard, P. (eds) *An Ageing Population*. Hodder and Stoughton, Sevenoaks, Kent, pp. 72–80.

Strehler, B. L. (1962) *Time, Cells and Aging*. Academic Press, New York.

Summerfield, C. and Babb, P. (eds) (2004) *Social Trends 2004*. The Stationery Office, London.

Thane, P. (1998) The family lives of old people. In Johnson, P. and Thane, P. (eds) *Old Age from Antiquity to Post Modernity*. Routledge, London.

Thane, P. (2000) *Old Age in English History.* Oxford University Press, Oxford.

Thatcher, R. (1999) The demography of centenarians in England and Wales. *Population Trends*. 96, 5–12.

Thompson, P., Itzin, C. and Abendstern, M. (1990) *I Don't Feel Old*. Oxford University Press, Oxford.

Tomassini, C., Glaser, K., Wolf, D. *et al.* (2004) Living arrangements among older people: an overview of trends in Europe and the USA. *Population Trends*, 115, 24–34.

Townsend, P. (1957) *The Family Life of Old People*. Routledge and Kegan Paul, London.

Townsend, P. (1964) *The Last Refuge*. Routledge and Kegan Paul, London.

Townsend, P. (1979) *Poverty in the United Kingdom*. Penguin, Harmondsworth.

Townsend, P. (1981) The structured dependency of the elderly: the creation of social policy in the twentieth century. *Ageing and Society*, 1, 1, 5–28.

Troyansky, D. (1997) Historical research into ageing, old age and older people. In Jamieson, A., Harper, S. and Victor, C. (eds) *Critical Approaches to Ageing and Later Life*. Open University Press, Milton Keynes, Bucks: 49–61.

Tudor Hart, J. (1971) The inverse care law. *Lancet* i(7696): 405–412.

Tulle-Winton, E. (2000) Old bodies. In Tyler, M. (ed.) *The Body, Culture and Society*. Open University Press, Buckingham.

Tunstall, J. (1963) *Old and Alone*. Routledge, London.

Twigg, J. (2000) *Bathing: The Body and Community Care*. Routledge, London.

Twigg, J. (2004) The body, gender and age. *Journal of Aging Studies*, 18, 59–73.

Twigg, J. and Aitkin, K. (1994) *Carers Perceived*. Open University Press, Buckingham.

Ungerson, C. (1987) *Policy is Personal: Sex, Gender and Informal Care*. Tavistock, London.

Vaupel, J. W. (1997) The remarkable improvements in survival at older ages.

Royal Society: Philosophical Transactions: Biological Sciences, 352, 1761–1920.

Verbrugge, L. M. (1984) Longer life but worsening health. *Millbank Memorial Fund Quarterly*, 62, 475–519.

Vetter, N. J., Jones, D. A. and Victor, C. R. (1984) The effectiveness of health visitors working with elderly patients in general practice. *British Medical Journal*, 288, 369–72.

Victor, C. R. (1984) *Old Age in Modern Society*. Croom Helm, Beckenham, Kent.

Victor, C. R. (1991) *Health and Health Care in Later Life*. Open University Press, Milton Keynes, Bucks.

Victor, C. R. (1994) *Old Age in Modern Society*, 2nd edn. Chapman & Hall, London.

Victor, C. R. (1996) The financial circumstances of older people. In Bland, R. (ed.) *Developing Services for Older People and Their Families*. Jessica Kingsley Publishers, London: 43–57.

Victor, C. R. (1997) *Community Care and Older People*. Stanley Thornes, Cheltenham.

Victor, C. R. (2002) Using existing research and statistical data: secondary data analysis. In Jamieson, A. and Victor, C. R. *Researching Ageing and Later Life*. Open University Press, Milton Keynes, Bucks: 51–65.

Victor, C. R., Scambler, S., Bond, J. and Bowling, A. (2000) Being alone in later life: loneliness, isolation and living alone in later life. *Reviews in Clinical Gerontology*, 10, 4, 407–417.

Victor, C. R., Scambler, S., Bond, J. and Bowling, A. (2001) Loneliness in later life: preliminary findings from the Growing Older Project. *Quality in Ageing*, 3, 1, 34–41.

Victor, C. R., Scambler, S., Shah, S. *et al.* (2002) Has loneliness among older people increased? An investigation into variations between cohorts. *Ageing and Society*, 22, 1–13.

Victor, C. R., Scambler, S. J., Bond, J. and Bowling, A. (2004) Loneliness in later life. In Walker, A. and Hennessey, C. (eds) *Quality of Life in Old Age*. Open University Press, Maidenhead, Berks: 107–126.

Vincent, J. (1995) *Inequality and Old Age*. UCL Press, London.

Vincent, J. (1999) *Politics, Power and Old Age*. Open University Press, Buckingham.

Wadsworth, M. (2002) Doing longitudinal research. In Jamieson, A. and Victor, C. R. (eds) *Researching Ageing and Later Life*. Open University Press, Buckingham.

Walker, A. (1980) The social creation of poverty and dependency in old age. *Journal of Social Policy*, 9, 49–75.

Walker, A. (1981) Towards a political economy of old age. *Ageing and Society*, 1, 1, 73–94.

Walker, A. (1999) Public policy and theories of aging. In Bengston, V. L. and Schaie, K. W. (eds) *Handbook of Theories of Aging*. Springer Publishing Co., NewYork: 361–378.

Walker, A. and Maltby, T. (1997) *Ageing Europe*. Open University Press, Buckingham.

Walker, A., O'Brien, M., Traynor, J. *et al*. (2002). *Living in Britain: Results of 2001 GHS*. The Stationery Office, London. Available from http://www.statistics.gov.uk/lib2001/resources/file attachments/GHS2002.pdr.

Wall, R. (1998) Intergenerational relationships past and present. In Walker, A. (ed.) *The New Generational Contract: Intergenerational relations, old age and welfare*. UCL Press, London.

Wallace, P. (1999) *Agequake*. Nicholas Brearley, London.

Wallace, R. B. and Woolson, R. F. (1992) *The Epidemiologic Study of the Elderly*. Oxford University Press, Oxford.

Ward, R. A. (1984) *The Aging Experience*. Harper and Row, New York.

Ward-Griffin, C. and Marshall, V. W. (2003) Reconceptualizing the relationship between public and private eldercare. *Journal of Aging Studies*, 17, 2, 189–208

Wenger, G. C. (1984) *The Supportive Network*, George Allen and Unwin, London.

Wenger, G. C. (1994) *Understanding Support Networks and Community Care*. Avebury, Aldershot.

Wenger, G. C. (1996) Social networks and gerontology. *Reviews in Clinical Gerontology*, 6, 285–293.

Wenger, G. C. and Burholt, V. (2004) Changes in levels of social isolation and loneliness among older people in rural Wales: a 20 year longitudinal study. *Canadian Journal on Aging*, 23, 2.

Williams, A. (1997) The rationing debate: rationing health care by age: the case for. *British Medical Journal*, 314, 820–825.

Williams, R. (1990) *A Protestant Legacy*. Clarendon Press, Oxford.

Williamson, R., Stokoe, I. H., Gray, S. *et al*. (1964) Old people at home: their unreported needs. *Lancet* i, 1117–1120.

Wilson, G. (1995) 'I'm the eyes and she's the arms': changes in gender roles in advanced old age. In Arber, S. and Ginn, J. (eds) *Connecting Gender and Ageing*. Open University Press, Buckingham.

Wilson, G. (2000) *Understanding Old Age*. Sage, London.

Wimo, A., Winblad, B., Aguero-Torres, H. and von Strauss, E. (2003) The magnitude of dementia occurrence worldwide. *Alzheimer Disease and Associated Disorders*, 17, 2, 63–67.

World Bank, (1994) *Averting the Old Age Crisis*. Oxford University Press, New York.

World Health Organisation (1980) *International Classification of Impairments, Disabilities and Handicaps*. WHO, Geneva.

World Health Organisation (WHO) (2002)*Annual Report 2002*. Available from website www.who.int/whr/2002/en/whr2002_annex1.pdf.

Young, M. and Willmott, P. (1957). *Family and Kinship in East London*. Penguin, Harmondsworth.

Zeilig, H. (1997) The uses of literature in the study of older people. In Jamieson, A., Harper, S. and Victor, C. (eds) *Critical Approaches to Ageing and Later Life*. Open University Press, Milton Keynes, Bucks: 39–48.

Index

Note: Page references in *italics* indicate tables